WRITE
10K in a DAY

Avoid Burnout

Unleash Your Prolific Potential

An Author's Survival Guide

Lydia Michaels

www.LydiaMichaelsBooks.com

LYDIA MICHAELS

BAILEY BROWN
PUBLISHING

WRITE 10K IN A DAY

WRITE 10K IN A DAY

AVOID BURNOUT

By LYDIA MICHAELS

1. Language Arts & Disciplines / Authorship 2. Language Arts & Disciplines / Compositions & Creative Writing 3. Business & Economics / Personal Success 4. Self-Help / Personal Growth / Success 5. Business & Economics / Marketing / General 6. Psychology / Mental Health 7. Self-Help / Self-Management / Time Management 8. Self-Help / Creativity 9. Humor / Topics / Internet & Social Media

Hardback ISBN: 978-0-9995236-6-7

Paperback ISBN: 978-1-7371244-2-9

eBook ISBN-13: 978-1-7354677-3-3

Cover design by LYDIA MICHAELS, Edited by THERESA KOHLER

Printed in the United States of America

BAILEY BROWN PUBLISHING, USA

Dedication

This book is dedicated to the women "Behind the Keys".
The Behind the Keys Author Retreat is such a comfort to my author soul.
I love sharing in our mastermind discussions and laughing over cocktails with all of you!
We are stronger, wiser, and better when we work together.

Table of Contents

Epigraph

"I have to write to be happy whether I get paid for it or not. But it is a hell of a disease to be born with. I like to do it. Which is even worse. That makes it from a disease into a vice. Then I want to do it better than anybody has ever done it which makes it into an obsession. An obsession is terrible. Hope you haven't gotten any."

Ernest Hemingway, Letter to Charles Scribner, 1940

About the Author

Lydia Michaels is the author of over forty novels and the consecutive winner of the 2018 & 2019 *Author of the Year Award* from *Happenings Media,* as well as the recipient of the 2014 *Best Author Award* from the *Courier Times*. She has been featured in *USA Today, Romantic Times Magazine, Love & Lace*, and more. As the host and founder of the *East Coast Author Convention*, the *Behind the Keys Author Retreat*, and *Read Between the Wines*, she continues to celebrate her growing love for readers and romance novels around the world.

Lydia is happily married to her childhood sweetheart. Some of her favorite things include the scent of paperback books, listening to her husband play piano, escaping to her coastal home at the Jersey Shore, cheap wine, 80's pop culture, coffee, and kilts. She hopes to meet you soon at one of her many upcoming events.

Please follow and/or reach out to Lydia Michaels through email or social media. She is most interactive with bloggers, authors, and fans on the following platforms:

Email:
Lydia@LydiaMichaelsBooks.com

Instagram:
@Lydia_michaels_books
www.instagram.com/lydia_michaels_books

Facebook:
www.Facebook.com/LydiaMichaels

TikTok:
@lydiamichaels
www.tiktok.com/@lydiamichaels

Acknowledgement

So many brilliant professionals supported the idea of this book. It's difficult to place names in any sort of order, but my gratitude for their persistent encouragement and enthusiasm for the subject matter is endless. As a dyslexic child who could never keep up in reading class and performed tragically on spelling tests, I never dreamed I'd pursue a career in writing, let alone an award-winning one. My experiences have proven that we should never cripple our potential by assuming we know where our gifts begin and end.

For more than ten years, industry professionals, including some at the top publishing houses in the world, have labeled me as "prolific," but it took a decade of interacting with other writers in my field to realize I might actually have something of value to teach (proof that we all battle impostor syndrome to some degree). For every aspiring writer and seasoned author out there who suggested I publish a book on the subject of prolific writing, I thank you.

My early school failures in spelling and reading fluency brought about painful shame and left emotional scars that will haunt me always. But when I fell in love with writing, I fell so hard, there was no returning to the place I existed before. I had no choice but to teach myself the skills needed to succeed, and in doing so, I unleashed a prolific potential no one could have predicted, including myself. I produced an abundance of successful novels and achieved a sustainable author career in a short time. As well-developed novels amassed at abounding speeds, requests that I share my secrets on writing soon followed.

That little dyslexic girl still lives inside of me, and those who know me best often glimpse her shaking with insecurity, while the rest of the world only sees the confident woman I choose to show them. The authors that encouraged this book truly have a way with words, because they convinced me I have something of great value to share.

Author Tere Michaels, you reached out to me requesting I teach prolific writing at BLC2020. I was honored and humbled when you told me my workshop "needs to be a book."

Zoe York, you have an endless labyrinth of a mind and an open-door policy to your thoughts. You inspire me and remind me that being an author can be whatever we want it to be. Thank you for your kind guidance and sunny attitude. You're a rock star.

And to Pam Godwin, the sweetest woman I've met in this industry (who happens to write the absolute most terrifying books), you are an endless well of encouragement, statistical analysis, and craft theory. There is no one else in the world I'd rather drink wine and share trade secrets with at 4 am than you—you sexy minx.

To my dear friend and colleague, Michelle Windsor, you are one of my greatest supporters, always looking out for me and pointing out my strengths when I'm feeling weak or adrift. Thank you for reminding me I'm a shark and for swimming by my side (#FinsOut).

Special thanks to Theresa Kohler, who is so much more than an editor to me. And finally, I must thank all the women who have attended the Behind the Keys Author Retreat over the years. You have all opened your hearts and minds to me. This book is especially dedicated to all of you.

PREFACE

What this Book is and What it is Not

Write 10K in a Day is a first edition accompaniment to a workshop designed for the 2020 Book Lovers Convention. It mingles craft theory and healthy alternatives to an otherwise sedentary job. The tested philosophies featured in this text advocate high word counts while balancing productivity with frequent kinesthetic breaks to boost creativity.

What does that mean, exactly? The goal of this book is to help authors of all levels write faster, live a healthier author life, and write higher quality stories while staying relevant in a saturated market.

Writers will learn methods to effectively meet deadlines and develop more efficient, healthier ways of hitting high, daily word counts. *Write 10K in a Day* teaches key components, such as creating multidimensional characters with clear goals and characters driven by compelling motivation.

It offers custom formulas for producing high-stake story conflicts that will drive any writer's plot from one-hell-of-a-hook to the gripping end. But, above all, it advocates career practices that take a proactive approach to authors' mental and physical health, something—in my professional opinion—that is overlooked far too often in this field.

While some may find a few methods unconventional, the strategies offered in this text have been developed, tested, and honed for more than a decade. I acknowledge that advice given in an era of such rapidly developing technology is transient at best, however, one of my favorite "How-To" writing books is *How to Write Best Selling Fiction* by Dean R. Koontz, published in 1972. This book is no longer in production, supposedly at the author's request, who is rumored to have thought the content "obsolete" after the internet and eBook industry revolutionized the market. However, my eccentric father gifted me with a rare copy he won at an auction several years ago, and as I assumed, there were some golden nuggets of wisdom in Dean's book that have stood the test of time.

So, while all "How-To" books may be transient, it is every person's duty to decipher the shit from sheer genius in any piece of advice. I suggest, as you move forward reading *Write 10K in a Day,* that you maintain a judicious perspective and draw your own conclusions about what advice is useful and timeless and what does not apply to your personal journey.

Every writer's journey begins in a different place. While *Write 10K in a Day* offers many formulas and theories, it's important you, as an author, take the time to customize your own process based on your specific strengths and weaknesses.

Industry guru and author, Zoe York, accurately described the process of successful publishing as, "a weird formula nobody has ever quite figured out." She also warns that privilege weighs heavily on circumstances of author success. For these reasons, and many more, authors must think long and hard about how they, as writers, will measure their success, because there are millions—yes, millions—of undiscovered masterpieces in publication today. You may have even written one!

Success is relative, and the road to it is ever-changing. The passion that fuels your journey is the same passion that will guard you from burnout. But sadly, with the overabundance of publicity and exposure to others through social media networking today, passion can become a paradoxical shield that betrays us the moment it breeds with competitiveness or greed. Only common sense and balance can truly protect you from the dangers ahead.

It is a certainty, however, that the actual *business* of publishing thrives heavily on commercialism, so if you are seeking a sustainable career in writing, you must be willing to cater your work—at least to some degree—to the commercial market. Therefore, social influence and marketing remains a necessary evil.

Don't panic! In the chapters ahead, you will learn to balance all of these hats without going fully mad. Although, we must allow a little madness, because how could writers ever be considered completely sane, when we have so many voices chattering in our heads?

While *Write 10K in a Day* briefly references some promotional tips, this is not a marketing book. I prefer to leave that advice to more knowledgeable marketing pros, since my specialty is mostly tied to prolific story building. The basics in publicity that I do share are personal preferences and can be collectively stored under an umbrella labeled: *Things I Wish I Knew When I Started.*

Write 10K in a Day advocates quality craftsmanship in stories. And while it offers strategies to speed up the creative process, it will never suggest doing so at the cost of an author's mental or physical health. The chapters ahead focus on gaining *loyal* readers by honoring a promise not to betray the customer with poor products. This is accomplished by placing the author's needs first.

Write 10K in a Day dials back the volume of the *authorpreneur* commercial world so we, as creators, can recognize the tried-and-true characteristics of successful writing habits. Much like the pearls of wisdom I unearthed in Dean Koontz's dated copy of *How to Write Best Selling Fiction,* I hope to highlight some of today's most valuable writing advice.

Good advice has been buried beneath decades of digital noise bombarding writers from self-proclaimed experts. Modern authors face the universal challenge of wading through the mess and filtering out the gems. I share my knowledge openly and honestly, but in the end, it's only your judgement that matters, as you will decide which strategies apply to you and which do not.

Speed is not the be-all end-all of an author's success. Good books require skillful writers, knowledge of the craft, creativity, time, and above all, a healthy mind and body. It's a combination of talents and positive circumstances that truly unleashes an author's prolific potential, and in the chapters ahead, I will do my best to teach many helpful strategies that should improve both your talent and circumstances. It remains the responsibility of each individual to apply and practice the theories learned.

Before accepting any advice, it's always wise to have some background on the source, so please allow me to share a little about myself. I began my writing career in 2007, long before I knew Facebook or even MySpace existed, therefore, it was an isolated introduction. My first attempt to understand the book market began with a directory of the publishing industry with a spine eight inches thick. I spent a solid month paging through the reference text, learning about the various players in publishing, and researching the query process.

After laboring over all the various industry standards, I polished my first manuscript and shipped more than thirty samples out via snail mail. Then the waiting game began. It was painful, pricey, and a gross waste of paper. I'm glad to see the process has improved over time by going green, but, sorry to say, it hasn't gotten much easier.

It's important for me to date myself here, so that you, the reader, know that I have more than fourteen years of experience, and I've earned my scars in the author arena. I call them scars, because when you make it as a published author, even your greatest victories but especially your most noteworthy masterpieces, can take a toll.

I am knowledgeable about the author profession, but in an industry that shifts as rapidly as ours, I find it difficult to claim anyone is an *expert*. As a hybrid author, published both traditionally and independently, I have seen my fair share of success. I've signed with the largest publisher in the English-speaking world and shared endcaps with greats like E L James and Sylvia Day. Yet, in the saturated sea of the book market, some have never heard of me.

Allow me to introduce myself. My name is Lydia and I have more wrinkles from laughing than frowning, but I worry more than most, which also means I possess a great ability to joke about my incessant worrying. Prior to becoming an author, I was a teacher certified in special education. I'm dyslexic, which makes my profession as a writer extra entertaining at times and editors an absolute necessity to my success. I'm a reformed workaholic who is beyond humbled that my experiences, both positive and negative, might help others.

People assume I have an abundance of confidence, but that's a common misconception. I just come from a loud, Italian family, so my insecurities are easily missed, but believe me, they're there. I'm also a Virgo, so I overanalyze *everything,* hence, the worrying. All of this adds up to being as perfectly flawed as any well-developed human should be. I'm proud to declare myself a *lifelong learner*.

I am not a self-proclaimed expert. I'm merely a collector of experiences and tips I've gathered from the so-called "greats" and the under-celebrated writers I've met over the years. If that makes me a trustworthy source in your mind, I hope we can hang out for a while.

My goal, in publishing *Write 10K in a Day,* is to simply open my mind to you, share my mistakes to help you avoid the same, and perhaps, motivate you to think outside-the-box in terms of success and living a happy author life. If, at the end of this book, you find yourself disagreeing with my theories, that's fine. I am but one author, and there are millions out there to learn from.

As an advocate for publicly sourced knowledge, I've made a profession of openly sharing my theories through social media, public lectures, and private workshops. While this book is not a one-size-fits-all, I've done my best to consider the diverse creative styles of authors. I've also provided graphic organizers and tools to help you better understand your own process and preferences along the way.

Write 10K in a Day embraces the idea of an open author community, firmly believing that writing does not have to be an isolated job. Writing is personal, but being an author should never feel lonely. As a matter of fact, if you'd like to join more craft and trade discussions, connect with me on social media, where I often post writing tips and tricks! Just follow this shameless Instagram plug @lydia_michaels_books or catch me on TikTok @lydiamichaels.

After you have finished *Write 10K in a Day,* I'd love to hear from you! My goal with this book is, and always has been, to give something back to the author community that has given so much to me over the course of my career. So, let's be friends and keep the dialogue going!

Email: Lydia@LydiaMichaelsBooks.com
Instagram: @Lydia_michaels_books
Facebook: www.Facebook.com/LydiaMichaels
TikTok: @lydiamichaels

PART ONE

THE
HEALTH & WELLNESS
OF A WRITER

Chapter One
Burnout

"A good novel tells us the truth about its hero; but a bad novel tells us the truth about its author."

G.K. Chesterton, Heretics, 1905

Before We Begin

Unlike other non-fiction books you might have read, *Write 10K in a Day* has been designed to take an interactive approach with the reader. As the author, I understand each of you are beginning at different stages of your career, each person bringing different skills and experiences to the table, so I wanted to make this book a tool that a diverse group of writers could use and discuss together.

That being said, welcome to the table! Here, every author has a place and a seat. No writer is more valid than another.

To gain the most from this book, is to acknowledge that there is always more to learn from others than can ever be taught by problem solving alone. Even the most experienced authors have something to learn from the fresh writers just starting out and vice versa.

In the chapters ahead, we will discuss varying levels of burnout. The experiences shared are not written to intimidate, but rather, to motivate. I will state, right here from the first section of Chapter One, that burnout *can* be reversed, so if you are currently feeling hopeless about the career you've chosen or battling doubts, you've come to a safe and honest place. By applying some or all of the practices ahead, authors can greatly improve their circumstances, mindset, and flow of creativity, so have faith.

For those just starting out, those who still maintain the youthful views of a new author (Not mocking, trust me, we envy you!) and a sense of invincibility, heed the warnings ahead, but do not let anyone, including longwinded authors of self-help books, diminish your optimism. Knowing the challenges ahead should help you prepare, not despair. You've got this.

Throughout the upcoming lessons, I will pepper teachable moments and theories with anecdotes from my personal journey. I share my own vulnerabilities to save others a trip, and hopefully, prevent them from suffering the same fall. I also share my victories as a steady reminder that burnout can be reversed and writing should never stop bringing an author joy.

This book is not a perfect cure. It is, however, a tool to help authors adopt healthier work habits, avoid burnout, and unleash their prolific potential.

Before we begin, I encourage you to form a discussion group with writers in your "circle of trust" to get the most from the lessons ahead. Forming a discussion group, or mastermind group as they were once called by visionaries like Edison and Roosevelt, is a proven way to effectively create opportunities for peer-to-peer mentoring and vastly influence your success while fostering positive relationships.

The tradition of peer groups among the author community is often echoed in the common practice of writer conferences and retreats. Authors do not need to go into debt to participate in, or reap the benefits of, such practices. Simply gather in your living room, at a local coffee shop, a Google Meet or Zoom, or create a social media group, and open the discussion with likeminded professionals.

Need help finding likeminded professionals? Follow the *Write 10K in a Day* Instagram page where I frequently post helpful videos, answer questions, and interact with the author community. Writers of all stages are welcome!

In the business chapters ahead, we will look at strategies for forming mastermind groups in more detail, but for now, take the opportunity to reach out to a fellow author and read this book together. It will give you more opportunities to process the ideas and develop your own. Communication is a key component to success.

Now, we have a lot to cover. Pull up a chair, grab a cup of coffee or a cocktail, and let's begin.

Burnout: Early Identification

The greatest threat to any author is burnout. Burnout can impact a writer's creativity, health, mindset, family life, financial situation, and professionalism among other things. But what *is* burnout?

Burnout is the reduction of fuel through prolonged use or combustion until no source of energy is left. Picture a car driving cross-country. What happens to that car if it doesn't stop to change its oil or refuel? Eventually, it breaks down.

As humans we call this refueling *self-care*. Yes, we can get from A to B on fumes, but what good are we once we arrive?

Unlike a car, when a human experiences burnout, they fall into a state of physical or emotional exhaustion that also involves a sense of reduced accomplishment and loss of personal identity.

Some emotional risks associated with burnout include depression, mood decline, and irritability. Sound familiar? The emotional symptoms are usually the first to show and the easiest to ignore.

It's a common practice for adults working high-pressure jobs to form a habit of excusing such symptoms as normal or acceptable.

"Sorry, I had a terrible day at work."

"People just don't realize how difficult my job is."

"No one understands the stress I'm under."

"I can't focus on anything else until I meet this deadline."

If any of the above sounds familiar, then chances are you're already suffering early symptoms of burnout. Physical risks associated with burnout include aches, pains, weight gain, changes in vision, and more severe issues.

Have you ever spent hours at the computer only to find your vision suddenly blurring? This is a common issue with today's screen time, and we're taught handy tricks, like taking twenty seconds to stare at something twenty feet away every twenty minutes, to give our eyes a break, but the issue repeats as soon as we overdo it, again.

Why? Because all of the above issues are symptoms of the umbrella problem known as burnout. And as with any problem, we will never fully heal by merely treating the symptoms. We have to find the source and correct the issue at the root.

CONSIDER THIS:

Would you rather put out a house fire in your home or take preventative measures to avoid a fire altogether? Code enforcement requires homeowners to keep fire extinguishers in the kitchen where small fires are more likely to occur, but even a small fire can quickly spread out of control, and the tools you have at hand might not be enough to save your life.

This is why code enforcement also requires homeowners to hang smoke detectors in every room. There is less chance of an emergency by taking a preventative approach with an alarm system that can alert you of trouble before an issue spreads out of control. This is considered a *proactive* approach, where a fire extinguisher would be considered a *reactive* solution to an emergency.

Smoke, in the case of house fires, is the symptom of a greater issue, just as irritability and exhaustion can be a signal that the body is burning too quickly through needed resources and entering dangerous territory.

Your body is your first home. Don't protect it with reactive tools when you can avoid a crisis by monitoring it with proactive habits. Ignoring your body's signals that there might be a problem (symptoms of burnout) is the same as taking the batteries out of a chirping smoke detector. It leaves you open for catastrophe.

In this modern world, we often rely on responsive therapy when taking a proactive approach would be so much more effective. Yes, people who eat well, exercise, and do yoga still die, but imagine the quality of life they have before they do. They usually don't have to sacrifice as much time putting out fires as the person who eats garbage, sits at a desk sixty hours a week, and suffers chronic stiffness and pain.

There's an old saying, "give someone an inch and they'll take a mile". When we neglect our bodies and seemingly get away with it, we do it again and again. Each time, we push our boundaries a little farther until we're so far beyond the safety line we're lost in a danger zone.

In 2017, I saw my weight going up, felt my joints stiffening, but I just kept making those Monday morning promises that never came. And the headaches and vision changes… It was nothing a pill and new glasses couldn't fix.

But, once the physical warnings got bigger and more frequent, I needed more than just a Monday meal plan. I needed to completely stop my life and reboot, with a lot of soul-searching and heartache. Trust me when I say, my dream job wasn't always pleasant.

Eventually, as the symptoms of burnout build up over time, the quality of work suffers. If we don't pay attention to the early identifiers, we risk running into many unforeseen setbacks. Our effectiveness dwindles the longer we ignore our alarm system, and we begin to have less productive days. Once we lose our speed and efficiency on the job, we chance losing our joy.

Symptoms Become Consequences

Energy is sometimes a nonrenewable resource. Small symptoms that can be resolved with slight behavior changes can snowball into an avalanche of consequences if ignored.

Authors that fail to identify early warning signs risk burning out to a point of no return. They are not only wasting their potential on tasks that might not be serving their best interests, they're spending their youth on practices with little impact on measurable success.

Now, that might strike you as dramatic, but that's exactly what's happening. The less we take care of ourselves, the faster we age—mentally and physically.

Look at the supplements swallowed by middle aged consumers geared to increase brain function and enhance focus or energy. We didn't need these things as children, perhaps, because we spent so much time playing outside and running around in the sun.

Some of you are likely arguing that everything you do is necessary. It's common to feel defensive, especially after all the hard work you've done to succeed. But success should not feel like failure. And in order to resolve the troubles, present or ahead, we must first be willing to look our demons directly in the eye. That means admitting and owning our reality in its truest actuality.

So, unless you have mastered the art of living a balanced life, or you are one of the top-tier authors of commercial fiction fairly compensated for every minute of your time spent writing, these warnings, most likely, apply to you. The sad truth is, very few authors out there, less than 1%[1], have actually met the industry standard for success.

Often, in the case of the overworked author, there's a bit of an antihero plot twist where *the author* is both the hero *and* the villain. Spoiler alert, prepare to be stunned by some upcoming revelations.

And for those new authors who haven't felt a hint of trouble on the horizon, consider this part of the story arc the "calm before the storm." Heads up, a climax is coming, and your choices now will determine if you triumph or flounder later (more on these story arc patterns when we get into the craft section of the book).

This is your story. Every bad day is merely a plot twist and challenge meant to help you grow. You can either heed the warnings or ignore them, but every choice at every fork in the road will decide your fate in the end.

It's okay to take high stake risks, as long as you accept that eventually your resilience will wear away. Even the greatest heroes can get so run down they lose their grip on reality completely.

Don't believe me? Check in with the classic cases of beloved heroes and heroines, like Anakin Skywalker or Daenerys Targaryen. Both recklessly rose to the top, so resolutely focused on their objectives they lost touch with their purpose in the end. Neither Anakin nor Daenerys end up as heroes, despite how we might have hoped otherwise.

---

[1] According to www.quora.com, 2 in 10,000 authors make a sustainable living and only 1 in 100,000 authors become a household name.

Burnout is often the result of fanatical efforts. Consider cults. Cults typically start with an inspiring message that motivates others to follow. But over time, the messaging becomes overzealous and hyper-focused, cutting off logic until a fanatic is born.

When such an imbalance sets in, with work, religion, or other parts of life, consequences will inevitably follow. As the saying goes, *nothing in excess.*

We live in an indulgent, work-driven culture, and it is common for people to overdo patterns of behavior to a point of danger, even with enterprises that seem innately good at first. Addiction is rampant, and excuses are far too simple to find, especially in cases where behaviors are justified by the promise of more success in the end.

Steve owns a diner. In order to stay afloat he must keep his establishment open 24/7. Steve develops a pattern of late nights and long hours. He also develops a taste for amphetamines. After months of this behavior, Steve can't function without the drug. Steve could be considered an addict.

Tiffany is a newly published author. She is told that she must release a second book within six months if she wants to establish her brand and remain relevant in a saturated market. Tiffany develops a pattern of late nights and long hours. She also is spending more than a hundred hours a week sitting at her desk, drinking far too much coffee, and skipping meals. As soon as Tiffany releases her second book, she continues this pattern of behavior so that she can quickly release her third.

Is Tiffany an addict?

Just as there is a running high, a sense of euphoria created through jogging, there is science behind a writing high. Studies have shown the act of writing creates a surge of dopamine to the brain. Dopamine is an acting chemical in the brain linked to the reward and motivation sensors. This same chemical is released through the use of certain drugs, the act of running, and, yes, even writing.

Could it be that authors become so obsessed with their jobs because they are feeding an actual chemical addiction? More studies are needed, but there is a basis to assume writing addictions do exist. By studying author behavior alone, there seems overwhelming evidence that something bigger than financial incentive is driving this industry.

Regardless of the cause, without a balanced reward system and proper guidelines for moderation, imbalances will occur. Long-term imbalances lead to setbacks, and chronic setbacks eventually end in burnout.

Burnout is not only a joy thief, it can sap away a person's passion so completely that what was once a fulfilling, indulgent obsession can suddenly flip into a controlling curse and punishment. Meaning, in extreme cases, the burned-out author can lose all sense of pleasure gained from writing, yet feel incapable of walking away or even taking a short-term break.

Beyond substance abuse, addiction can also be defined as a biopsychosocial disorder characterized by the repetitive engagement in a behavior, despite harm to self or others. When writers engage in their work to the point of self-neglect, they are feeding an addiction and on the road to burnout.

In addition to the basic disadvantages of burnout, are the already existent risks of having a sedentary job, such as type 2 diabetes, cardiovascular disease, and various types of cancer. The compounding effect of emotional and physical consequences can lead authors to some very dangerous health problems.

Unfortunately, as authors, we have no one policing the safety of our office or jobs. There is no human resources department, no OSHA, and very little in terms of healthcare in this field, so it's no wonder so many authors are unhealthy and hurting.

The reversal of burnout begins with balance, an alignment of the mind, body, and spirit achieved through *awareness*, *intent*, and *reflection*. In the chapters ahead, we will address techniques to achieve such an alignment, but first we must totally grasp burnout—its symptoms, effects, and consequences.

Symptoms of Burnout Include:

- Becoming overly cynical or critical about work
- Avoiding work
- Irritability and impatience
- Lacking the energy to be consistently productive
- Broken concentration
- A lack of satisfaction in achievements
- Disillusionment
- Changes in sleeping habits
- Headaches, stomach issues, and/or other physical problems

Everyone has encountered at least one of the above symptoms, either since becoming an author or in other areas of life. Burnout is not a problem uniquely faced by writers. Stressful situations that reoccur tend to trigger one or a number of symptoms of burnout.

The symptomatic author is in less trouble than the author who allowed symptoms to form into actual consequences. While symptoms of burnout represent the red flags, we must pay attention to consequences of burnout, which signify the beginning of long-term troubles ahead.

Consequences of Burnout Include:

- Excessive stress
- Chronic fatigue
- Frequent headaches
- Frequent stomach issues
- Reoccurring insomnia
- Depression, anger, or irritability

- Alcohol or substance abuse
- Weakening immune system
- Chronic or severe illness
- Heart disease
- High blood pressure
- Type 2 diabetes
- Cancer
- Death

Taking Back Control

As a writer, I've watched authors battle autoimmune diseases, cancer, obesity (the second leading cause of preventable death in the United States), and more. Sadly, not all of them survived the battle.

We, as a writing community, are starting to see patterns of illness. When an author gets sick, we rally behind the author and typically orchestrate an anthology or fundraiser to offer some form of relief and support. Unfortunately, this *responsive* approach to a problem doesn't always double as a solution.

Taking a preventative and *proactive* approach will have a greater impact on the health of authors as a whole. Incorporating yoga classes and job-healthy workshops into our conventions is a great start, but for those classes to be effective authors must actively show interest, attend the workshops, and apply such strategies on a daily basis.

The CDC offers a comprehensive resource guide that proposes ideas for physical activity breaks in the workplace, which I will link here as well as include on my website at lydiamichaelsbooks.com. I recommend keeping a list of movement ideas posted at your desk as a reminder to yourself that movement should be an intrinsic part of the job.

Authors must make use of such building blocks and advocate for more focus from the industry in the direction of health and wellness within our writing community. That is how our community speaks through action. That is how positive change begins to take shape.

So many workshops are geared toward improving word count, hitting deadlines, or beefing up marketing strategy, adding to the overall responsibilities already hammering authors into the ground—perhaps into early graves. Very few workshops address the necessity of self-care.

Balance is a trifecta—mind, body, and spirit. Without balance, effectiveness and happiness suffer. We cannot focus on the business (mind) and creativity (spirit) alone. The body is the vehicle that gets us to work. If the body is broken down, so are we.

A career in writing should never be a sprint. It should be a marathon, and if we want to write well into our old age, we must adapt healthier habits and be kinder to our needs.

My reputation for high word count created an opportunity to teach others how to up their word counts but also created an opportunity to open a dialogue about authors' other needs. Having a platform has helped me connect with professionals and address the many expectations pressed upon authors with little consideration for the cost to our health. But, more importantly, it's provided me the chance to help others and try to find solutions for a community I love.

People are generally treated exactly the way they teach people to treat them. If boundaries do not exist for an author, it is because the author has failed to maintain said boundaries. And if we are unable to honor our own boundaries, it's unlikely others will.

Boundaries will only exist if we build them. The moment we let others decide what we should and shouldn't tolerate, we've lost control. Reestablishing control starts with reestablishing limits.

Do not allow yourself to fill a position at the mercy of the reader or blogger. Always remember, you are the artist. It is your product the consumer needs, and there are varying levels of demand.

Yes, success is saved for a mere 1% in this field. But that sparce success is reserved for authors who practice balance, take care of their needs first, and invest time in the craft and creative process, so that they might increase the quality of their work every time they publish something new.

Taking a step back or operating below full-throttle might remove the sense of being "in high demand," but if an author has built a loyal audience and established practices that automate an occasional online presence, their relevancy will sustain the break.

Trust your worth. The readers that love you will wait for you. Undervaluing or losing faith in said worth is an early sign of burnout. To counter burnout, try to act in confidence rather than fear.

Relevancy is a precarious position at best. An author's place on a list can easily get jostled by incoming talent or trends. These stimuli do not necessarily mean an author's book is less valuable than it once was. They are merely indicators of a shift in market. And in an industry as fluid as the book market, it's best to expect shifting currents. Sometimes one's survival even comes down to knowing how to stay still and simply float for a while.

Readers will continue to hold authors to a certain, sometimes draining, level of expectation because too many authors allow it. Authors that indulge standards that pressure them to hold rapid book releases and be constantly present on every social media platform trending are doing a disservice to the community as a whole. But we cannot control the behaviors of others. We can only control ourselves.

People will treat us the way we teach them they can. If we show them certain expectations are acceptable to us, they will continue to expect more of the same. It takes a courageous person to speak out and establish boundaries where there aren't any, but the more authors ban together and set limits, the less advantage others will take of their time.

Have you ever attended a signing where readers are encouraged to collect signatures on a scavenger hunt? Event hosts provide a list of author names and readers are encouraged to visit tables and collect signatures. Hosts assume they are creating opportunities for networking, but what is actually happening is the reader no longer needs to purchase a book to obtain a signature or speak to an author. They merely shove a piece of paper in an author's face, ask nothing about the books, take a signature, and walk away.

Authors have been trained to find contentment in the illusion of "success," when in actuality, the hourly rate of an average author typically ranks below minimum wage when figured into the actual hours spent on the job. Perpetuating more illusions of success has only made the possibility of eventual true success less probable.

In the case of the scavenger hunt, the illusion of a patron line at an author's table is created. But illusions do not pay the bills. And how many people are actually being fooled when the entire guest list, both readers and authors, are in on the deception?

We have taught event hosts and readers that this sort of non-patronization is acceptable by simply accepting it. A sense of fragility has made us tolerant of too many practices that prove more counterproductive than profitable, when anyone with good business sense should have the courage to speak up or stop indulging in unbeneficial practices.

Too many authors feel their position is too delicate to make waves, when in actuality, authors should hold the wheel that steers the industry and dictates its course. In rare cases, we do, but in such a large, diverse group, it can feel almost suicidal to swim against the current. So, in most cases, we unanimously go along with what we are encouraged to do, because it seems like what is best for survival. Again, I ask, is this actuality or illusion?

There are those who believe success is pumping out a book every few weeks and editing isn't necessary. Then there are those who view writing as an actual art form and spend years polishing their manuscript before ever letting it see the light of day. And, of course, there are the rest who fill the in between. The question is, what kind of author are you?

Too many talented artists are following commerce-driven hacks. It's time to unflinchingly recognize the value of your work and start honoring your needs. If you can't, no one else ever will.

Industry standards have pushed us into a sort of emotional debt with many health deficits and no financial guarantees. As a community, authors must start behaving in a way that shows we have limits and plan to honor them.

If you are merely selling a product, continue to follow the commerce model of mass-producing forgettable books. If you consider yourself an artist, come to terms with the time and skill required to create said art. And for those who want to produce both sustainable product lines with the occasional masterpiece, welcome to the land of balance. Lesson one is to stop perpetuating obstacles.

So many authors refuse to take a step back. They are missing the big picture. By merely drawing back and appraising the situation, they would see the chaos at foot and a clear path around the mess. But fear keeps them buried in the weeds, following the masses, never certain if there is a cliff or victory ahead.

Having a broad perspective of the actual circumstances faced by authors is a crucial part of proper, healthy decision-making. Do not let others dictate your process. Even as you read this book, you should be adapting these suggestions to your own belief system with a judicious mind. Only you know your true circumstances completely—if you pull back enough to look. If you're too scared to take your foot off the gas, I'm afraid your perspective will be blurred.

If you feel as if you've lost control, it's probably because you have. But, no one took control from you. Your choices and behaviors handed it over.

Someone said do X, Y, and Z and you trustingly said okay, because they sounded confident, knowledgeable, and that's what others were doing. Hell, X, Y, and Z might have even created desired results for a time. But the moment the results were not exactly what you hoped and you continued to do X, Y, and Z anyway, it was time to stop and reexamine the situation. Yet, so many authors continue practices that do not yield desired results.

Just remember, it was Einstein who once said, "The definition of insanity is doing the same thing over and over again and expecting different results." Maybe there's a reason your job has you feeling a little nutty. Perhaps it's time to stop doing all the things that aren't working and try something revolutionary—like putting yourself first.

If you want to regain control over your career and success, you have to choose to take it back. You have to find the courage to face the problems with a critical eye and the confidence to say, "I don't care what others are doing. I'm only going to do what is actually beneficial to me and my journey".

Putting your needs and the needs of your company first does not make you a prima donna or a diva. It makes you a savvy entrepreneur with good business sense. If you're only in it as a hobbyist, continue to play into the "fake it till you make it" performance and draw what you can from illusions of success.

However, if you desire actual success, measurable prosperity, and a valuable sense of accomplishment that feeds your sense of self-worth rather than diminishes it, you're ready for change. You're ready to accept the reality of the industry challenges ahead and hone your behavior so that your journey is both efficient and rewarding, rather than depleting and self-deprecating. You're ready to learn the strategies needed to become a healthy, happy, balanced author.

Chapter Two
Wake Up Call

"Like a gulp of wine late in the afternoon, it makes you shudder. My feet tingle. I thought I was going to die the very next moment. But I didn't die..."

Jack Kerouac, The Dharma Bums, 1959

Denial

I was aware of something happening but helpless to stop it. My fingers tingled and a white haze crowded my peripheral as the quiet sounds of the house muffled into a droning hum. Instinctively, I slowed my steps and reached for the counter. Twenty seconds ago, I'd been seated safely at my desk, typing away, crushing my word count goals for the day, killing myself for that deadline—figuratively and literally.

My hand swiped through the air in what felt like slow motion as a fog settled over my thoughts. I missed the counter, lost my balance, and my vision went black.

The beauty of passing out is the unconsciousness of the fall. I didn't tip over like a tree when someone yells timber. I collapsed like a sack of bones, brainless for a split second, numb, with my last thought floating into nothingness.

This isn't normal...

A few seconds—maybe minutes—later, I opened my eyes to find myself on the kitchen floor. My husband had left a bag of work clothes needing to be washed by the door, and they had, thankfully, broken my fall. Without the soft laundry landing, I might have split my skull open on the hard tile.

I sat for several minutes, finding my bearings and catching my breath. It wasn't the first time I collapsed, and like all the other times, my heart pranced in an erratic rhythm of uncertainty, nervous energy, adrenalin, and physical red flags any medical professional would have shown concern over.

I slowly stood and located my phone, never stepping out of reach of the wall. I texted my husband, alerting him that I fell, again, and drank a glass of water as I waited for my nerves to calm.

If this had happened at an office, my employer would have most likely sent me home. But, here, I was the boss, and all I could see was the deadline, so I finished my water and went back to work.

A month later, I collapsed, again. I landed awkwardly on my ankle and hurt my foot, but the injury wasn't serious enough for me to consider making an appointment with the doctor. And let's face it, doctor visits ate up a chunk of the workday I wasn't willing to sacrifice.

As time went on and I continued to ignore the visible symptoms of my health declining, the dizzy spells got worse, and I eventually did seek medical attention. One doctor thought the spells had to do with my spine and possible nerve damage. Another told me I wasn't eating enough. Both were partially right. My back was shot from spending more than a hundred hours a week sitting at a desk hunched over a computer, and I was so consumed by work I often skipped meals, mostly breakfast and lunch.

Typically, I wouldn't break my fast until 5pm, aside from gulping down too many cups of coffee. I'm an early riser, so that usually comes with an early bedtime. My last meal habitually took place between 6 and 8pm. This left me starving for roughly twenty-one hours on most days.

But it didn't feel like starving. I was gorging my demons by overworking—as most workaholics often do when too hyper-focused to notice mild distractions, like hunger or fatigue.

Despite hardly ever eating, I was gaining weight. When I did eat, during those sparse three hours at night, I was too mentally drained and physically exhausted to put thought into healthy meals.

Quick takeout led to an abundance of sodium, fats, and processed sugars, which often put me into a food coma. I was starving, bingeing, not exercising, and within a few years, I'd gone from being an average plus-size American girl to a morbidly obese one.

I'd put on eighty pounds and I wasn't small to start. I also should have mentioned that I have systemic lupus, an autoimmune disease that has one goal—kill its host. Fat, sick, depressed, overworked, and not even close to wealthy, I, along with millions of other authors, spent several hours a week wondering if the cost of my job was worth the benefit.

Financially speaking, it wasn't. And what about mentally? Well, I was pretty much emotionally bankrupt at this point—bitter, negative, discouraged, and jaded. Even in areas outside of my job, areas I at one time loved, I had become despondent and indifferent toward. Physically, I was in a massive danger zone, and as much as I acknowledged what was happening, I was in denial about my lack of control.

I'd start to care on Monday—or whenever those new sneakers came in or maybe when the weather broke or after the holidays or just as soon as I met this deadline… The excuses were endless.

The dizzy spells and falls were like flags on the play, but I just sidestepped them like any other obstacle. I did this until avoidance was no longer an option.

In spring of 2018, while on a book tour, my legs and feet swelled up worse than ever before. I was constantly dizzy and terrified I would fall in front of people. I blamed my body's reaction on stress and high sodium hotel food—always an excuse that misplaced the accountability I didn't want to own.

After the tour, I took a "stress-reducing trip" with my mother, a mostly healthy woman in her early sixties. As we walked along the Pensacola beaches, I could hardly keep up with her, despite being more than twenty years younger. The simplest activities sapped the little energy I had, and I couldn't bear staying up later than 10pm.

On the way home, she had a difficult conversation with me about my health and her concerns. We both cried, and I finally admitted some painful truths.

I'd neglected my health for nearly half a decade in favor of success and pushing ahead in my career. I sidestepped my body's warnings until I could no longer walk without pain or collapsing. And that long-term abuse had buried me so deeply in health complications, I sometimes wondered if I'd already dug my grave.

I had the gym membership, the new sneakers, the cute workout clothes, and none of it mattered. Monday didn't mean shit because my organs were struggling to function, and I'd pushed myself so far beyond my limits that I lost control and couldn't find my way back.

And for what? Success? Yes, I was more successful than I'd been a few years prior, but I wasn't happy. I was miserable. I'd become so downhearted, I barely recognized my accomplishments, let alone took the time to celebrate them. No matter how much I achieved, it wasn't enough.

I was—literally—killing myself. And I already felt dead. So how the hell was I going to get my life back?

If any part of this feels relatable, it's because everything I just described was a mild to severe symptom of burnout. Burnout is one of the greatest obstacles that authors face. It is lethal and it will steal your success faster than any other villain. It should be feared more than plagiarism, bankruptcy, or social ruin, because burnout can lead to all of those things and more. Burnout can literally end your life.

I should know. It almost ended mine.

If, however, you are just starting your author career and have no experience with such work-related setbacks, that does not necessarily mean you are in the clear. While I understand that you are already facing an overwhelming number of aspirations as you try to orient yourself with this unfamiliar industry, it's best that you understand the patterns of burnout early on in your career. My intention is not to terrify you but to warn you.

As a matter of fact, beginning authors are in the best position to practice healthy habits as they have not yet established the bad habits many intermediate and advanced authors are trying to reverse.

It is the veteran authors who will struggle the most when it comes to changing behaviors. And sadly, when a seasoned author reaches a point of burnout, it's usually an extreme case. If you consider yourself an experienced author who now struggles to feel joy on the job, take heart. I, too, have been where you are.

For those of you still operating in the safe zone, consider this a cautionary tale. One that, I hope, will stay with you and save you the emotional, physical, and monetary expense of poor business practices and pain of burnout.

Throughout this nonfiction text, I will divulge several personal details of my life and journey. I was the ambitious, seemingly invincible performer who continuously put herself second until she nearly lost it all.

But if you know anything about me, know that I'm a survivor and in the words of Elton John, "I'm still standing."

Awareness

It happened so fast. A little overtime here and there snowballed into twelve-hour shifts, six or seven-day work weeks, and the demise of my social life. I had to keep going because pausing would jeopardize all the success I'd built so far.

I have to stay relevant! Those are the infamous last words of an author on the cusp of burnout.

But the truth is, it didn't happen fast at all. I didn't suddenly wake up one morning wondering where my motivation had gone. I felt it slipping away over a period of three to five years, but I blissfully existed in a state of denial.

It first started with a project, let's call it *Book A*, that took longer than expected to publish. I wrote the book in typical time, sealed a book deal, and started the editing process, only to have the rug pulled out from under me when the publisher announced they were declaring bankruptcy. The backlash of their decision took a financial and emotional toll on me as well as other authors.

Authors are not idle creatures, so we tend to have multiple projects moving at once, each in a different stage of development. Flash forward a year after the publishing house closed, and I was signing another deal with one of the *"Big Six"* publishers in New York. Let's call this project *Book B*.

But even the conglomerates aren't invulnerable to setbacks. When my editor suddenly resigned, for reasons not disclosed to me, I was assigned to her protégé, only to see her also resign six months after her predecessor. Three editors on one project are far too many in my opinion, and by the release of *Book B*, I had already written and published *Book C*. Meanwhile, *Book A* was still sitting in a file on my desktop.

In the chaos of a folding cottage industry of small presses where publishers were filing for Chapter 13 constantly, and my editors were frequently being let go or resigning with only a day's notice, I also lost a literary agent to retirement. Talk about some unforeseen setbacks!

By the time *Book A* was finally published, I had lost all emotional attachment to the story and was completely exhausted from monitoring the domino effect of crises scattering around me and trying to keep my brand alive.

I had to stay relevant!

I created a pattern of not pausing to correct unforeseen setbacks. To save time, I also created a pattern of no longer celebrating victories. Who has time for champagne and parties when the industry is so cutthroat? I had to keep moving.

This endless cycle of write, revise, produce, continued for years. I never rested between projects, and I hardly felt the success I was accumulating, because I was moving so fast I barely touched down to reality long enough to graze the surface, let alone enjoy the spoils of the job (Don't worry, they're there.)

I saw being an author like a jester spinning plates in the air. Each ad campaign, book signing, social media platform, and novel represented a plate I had to keep spinning. After thirty novels—which I had to maintain individualized marketing for if I wanted to keep my sales moving—I had countless plates spinning in the air.

I could only offer a glimpse of focus to each plate as the others needed my attention as well. I was so divided and cross-eyed, I lost sight of everything that truly mattered. It was no wonder I started falling down.

I was a performer, no longer a writer. Everything felt artificial, as if the only person outsiders saw was a woman made of wax. I was a mermaid, floating on an endless sea of nothingness, and never focusing on anything long enough to form any sort of real connection.

In 2018, when I started frequently blacking out and lost my ability to walk without pain, my precious plates came crashing down. In the course of less than a decade, my grip on reality and what mattered most had slipped. The woman I was had disappeared, and all that remained was *the author*—a miserable one at that.

I'd somehow sacrificed every ounce of pleasure I once felt for my career. The job I used to love, I now hated, as it brought me nothing but anxiety, illness, and stress.

Hobbling around the house, sore and stiff, gloomy and despondent, I couldn't bring myself to write with the joy or motivation I once claimed, and I had forgotten how to be anything other than an author. Never in a million years did I think being an author could steal my quality of life to the extreme it had.

There wasn't a playbook of healthy work habits for writers, and from my point of view, I was only doing what every other successful author appeared to be doing, but I wasn't succeeding. I was drowning.

After much time and *reflection*, I accepted what I didn't want to admit. Something so many had cautioned me about, but I had arrogantly believed myself invincible. Writing wasn't killing me. Burnout was.

Yet, there remained this thread of certainty I hung my heart on, a fraying belief that writing would somehow save and revive me. How could that be? If a writing career had practically killed me, how could it also save me?

For a solid month, I cried every day, assuming I would inevitably need to change careers if I wanted to put my health and mental well-being first. I loathed my job as an author, but part of me still wanted to continue writing. For weeks, I contemplated possible solutions to my situation, certain there had to be a better option than quitting.

Then it came to me. Toni Morrison, author of the Pulitzer Prize winning novel *Beloved,* once said, "If there's a book that you want to read, but it hasn't been written yet, then you must write it."

I decided to turn my life into a case study and write the playbook on healthy writing habits in order to practice and develop my own. As it turned out, I wasn't alone in my desire for such guidelines. Every author I told about the project rejoiced with excitement, as they, too, were battling some level of burnout.

And sadly, even some colleagues—who thought themselves invincible to such fates when I began this project—were singing a different tune by the time the book was finished. It is unsustainable to live in a state of steadily increasing expectations without consequence. That is not just a truth authors need to face, it is a truth that affects all players of the industry, even the ancient ones.

Earlier, when I mentioned the crumbling of the cottage industry presses, I was not speaking of some long-ago phenomenon. Multiple small presses collapsed in the last decade, and authors were left with countless orphaned books needing homes, several choosing to try their luck at self-publishing.

None of these industry shifts were the result of writing being difficult. As many of you would agree, writing is the easiest part of the job. But publishing is another animal entirely.

And while the industry can sometimes feel like a lawless jungle where powerful giants decide the smaller creatures' fates, there are actually ways to predict upcoming shifts in the industry. In the business chapters ahead, we will examine some of the ways history repeats itself in publishing, because there are valuable lessons worth learning. It's when we ignore the patterns and fail to see trends of history repeating itself that we face making the same mistakes as those who came before.

Ignorance is not bliss, especially when your livelihood hangs in the balance. Lack of knowledge invites a surplus of misguided practices. An inability to accurately identify when a business practice is not paying out will only create more of a syphon over time, sucking away an author's time, money, energy, and health.

So, why do authors continue to work in a state of denial? At some point, even the least accountable writer has to reach a degree of *awareness* and see the truth in the math. They will eventually have to accept that the hours most authors spend on the job typically far outweigh the financial reward.

Again, I'm not speaking of the less than 1% of authors who have reached the industry's measurable "standard for success." I'm speaking of the other 99%.

Let's examine that "standard for success" for a moment, just for a reality check. *Forbes* reported that James Patterson cleared $94 million in 2012. He, of course, qualifies for that top 1%.

But what is the standard? What measurable data does the industry use to rate if an author is in fact successful? Is it $94 million? Not even close.

According to Google, for an independent author to be considered successful, they must sell 1,000 books. Take a moment to actually process that.

Let's just assume your book has a retail price of $4.99 with a 70% royalty. That equals a profit of $3.49, not considering any of the production costs. Now, multiply that $3.49 by 1,000 book sales. That should bring the grand total to $3,493.00.

Now, I ask you, is thirty-five hundred dollars what you consider "making it?" Does that dollar amount compute to any sense of financial stability in your mind? For many Americans that isn't even enough to cover the monthly cost of living.

There are inconsistencies in our industry's research and some controversy over what qualifies as a "livable wage". $3,493.00 per book is not "livable" for my family, meaning it is not enough to meet my family's general needs—by a long shot.

So, what is "livable"? The research varies, but none of the estimations are what this author would label as "lucrative"—save that 1% of authors crushing it in the book industry.

According to *Writers Digest*, the median income for self-published authors is under $5,000 with 20% earning nothing. According to *Forbes,* the median income for a traditionally published author is between $5,000 and $9,999. Hybrid authors, reportedly, earned an income with a median between $15,000 and $19,999.

I don't know what's more shocking, the fact that most authors are financially floundering or that there seems an almost purposeful misrepresentation of our success as a whole. Could it be that the book industry is playing on the ignorance of its main contributors?

There have been days when I've suffered bone deep exhaustion, and felt no more valued than an old dog crated in a puppy mill, used for my natural talent, under loved and taken for granted. But I tell myself it's a labor of love and my moment will come.

Then after a year of working on a novel, I send it out into the world where 90% of the fanfare is paid for, and even my parents, husband, and best friend forget to say congratulations.

I know plenty about the emotional poverty suffered by authors. Sometimes that's harder to bear than the scarcity of income. The fact that we continue to write, tells me there is a reward in the process more than the result.

It pains me to think what the other 99% of authors are actually making. And it's no wonder why so many authors choose to live with their heads buried in the sand. The actuality makes too many hard-working authors—and believe me, authors are an impressive group of hustlers—sick with despair.

In any properly functioning industry, hard work should equal profit. But in an industry of art, existing in an oversaturated market, hard work comes with no guarantees.

I'm not trying to discourage authors or convince anyone to give up. I'm merely suggesting it's time we, as a community, level up.

It's time to close the disparity gap between effort and profit. To do this, we need to face the industry problems head-on and set some long overdue boundaries. This begins by removing the shame associated with the less than survivable average paygrade and starting a dialogue about what is actually sustainable in this business.

Such discussions aren't easy. Resolving problems usually requires courage. It requires someone to stand up and announce the "norm" is no longer working and risk being criticized or ostracized for going against the current.

I will gladly be that author, because I have seen the dangers of pretending everything is fine when it so clearly is not. I have paid the price of burning out from a job that does not consistently reward effort, and I want to save others from doing the same.

Perhaps burnout is not often discussed because it resides along the fringe of mental illness, and as Americans, we tend to overlook such realities until they can no longer be ignored. Aside from the detrimental situation of an abundance of authors burning out more than ever before, it behooves all authors to recognize the average income of published writers as an industry crisis.

There is a solution. There is a way to create balance between effort and profit, but we must, first, become fully aware of the problems and accept that we work in an industry that comes with no guarantees.

When author Tere Michaels asked me to present a workshop on prolific writing for the 2020 Book Lovers Convention, I had one condition—I would only teach authors how to be more prolific if we balance the lesson with healthy work habits. She gave her full support, and that workshop eventually grew into this book.

So, if you're suffering from burnout and worried you might be too far gone to ever find your mojo again, don't close that chapter of your life just yet. I'm living proof that positive change is possible, even for the most unhealthy, emotionally fried author out there.

Or, if you're merely starting out and concerned that such an overwhelming obstacle as burnout exists, follow along to learn helpful methods of avoiding long-term job stress. I promise there is a sensible method to getting back exactly what you put into the job.

And, spoiler alert, I love my job again! I also work less than forty hours a week, live a joyful life, and celebrate a new, healthy me. In the chapters ahead, I will tell you how I brought about such change so that you can improve your life in the same way.

Acceptance

After becoming aware that a problem existed, the first step to getting my life back was accepting that I had lost control. I needed to acknowledge the severity of my burnout.

I realized, if books were spinning plates, my load would only grow with time, and the way I was managing the load was in no way sustainable. Authors have the beautiful luxury of writing well into retirement age. But how likely is it that we will be able to perform like jesters with eighty spinning plates at that point? How likely is it that the average author's income will allow any sort of dependable retirement plan?

Can you picture a seventy-five-year-old you running endless campaigns on social media or attending virtual events, traveling, performing, advertising, and staying up to date on marketing trends?

To be perfectly honest, the idea of having to do those non-writing things for the rest of my life in order to sustain my career as an author made me physically sick to my stomach. I found myself desperately seeking an exit from a career I once loved.

And then it clicked. I spoke the words aloud, literally heard myself say, "The circumstances faced by authors today, make being an author an unsustainable career."

Some would call this a lightbulb moment. For me, it was much more dramatic. The floodlights flashed on and the brain fog I'd been suffering finally lifted. My path forward was illuminated.

I could see the flaws with the job expectations of a "modern day author," each one stemming from the delusions we keep.

You see, I, like many writers, loved the idea of being an author like Colin Firth in *Love Actually*, tucked away in a remote cottage in the south of France with a sexy Portuguese assistant serving up endless cups of tea and scones (My best friend is Portuguese, and she actually braves the writing cave to bring me food and water on occasion, so I'm almost living the dream).

Unfortunately, the reality of author life is much different from what Hollywood cinema has led us to believe. It's unbrushed, braless, and smells develop if an author is left unsupervised for too long. In no way would any truthful author call it *glamourous*.

For the purpose of this book, let's all agree that we will not romanticize the job of "modern day author," which will be what I'm referencing when I use the term "author" throughout the book. For once, let's drop the façade and discuss the job realistically as the actual shit show it is for the 99% of authors not qualifying as the top 1%.

The Four Greatest Flaws of Being a "Modern Day Author" (as I see things):

1. Books are no longer priced congruently with today's cost of living. Inflation has overlooked 90% of the authors in existence, and readers revolt whenever a common author prices a novel above five dollars, as if that writer didn't work as hard on their book as a nationally celebrated best seller might. Yet, it's common practice for the top-tier authors to price their eBooks in the ten-dollar range.

2. There are too many authors. With indie publishing as accessible as it is, anyone can publish their writing, slap an ISBN on the cover, and call it a book. It's created a bit of a swamp. Readers struggle to differentiate trash from talent. To take a risk on a new author means risking

one's money or time wading through an endless sea that can sometimes feel more like a cesspool, which is why many readers have learned to stick with what they know and *not* spend money on new names.

3. Marketing is heaped onto the author's shoulders more than ever. Authors are expected to not only maintain a website, but also a blog, newsletter, and a handle with every social media site trending. And when new platforms arrive, old ones do not disappear, so the list of places authors are expected to be virtually present continues to grow, with no end in sight. Such job expectations have drastically reduced authors' available time for writing. And, often times, higher royalties can be earned through strong promotional practices rather than time spent polishing and perfecting a book, which has shifted job motivation heavily toward marketing rather than writing. Consumers in this day and age are often more interested in *feeling good about their purchase* than forming any sort of private opinion on a product after the fact, so marketing is huge at this moment in time.

4. The publishing industry is shrinking while the author industry rapidly multiplies. What were once the *"Big Six"* publishing houses in New York are now more accurately "The Big Four." Conglomerate companies have cannibalized smaller presses and merged with sister companies, leaving fewer options for authors to pursue traditional publishing. With the downsizing of publishers, there has also been a downsizing of professionals. As more authors arrive on the scene, agents and editors grow more leery of taking risks on untried talent. This, in turn, directs writers to publish books independently, in an overly competitive market where the cost of discoverability far outweighs the average income of the self-published author.

Do you see? Have I turned on the floodlights for you? If that raw dose of reality left you a little depressed, don't fret. My goal, when I decided to rewrite the rule book for authors, was not to alter these flaws but reassign the control.

A person becomes a victim of circumstance the moment they lose control of a situation. Due to the market demands and the speed technology is advancing in our field, authors have very little control over their circumstances. My goal in writing *Write 10K in a Day* was to help authors return a sense of control to their job and offer useful advice for overcoming the current obstacles congesting our path to success.

Good books require a decent amount of preparation, so I started this journey with long hours of *reflection*. I shut all my notifications off, deleted some of my apps from my phone, and gave myself permission to do something I hadn't done in far too long. I sat still with my thoughts.

PAUSE FOR A DEEP BREATH

If you are feeling overwhelmed, take a moment to reflect. None of the current marketing circumstances accurately measure the value of the effort you gave or the quality of your finished book. Do not let the flaws of the industry dictate your self-worth. Remind yourself that publishing is an incredibly difficult business. If even ten strangers read and enjoyed your work, you have succeeded to some degree. More success is coming. But first, you're going to learn how to build safeguards and boundaries to protect yourself along the journey. Then once you, our magnificent hero of this story, are properly armed with knowledge and helpful practices, you will continue your journey to the top. My goal is to get you there in one piece and in a perfectly balanced state of being.

My period of *reflection* started with a lot of tears, as I, like many of you, did not want to face the fact that, after all my hard work, the job of "author" turned out to be flawed, and the chance of reaching unequivocal success, on any sort of grand scale, was about as likely as me winning the lottery. And I don't buy lottery tickets.

You see, that's where we are. There are simply too many published authors in existence. Even the best writers can go unnoticed. Masterpieces are more likely to go unread than ever before.

Now, some of the newer authors reading this might still live in a mostly hopeful headspace, and it's not my intention to shoot down their dreams. On the contrary, I envy that early can-do spirit that thrives in optimism, and I hope it never fades, but for some of you, it will. I share my struggles to better arm you for the tumble so that you won't find your spirit as broken as I found mine when I hit the ground.

Chances are, you're doing almost everything right. But so is everyone else. In a market as oversaturated as the book market, it takes something truly extraordinary to stand out among the masses. Failing to do so is not necessarily a failure in terms of talent or skill.

Let me make this perfectly clear, IT'S NOT YOU! It's the market!

Denial stops the moment an author becomes completely aware of what the actuality of being an "author" means. But progress requires self-awareness. We should be unflinchingly clear about the parts of the job we like and dislike, so we can reject the areas that don't serve our goals.

When you reach the end of the chapter, the stream of consciousness activity will help clarify your overall goals. But never forget, you have the right to be selective! Like any job, you can negotiate the expectations of the position. You will do this by manipulating personal preference, salary, and benefits, making various compromises until you reach an outcome that feels fair.

Pausing life long enough to gain some perspective and identify what my greatest motivators were, might have risked my relevancy, but we're all temporary at best. For me, this initial moment of *reflection* lasted roughly three weeks, but it was followed by a year of planned breaks designed to help me establish a more balanced lifestyle. And, in the end, I'm happier, healthier, and more successful for it.

Now that I've stopped neglecting my needs and put myself first, my writing has peaked and my creativity has exploded into a supernova I can hardly contain. My path is illuminated, clear, and I have no regrets for the time I took away from writing to get here. So, don't freak out if you need some time to regroup, be it a few weeks or an entire year, you will come back to it stronger in the end.

No matter how much I hated being an author in this day and age, I still loved writing. Writing completed me like a soul mate that had been missing for the first half of my life. It was all the non-writing parts of the job that were sucking my soul away.

Prior to being an author, I'd been a teacher, and I never experienced a sliver of the satisfaction in the classroom that I found while writing books. Acknowledging that I might have to give up my career depressed me in a manner too gutting to describe—and I pride myself on accurately writing every human emotion.

The thought of not writing left me hollow, vacant, lost, alone, and scared. I felt obsolete, like a woman who misused her potential and had no purpose. Calling it an existential crisis would be an understatement.

If writing was my soul mate, my soul mate tried to kill me—and so I grieved.

But, maybe, it was me who tried to kill my soul mate first. Writing had always been a beautiful pleasure. It didn't become unpleasant until the term "author" was redefined by an influx of nonexperts claiming that to be an "author" one must do X, Y, and Z.

I use the term nonexpert to reiterate that we live in a time where anyone can create seemingly qualifying credentials by simply building a website, designing business cards, growing a social following, or—since the dawn of digital print—publish a book. There is very little experience or expertise behind most people's claims, so be selective when it comes to taking advice from others. I've found the majority of self-proclaimed experts out there to be tragically underqualified.

In the preface, I mentioned the book *How to Write Best Selling Fiction,* published by Dean Koontz in 1972. This isn't the only relic I own. I have a habit of placing higher value on craft books published prior to the genesis of self-publishing because I believe there was a higher level of quality control back then.

Nowadays, any moron can write a *"How-To"* book and call it expertise. You might even think I'm one of them, which is why I specifically requested you identify me as a *lifelong learner*—rather than an expert on anything—while reading this book.

When people obnoxiously proclaim their excellence, displaying an alarming abundance of confidence and knowledge for a subject, step back and ask yourself if they are truly qualified to advise anyone on the subject.

I sure hope you asked yourself that when you started this book. And if you rated my background and experience with a mid B then I would expect you only to agree with about 85% of my theories. Very rarely do we find a source that is 100% reliable and accredited in this day and age. That is why true experts are so rare, so, please, use your best judgement.

Returning to the idea of nonexperts and the dangers they present, we must know how to identify them. Those who insist you must do X, Y, and Z to fully qualify as an author, those who tend to perpetuate an air of expertise from a somewhat lacking background, they often do so to *appear* smarter. Confidence is so highly prized in American culture, many people prefer to pretend they are knowledgeable in a certain subject area rather than risk appearing inferior. Their arrogance has very little to do with actual intelligence.

In other words, the ego is forming a barricade between people and useful knowledge. If someone delivers advice with enough confidence, others will believe them, whether they're talking out of their ass or not. Opinions are not facts! But they are like assholes and everyone's got one. Choose wisely when it comes to the opinions you trust. If someone's opinion smells a little like bullshit, it probably is.

This pattern of trusting underqualified sources is commonly referred to as the *Dunning-Kruger effect*, which is having a bit of an American renaissance lately, as people argue conspiracy theories over actual facts to distort the truth.

People who use the *Dunning-Kruger effect* to appear smarter than they actually are could be labeled "predators of intellect." Be smarter than the predator or you will find yourself filling the role of prey.

All advice should be digested with a judicious mind and never swallowed down as a quick fix pill, because no advice, including my own, is one size fits all. And, as with any pill, there are always side effects.

That being said, consider the advice you have been given in the past, specifically advice directly relating to "being an author". Was the source qualified? Trustworthy? Were they smart enough to know they couldn't possibly know everything? Maybe not. Maybe some of that good advice you've been killing yourself to follow wasn't that good for you after all.

So, why do we fall for it? Half of the world seems to think confidence is more valuable than actual intelligence.

People who value intellect over arrogance tend to be a lot more humble. Pride is a loud characteristic, where modesty is much more subtle and quiet.

Humble people know they have more to learn, so they tend to be smarter, because they've set themselves up as lifelong learners and are always consuming new information and using their ever-growing intellect to filter out the rubbish.

Know-it-alls tend to underestimate humble people's intelligence, seeing such modest traits as unimpressive or weak. They are much more drawn to grandiose displays of confidence and are rarely concerned with fact-checking.

On the other hand, humble people tend to be so modest, they often struggle with confidence. They're uncomfortable revealing their opinions before they're certain they've done enough fact-checking to form a solid foundation. These are the authors that have the most anxiety when releasing a book, because they will always be aware that it could be better.

Often, this also makes them the most vulnerable when it comes to believing others have their best interest at heart, when, in reality, others are often only feeding their own ego by playing the role of self-proclaimed expert. A safe rule of thumb is to never take industry advice from anyone who doesn't preface said advice with a caveat that there are exceptions to every rule and what worked for one person might not work for another. If you find yourself getting advice from someone proclaiming their way is the only way—run.

Interestingly enough, the opposite of the *Dunning-Kruger effect* is the impostor syndrome. Do you see the parallel now?

I, personally, will always prefer to talk shop with a humble author rather than an arrogant one, because those reserved little gems are actually in possession of the most valuable knowledge.

However, many authors are drawn to the loud mouth know-it-alls barking out groundless claims and using the *Dunning-Kruger effect* to convince others their way is the right way. You can thank them for complicating the job and definition of "author."

Falling for poor advice and believing all authors must do X, Y, and Z in order to succeed, costs time, money, health, and can even cost an author their passion in the end.

Following bad advice nearly extinguished my confidence. It certainly doused my passion. I was going the wrong direction, way too fast to steer, which was why things started spinning out of control. Slamming on the brakes and pulling over to catch my breath so I could reassess the roadmap was, possibly, the best thing I'd ever done for myself and my career.

So, let's all take a moment to stop and look at where we are. You're all standing at a different vantage point of *your* personal journey. What matters most is that *you* stay aware of *your* surroundings. Stop worrying about what all the other people on the road are doing. They're on a different path. You're on yours.

Once you are truly aware of your surroundings and the obstacles on the road ahead, think about where you want to go. What is *your* objective? How would you like to get there? Do you want to take a fast track or a leisurely back road to reach your destination?

All of this can be decided when you take your moment(s) of *reflection*. Take your time with the process of choosing. There is no deadline for making up your mind and no rule that says you can't change direction at any given time. This is *your* journey, so you might as well make it a pleasant one.

Objective

We have bastardized the artistic simplicity of writing by crowding the job with so many outside obligations associated with the business of publishing that authors frequently complain they have no time to write anymore. But it doesn't have to be this way.

Let's start this section off by filtering the term "author" back to what it actually is—a person who writes.

If you're overwhelmed, overtaxed, and feeling undernourished mentally, emotionally, or physically, put down your spinning plates and come with me on a journey back to the basics. If you don't like what you've learned in the end, your plates will be right here where you've left them. However, if you'd like to open your mind to the possibility of a better life and expand your perception, I'd love the opportunity to introduce you to the actual rules of the game. This may shock you, but spinning plates and exhaustion are not required to obtain a successful and satisfying author career.

You are your greatest instrument. You wouldn't sit down to write a story using a pencil with a dull tip, so why would you expect to type one with a dull, hazy mind?

When I refer to "health" in this book, it's important to understand that I'm referring to the health of the mind, body, and spirit. That is, the physical health, emotional health, and creative health of the author.

Hard work only leads to success when paired with knowledge and planning. Working hard is stupid if you don't have a plan. You are not a stupid person, so take this moment to promise yourself you will no longer waste time on stupid practices that have little to no benefit to your life.

Repeat after me: "From here on, I will be self-aware and accept the reality of my situation. I will no longer give my energy to tasks that lack a clear objective or benefit to my overall quality of life."

Yes, I said life. I understand writing is your livelihood, but that's just a fancy word for career. Decide right now, which do you value more—your life or career? And remember, you can have a life without a career, but you can't have a career without a life.

Once you're aware there might be a problem, which I'm assuming you are since you purchased this book, you have to accept that you might not be as in control of your career as you once were. We are going to reorganize your career objectives and set *you* at the top of your priority list. We are going to return control to the author. *What a revolutionary idea!*

Success begins with a healthy mindset. So, if you are burned out, showing symptoms of burning out, or just want to avoid these things altogether and learn some useful writing tips, set your mind to the possibility that burnout can be avoided and, if necessary, reversed. Also, acknowledge that burnout is the greatest threat to your success.

If you're on the cusp of giving up, don't. Bear with me for the length of this book, and I promise to teach you options you might not know you have.

It's not you that has failed. It's the methods you were sold. It's time to toss out the broken practices and focus only on the strategies that have stood the test of time.

I've shared my journey, now it's time to review yours. You begin your journey with a writer's most critical tool. It's not a pen or paper or computer or even your mind. It's your body.

The body is the one thing every person should always put first, regardless of the job ahead. Taking care of you, mentally, physically, and spiritually is the first step in your journey to success. It's objective number one.

ACTIVITY

Find a quiet place away from distractions. Silence all notifications and set a 10 minute timer. Use a blank sheet of paper to practice stream-of-consciousness writing, with the single intention of answering the following question:

WHAT DO YOU WANT TO GAIN FROM A CAREER AS AN AUTHOR?

TO BEGIN stream-of-consciousness writing, simply start writing. Try to write continuously for ten minutes, and do not stop until time is up. Waste no time on grammar or spelling. The thoughts that land on the page should be uninterrupted, unedited, and unstructured.

When you're finished, your words should reveal quite a bit about your goals. This practice has been used by famous writers, such as Edgar Allan Poe, Virginia Woolf, Tolstoy, and more.

EXAMPLE:
Writing books. Peaceful. Cathartic. Let go. Characters. Falling in love. Joy. Thinking. Clarity. Ease. State of mind. Inspiration. Peace. Hope. Relatability. Inspiring others. Happiness. Balanced. Independence. Human connection. Making a living. A sense of pride. The absolute joy of writing. Challenging myself. (and so on…)

Notice how, in the example, the author sometimes repeats ideas and words. That is fine, as it emphasizes their importance.

READ your stream of consciousness, and take time to reflect on the feelings your words have revealed.

Chapter Three
A Healthy Road to Success

"Every human being is the author of his own health or disease."

Swami Sivananda, Bliss Divine, 1974

The Value of Happiness

It is crucial to recognize the actual challenges faced by present day authors. As professionals, we must accept that most writers are struggling to overcome many obstacles.

Authors should be prolific, but first and foremost, they must know how to be efficient without jeopardizing their health. Beyond writing habits and hacks, there are obstacles that should concern every writer.

Sedentary jobs that keep people in chairs for eight hours a day, such as writing, have been proven to increase chances of type 2 diabetes, cardiovascular disease, and all types of cancer. These are sad truths no one likes to discuss, but they are also common worries that weigh heavily on most authors.

Unhealthy advice, such as publish a book every five weeks, increases the pressure on authors to write faster, which requires more time chained to the desk and less time meeting the physical and mental needs required to remain sharp and healthy.

Those who have been writing for a substantial amount of time and occupying a desk job for years can already see the neglect taking effect on their mind and body. Simply sitting for a few hours without taking a movement break can do severe damage, and even rob us of a future.

As authors, there is a growing pressure to stay relevant in an oversaturated market. Successful writers universally face the task of mastering time management. Using time effectively, as sole proprietors and artists, creates a vacuum between marketing and creating.

Social media is a cost-effective, free way to form connections, but it is also a time-suck. This, among other useful business practices, can eat up an author's eight-hour workday. But keep in mind, many authors work twelve hours or more a day to accommodate the endless job requirements. That's a fast track to burnout.

As entrepreneurs, authors are typically one-man or one-woman shows. The wish for more hours in a day or more hands or brain cells or a clone, seems a continuous theme. But the answer isn't wishing for the impossible. The solution lies in managing time effectively and maintaining a healthy balance between work and pleasure.

The typical author, like most artists, is starving on some level—usually, if not on a financial level, an internal one. Take a moment to ask yourself if you are fulfilled, satisfied, and happy in your career?

Chances are, your emotional balance isn't in alignment with your bank account. Or, maybe it is, if both are looking a little bankrupt.

The unfortunate truth, as discussed in the previous chapter, is that less than 1% of authors sell more than 1,000 copies. And for those that do, it is important to consider how vast that single percentage is. Meaning, even those who breach that 1% and sell more than a thousand copies of a single title, are not necessarily making Stephen King or Nora Roberts dollars.

Depositing money into one account does not automatically create a surplus of joy in life, either. There is no guarantee that once you've met some obscure criteria used to define an author's "success" that you will actually feel successful.

As with any business, a profit cannot be effectively measured without first deducting the expenses, so there lies another inadequacy in the 1,000 copies sold rule. So, if authors are not measuring success by copies sold, and the majority of published authors can't justify their work by profit, then how should "success" be measured?

The idea of success is a relative one at best. The cost of any business should never be more expensive than the reward, yet authors need much more than money to stay afloat. They are spending a ton of energy on practices that lack a measurable return.

Being an author requires a lot of business sense if you are hoping to draw an income. In business, all investments must show a sizable return to qualify as justified. This is commonly referred to as ROI or return on investment.

How much have you invested to make it to this point in your journey? If a dollar amount comes to mind, write it down. But also consider the emotional toll, the time away from family and friends, the late nights, the breakdowns, and the neglect you suffered in the process. Can you put a price on all of that?

Now, think about the return. Does it outweigh your investment?

The problem with burnout is that it removes a person's sense of satisfaction. And in a job with very little guarantee of financial reward, sometimes that emotional satisfaction is the only reliable incentive authors have.

So much of an author's emotional and physical turmoil stems from inadequate time management. We notoriously abuse our bodies in search of more hours in a day or fall into wasteful business practices that prove a poor use of our time. It's no wonder so many authors feel like their worlds are spinning out of control.

We must stop. Stop everything. Put the spinning plates down. And survey what is actually going on.

Our health depends on our ability to accurately and honestly measure our behavior. We must put everything on pause so that we can clearly assess the reality.

I know, I know… Many of you are already making excuses that pausing isn't an option. If you honestly believe that, stick a bookmark here and come back when you're more open-minded, or maybe when you're miserable enough to consider another—possibly better—perspective.

These strategies won't fade with time, so I won't be offended if you stick this book on your shelf for a while. But you know what does fade with time? Ambition. Youth. Intelligence. Maybe, just maybe, the methods in this book could prolong those fleeting qualities and bring about riches you haven't considered the actual value of for some time.

Ask yourself, what would you rather be, wealthy and miserable or monetarily stable and happy? For me, happiness is always the winner.

I aim to be one of those cheerfully optimistic people who annoy others with their can-do attitude, which is quite a stretch because, in reality, I'm rather dry, sarcastic, and comically bitchy on my best days. But hey, this masterpiece is a work in progress.

Considering that you're still reading and you have not chosen to put the book on a shelf, let's move on and figure out how happy authors live.

The Use of Time

Time management is one of the greatest tools in a healthy writing career. That's why I've chosen to address it from the start, just after establishing that burnout is the ultimate villain in this book. Hence, the subtitle: *Avoid Burnout and Unleash Your Prolific Potential.*

Seems a little contrary, doesn't it? But there lies the paradox. What if there was a way for authors to avoid burnout and write faster? What if an author could write ten thousand words in a day?

Do that for seven days and you'd have a seventy-thousand-word novel. Do it for ten days, and it's up to one hundred thousand words, that's roughly a book of three to four hundred pages.

I'll remind those of you frowning that you're only going to give yourself wrinkles. While it might seem like I'm contradicting myself, I assure you, I'm not.

In no way, shape, or form am I advocating longer than eight-hour workdays or suggesting you lock yourself to your desk for seven or ten days straight. As a matter of fact, the methods in this book can actually shorten your work days and work weeks.

That's right! Some days I only work four hours, and I still hit my word count. And most weeks, I have no problem taking a half or whole day off if something comes up.

How? It all comes down to knowledge, planning, and hard work.

Stick with me.

My journey toward taking better care of myself got extra self-indulgent during the isolation of 2020, and I've since learned to lead a life where the main character has her dream job, plenty of time for socializing, practices self-care on a regular basis, smiles more, and basically spoils herself rotten.

We are the main characters of our lives. My personal story was turning into a tragedy until I made some revisions. Like most of my other books, the heroine didn't need a hero, because she figured out how to save herself. And I'm going to teach you the same!

Think it's impossible to write 10K in a day and not get burned-out? Or, maybe you're thinking it is possible—*if* an author is okay with writing complete rubbish. Wrong on both accounts.

Authors can absolutely write ten thousand, valuable words a day without burning out. I've done it several times, and I can teach you how to do it, too.

While you will need a decent grasp of typing skills, this method has very little to do with the speed at which one can type. However, if you are of the hunt-and-peck sort, you might need to get your WPM (words per minute) up to an average speed.

I type an unimpressive 40 words per minute, a standard average. But let's put that into perspective to abolish any assumption that I might be hiding savant typing skills, which, I assure you, I am not.

The fastest recorded typing speed, according to world records, is around 216 WPM—on a 1946 typewriter no less! In the show *The Office*, Pam Beesly claims she can type 90 WPM. Jim Halpert claims he can type 55 WPM. So, you can see, I'm typing at a very basic word count per minute—less than even Jim can manage. Yet, I can write ten thousand words a day while maintaining highly profitable, quality work.

Full disclosure, my highest word count record is 27K in a day. I in no way recommend this, as it was achieved at the peak of my burnout and part of the reason why this book exists. 10K is my sweet spot. By the end of this book, you will know yours.

Some authors struggle to meet 1k a day, and that's a fine place to be right now. By the end of the book, you will be armed with tools to help you gradually increase your speed.

After some practice with the tools I provide, you will become an expert on story arcs and character development. And in time, you will grow your word count up to 10K a day without threatening your sanity or health.

Speed does not have to come at the cost of quality—*if* the skill is there. Nor should high word counts cost you your health.

Once again, I remind you of the combination approach that requires knowledge, planning, and hard work. If you have the knowledge and plan in place, meeting word count is just a time-consuming part of the hard work that follows.

Some of my best sellers were written using the prolific practices advocated in this book. As a matter of fact, if I did an audit of all of my books, the majority of the more lucrative titles were created with this approach.

Unfortunately, many of my earlier titles were written using *only* the strategies taught in the craft sections of this book, while neglecting all other areas of my life. That off-kilter focus is what eventually burned me out.

The goal of sharing my new holistic approach that focuses on balancing the mind, body, and spirit of the author soul is to share my past mistakes and save others similar pain. I have learned to balance life and work and all the in between, but doing so requires my ongoing focus and dedication. It is possible to accomplish—live a balanced life and achieve high word counts simultaneously—with the methods I will explain throughout this book.

The balanced approach is the only approach. Anything less, and you, the author, will ultimately suffer, as will your work.

Some examples of books I've written quickly include:

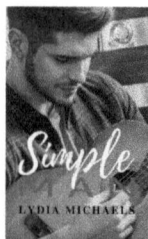

Simple Man (240 pages), a stand-alone novel I published with a small press in 2015 that took twelve days to write. InD'tale Magazine later nominated it for Best New Adult Romance.

La Vie en Rose (380 pages), a story that remains one of my favorites to date took ten days to finish. This story led to one of my most successful book launches and remains a treasured book among readers.

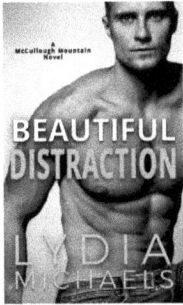

Beautiful Distraction (McCullough Mountain 2)—previously published under the title *Skin*—was written in five days. It's two hundred pages and won *Honorable Mention* for *Best Contemporary Romance* at the RONE Awards in 2015.

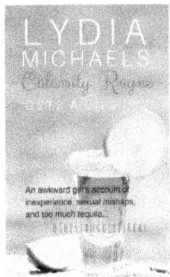

Calamity Rayne: Gets a Life—This hilarious RomCom is an awkward girl's account of inexperience, sexual mishaps, and too much tequila. It was written in twelve days using the practices taught in this book. (It's also free, so be sure to download a copy!)

THE JASPER FALLS SERIES

And coming in 2021, the Jasper Falls series, which used the guidelines in this book as an experiment to confirm the theories. Each book in this series has been written in under one week!

So, you see, it is possible to write quality work in a short period of time. But if you aren't managing your time appropriately, there will be a steep cost. I'm happy to report that I suffered no negative consequences after writing the Jasper Falls series, because I was practicing the balanced methods advocated in this book.

However, in 2016, during a definite time of imbalance, after upping my word count to dangerous heights and stretching my time too thin between writing and marketing and travel, the early symptoms of burnout reared in my career. I was so exhausted, I couldn't shake the sense that I was failing. No matter how much my royalties rose, and my following continued to grow, I was dissatisfied with my progress. And by 2018, I literally started to fall.

If we mismanage time and energy, we will eventually lose our balance, misstep, and fall. Mismanaged time is the fastest route to burnout. And, as I've already stated, there is no greater setback, or one that knocks an author on his or her ass as thoroughly, as burnout.

The Untimeliness of Setbacks

Burnout is an untimely and inconvenient side effect of the job. I, like so many other authors, naïvely assumed it would never grab hold of me, so I denied how severely it was affecting my life as a whole once I was trapped in its clutches.

Cue Julia Roberts in Pretty Woman, "Big mistake. Huge."

By 2018, I was dangerously ill, ready to give up a career I'd previously loved, and so sick with wariness that I could hardly breathe. My confidence had turned to dust. My drive all but disappeared. And my mind was trapped in a dark cycle of discouragement, envy, and doubt.

On paper, I was successful. But emotionally and physically, I was falling apart. For all of my success, I still woke up every day with a sense of failure. I felt like I was drowning, and for what? The harder I worked, the less satisfaction I drew from the job.

Yes, I was making substantially more money than when I started writing, but I was also spending a fortune to stand out among the competition, because the closer authors get to the top, the fiercer the game and the higher the stakes.

At the end of the year, my income seemed sizeable, but after all my deductions and the toll my job was taking on my soul, I honestly wasn't making enough to justify the cost to my health and sanity. In other words, I couldn't justify the emotional ROI.

Like so many authors, I was suffering from the pressure to produce rapid books to stay relevant or forced to steadily perform in virtual or physical events or run expensive promos that rarely provided tangible returns on my investments. I was also recovering from a list of unforeseen setbacks, as described in Chapter Two.

Publicity stunts, like running a promotion with massive newsletters, were becoming increasingly selective and nearly impossible to land. But the thought of pushing myself harder than I already was, seemed the only way to get ahead, and the fastest way to put me in the ground.

Think I'm exaggerating? After visiting with several doctors, I faced the indisputable physical proof of what I'd done to myself by ignoring the symptoms of burnout.

Not only was I morbidly obese, my cholesterol was dangerously high, my organs showed troublesome red flags of bigger problems to come, I could hardly walk without assistance or stand for more than a minute without pain, I was blacking out and frequently collapsing, my heartbeat was all over the map, my hair was falling out in clumps, my brain was in a constant fog, and my legs and feet were perpetually swollen. On top of all of that, I had lost any sense of joy in my once blissful life.

Setbacks come in all shapes and sizes, so do not expect one author's to resemble another's. The death of a loved one, divorce, loss of income, troubles at school with the kids, becoming a caregiver, combatting an illness, domestic responsibility, financial stress, an act of God, all of the above are unforeseen setbacks I have watched authors combat on top of everything else. And there are plenty more I have not mentioned.

The list is endless. Life is unpredictable. And we could all make do with being a little nicer to each other.

Everyone is fighting their own private crisis on some level. Remember that, the next time you're scrolling through social media and feel envy setting in. Just because someone's brand or life looks perfect, does not mean it is. Never forget you're only seeing a glimpse—a very meticulously selected and most likely airbrushed, glimpse.

When I suggest we treat each other with a bit more compassion than we have in the past, I'm specifically asking you to take it easy on *yourself*. Do not let other people's success diminish your own. It's a marathon, not a sprint (for more uplifting clichés and inspirational affirmations, please follow my Instagram page @lydia_michaels_books).

So, while all of the problems listed above can qualify as a personal "setback," someone else's success never should. Your job is to worry about *you*. Rubbernecking will only slow down your journey, so keep your eyes on the road ahead.

The Rush of Surrender

I was done. Once I hit my breaking point, burnout had won. Even if I lost everything, I didn't care.

The shift in my attitude from a woman who would put aside *everything* to succeed, to a brokenhearted writer who only sensed failure, goes to show how deeply depressed I actually was at the peak of my burnout.

If pausing my career cost me every ounce of success I'd spent the last decade trying to earn, I didn't care. I only knew I couldn't continue the way things were going.

This was the scariest moment of my career—possibly the most reckless—but also the greatest. If my present self could go back in time, I'd tell my past self that establishing boundaries is a strength, not a weakness. Do yourself a favor and write that down, right now, in your notes.

Establishing boundaries is a strength, not a weakness.

You'd think, as the author of *The Surrender Trilogy,* I would have read and written enough scenes on *surrender* to understand that while surrender can be scary it can, also, be liberating, but no. Hitting the brakes on my career terrified the ever-loving shit out of me. Fair warning, I expect it will have the same effect on you.

If you've ever read a love story about surrender, you know the moment the main character lets go she (or he) is liberated from her (or his) demons. This is where all that glorious symbolism and irony about being tied in physical and emotional knots comes into play. You would think a romance author would know better and arrive at this conclusion without suffering a complete meltdown, but no.

In life, characters can also be infuriatingly dense. But, hey, that's what makes the happy ending all the more rewarding.

The Freedom of Boundaries

I decided to take the entire summer off to focus on healing myself. I walked every day, listened to a ton of self-help books, rediscovered my love for cooking, lost a lot of weight*, and surrounded myself with things that once brought me joy. Slowly, my happiness was restored.

When I felt strong enough to return to social media, I showed a more authentic side of myself than ever before. I posted inspirational affirmations about acceptance and success on my Instagram to help me stay focused on what truly counted. I also shared glimpses into my healthy lifestyle with recipes, humor, and writing tips to help authors avoid burnout and unleash their prolific potential.

I became grounded in the affirmations I needed to hear most and told myself every day that my life was too valuable to waste in misery. I started to receive messages from strangers, thanking me for inspiring them.

But I still struggled to see myself as any sort of positive example, because I knew my journey was far from over. The first part of my career was spent perfecting an image, a personification of what I thought an "author" looked like. From my point of view, I saw myself in a raw state of post-depression recovery—and I'm being generous with the term recovery, because I still felt incredibly fragile.

I saw myself as needing inspiration as much as anyone else. My interactions had become more thoughtful and less about my brand. The fear that I might teeter outside the veil of professionalism was traded in for raw, honest content about food, family, and things that make me go *hmmm.*

In a way, I suppose my authenticity made me more relatable to others (more on authenticity and relatability later). For now, the point is, what we think looks best isn't always best. By simply being real with my followers and sharing glimpses into my ordinary life, I make more lasting connections than I ever could with some superficial ad campaign designed to snag readers' attention.

The boundaries I established that summer grew over time. As a workaholic, I had a hundred lists of goals, each one important to me. But I had lost sight of my first priority. I needed to stop in order to clarify my objective and get back on the right track.

If I must choose to be one thing, I will always choose to be happy. That is my #1 Objective, plain and simple. Unfortunately, it took a lot of unnecessary misery for me to remember that.

Writing makes me happy. But being an author, the way authors have been encouraged to behave with the excruciating duty of publishing and the endless marketing tasks, was making me the opposite of happy, so I redefined the rules.

Prolific writing and a clear plan to avoid burnout must go hand in hand for any long-term, sustainable success. Perhaps you're ahead of the curve and already figured out how to do one of the two. Or, maybe you're feeling completely overwhelmed and unsure how to accomplish either.

---

* At the time of writing *Write 10K in a Day,* I had been on my journey to reverse the effects of burnout for 18 months.

Take a deep breath. This is only the beginning. This is the beginning of the rest of your life. This is the start of your future, which will include joy, laughter, peace, and an abundance of success. We just have to take some *time*, make a few *changes*, overcome a few *setbacks*, *surrender* to reality, and establish some healthy *boundaries*. Then *happiness* will follow.

The success of an author is not only measured by book sales, but by quality of life. Any author's quality of life will improve the moment they turn their focus to finding balance between work and pleasure, which this book advocates and teaches. Balance not only helps authors avoid burnout, it also unleashes their prolific potential.

The concepts taught throughout the upcoming chapters require authors to acknowledge the important role health plays in the success of a writing career. A healthy career is a happy, sustainable one, measured not just in monetary value, but in joy, satisfaction, and its ability to deliver a fulfilling existence.

****

Before moving on to the next chapter, complete the worksheet on the next page. If you are listening to the audiobook or reading from an eBook, simply draw a T on a piece of paper, labeling one column: WHAT I LOVE ABOUT BEING A WRITER and the other column: WHAT I DISLIKE ABOUT BEING AN AUTHOR. This will help you analyze your current location and determine what direction you need to go.

Then when you've finished your list, see if you can determine what your ultimate priority is, your #1 Objective. This will help you decide how best to measure your success.

WRITE 10K in a DAY

REVIEWING THE JOB

Fill in the sections below to assess your current feelings on being an "author" versus being a "writer". Then decide what your objective is to better determine what behaviors you can change.

What I love about being a writer:

What I dislike about being an author:

My Objective is:

_____
_____
_____
_____
_____
_____

www.LydiaMichaelsBooks.com

Chapter Four
Stress

"Had I died, it would have been self-destruction."

Jane Austen, Sense and Sensibility, 1811

The Physical Effect of Stress

An author's knowledge starts with knowing how our bodies process stress and function on the job. The immune system is a complex network of cells, tissues, and organs that help the body fight infections and other diseases. When germs, such as bacteria or viruses, invade our bodies, they attack and multiply, creating a snowball effect that can quickly evolve into an avalanche.

Several symptoms of burnout begin with the immune system. As one example, some authors that experienced burnout firsthand complain of thinning hair.

They often blame this on the stress of the job, but if they dig deeper, they would learn that prolonged, severe stress has caused the immune system to attack the body, and hair loss is merely a symptom of a greater issue. Hair follicles are providing visible proof of the effect stress is having. Unfortunately, stress is likely wreaking havoc on other, unseen parts of the body as well.

A misguided immune system often starts to attack its own body. This behavior is labeled as autoimmunity. Once autoimmunity exists, it can often lead to other, more complex autoimmune diseases, such as rheumatoid arthritis, multiple sclerosis, autoimmune thyroiditis, Sjögren's syndrome, and inflammatory bowel disease, which carry a substantially increased risk for additional diseases.

Too many authors are currently battling one of the above disorders, and many of those authors claim said conditions cropped up during their career, having never existed before.

Overworked authors that ignore the effects of stress can suffer a myriad of symptoms linked to larger problems. I've heard authors complain about long periods of blurred vision that make it impossible to work, fingers locking up, vomiting, fainting, shaking, swelling, limbs numbing, and more. But their devotion to the deadline keeps them slaving away, and in turn, they make a choice to further neglect themselves.

The sedentary lifestyle of authors can also lead to noticeable weight gain, which can trigger more cause for concern and other life-threatening diseases. And we haven't even touched on how poor lifestyle and chronic stress can lead to mental illnesses, like anxiety and depression. So, why aren't we doing something about this?

It's always a joy to attend an author conference and see workshops for yoga or meditation or walking groups in addition to the usual activities. Such practices need to be more commonplace in our field, and it is our job to advocate such things. Authors are not unionized, nor do we have the luxury of healthcare or monitored job safety. Our well-being is solely supervised by us, and we've done a poor job at best.

If we do not put ourselves at the top of our priority list, no one will. If we allow dangerous industry demands to pile up without speaking out about the toll certain practices are taking, then we will be the only ones paying the price in the end. We are our best advocates, and in terms of health and stress management, many of us are failing.

To those of you who feel you're already taking the steps to counterbalance health issues, I applaud you. This section is not to shame anyone or preach from some high place, as I'm far from what anyone would consider "in peak condition."

Do not misinterpret what is basic observation as a lecture of any sort. The purpose here is to merely create a dialogue, so we, as a community, can make progress.

For any progress to occur, authors must feel safe to openly discuss the reality of their situation and the overwhelming demands of the job. The rapidly expanding market has created a vacuum effect, sucking up authors' time, money, and motivation. Too many are sacrificing self-care in order to stay relevant and survive.

Discounting books, the price gouging of underqualified editors, and the escalating fees for promotions are just some of the financial stresses authors are facing on a daily basis. There are also the strains triggered by social media, which have been linked to negative effects on a person's mental health and overall well-being.

I've had more than one author tell me their accountant showed concern for their business's future and sustainability. Many authors don't even bother with creating a profit and loss summary because, on paper, there's very little that justifies sinking so much into a job that gives so little back in return.

> SIDENOTE:
>
> Do not—I repeat, *do not*—ever allow your accountant or anyone else to refer to your start-up as a "hobby" once you begin investing in a future profit. All businesses take a loss in the beginning, at which point the IRS labels them *hobbies*, and most start-ups require a developmental period of two to three years before turning a notable profit, but the moment your profits start to occur and you are actively filing taxes for your business, your hobby days as a writer are over.
>
> When someone refers to your business as a hobby—outside of the IRS's meaning—they demean both you and the effort you've applied to reach that point, regardless of how much further you still have to go to see yourself as a success. Every entrepreneur has to start somewhere.
>
> I, especially, do not want to hear *you* calling your job a hobby. If you cannot respect the work you're doing, don't expect anyone else to. Too many authors have confessed to others making disparaging comments about the work they do. If only the outside world could see how difficult and straining an author career actually is at times.

As the CEO of your company, you have final say in those you do business with. Do not let your spouse or parent call your business a hobby, and certainly do not permit it from anyone sharing a client relationship with your company in any way. If they do, fire them. Hire a financial planner that sees your vision and can help you get there. Do not do business with professionals that are not supportive of the overall goals of your company.

We get the respect we command. Know your worth and add tax, because as long as the IRS recognizes your business as a business, it is not a hobby.

Differentiating Sacrifice & Neglect

No matter the stage of our careers, we persevere, despite competitive climate. We give up sleep, socializing, and many times, our sanity, simply because we can't quit.

Why? Because writing is our calling. It fulfills us in a way nothing else can. So how can one continue a career as a writer when the job description of a modern-day author is so depleting?

I'm not speaking of the 1% at the top. This does not include the household names whose books make it to the grocery stores and corner drugstores. When I describe the struggle and high stress associated with staying afloat in a saturated market, I'm speaking to the average majority, the indie or small press or even the *"Big Six",* digital-first imprint authors who are not clearing six figures, yet working over forty hours a week to earn something more than a grocery bill a month.

Stir in some basic life and you have a recipe for a highly stressful atmosphere. Authors have asked me how to manage their deadlines when also supporting a sick relative or working a second job. Some want to know what they can do when their royalties can't afford the cost of popular promotions and they can't make the investment with money borrowed elsewhere. The truth is, there is no easy solution.

What worked for one author might not work for you. And what worked yesterday may produce stale results today. The market is fluid and the competition is fierce.

After fourteen years in this business, the only thing I know for sure is that writers need to write. Fully, well-developed books create return customers. The challenge is getting the customer in the first place.

Running an expensive promotion does not guarantee its success. Even marketing trends stagnate. PR companies overpopulate, and too much advertising from one source loses its zeal and inevitably becomes white noise.

The problem and the solution is fluidity. Marketing should be fresh. This requires constant updating.

Think of marketing as the food in the cupboard. The best foods are alive. They have a shelf life and rot quickly. They also carry the most benefits if utilized at the right time.

Now, think of the staples in the pantry, the cardboard products that can sit on the shelf for more than a year. These products have very little nutritional value. But they can sustain you. But be warned, they are mostly preservatives.

Authors love preservatives, those little injections of fanfare meant to send a zap of excitement out to *Booklandia*. These often take the form of cover reveals or teasers. And yes, they satisfy readers like a bag of chips might satisfy a couch potato waiting through a commercial break, but how often do they lead to an actual sale?

When these said preservatives are so commonplace, how much buzz are they actually creating? How much time and energy are they costing? Is it balanced?

Disruptive content is the most successful kind of content a person can post on social media. The moment the disruptiveness of a post fades, people hardly give it a glance. This occurs once an author's teaser starts looking like the one before. The effectiveness of the content decreases as soon as marketing trends start getting mass produced.

Yet, the demand for such services goes up, and with the demand, so does the PR companies' pricing, and the general importance of such practices in the mind of the author community.

The above is a perfect example of going with the current rather than swimming against it and making waves in a disruptive way that creates measurable benefit for your book. Yes, there will always be the superfans and one-click readers. They are the loyal following your words have created. And chances are, they'd one-click your book with or without the marketing campaign. You just need to notify them.

Reveals and blitzes and so much of the other preliminary work are meant to attract *new* readers. But is it? If the content isn't *disruptive,* it most likely won't. The trick is existing ahead of the curve and thinking of new, fresh ways to cause a disruption in the sea of social media.

Don't worry about the perfect dive that looks like every diver who dove before. Be the cannonball author. Make a splash and get a reaction—whether it be pissing people off or making them giddy with expectation. If you can't accomplish that, then I suggest you keep swimming and think about it a little longer.

Do not fall for the *Dunning-Kruger effect*! Save your energy. Save your money. Save your time. Only invest in practices that will produce tangible results or measurable sales, especially if you are dealing with a low advertising budget.

If all you can afford to do is write books right now, then that's what you're going to do. Writing is, after all, the first part of the job description and the truest definition of the term "author" you will find.

However, if you've established a budget that allows for some preservative marketing, go ahead and contract the work out to PR companies. Just remember, you're only paying for a generic bag of chips. This sort of quick snack investment will never create the same response as an elaborate feast made of only the freshest, organic materials.

If you want fresh and organic, you have to be fresh and organic. That means, not relying on dime-a-dozen marketing formulas that regurgitate the same old noise. It requires getting out there, being present, making human connections, sharing authenticity, proving relatability, and attracting that organic audience with fresh content, again and again.

I'm sure some of you are quivering at the thought, but that's how it's done. And the best part is, it's free. It only costs you time. Oh, wait… Authors have no time. Let's get back to fixing that!

We've established that stress is a common part of most authors' lives, be it financial limitations, time limitations, or something else. The key solution isn't avoiding stress altogether. It's learning how to counterbalance the stress triggers and cope with the demands of the job by taking a proactive approach to your health.

We are all stressed on some level. But how much of your stress is unnecessary stress? Correcting any imbalance requires authors to become more self-aware, so that they can better identify the stress triggers in their career (and life) and fairly evaluate the return.

Ambition often goes hand in hand with sacrifice and that's admirable. But your dreams should never lead to neglect. Too many authors have crossed the line that separates the two.

What starts out as typical start-up sacrifices needed to lift a business off the ground, too often leads to undeniable personal neglect. Long-term neglect inevitably leads to burnout. Minor sacrifices should not.

It is crucial that adults try to maintain a healthy immune system. This does not require you to run out and get a gym membership or live completely off sprouts and nuts, nor does it mean changing your life in any punishing sense.

On the contrary, the simplest ways to boost the human immune system also happen to reduce stress. There is nothing overly complicated about stepping outside and standing in the sunshine for ten minutes or drinking a glass of water or taking a stroll around the block or practicing some breathing exercises, so why are you hesitating? Why aren't objectives like eating more veggies or getting daily exercise already scheduled into your day-to-day routine?

SUNSHINE   EXERCISE   HEALTHY FOOD   HYDRATION   RELAX   SLEEP

BOOST YOUR **IMMUNE SYSTEM**

If they are, brava! You're ahead of the crowd. But the majority of authors interviewed while writing this book admitted to sitting for extended periods of time, not taking movement breaks, skipping meals, and often finding themselves too exhausted to plan healthy dinners, and, therefore, more dependent on quick, low quality food solutions. Some even admitted to not leaving the house for days on end.

And quality sleep? Forget it. Too many authors admitted to insomnia, some claiming that in place of sleep they find themselves working eighteen-hour days. It's no wonder we're stressed out.

Neglect inhibits common sense, and too many authors have been neglecting their needs for far too long. In order to reverse this pattern of behavior, we must stop labeling acts of self-neglect as sacrifices.

The moment you actively choose to sacrifice your health to maintain a nonreciprocal relationship, be it a marriage, job, access to a substance, or even a relationship with an inanimate object like a book you spent years obsessing over, you are no longer in a safe place. You are in what can only be defined as an abusive relationship, and you are the abuser.

The First Line of Defense

What if you just visited your personal care physician and had an impeccable physical? Can you assume the complications triggered by stress won't eventually affect you? Let's look at specific, common examples of immune system stress in the author field before deciding.

I'll assume, especially after the introduction of COVID-19, we all have a basic understanding of how germs are spread—air droplets, touching surfaces, and so on. Once you've attended an author event surrounded by hundreds of readers in close quarters, you've probably made a point to pack hand sanitizer and a few other personal hygiene helpers, even before the spread of a global pandemic.

Authors typically work alone. So, we aren't as exposed to foreign germs as someone working in an office with others on a daily basis. Therefore, when we attend events and expose our usually isolated immune systems to germs, travel, and communal living, we often find ourselves under the weather when we return home.

In reality, post-event illness has less to do with our exterior environment and more to do with what's going on inside our bodies. What does that mean? Well, it means our immune system is getting a bad rap.

We assume the immune system was slacking on the job, and we picked up a bug at the hotel, but we most likely didn't get sick from the hotel or the people at the event at all—thank you properly functioning immune system!

So, how do we explain the familiar post-event cold too many authors are known to suffer? It's simple. While we might not have picked up anything at the event since our immune system was armed and ready for duty, we stopped thinking about germs the moment we got home.

After overtaxing our immune system on the trip, it's tradition to give it the day off as soon as we return to our usual, familiar environment. Having done its duty well, the immune system exhales, strips off its battle fatigues, and shuts off for a while to recharge.

But instead of resting, you head off to the grocery store or stop to talk to a neighbor, and boom, during that small window of being unprotected you pick up a nasty little bug. The truth is, if we hadn't overtaxed the immune system, it wouldn't have needed a vacation after the trip. But I'm sure you can relate, because even the most exciting trips tend to be taxing, and *we* often need a day or two to recuperate.

Don't assume it's the hotel getting you sick. It could be something around your own house. The best practices remain the ones drilled into our heads—practice good hygiene, wash your hands frequently, and avoid touching your face.

Now, I bet some of you are saying, *"This is exactly why I don't attend author events."*

Well, you're not out of the woods either. We don't need to leave town to create a stressful environment in the body. Hell, chances are we can create the perfect storm of anxiety and paranoia right from our own familiar bed at 3 a.m.—for absolutely no reason at all.

No matter what the cause of stress, your immune system is built to respond and neutralize the threat if it is functioning properly. Over activate the immune system and that's when the human body starts to run into problems.

No matter what the cause, the immune system sees stress as another form of infection. Once detected, the immune system releases proteins and cortisol to fight inflammation. By triggering the immune system, it overcompensates and eventually weakens, requiring a brief vacation to recharge after the stress is gone. *That* is when we are most likely to get sick.

In the situations of immune system versus workaholic, both sides lose. The immune system is not built to sustain endless stress, and neither are we. Let's examine two common scenarios of this happening in author life.

Scenario One

Sam has a book signing. She alters her usual routine to start preparing. She's packing and planning and working overtime to make sure she's ready for the event. This is different from her usual workweek, so her immune system groggily lifts its head to see what's going on.

Sam gets on a plane, flies across the country, checks into a hotel, and has drinks with colleagues. At this point, her immune system is fully awake and wondering what the hell is going on.

All of these events delight Sam. She loves the crush of excitement and the close encounters with hundreds of people she usually only gets to interact with online. But excitement, no matter how pleasant, creates stress in the body. And stress triggers the immune system into action.

For the duration of the event, Sam's immune system is running at full speed to keep her healthy. Only when she gets on the plane to return home does it slow down enough to process that the threat of stress/excitement has receded.

Once home, Sam unpacks, slips into her favorite PJs, and curls up on the couch with a book for a day of rest. The immune system exhales and interprets this as time to relax and off on vacation it goes.

The next morning Sam does something totally ordinary like running to the market for some groceries. She picks up a bug—just a common cold—but her immune system is off on a bender enjoying its vacation after a long, stressful week. That common cold hits Sam like a tank, and she's down for the count, missing the next five days of work.

Sam, like many other authors, assumes she caught the cold at the hotel or on the plane. But she could have caught it at home in her safe space, because her immune system was overworked and MIA.

Scenario Two

Alice has a deadline and she's been procrastinating. Now, it's down-to-the-wire and she only has one week to finish.

On Monday, she works overtime and the hubby orders a pizza to feed the kids. She wakes early on Tuesday but—*uh oh*—the editor left a note for a complete rewrite of a scene that has been challenging her muse from the start. She's still working on that damn scene come Wednesday.

By Friday, she's made it to the last half of the book, but there were so many revisions, she now needs to read it all over again for clarity. She cancels her weekend plans and works straight through to Sunday, turning her edits in minutes before the midnight deadline.

Now, think of Alice's immune system. The moment she went balls-to-the-wall, her immune system went on full alert. Think of the instant relief Alice felt as she hit SEND and shipped those edits back to her editor.

First thing Monday morning, her immune system was off drinking a mai tai at a swim-up bar, completely checked out. By the following Friday, Alice is run down with a cold and fever.

Ever happen to you?

The first line of defense against stress will always be *moderation*. However, life does not always allow for such things.

Many times, as described above with Sam, the activities we enjoy can still trigger an immune system response, which means, as long as we are living, stress will be an inevitable part of life. But we can manipulate the frequency by monitoring our behavior to avoid repeating bad habits and creating dangerous patterns.

The common failing in the immune system's response described above, came after a boom-and-bust pattern of stress brought on by the authors. This cycle is commonly referred to as the *Let-Down effect*.

The Let-Down Effect

The Let-Down effect proves that intense times of stress can lead to a suppressed immune systems. In the case of the traveling author, he or she returns home and the energy dramatically shifts from intense to calm. And in the case of the stressful deadline, the manuscript gets turned in, and the author can finally shut down and relax after days of tense pressure. They are two very different scenarios with very similar outcomes.

The cause of stress is irrelevant, but the result is often the same. When the immune system isn't responding properly or is suppressed (e.g., on vacation), there is an open invitation for health complications. Depending on the person, these complications can be as mild as the common cold and as severe as pneumonia or kidney failure. Every human body is different, which is why we must each maintain a uniquely designed level of balance

The Let-Down effect is a prime example of the immune system's function in relation to work. This boom-and-bust phenomenon happens to the body after a stressful situation, such as a deadline or intense work trip, but also a family crisis, a breakup, a robbery, a health scare, a marriage proposal, a promotion, a surprise party, or anything else—positive or negative—that might jolt your ordinary response into a hyper state.

The phenomenon of *the Let-Down effect* has been linked to health consequences such as colds, the flu, panic attacks, migraines, eczema, psoriasis, and more. And remember, even stress masquerading as excitement can have adverse effects on the body.

Imagine a direct line from A to B. Let's call this your "ideal growth." A is the beginning of a project and B is the deadline. The path from A to B is steady, consistent, and evenly paced.

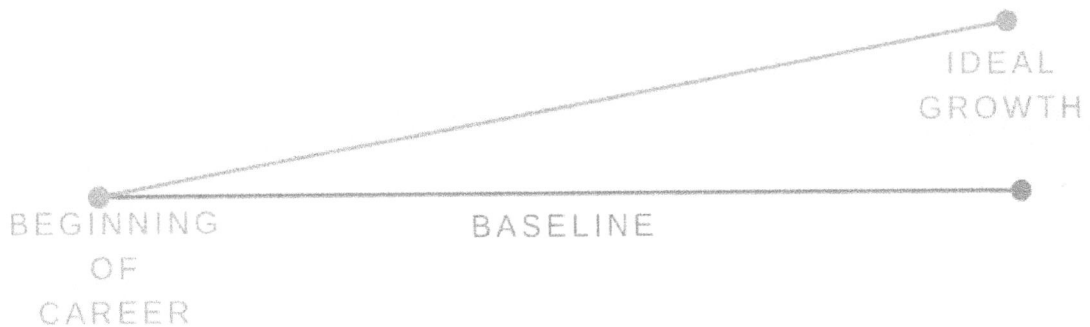

IDEAL
GROWTH

BEGINNING   BASELINE
OF
CAREER

But in the midst of the journey, life happens and you're pulled off task. Several chaotic days pass and you find yourself in a crunch to get back on track. This creates a boom.

Your body goes into high alert as you up your intentions for the day and double down on your word count, which, in turn, triggers stress and sends your immune system into overdrive.

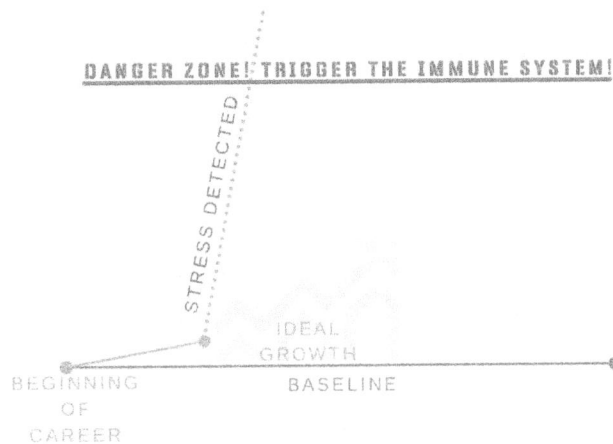

DANGER ZONE! TRIGGER THE IMMUNE SYSTEM!

STRESS DETECTED

IDEAL
GROWTH

BEGINNING   BASELINE
OF
CAREER

You work hard, pushing yourself, and eventually you meet your goal despite the setbacks life presented. Finally, you have a chance to catch your breath, so you exhale and your stress diminishes, and off to vacation the immune system goes.

But you have to work hard to get your performance back above your baseline. Your body does not return to its usual pace. Instead, it's operating in a state of playing catch-up. This is usually where the neglect sets in and well-intentioned promises are made, but they're actually lies.

Soon as I get caught up, I'll go out with the girls. I'll make it up to them. I just need a few days to catch-up.

The truth is, once time is lost, it's gone. Time is the most nonrenewable resource we have in this life. It's also the most taken for granted.

The minute you lose time to a setback, you are operating behind the curve. It will, inevitably, cost you something to regain your place ahead of the curve. The question is, what are you willing to pay? The price you pay will be demonstrated by the increased incline of actual growth illustrated below.

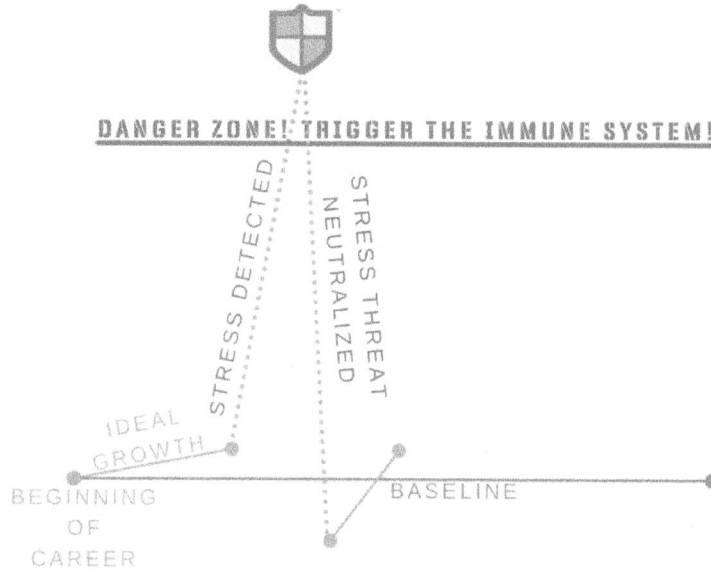

Maybe you get out of the woods without any real consequences. But after a successful turnout, you're now more likely to take your body's stress response for granted and abuse your immune system by making a habit of such stress-triggering practices. It isn't long before you're in a similar situation, again.

A deadline approaches and life interferes. You're forced to double down and push yourself to meet that deadline, again, with a boom of stress. Once you reach the deadline, your stress levels drop suddenly with another bust. And the pattern continues.

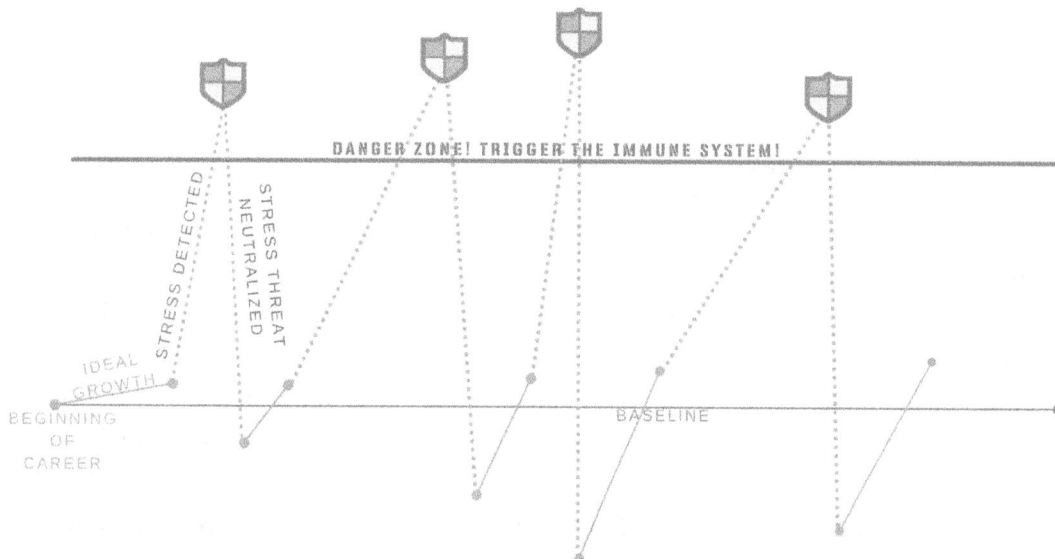

Over time, your performance levels slow down. Due to recovery time, your "ideal growth" is no longer aligned with your "actual growth." Eventually, your actual progression reveals itself as far below the desired "ideal growth" projection line and you have to work much harder to catch-up.

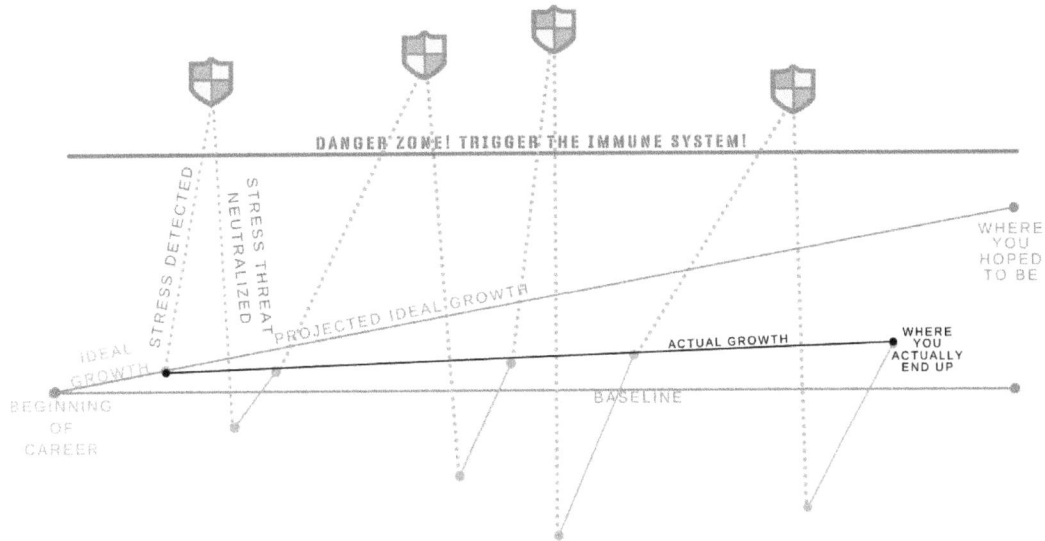

Note the large gap between the actual end point and the possible end point you could have achieved if you would have treated yourself kinder. If you are constantly feeling like you're operating behind the curve, you very well may be, and at your own doing. This boom-and-bust pattern is actually forcing your growth line to stay lower, and slowing your progress.

Consider your journey. We all have a choice to make when it comes to the road we take to reach our success.

Which path do you think burns up the most fuel and puts the most pressure on an engine, the one with mountains or the steady incline?

Which one takes you on the most detours?

Which one will get you where you hope to go the fastest?

Sometimes, shortcuts don't actually save us time in the end. Think of the graphs above as a glimpse into one year of an author's life. Each jolt in the line is a trip or a deadline that was accomplished with poor time management. At the end of the year, who will feel the most depleted, the author who sets boundaries and takes a proactive approach to her health with balanced time management practices and frequent breaks for self-care, or the author who frequently runs into setbacks and burns unnecessary energy trying to make up for lost time?

Remember, time is a nonrenewable resource. Once it's lost or gone, it's gone.

They are called setbacks for a reason. Rarely do we consider the long-term effects of minor setbacks in our lives, but over time, the results compile and drastically alter the outcome of our success.

Take a look at the side-by-side of two different authors, one who has not planned well and has had numerous stressful situations, and the other who has worked in ways to decrease daily stress.

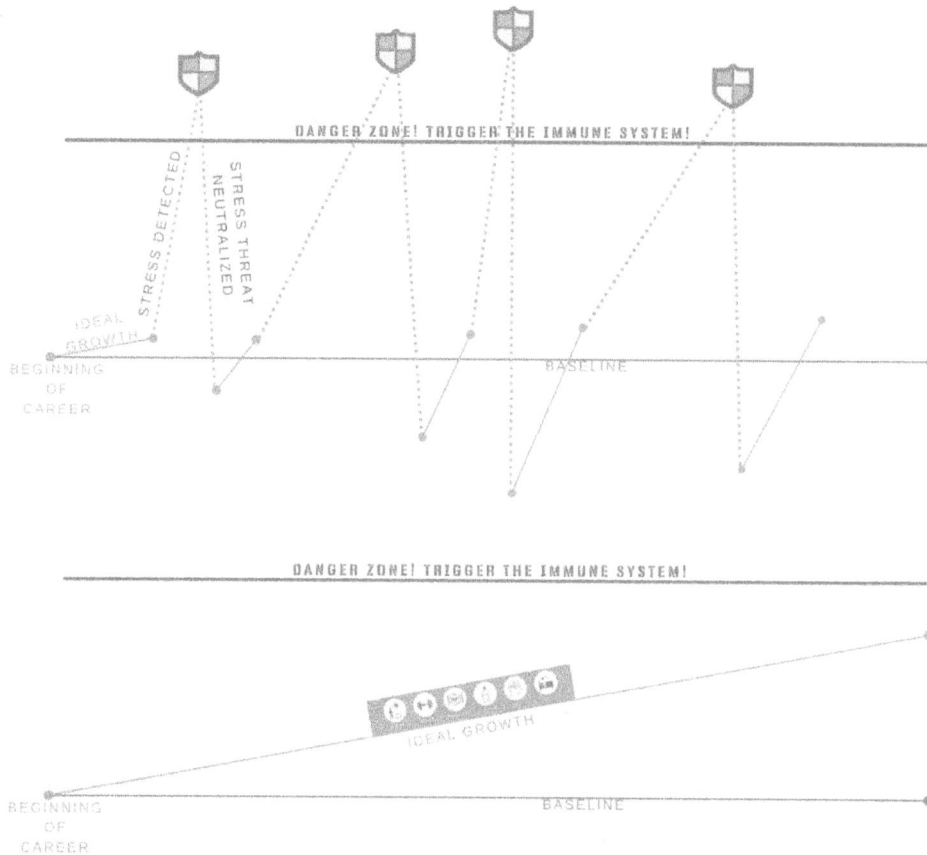

It's clear which author is facing the most chaos and which author enjoys the peace and calm of finding balance in her life and career. Over time, meaning when these habits of extreme stress and recovery occur for years or even decades, the zig and zag pattern becomes more exaggerated. Or, in the case of the Zen author, balance becomes easier to maintain.

What kind of author do you want to be? Which depiction is more aligned with your primary objective?

Depleting your battery and enduring long-term episodes of stress leaves people moody, tired, and feeling chronically out of whack. If that sounds like you, my friend, you are, most likely suffering, from the *Let-Down effect* and these resulting troubles are symptoms of burnout.

We must learn to pace our success and stop running full speed ahead while shoving our health into a place of complete disregard. Every time we unnecessarily kick our immune system into overdrive, we risk confusing it.

Another way to describe this confusion is to label it misguided. A misguided immune system creates abnormalities that can lead to what's called autoimmunity, a situation where the immune system attacks its own body.

What would your life be like if your immune system stopped protecting your health the way it's properly meant to? I assure you, as someone who now has a permanently compromised immune system, your problems would far exceed that of meeting deadlines.

I was diagnosed with systemic lupus erythematosus in 2006, just after the birth of my daughter. Doctors believe the stress of pregnancy on my organs overtaxed my system and triggered the disease.

My body had stopped responding to natural commands, and I struggled with simple tasks—like twisting a light switch, picking up a sheet of paper, standing, or holding my newborn. My hands would sometimes curl into talon-like deformations and be useless for hours. I'd catch a cold and run a fever, requiring days of bedrest to recover from what is typically the sniffles for a person with a properly functioning immune system.

My compromised immune system keeps me in a permanently fragile state. It's invisible, so my limits aren't always appreciated, even by those closest to me. When I limp or my face is red due to the infamous lupus butterfly rash, or my hands discolor, deform, or fail, people remember my condition. But I never forget.

I never stop feeling the effects or paying the consequences. And while my health can improve from the choices I make, it can also suffer. So can yours.

When we neglect our bodies, we trigger subtle red flags. Ignore those red flags, and they will get bigger, louder, and more frequent. Eventually, poor behavior patterns can create a situation that cannot be ignored. Believe me—I'm not the only author this has happened to.

Whether suppressing the immune system with exterior events or internal expectations, the body is not meant to handle extreme levels of stress continually, year after year after year. Such neglect will ultimately lead to more sick time away from the office, which is the opposite of becoming more productive.

So, how do we combat these situations if a stress-free work environment isn't possible? The answer, of course, is creating balance, and in the chapters ahead, I will teach you how.

Chapter Five
Detox

"We all know that words have an enormous influence on the way we think and feel, and that things generally go more smoothly when positive words are used."

Masaru Emoto, The Hidden Messages in Water, 1999

The Root of Toxicity

Health and wellness must go hand in hand with craft and business practices to achieve any sort of satisfying success, and while you might not always agree with the logic or methods ahead, there is an undeniable case that burnout has become an invasive and dangerous problem in the writing community.

The toxicity of misery can grow like an all-consuming cancer if left untreated. Too often, writers set their standards according to what others *appear* to be achieving.

I use the word appear, because unless you have access to other people's private bank statements, therapist records, spouse's or children's opinions of their homelife, you really have no clue how successful they are. You're only able to assume based on the staged glimpses provided through social media or public events where authors are basically performing for an audience.

Do not measure your success on the appearance of someone else's. Doing so will lead to envy, insecurity, a sense of inadequacy, bitterness, unrealistic standards, and an overwhelming sense of failure. And if you are currently burned-out, your perspective will be damaged, so your ability to measure your own self-worth or accurately compare yourself to others is faulty from the start.

It was 2015 when I first identified burnout symptoms in the form of bitterness in my life, though I didn't have an explanation for it. I called the frequent bouts of envy and discouragement "author depression," a mood I often fell into when spending too much time on social media, watching other authors succeed when I should have been using that time to focus on my own success.

Negative thoughts, envy, or feelings of bitterness are more dangerous than most people realize. Thoughts can have a molecular effect on your body's health. A negative state of mind can mirror itself in a negative life. But it will also manifest negative responses in the form of illness and toxicity within the body.

American medicine is so grounded in capitalism, the idea of merely treating a symptom, rather than curing a disease, has become an almost unanimously acceptable solution. However, with the explosion of open-source knowledge, we are becoming more educated about options geared toward prevention, cures, overall well-being, and longevity.

In other words, we're getting wiser. The patient who has chronic stomach aches is growing dissatisfied with the prescribed pill that dulls the pain. He or she now wants to identify the cause in order to correct the actual problem.

There will always be eye drops designed to help blurred vision and headache medicine to treat pounding temples after staring at a computer screen all day and, of course, coffee for when we just have to hit that word count. But by reaching for those "cures" we're only masking the problems. We need to stop relying on temporary fixes and turn our attention to better preventative approaches.

In a world where big pharma has so much to gain by treating people's symptoms with overpriced remedies, this healthy, preventative approach remains an unpopular one. But this book doesn't give a shit about what big pharma wants. It only cares about returning a sense of control to you, the author, so let's get to the root of the issues.

The Power of Negativity

As established in earlier chapters, long-term effects of stress produce negative outcomes. Unresolved symptoms of stress become consequences of burnout. But how can that be? How can something as simple as moodiness lead to something as extreme as cancer, in some cases?

Dr. Masaru Emoto, the New York Times bestselling author of *The Hidden Messages in Water*, was one of the first to document the connection between conscious thoughts and the molecular structure of water, which later proved that human thoughts and words can directly alter the structure of human cells.

Dr. Emoto claimed that water acted as a blueprint of reality, providing visual evidence for the impact of words. His experiments used crystal clear samples of water, which he exposed to his laboratory staff after instructing them to insult or complain to the samples.

Scientists visited the water samples every day, bitching and moaning about their problems. And after a period of time, the water changed. It had gone from crystal clear to cloudy. The change was evident after, once again, freezing the samples and using microscopic photography.

More experiments were performed, and further proof was revealed. Clear water molecules before and after prayer, showed significant changes. Before the prayer, the molecules were basic and random. After the prayer, the molecules formed into intricate snowflake shapes.

Words like *thank you* or *Mother Teresa* also created similarly aesthetically pleasing shapes. While words associated with negativity like *I'll kill you* or *you make me sick* or *Adolf Hitler* created mutations in the molecules, leaving the molecules foggy, dark, and pocked.

Some experiments started with polluted samples and distorted molecules. After exposing the samples to large groups of people sending positive thoughts and words to the water, the molecules were reshaped into intricate snowflakes.

The images of Dr. Emoto's samples are protected under copyright, but slides of his water experiments can be viewed at masaru-emoto.net. The extreme differences between samples of positivity and samples of negativity are something to behold.

Dr. Emoto verified that negativity can deform molecules, while positive thoughts had the ability to convert molecules into works of art. Of course, beauty is in the eye of the beholder, but the evidence of change was indisputable. Thoughts and words directly affect the molecular makeup of water.

So, why is this relevant? The adult human body is made up of approximately 60-70% water[2]. We are mostly water. Our eyes are 95% water. Our heart and muscles are more than 75% water. Our blood is more than 80% water, and our brain, kidneys, and lungs are mostly water. If negativity can alter the molecular structure of water, our negative thoughts can surely alter the molecular structure of us.

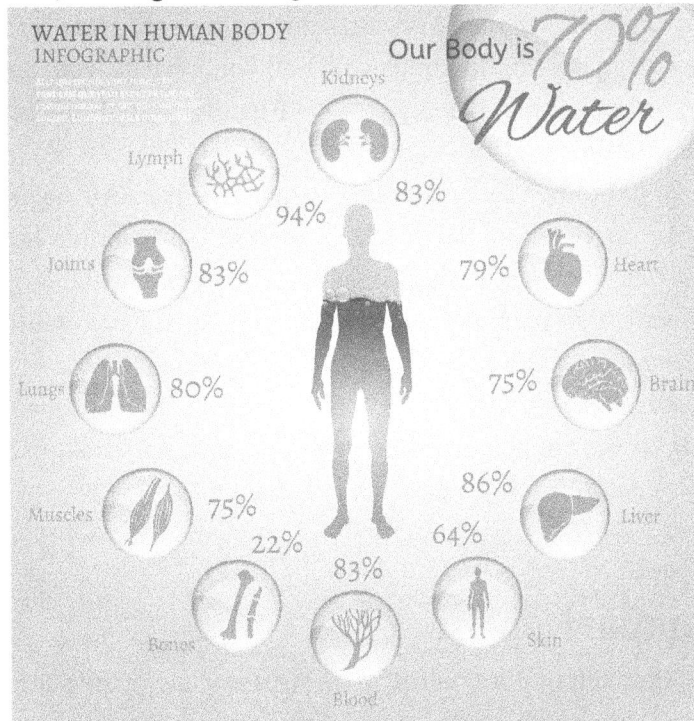

WATER IN HUMAN BODY INFOGRAPHIC — Our Body is 70% Water

It's no wonder that when we're in a negative headspace we start to feel sick. Toxic thoughts have a direct relationship to the toxicity in our bodies. So, when we are suffering burnout, we are possibly damaging our bodies on a molecular level.

Bitterness cannot coexist with balance, because negative emotions are proven to suppress brain activity. Clear thinking is absolutely necessary to live a well-balanced life.

If I'd known years ago what I know now, I would have called my growing bitterness "early-stage burnout" and forced myself to take a vacation or, at least, a few days off to reset and invest in some self-care. I'd also practice *awareness* so I could detoxify some of the negativity from my life, but because bitterness often stems from delusion and, at the time, no one had warned me it could be so invasive, I never assumed burnout to be the culprit.

I didn't know what burnout was or that it was a legitimate problem faced by countless authors. How could I? Very few people addressed it as a professional concern, so it just felt like a trendy buzzword. And in the shadows of so many limelights, I could only see my inadequacies, which felt an awful lot like failures.

When we mislabel an actual issue as a failure, concern mutates to self-blame. Resolutions are often pushed off, because we feel responsible in some sense. *I did this to myself...* In reality, it was the burnout that most likely blocked our success.

---

[2] The Water in You: Water and the Human Body (usgs.gov)

Studies in evolution have shown that criticism can carry more impact than praise. Our brains exhibit a neurological bias, which assigns a higher significance to negative stimuli, so we automatically dwell on negative thoughts more than positive ones.

Why? Why does an insult carry so much more weight than a compliment? The answer is survival.

In the wild, negativity can often equate to death, so it makes sense that our brains hook an emotional response to these triggers. If a dog bites you, and you have to walk past that dog every day, it's in your best interest to remember that the dog is not a friendly animal. Forgetting the negative impact of the bite could lead to more injury.

Humans are hardwired to hold on to negative thoughts. This is called *negative bias*.

However, humans very rarely live in the wild anymore, so our negative experiences mostly stem from relationships or ourselves. Negative self-talk can be extremely detrimental, but controlling our thoughts isn't easy. Dwelling on a broken record of doubt and inadequacy, while appraising the "competition" online, can spiral into dangerous headspace very quickly.

By consciously elevating happier thoughts, a person can outmaneuver the negative ones. This is achieved through pattern behavior and distractions. Read a captivating book, listen to uplifting music, or go for a walk. Whatever you do, don't dwell on negativity!

The Crisis of Comparison

Bitterness can easily slide out of our control when we associate other people's success with personal loss. We often need to remind ourselves it is not a race, and there is room at the top for everyone.

However, the doorway to the "top" is quite small and only so many can squeeze through at any given time. In other words, the tsunami of indie publishing has created a bit of a traffic jam. But the space on the other side of that door, that top floor we're all heading for, is endless, and if you get through the door, you will find room and more opportunities to stretch and grow.

Think of clothing brands. There isn't just one fabulous clothing line. There are countless brands crushing it in the clothing industry, and more are coming. Just because one designer got there first, doesn't mean all the spots are taken.

Thinking otherwise is a lose-lose mentality.

"Look at what my competition is doing."

"I'm so far behind."

"I'm going to have to work harder and later if I ever want to catch up."

But our journeys are not aligned. They are unique and not meant to run a parallel course with anyone else's success. We are all just waiting for the rare moment when the door will open to us and we can slip through. Then we rise.

Stop using Suzie Nobody as a model when she's not the norm. So, what if she really lucked out and signed a book deal on her first manuscript, after only one query letter? That's almost unheard of. She's the exception to the rule, not the actual rule.

At the same time, a struggling author by the name of King wrote a thriller, and it was rejected more than thirty times. Imagine his frustration, especially after initially tossing the manuscript in the trash—only to have his wife fish it out and convince him it was worth submitting.

If King had been watching Suzie Nobody at that time, he would have really beat himself up. But years later, Suzie has only published three novels, which performed "good enough." She's satisfied with her success.

But what if he gave in to bitterness, saw Suzie's success, and stopped trying instead of keeping his head down and publishing more than eighty books, many of them bestsellers? In hindsight, Suzie's success is rather modest by comparison.

Luckily, King didn't give up and has since sold millions of books, scored film contracts, published more than two hundred short stories, and won numerous awards. Despite getting there first, Suzie is still Suzie Nobody.

Success is relative, and we never see the final work of art in its totality, because we typically don't live long enough to see how the world will perceive us as creators. An artist's success can't be measured until long after he or she has passed away. So, in reality, we are never able to accurately rate our own success.

Think of poor Emily Dickinson. Her first novel wasn't published until four years after her death. Consider how wasteful a sense of inadequacy might have been in her career. If only she knew the legend she would someday become.

F. Scott Fitzgerald, John Keats, and Jane Austen are a few others who did not live to see the extent of their fame. We must stop pretending we are any sort of authority on our own success. The beauty of being a writer is that your words will transcend time, so even when our lives are over, our stories are not.

In 2015, I wasn't the positive thinker I aim to be today, and the claws of negativity held me in an unbreakable grip. I'd take frequent self-deprecating strolls through social media and remind myself of all the ways I was falling short.

I'd then work late or skip out on family time to get some extra work done. I had to get ahead!

Soon, it wasn't just my weekends that were stolen by my need for more. I started earlier and worked later, emerging from my office hours after a normal dinner time.

Takeout became a staple and a time-saver. It also was a great contributor to my declining health. But I was so busy, I saw no choice but to put in those extra hours. The "competition" was killing me.

I reached a point where I'd sit in my desk chair twelve to eighteen hours a day, trying to get ahead. But the more I watched others, the longer the race became and the further behind I felt.

Some days, it seemed endless. And then everything capsized, and I couldn't do it anymore. Cue the iceberg.

The Iceberg

Icebergs make wonderful metaphors when we can't see a situation in its totality. Writers often compare the job of authoring a book to an iceberg, reminding outsiders that the finished product, the book, or the actual act of writing a book, only represents the 10% of effort shown on the surface. In truth, the world will never know the other 90% of time we spend struggling.

However, for the purposes of this book, the iceberg represents the symptoms of burnout. That hair loss or weight gain, they're just minor tells of a greater issue hiding under the surface.

And to make things more fun, I want to keep with the iceberg analogy and remind everyone of the Titanic. The career path of the "author," in this scenario, is the ship, barreling recklessly ahead with all boilers lit. The bitter cold sea represents the industry. And I'm sorry to say, you are but one passenger on this journey.

Assuming we're all familiar with the fate of the Titanic, I want to remind everyone that only a select few escaped unscathed. The lifeboats were not for the average passenger, but rather, the rare passenger who met a certain criteria.

Everyone wave as our author idols float off on a glamorous lifeboat...

Now, picture the mess they left behind. My imagination jumps immediately to James Cameron's depiction in the 1997 blockbuster. If you missed it, here's a similar depiction of the ship going down. (In my head, it's much more dramatic, like the Hollywood version.)

At the peak of my burnout, this sinking ship scene seemed the best way to accurately describe my inner panic to others. I was drowning, numb yet shivering, struggling to stay above the surface as other, better swimmers seemed to shove themselves right over me. I could only see a few inches ahead of me, if at all. I'd sink and struggle to rise, clutching at any form of tangible security, only to come up empty handed as safety was out of reach.

As I treaded water, my exhaustion grew. Some people struggling to make it, eventually faded away, either giving up or simply not having what it takes to endure. I'm ashamed to admit that in their silence, I arrogantly congratulated myself for surviving. But a part of me always knew I couldn't sustain such a struggle forever. If I didn't catch a break soon, I was going to drown.

It's almost claustrophobic to imagine yourself in that scene. But that's how it was for me. That chaos is how I still see the current book industry. There are simply too many of us and not enough lifeboats. In the words of Rose Dewitt Bukater, "Not enough by half".

Approximately 30% of the Titanic passengers survived the maiden voyage. Would you buy a ticket if reaching your destination came with those odds? Interesting that the odds of reaching success as an author are even lower, and yet, we continue on that journey every day.

A rescue is coming, but the wait is long. The trick is not making it to a lifeboat first. Though that kind of good fortune sure helps, it's mostly saved for the privileged or connected. The true art of surviving relies on one's ability to stay afloat. We must learn to tread water, brace against the cold, sustain our energy at the bleakest moments, and always stay optimistic that our moment will come.

So, whether you see it as a lifeboat or a door, remind yourself that rising to the top is almost always more about the moment than circumstance. Like I said in the very beginning, there are more unread masterpieces in publication today than ever before—you might have even authored one. Timing is everything, and making it in this business comes down to honing your talent and being prepared for "your time."

The moment your opportunity presents itself, you must be ready. So be rested, be available, and don't let bitterness pollute your mind.

Stop spoiling your energy on nonsolutions. Think of the drowning passengers who wasted energy screaming for help that wasn't available. Picture Rose and Jack. Could anyone hear them? No, because there was too much chaos, too much noise. Only in the calm could her call be heard.

So, rather than wasting energy with whispers lost to the screaming chaos, or preservative promotions that really don't resonate, save your strength. Be aware of your reality, keep writing, and keep your eyes open as you watch for your time.

Burnout is not a sudden circumstance. It seeps into your life slowly, almost untraceably, but over time, the effects accumulate. And eventually, if we allow it to weaken us, it defeats us.

The pivotal moment, for me and most authors, is what we writers refer to as a fork in the road. It's the moment where the main character must make a decision, and whatever they choose will greatly affect the outcome of the story and their fate (more on this when we get into story arcs).

If an author has reached the peak of burnout, this fork will often lead to two extremes: continue on as is (in a total state of self-induced misery) or jump ship. This is when a lot of authors quit, and I'm not knocking them for that decision. In some cases, it might be the samurai way to go. But remember when I said one problem with burnout is that it affects a person's logical, decision-making skills?

If an author is truly burned-out, I mean, struggling with an overwhelming sense of defeat accompanied by health issues and feeling completely devoid of motivation, they need to step away from the situation and not make any decisions until they've calmed down and regained a clarified perspective. If that takes weeks, months, or even a solid year, then that's what it takes. But how do we clarify a cloudy perspective?

The reality is, fully burned-out authors have lost the ability to judge situations accurately. And until they can do that, they have no business making life-altering decisions about their career. Their view is cloudy and dark. They can't see the iceberg directly ahead.

If you're at this stage, my advice is to only make temporary decisions, the first being to immediately stop and take some time off. Trust me, you're overdue, and a break could save your career and your life.

However, if an author is not at that pivotal moment yet and can see the fork in the road approaching, there's still a chance to make some tough choices and change the direction of the journey, creating a new path.

It's not too late for such authors to pause and assess their reality. They can conduct an audit of their situation and apply some proactive strategies to avoid possible disasters ahead.

No matter where you are, the trick is removing the toxic patterns and performing a professional detox. If we're sticking with the Titanic analogy, think of the detox as waiting for the waters to clear, the sun to rise, and slowing the hell down so you can plainly see the lethal obstacles ahead and make rational choices to avoid them.

Authors just setting out on the beginning of their journey have the most options of all. They can listen to the horror stories of ghosts and survivors, learn from others' mistakes, and take the path less traveled.

This is the path of the *new author*, the author grounded in *awareness* and armed with methods to help maintain balance between the mind, body, and spirit. The *new author* is wise beyond his or her years and knows how to feed the author soul.

The best thing about the *new author* approach is that it isn't solely for newbie authors. It's for recovering authors who want to reverse the effects of burnout and return to happy writing careers.

After rescuing myself from nearly drowning on the job, I had to face the facts. The healing process began with admitting there was a problem. As stated in Chapter Two, recovery cannot take place if we remain in a state of denial.

Once authors fully face the obstacles impeding their success, they become aware of the true reality. They hit the pause button and in turn, step back from the chaos long enough to stop depreciating their self-worth.

By taking a momentary break, authors reestablish the ability to identify poor habits, questionable business practices, and all those neglected self-care priorities that have become too many to list. They become self-aware.

Awareness is the undeniable state of reality. It's a beautiful runway model without her makeup or wig or undergarments that magically defy gravity. And the first time you look reality in the eye, it's scary as hell.

But the good news is, once we've faced the actuality of our situation and moved into a state of *awareness*, we're ready to accept that which we cannot control and form a plan. For those recovering from burnout or those hoping to avoid burnout, that plan usually begins with *intent*.

No matter what your #1 Objective is as an author, your *intent* had better cover practices that require you to be kinder and more aware of your needs. If you fail to do so, you will only find yourself at the same fork in the road, on a writing bender, strung out on caffeine and squirrely from lack of sleep, immune system burning on all cylinders, plowing full speed into an iceberg at 1 am—or something equally as destructive as that.

In Chapter One, we established that without a healthy mind and body the author's spirit, or creativity, will not function properly. There must be balance among this trifecta that is the author's soul. We must be self-aware.

It's really that simple. Stop ignoring your needs. Your work is suffering because your work practices have created a severe imbalance, and you keep tipping the scale in the wrong direction every time you heap more expectations on yourself.

Just. Stop. That's the only way to let the detoxification process begin.

The Detoxification Guide

Depending on where you are in your journey and what level of burnout you're currently facing, detoxification will resonate differently with different people.

Those feeling especially overwhelmed are advised to take some time to simply *"be"* before jumping into the detoxification process. It would be better to come back to this after enjoying a meaningful break. But if you are not feeling especially overwhelmed, and believe you're in a healthy headspace to make some positive change, dive right in.

Detox is usually defined as a process where toxins are removed. In the case of substance abuse, an addict often experiences an unpleasant sense of withdrawal during detox. It's common for workaholic authors to feel work calling them back. This unpleasantness is normal.

It's important that you use this time to focus on the process of cleansing the areas inviting toxicity into your life. It requires patience and focus. Do not rush the process.

Do not attempt to heap this process onto your already full plate of responsibilities. Make allowances in your schedule to apply these changes. In other words, this process requires time and patience, so you will have to excuse yourself from your usual responsibilities for a period of time. Different people will require different amounts of time depending on their unique circumstances.

There are no shortcuts. If you cannot approach this process with the genuine effort it deserves, you will not reap the benefits. As a matter of fact, you will probably cause yourself to spiral further into a negative place.

This detoxification relies on extracting toxins through thoughtful evaluation. It requires us to evaluate our environment, identify possible toxic sources, and carefully remove them from our lives.

I've broken down the basic steps to form a guide. There is no time limit on the process, but I recommend giving each step *at least* one day of focus before moving on. If more time is needed, take it.

The goal is not perfection, as mastery is not expected, especially during a first attempt. The goal is progress. Think of detoxification as a part of your ever-improving journey as a well-balanced human being and author. Detoxing your life on a regular basis will keep things operating smoothly, much like an oil change does for your car.

Feel free to repeat or revisit the guided steps as often as needed.

Pre-Detox Steps

1. Meditate. Visualize yourself living in a less cluttered, less toxic environment. This includes physical, mental, digital, spiritual, and emotional clutter, so evaluate *all* the baggage you're packing on this journey. It's time to get rid of anything holding you down. Picture yourself enjoying a balanced mind and healthy body. What does that look like? Try to picture all the qualities of such a life for a moment, be it one minute or ten. Write them down if that helps. Imagine how a less cluttered life will feed your creative spirit.

2. Establish a healthy reward system. Practice pausing after activities that are mentally or physically strenuous to appreciate that you were able to do such activities. Practice this method of mindfulness and gratitude often. If you struggle to celebrate accomplishments, consider starting a gratitude journal.

3. Reestablish a healthy sleep schedule designed to maintain 6-8 hours of sleep a night. If needed, use technology to set alerts for waking and winding down.

4. If you are not drinking the daily recommended amount of water, start meeting the suggested 2.7 to 3.7 daily liters of water now. This will begin the process of physically flushing toxins from your system. Water is so important to the body's healing process and so many people undervalue its benefits. If staying hydrated is a challenge for you, try using a 32 oz. water bottle and drinking its contents 3-4 times a day.

Steps to Detoxify your Life

1. **Detox your physical environment.** This requires you to clean your office, home, and car. I suggest you start with your home, since many of you are taking a break from work. The objective is not to polish the furniture but to declutter. Every item you own should have a home. If it doesn't, make it a home and inform any other household occupants that *this* is now where *that* belongs. Dispose of or donate any unwanted items.

2. **Detox functional spaces.** For some, this might mean organizing a cosmetic area or shoe rack. For others, it might be a tool shed or silverware drawer. The idea is to hit each closet, compartment, and/or garage until order is restored. Think functionality over vanity.

3. **Detox your digital devices.** Organize your computer files, remove any apps you don't use from your computer or phone, empty your inbox and set filters by unsubscribing to the mailing lists you steadily ignore, run all updates, cancel unwanted subscriptions, especially those forgettable ones that bill on a cycle, and evaluate your notification settings.

4. **Detox your relationships.** Start with an overhaul of your virtual friends. Without getting lost in social media, focus only on your follower/friends lists. If we don't clean out the weeds, new flowers will have no room to bloom, so get rid of the raggedy ones clogging up your fresh perspective. Also, declutter the list of people you are following. *Stop following people who only make you feel bad about yourself!* Then move on to your real-life relationships and appraise each one realistically. If someone in your life does not inspire positive emotions, ask yourself if you share a healthy relationship. Cut away the dead relationships, say goodbye to the toxic people in your life, those who only stir negative thoughts and feelings. And for the toxic relationships you

can't totally cut off, at least establish boundaries. Maintain a healthy distance and revisit the relationship again in the future. Ideally, the people in your life should inspire and motivate you. They should lift you up and fill you with light. Life is too short to waste time on toxic relationships or toxic people.

5. **Detox your mind.** We prepared for this process through meditation, now, let's revisit and practice. Sit with your thoughts again, and pay special attention to the airiness where sludge might have existed before. Your state of mind should feel less overwhelming. Express gratitude for this rediscovered openness. It will provide a clearer, more accurate view of what lies ahead. Take some time to really evaluate your thinking. Journaling is helpful at this stage. Write down or say affirmations that are in line with your new perspective and desires. Voice promises to yourself about habits you still hope to break or form. The goal here is to be forgiving and recognize that you are a work in progress, but also a masterpiece in the making. Expand your belief system from always thinking in terms of the impossible to embracing the ideology that with patience and balance *anything* is possible. Make a road map of your goals in life, career, love, and so on. Think big picture to help maintain that desired balance we're after.

6. **Detox your routine.** As you prepare to return to work, do not rush back into the toxic patterns you ran from before. Now is the time to develop a new routine. Take the time to plan it, placing thoughtful consideration into mental, emotional, and physical breaks. Do this, and your routine will not have the chance to break you.

The detoxification process is not a one-and-done practice. It is something I revisit often to fine-tune my mindset, assess how well I'm balancing work and play, and make sure I'm no longer neglecting my personal needs.

My first attempt at the detoxification process took the most time, because my life was overrun by chaos and I was deeply burned-out. But now, when I revisit the process, I can run through it in a matter of days.

The clarity I gain each time I complete a detox cycle is immeasurable. The positive benefits include a burst of creativity, a renewed sense of control, ease and functionality that had been hindered by clutter and disorganization before, and so much more.

When I feel the need for an emotional or motivational reset, this is where I go. It's a sure way to reboot your life and give yourself a fresh start with a brighter perspective.

For the truly ambitious and committed, I recommend following this process with books or articles that take a deep dive into mindfulness, functional organization, and gratitude.

If these theories are a little too new-age for your taste, skip over them. There're plenty more useful tips ahead. But remember, you can always come back if you change your mind.

Chapter Six
Balance

"'Here's a nice image for a life in balance,' she said. 'You're juggling these four balls that you've named work, family, friends, spirit. Now, work is a rubber ball. If you drop it, it bounces back. The other balls they're made of glass.'

'I've dropped a few of those glass balls in my day. Sometimes they chip, sometimes they shatter to pieces.'"

James Patterson, Roses are Red, 2001

Creating Structure

Authors living happy author lives and producing quality work have most likely learned to put health first and deadlines second, otherwise their careers could flatline before they know it. We've established that time management is key and burnout is the enemy, but we also must accept that balance is the be-all and end-all of contentment with success.

An imbalanced mindset will often lead to an off-kilter appraisal of self-worth. This is why some of the most monetarily successful authors sometimes still struggle to overcome a sense of inadequacy and chronic depression. If we can't *feel* success, it is worthless to us.

Every accomplishment, big or small, must achieve a level of emotional value. Failure should also achieve value, because failure can prove to be more beneficial to our success than actual prior successes at times, especially if said failure makes us try harder or learn lessons a triumph wouldn't have taught us.

No matter the value of progress, never lose sight of the cost. The physical and emotional expense of success cannot be greater than the value of the payoff. Balance is the only way to ensure success doesn't cost the life you value and leave you emotionally bankrupt in the end.

Your career is your livelihood, so the behaviors adopted at work should be considered a lifestyle. If you spend 40 hours of a 168-hour week working at your job, and 50 hours sleeping each week, you are spending, roughly, 34% of your waking life in this lifestyle, so it might as well be a happy one.

What if you not only work 40 hours, but you also spend at least two hours a day preparing for work and commuting? The percentage of your waking life occupied by your career just leapt to 42%.

Now, consider all the time doing the dull but necessary tasks in life, like grocery shopping, trips to the dentist, dropping off the water bill, and even using the bathroom, a room which recent studies report humans spend 30-60 minutes a day visiting! If that's true, another 5% of your free time just got flushed down the toilet.

The point is, your time is precious. Most adults need to work. If you're like me, you might show signs of being a workaholic at times and have difficulty not overdoing it. I definitely get twitchy when

I'm not doing something productive, so it was quite a challenge to transform myself into the balanced worker I am now.

Having a full-time job should not mean sacrificing your personal time, social life, moments with family, or opportunities to retreat and practice some self-care. We need all of these things to sustain a well-rounded, balanced life and mind.

In many cases, authors do not *choose* to sacrifice those personal aspects of life, but they drop in priority all the same. There doesn't have to be a formal decision when we prioritize our life. In many cases, not just with authors, people suddenly lift their heads from their work and find they're no longer standing in the same position they thought they were—children grown, spouse supplementing attention elsewhere, friends having parties without them, and so on.

The worst thing we can do to those we love, is teach them through neglectful actions that they don't need us. Once a person learns to live without you, it becomes almost impossible to convince them you're indispensable, again. Not to mention, the emotional injury they've suffered at being demoted to "second choice."

In terms of prioritizing life and balancing personal time evenly with professional efforts, our actions will always speak louder than words. It's fine to turn down an invitation once in a while, but if we make a habit of putting work and deadlines before personal relationships, our actual "priorities" announce themselves, and relationships suffer.

This shift is usually an unconscious choice, but a choice all the same. It is rarely the author declaring they *want* to put work ahead of family or friends. It's their behavior making the statement.

Behavior is what most people will listen to in the end, so be self-aware and don't keep your nose to the grind for too long without coming up for air and checking in with those you love. But don't just check in, be present, make your loved ones your only priority when it's their time with you. They deserve that after putting up with an eccentric author for so long.

If you're reading this and guilty of the scenario just described, you're probably aware of what an imbalanced life looks like. Too many authors confess that their endless work efforts have created resentment in their home, either with their once supportive spouse or their family.

It is unfair to consistently expect others to accept unpreferred conditions when there is no end date in sight. It is our duty to set boundaries and create fail-safe policies to prevent relationships from being damaged. That usually means clocking out and honoring an acceptable work schedule. Doing anything less is effectively showing your family that they are second and your job is first, when chances are your heart feels something different.

So, what does a *balanced* life look like? Is it possible to create balanced work habits after such a long time of working an off-kilter schedule?

The answer is, yes! Every day we have the opportunity to recreate ourselves and correct what we've been doing wrong. Refer back to the detoxification guide in Chapter Five if you're in need of a reboot, but remember, change takes time and you did not get here overnight.

Humans are creatures of habit. Virtue or vice, we tend to prefer what is familiar. It can take anywhere from 18 days to 254 days to build a habit, depending on how hardwired a person is and how determined they are to change. Psychologists claim that with conscious and consistent effort, a person can break a habit in as little as 21 days, so the rewiring process really depends on how deeply a person desires change.

One challenge, when it comes to making progress, is our inability to visualize what we do not know. Right now, imbalance might be all you know.

Imbalance is familiar, a chaotic routine of intense deadlines, stressful writing sprints, and endless carousels of other authors peacocking about on social media and filling you with toxic energy. *Did anyone else just shiver?*

To achieve *balance,* we must first be able to visualize it. By the end of this book, you should have a clear picture of what a balanced life looks like. Even if you are only able to achieve 75% of that vision, it will most likely be an improvement from the imbalanced, possibly burned-out, place many of you exist in right now. And like anything that requires effort, practice makes perfect, so keep that in mind.

When I used to picture "balance", my mind took me to a very Zen place full of nature and willowy trees. But in actuality, balance isn't breezy or loose at all. It's tight, controlled, and structured.

Structure is merely a hardy word for organization. Every author should have a personally tailored foundation secured by systematic framework.

While it's fine to buy into that masterclass and sit through another professional's workshop that divulges one professional's secrets to success, your journey will never perfectly align with someone else's—not even mine, which is why I've written this book a little differently from other *"How-To"* guides.

Rather than try to sell you a one-size-fits-all guide to success, I prefer to arm you with the knowledge to design your own personal guide. It's like the old saying, give a (wo)man a fish and (s)he'll eat for a night. Teach a (wo)man to fish and (s)he'll eat for life. Well, before anyone catches anything, they need the proper gear, so let's get each of you outfitted with your very own couture equipment.

Think of the theories ahead as scaffolding. They are temporary structures to help you make improvements as you design your own rock-solid plan. You can remove them at any time. And you always have the option to reread this book and do a refresher course of how your career is going, which I recommend doing once a year.

Your #1 Objective

Creating balance begins with identifying where imbalances are hiding. In Chapter Two we transcended from a place of denial to *awareness*, accepting that we might not be operating in total control of our careers. By this point, some of you might have already identified your #1 Objective, so you will have a good idea of the direction you need to go in order to make improvements.

Others might choose to take a more holistic approach, see what this book has to offer, and then come back and take the needed steps to improve. Either way is acceptable, and it's important that you do what is most comfortable for you. So, don't stress if other authors reading this book are taking a different approach.

Remember, your #1 Objective should be broad, basic, and apply to your entire life, not just your professional one. It is not specific like a short-term goal. Keep it simple.

My #1 Objective is *happiness*. Plain and simple, I want to be happy.

It's important that you choose a blanket objective for your life, because simply thinking in terms of your professional goals will create an imbalance over time. Prior to burnout, my #1 Object was to become an author. This created a surplus of effort toward my career and a deficit in other areas of my life.

No matter how much you can argue that you *need* to put extra into your career right now, doing so will most likely create other unwelcome problems. Problems become setbacks and setbacks increase stress. They can lead to health issues, and slow your overall performance growth over time.

I ran into several issues when I was hyper-focused only on my work success. Lacking a #1 Objective that fit my life as a whole caused me to frequently question where my focus should be. Meaning, every day I had to waste time deciding what task would best serve me in that moment.

When we jump right into goals without first identifying a sole objective, or purpose, we often travel way off track. By simply setting my goal as "author," I moved really fast and really far in the wrong direction, until I was lost.

Writing made me happy, so I identified as an author. But when being an author no longer made me happy, trouble set in. "Author" was never truly what I wanted to be. It was a goal but not my #1 Objective, not my sole purpose in life.

Solidifying a #1 Objective allows people to separate the means to an end from the actual end goal. It takes some thought and *reflection* to decide what this #1 Objective is to you.

Notice that my #1 Objective is not notoriety, wealth, security, or even being a writer. Those things can't touch my love life or my identity as a mother. Career objectives are simply too shallow to encompass the depth of who I am. For any non-shallow person reading this, you should find the same.

Happiness was what I found I most wanted in life. I wanted to feel it every night when I shut my eyes to go to sleep and again in the morning when I woke. Happiness was my truest form of motivation and my greatest asset. But everyone is entitled to choose their own #1 Objective, and mine may not be yours.

By solely focusing goals towards an objective that only advances a career, we create deficits in our personal lives and damage some very precious relationships. By honoring our professional life above all else, our personal value system grows out of whack, and we lose the ability to recognize our self-worth without accolades.

Having a #1 Objective that suits your entire life establishes guardrails for the journey that keeps you on track. If your objective feels constraining in any way, it might need some adjusting. Your #1 Objective should be unobtrusive, a simple guide you can refer to when you reach any sort of fork in the road or feel lost.

In my case, I might refer to my #1 Objective by asking myself the following questions when trying to make an important decision about a business deal:

Is this going to make me happy?

Is this going to cause me unhappiness?

Or, *is this still making me happy?*

It's okay to reassess a situation and change your mind at any point, as long as you're willing to accept the consequences. In the case of choosing *happiness,* there are always unpleasant moments in life, but knowing *happiness* is my #1 Objective makes it easier to weigh each possible outcome.

Sometimes I've entered into business ventures that stirred a sense of euphoria and passion at the start, only to have the project decompose into something ugly in the end. When misery is gradual, we tend to tolerate its seeping presence longer than necessary, which is why it's important to remain in a state of truthful *awareness.*

Steve Jobs was one of the most impactful visionaries in modern day history, and we can all learn something from his too short time on this earth. He once said, "I have looked in the mirror every morning and asked myself: *'If today were the last day of my life, would I want to do what I am about to do today?'* And whenever the answer has been *'No'* for too many days in a row, I know I need to change something."

Such great words to live by, perhaps he sensed his time would be short and instinctively had the foresight not to waste it. All of our time is limited, which is why it's crucial we not take the moments we have for granted. Having a #1 Objective establishes a simple method for fulfilling your purpose and assessing if you're still on track.

Thinking of our #1 Objective takes a quick measurement of where we are in terms of where we hope to go. If you find yourself off track, don't stress. Reassess and cut your losses. Tomorrow's another day.

Quitting can often turn into a win if you're able to redirect your journey without wasting time on guilt, shame, or blame. Just take the lesson for what it is and move on. Do not automatically assume walking away from a goal means it was a failure. Rather, look at it as a modification. You are wiser for having learned that lesson than the fool still heading in the wrong direction.

A loss is a loss because it implies a negative, but sometimes, in the grand scheme of things, positive change requires a small loss to get you on the right track. Your #1 Objective can help you justify which losses should be cut and which might need to be tolerated a while longer before they mature into profits.

Identifying that #1 Objective for yourself will help you turn your journey in the right direction. I hope that you've begun taking time to reflect on your personal journey so that you can identify where boundaries might be helpful in your personal and professional life. You are more aware of the health concerns associated with physical and emotional work stress, so you should feel motivated to make some positive changes.

If you used the worksheet provided in Chapter Two, you already have an idea of where those changes can begin. And if you've started detoxifying your life, you've already begun, and you're already making progress.

Finding the Right Headspace

If you are still struggling to identify your #1 Objective, the following tips might help you focus:

1. Go to a quiet place with few distractions.
2. Shut off all notifications so you are not disturbed.
3. Set a timer for thirty minutes.
4. Ask yourself what is it you want out of life.
5. If your mind wanders to other pressing thoughts, push those thoughts away. You can deal with them when the timer goes off. This time is dedicated to something else.

Repeat this exercise every day until you discover what it is you want. If you think you're close to identifying your #1 Objective, ask yourself if it can be broadened.

Remember, your #1 Objective should encompass your greatest goal in life and help you fulfill your purpose. If you identify your #1 Objective correctly and honor it, you shouldn't have to live with many regrets in the future.

Success is a Relative Term

Albert Einstein once said, "When a man sits with a pretty girl for an hour, it seems like a minute. But let him sit on a hot stove for a minute—and it's longer than any hour. That's relativity."

Success is a relative term, uniquely tailored to each individual's value system. Some will measure it in monetary rewards, claiming it's a million dollars in the bank, while others might say it's the security of no longer having to count the days until a paycheck arrives.

Perhaps success is more of a mental state for you. Maybe it's a feeling of contentment. Or, maybe success arrives in accolades, like bestseller lists or awards.

Your definition of success, whatever it is, must be measurable so that you can accurately identify the moment you reach it.

We cannot consider ourselves successful if to succeed in one area of life, we must fail in another. True success is a holistic ideal, one that encompasses a total life, not just a segment of it, as established in the prior chapters.

To be successful, one must have a plan. What are your goals? How can you achieve them with the littlest sacrifice or harm? What is the simplest, most effective route from A to B? How would you achieve *success*? How will you celebrate it, every day, with gratitude and grace?

My concern for authors' health and wellness does not come from an egocentric place. I did not write this book to feel superior or declare any sort of expertise. I wrote it from the purest place of love and concern for those who struggle with the common challenges associated with author success. I wrote this book to restore hope where it has been lost and show that we all struggle to succeed.

Burning out humbled me. But the methods in this book saved me. So, while I may never claim the accolades of Hemingway, I have learned the value of living. I have made a conscious choice to be happy before all else. And that decision has taught me more about success than any other theory I've tried.

How Will You Measure Success?

To define your personal version of success, first identify your intentions. Practiced *reflection* can help hone your list of intentions. As each intention comes to you, write it down, then link it to a goal and tie that goal to a logical plan.

Do not base your plan on what everyone else is doing, especially if their methods are leading to success less than 10% of the time. Try to think outside-the-box and come up with a new, unique approach that provides a clear picture of *you* succeeding and the message you want to share.

This process is the formulation of a plan. The more succinct and straightforward each intention and goal, the simpler it will be to execute.

Don't overcomplicate your plan. Clear away the chaos and distance yourself from the ideas that were not serving you well. Your previous step-by-step map to success likely had a few underperformers on it.

Moving forward, reflect and write out your *future* step-by-step map to an upcoming goal (e.g., your next book release). If there is a dreaded stage of the plan, ask yourself what is the actual ROI associated with that step. You might be surprised to discover there isn't one.

No measurable ROI? *No spot on the plan!*

Cutting familiar practices from your plan might feel like slacking, but what you're actually doing is preserving energy. Authors must tread water for a long time before the lifeboats arrive, so don't waste energy on practices that don't pay off. Use that extra energy to do something guaranteed to improve your situation—and write.

Read over your lists of intentions and goals every day. As your goals evolve, take a moment to regroup and clarify the steps needed to reach them.

When I began my journey, I used a special notebook to work out my plan and think through the process of redefining "successful author." This led to several lists. You may prefer maps or a vision board or whatever medium helps you reflect. I had various plans. Five-year plans, plans focused on my end-of-the-year goals, monthly plans, and even weekly plans.

As a creature of habit, it paid for me to review my methods and identify any tasks that were not producing the desired results or burning up more energy than they were actually worth.

Removing dreaded tasks from my lists, not because I accomplished them but because I decided I would no longer waste time doing them, was probably one of the most liberating experiences. Celebrating such autonomy and freedom made it easier to cut other things. Eventually, my lists only included tasks that produced measurable ROIs or brought me joy.

I rewrite my weekly lists every Friday, just before the week ends, so I know exactly where my focus needs to go on Monday morning.

It's okay to have multiple lists, sorted by broad, long-term intentions and smaller, more immediate goals. These are different from *to-do lists*. These are measurable, cause-and-effect sub plans that will grow your success with quantifiable results. Every single list, map, or plan should have a direct, positive relation to your #1 Objective. If it contradicts your #1 Objective, you've gone off track.

Try to focus solely on your needs, not just as an author, but as a well-balanced human being living a life rich in variety. Do not fall back into the habit of robbing Peter to pay Paul. Remember, we cannot consider ourselves successful if to succeed in one area of life, we must fail in another.

It is also helpful to write down your personal value system. What is it that you value most in this world? What are the qualities of life that bring you the greatest sense of satisfaction?

If you love to travel, but haven't left your home town in more than a year, you need to figure out a way to change that[3]. Your values should be your priorities, as they enrich the soul, and a well-rounded author soul promotes author success.

Indulgence is not a cause for guilt. It's a cause for pleasure. Remove the idea that we must pay for pleasure with some sort of pain. The universe doesn't require payment, so stop beating yourself up for enriching your life with pleasures.

In other words, if you want to take a break to socialize or watch your favorite team play or treat yourself to a massage, do it! Time spent doing something you enjoy is never *wasted* time! But we must remain accountable where our goals are concerned, so moderation is key.

Let go of your fears associated with abandonment in relation to making your audience wait. As long as you continue to give readers your best work, they *will* wait for you.

Not all readers are loyal ones. That's about them, not you. The loyal ones will be loyal to that loyalty trait—and you—until the end of their days. And if time away is going to make you a better author, take it! The readers will be there when you get back.

Readers are following you because they like your stories, your vibe, and watching your journey. It's human to require bouts of self-care, so there should be no shame in taking such time off or showing your followers you are human in such ways. Elusiveness can amplify an author's presence, as it makes an audience pay closer attention when an author appears with something important to say. As the boss, only you can establish and maintain the boundaries.

And *please*, stop resurfacing with an apology. "I'm sorry I've been absent…" should never touch your posts! You were absent for a reason. You owe social media nothing. We have to stop apologizing for taking time to meet our needs. Whether your priorities were taking care of personal needs, meeting your deadline, combing your pony's hair, shooting tequila with friends, or having a root canal, it's none of anyone else's business where you were, what you were doing, or why you were gone. Just say what you have to say and move on!

This idea that we must mermaid about for our fans has created a competition where everyone loses. Rather than be a mermaid, why not be a shark? Veracious and direct. When sharks appear, others

---

[3] The author recognizes that in present times, while the world continues to overcome a global pandemic, traveling may not be an option as it once was, but the limitations imposed by COVID-19 are not permanent and we will eventually recover as a society. During such times, however, people are advised to travel safely and reminded that road trips hold a nostalgic value that can greatly impact a person's wanderlust.

notice. They never beg for attention and they certainly don't explain their motives. They simply operate based on their nature. They are there to survive.

However you measure your success, remember that its value is both relative and fluid. One of the greatest emotional tragedies authors combat is the tendency to devalue their own achievements based on someone else's. Social media plays the ultimate culprit here, and this is probably the greatest argument available for establishing some boundaries.

Stop comparing yourself to others! You are only in competition with yourself and the person you were yesterday. No one else matters. While success is relative, other people's success is completely irrelevant to yours.

By mimicking others, we're only creating an impression. Imagine, for a moment, that a stranger offers you an impression piece of Van Gogh's *Starry Night*. You love that painting, but they are only offering a cheap replica. If the poster is hanging in countless dorm rooms across the world, does it really have any value?

Now, imagine that same stranger also has a hand-painted, one-of-a-kind work of art from a new artist. You've never heard of the artist before, but the work is authentic, and the stranger is offering you the only painting like this in existence.

Which would be more valuable, the original canvas painted by the unknown artist or the poster of Van Gogh's *Starry Night*?

I sure hope you took the work by the unknown artist, because an impression is never equal to an original—no matter how well known the artist.

Be your own priceless work of art. Don't be an impression of something that already exists. The world has already seen Van Gogh. They're still waiting to meet *you*. *Awareness* means acceptance of self. It pays to get cozy with your weirdness and own it.

Success grows when we live our best life. Living your best life does not require wealth or notoriety. It only requires time and mindfulness. All you have to do is get out and live. Once you start living, unique content will come to you almost effortlessly, and the glimpses into your life, no matter how infrequent, will add to your value as a unique and genuine soul.

As I restored balance and variety into my life, I became more aware of who I was and where I wanted to be. Misery transformed into happiness, and my resentment for social media shifted, especially now that I removed the sense of obligation associated with having to post.

By evaluating my goals and cutting away the toxic patterns of behavior, I gained perspective. The more unnecessary, nonperforming tasks I trimmed from my endless to-do lists, the clearer I could see the value of doing less. Less truly was more. Then something shocking happened.

After taking a notable time away to focus on healing myself, I slowly returned to work. I expected to see a massive decline in my royalties. I mean, there had to be a dent. I'd been out of the office for months, not posting, not interacting, totally consumed by my personal journey and focused on me.

But when I calculated my profits, my income had gone up. How?

We cannot measure our profits without first deducting our business expenses. I had been participating in so many expensive author practices, the simple act of not participating was saving me a ton of money. And that whole idea that if we don't do those things, if we don't perform, we will lose our relevancy and sales… Debunked.

Loyal readers continued to read and purchase my books. *My writing* was generating new fans. And while there wasn't sizable growth without marketing, there absolutely was not a loss, especially since I was not throwing money into unnecessary business expenses.

Then the pandemic hit, and 2020 was basically shut down. Author events were cancelled. Life was cancelled. This, in turn, took my experiment to the extreme, because a sense of uncertainty left families extra conservative in regard to spending money on anything considered nonessential.

People dialed back their lives. They reconnected with family, learned to appreciate simple pleasures, walked down empty streets, gardened, sang songs, and *wrote books*. The enforced rules associated with the pandemic removed any lingering guilt that I should be *doing something* other than taking care of me and writing.

In 2020, I wrote seven novels and published two. Other than announce when my books became available, I did very little to promote each release. However, I was enjoying life so much and frequently sharing snippets of my journey on social media that my relevancy grew.

Yes, a robust marketing campaign could have put my growth on steroids. But by not heavily marketing myself, I saw no profit loss, only gains. Oh, and I figured out how to be happy again.

So, to recap, by following my instincts and accepting the things outside of my control, I became more aware of my situation. I surrendered to my circumstances and changed what was in my power to change. In turn, I reevaluated my intentions, removed a ton of toxic sources from my life, established new boundaries, stopped neglecting my needs, and started living my best life, a life full of variety, self-indulgence, and balance. I crushed my daily word counts, while working less than forty hours a week, got a great tan, and met my #1 Objective of being happy again.

Still not sure if my methods are for you?

Everyone's definition of success will be different. It all comes back to your #1 Objective in life. Mine was happiness. I'm happy again. I was able to achieve this without failing at any subpart of my life, including being an author.

If you are still hesitating about taking a break to correct the imbalances in your life because of a concern that you might lose your relevancy, ask yourself how it is that some uber-successful authors don't even have an active website? You also can't find some of the greatest authors on social media.

Maybe they scored a book deal with a big publisher and they rely on the publishing house's platform. There is nothing stopping you from doing the same. You just need the right book. But how will you ever write it if you're spending 80% of your time marketing your work week away on side-hustles and book graphics and flash in the pan attempts to get an inch ahead?

If someone offered you and escape rope, would you grab it? What if said escape promised less chaos, you first have to let go of everything weighing you down? You have trust that your moment will come and surrender.

Get rid of all the unnecessary "work-related" things you follow that are affecting your mood in a negative manner. Unfollow the eight hundred bloggers clogging your feed with the distracting progress of others, and replace them with profiles that post things that motivate you.

It all links back to balance—an *awareness* of needs, clear intentions and goals, and a mindset that manifests positive outcomes. Success begins with understanding that every decision triggers a consequence, be it a positive or negative one. In business, act in ways that create a measurable ROI or

ROJ—return on joy—because success is a relative term, it had better relate to whatever feels good to you.

Defining Balance

We are what we do, not what we say. If you are tense and stressed at work, you will be tense and stressed in life. Imagine being joyous, balanced, and optimistic, instead. That being said, do not assume making changes will be easy, especially if you've been operating in a state of unbalance for the majority of your writing career.

A balanced business is an ecosystem and there will be rocky moments. As with any business, there is a period of adjustment, so give yourself time to make big changes, and don't forget to celebrate small progress, because even small steps in the right direction can eventually lead to bigger things. *Wanting* to improve is a monumental step forward.

So, what exactly is balance? In this book, *balance* refers to the connection of mind, body, and spirit that contributes to the body's overall wellness.

This connective concept implies we are more than just our thoughts. We are our emotions. And yes, this very progressive, hippy author believes in the medical benefits of ancient practices such as yoga, mindfulness, and meditation. Such a sustained sense of wholeness can often save a person from the negative effects of a crisis.

An imbalance in one of the three temples—*mind, body*, or *spirit*—can often trigger medical complications, depression, or despondency, so we must accept that they are all connected. Though I use the word spirit, I'm in no way pushing religion. Rather, I'm speaking of a sense of inner peace. Inner peace is found by stating our intentions and mentally mapping a path to meet our needs on a regular basis.

We accept the connectivity of this trifecta through *awareness*, *intent*, and *reflection*.

Awareness requires an honest appraisal of ourselves, as addressed in Chapter Two. We must stop denying what we struggle to accept and face our problems head on. *Awareness* is knowing what we need and making that a priority over what we want.

Intent means staying focused on meeting our needs and not being distracted by momentary wants. This goes beyond setting goals and comes back to having a #1 Objective in life. Remind yourself of your #1 Objective on a daily basis, and your goals will naturally align with your overall desires.

Acceptance, also addressed in Chapter Two, prevents authors from falling for the *Dunning-Kruger effect,* or worse, perpetuating such effects on others. View your situation with truthful appraisal. Realists can be dreamers, but for dreams to come into actuality, they must stop being dreams and start being goals. To set achievable goals, one must, at least on some level, identify as a realist.

Once a realistic method of achieving your goals has been considered, and you have roughed out a roadmap to get you from point A to point B, remove all mental, physical, and emotional obstacles from your path. Simplify your route as much as possible and never aim for any goal that is not ultimately in line with your #1 Objective.

Expect to have multiple goals and multiple roadmaps for each portion of the journey. Use your #1 Objective to prioritize each goal so that the path ahead is structured in a sensible order.

Try not to think in terms of instant gratification but, rather, in terms of long-term sustainability.

For example, if Brian's #1 Objective is to afford the life he wants (he has a fabulous vision board which details his dream home, car, and Olympic-size pool with a God of Olympus husband swimming in it), then he will need to prioritize his goals in terms of financial security as this is a very expensive objective (Don't judge him. To each his own).

Brian will likely outline each goal, hire a financial planner to help him invest his profits wisely, and move the goals that create the fastest returns to the top of his list.

Meanwhile, Kesha has a very different objective. Kesha dreams of leaving an impression on the world. She wants to make an impact on others and inspire women like her to break the mold and shatter any glass ceilings holding them down.

Kesha's #1 Objective is to inspire others and bring about positive change for women. Her goals will be prioritized in an order that broadens her exposure and allows her to reach more people. While she's busy writing books, she's also placing great value in diversifying her audience by reaching out to other publications and accepting speaking engagements.

Both authors in the example have other goals in life outside of a successful author career. No author will ever be content with writing alone. Yes, writing fulfills a part of the author's soul, but we are not solely authors. And living a life that only revolves around that fraction of our existence, will leave other areas empty in return.

Once you've identified your #1 Objective and sketched out some basic goals to help you get there, you're ready to start moving, but plan to make a few stops along the way.

Unlike the stressful setbacks that can often derail or slow our progress, frequent pit stops meant to take a mental inventory will run a quick assessment of how our overall plan is functioning. These frequent pauses used to check how things are running allow us a moment to tighten up any areas that have shaken loose.

QUICK TIP:

Set a date in your calendar as a recurring event each month. Use the scheduled time to step back and reflect. You can do this through meditation, walking, journaling, or some other means that helps you clear away daily distractions and focus on the broad picture.

The point is to make reflection a regular practice in your business. This is why larger corporations often hire analytical teams to keep a pulse on how their company is functioning.

Over time, through self-awareness and practices that help you fine-tune your goals, you will develop a new perspective of yourself as "author," and you will feel confident in your approach and its effectiveness, as made evident by your accumulating sense of progress. What other authors are doing along their journey will come to matter less and less as you reap the rewards from your own progress, and much of the toxicity you faced before will have faded into a memory.

After taking those frequent pauses for appraisal and *reflection*, be sure to celebrate your accomplishments so it becomes easier to recognize the progress taking place. When we operate from a place of balance rather than a constant state of chaos, progress becomes more noticeable, as we have time to take a breath for peaceful moments when we are more self-aware.

By using the many worksheets provided in this book, you will have a written record of what you want to accomplish. I make a habit of typing out a list of goals every January, slapping a relative affirmation on the heading, and tacking it right to my wall so I look at it every day. As the year progresses, I highlight the goals met.

Before practicing this method of tracking goals and accomplishments, I would, sometimes, publish several books in a year, win accolades, and still feel like I hadn't accomplished "enough."

Don't let that happen to you. Record your goals, monitor them, and celebrate each achievement along the way.

No matter how much we believe we want a specific end result, success is not a single destination, it's the overall experience of getting there. So, it's best to enjoy the journey!

The beauty of balance is that when we find it, we exist in a state of comfort, truly content in the present moment. We recognize that we are living, because we feel truly alive. And when we are alive, we have countless stories to share.

The health and wellness of a writer will always be the foundation of an author's success. The mind, body, and spirit are the three legs needed for any writing career to stand stably in this shaky market. They are truly the author's soul. Once they are established, and balance is achieved, the writer can then move into the art and business of writing.

Chapter Seven
Mind Over Matter

"Fear comes with imagination, it's a penalty, it's the price of imagination."

Thomas Harris, Red Dragon, 1981

The Repercussion of a Thought

Reflection is the story we tell ourselves. Your thoughts matter on a molecular level, as established in Chapter Five. If your thoughts are negative, your life will mirror that. If your thoughts are positive, your life will reflect positivity.

The *Law of Attraction* is one's ability to bring into existence what he or she is most focused on. The misconception with this law is that people often think if they focus on a Ferrari, the car will suddenly appear in their driveway. Sorry, no, that's not how it works.

The *Law of Attraction* requires several steps that manifest outcomes. Your success as a writer, according to this book, is based on solid practices, such as knowledge, planning, and hard work, but there is something to be said about acknowledging the obstacles ahead and consistently reiterating your goals along with an ever-evolving, logical plan to accomplish said goals. This is achieved through *awareness, intent,* and *reflection.*

Keep this loop in your mind and you will eventually attract the success you manifest. Why? Because you see the possibility of success, you've simplified the course, and you are consistently reminding yourself that you will get there.

You are not preoccupied by a stranger's suggestion that you accomplish X, Y, and Z to succeed. That's *their* recipe, not yours. You are focused on the A, B, Cs of your custom-tailored plan, which you've spent time developing and will accomplish through *awareness*, *intent*, *reflection*, and, of course, hard work.

Positivity manifests positive outcomes. Negativity attracts failure and toxicity.

When I was suffering from burnout, my thoughts were purely toxic. I'd constantly compare myself and my success to others. I was bitter, no matter how much I tried to be happy for other people's accomplishments or how many accolades I accumulated.

We will never truly be happy for others if we can't figure out how to feel happiness for ourselves. In order to be an outwardly joyful person, one must first learn to control their internal thoughts, rejecting all inclinations toward negative thinking.

Our minds should be a safe and private place, but technology has enabled algorithms to alter our thinking by exposing us to a steady stream of influences that can greatly alter our sense of balance and contentment. We have become polarized through overexposure, to a point that we sometimes identify as the most extreme versions of ourselves. This happens frequently with politics and other belief systems because the moment an algorithm catches a bias pattern, similar content overwhelms our social feed.

My content is different than your content. This is not accidental. So, when you start following an author because you want to study their behaviors and promotional habits, the algorithms notice. They see a pattern and, in turn, gorge you on that author's feed, until you're sick of seeing them. There enters the toxicity of overindulging.

Don't believe me? Spend thirty minutes discussing raccoons within earshot of your smart phone. I guarantee you will see raccoons on your feed within the next ten days. Some devices allow you to filter this function.

We are being observed and studied so that we can be paired with meaningful content. This is how and why our views have become so extremely polarized. When the algorithms identify an interest, they feed it and make it grow.

We are constantly being influenced by media. And in a commercialized world, media is always being monetized. Feeding insecurities is one of the easiest ways to trigger a response. Need an example, look at the beauty industry with an estimated value of over 532 billion dollars, and a blistering projected growth of 17% in 2021. That is a direct result of the manipulation effectively happening from media marketing.

Our independent thoughts are not as guarded as they once were. Like any endangered environment, we must make a conscious effort to keep our minds uncluttered and unpolluted so they don't become jaded swamps of negativity. But with the advancement of technology, this is becoming more and more difficult to do.

Sludgy, negative thoughts tend to carry potent effects. Not only are negative thoughts toxic, they're sticky and difficult to remove. As they grow, they trap and breed more negativity, until our beautiful mind resembles a wasteland.

Controlling private thoughts is not a simple task. It takes conscious effort to force the mind into a place of optimism and abundance, when so many influences are geared toward making us feel incomplete or inadequate and are geared to fuel the commercialized world we live in. Be patient with yourself as you work toward mastering such control, especially if you're starting from a particularly negative place.

While there seems no way to swiftly remove the impact of commercialization and influence through social media without becoming a luddite, especially in a field that requires some degree of social media interaction, being aware of the issue helps. Recognizing that we are constantly being influenced by not so trustworthy sources, allows us to set boundaries and limit our exposure.

Controlling the time you allow yourself to be exposed can greatly impact how much you are influenced by outside sources. This is a key example of *knowing* the reality of the obstacles you face, in terms of keeping a balanced state of mind.

The *Law of Attraction* requires positive thinking in order to attract positive outcomes, which is why it's critical to avoid habits that send you to a negative headspace. Yes, scrolling through social media is a terrific waste of time that seems to put us at ease. But pay close attention to the way you feel when you sign off. Is it really putting you at ease, or is it putting pressure where none is needed?

If you want to experience an abundance of positivity, start by limiting your exposure to toxic sources of negativity. Setting boundaries between you and negative influences will leave more room for optimism and light in your life.

Only when we are aware of the repercussion a single thought can create, are we prepared to stop the negative thoughts from trespassing into our minds. It all comes down to controlling our environment, internally and externally.

Methods for Abolishing Negative Thoughts

1. Identify the thought and picture it in its physical form, as if it were an actual object floating in your head.
2. Mentally label it as a "garbage thought." The opposite of a "garbage thought" is a "keeper." By identifying the kind of thoughts filling your mind, you're more likely to control the energy spent on each one.
3. Now, dispose of the "garbage thought." You can do this by visualizing an incinerator or a cliff. Be creative, just make sure you toss it out of your head in a way that it cannot be retrieved.
4. If that doesn't work, physically write the "garbage thought" down. Much like trying to describe a nightmare, the reality of the thought on paper will prove slightly underwhelming and silly.
5. Have a laugh at the trivial things we obsess over, crumple it up, throw it in the trash where it belongs, and get on with your day.

While some of you may be rolling your eyes at such a seemingly juvenile approach, I assure you, it has merit. An Ohio State University study found that writing down negative thoughts and physically throwing them away can help people clear up the troubling echo of ruminating negative thoughts.[4]

But what if you try the throw-away method and those toxic thoughts return? What then?

Try taking a steamy shower or cozying up with a hot cup of tea. Yale, Columbia, and Dartmouth researchers discovered that warming the body clears away some of those negative cobwebs from the mind.[5]

Similar to the *write it down* approach, you can also show your negative thoughts who's the boss, and verbally command the thoughts to "Stop." You can even go as far as speaking the command, "Get out of my head." Then try repeating an affirmation that directly contrasts the negative thought with a positive one.

David has been really negative lately. He follows Greg, an author he admires, to inspire content ideas and learn new author practices that will help grow his brand. But after a while, Greg's success

---

[4] Jeff Grabmeier, director, Ohio State Office of Research and Innovation Communications

[5] The journal Social, Cognitive, and Affective Neuroscience; *Social Cognitive and Affective Neuroscience*, Volume 14, Issue 11, November 2019

stopped inspiring David and started leaving him with a sense of inadequacy. He now feels unmotivated and discouraged that he will ever reach the level of success Greg has achieved.

David tries to mentally throw away the negative thoughts he's battling. He even writes down confessions of envy and physically throws the negative feelings away, but they reappear.

Completely fed up, he takes a shower to relax, makes his favorite latte, and returns to work ready to focus on his deadline. However, he finds his writing stalling as his thoughts, once again, return to Greg's upcoming release he just announced on Instagram.

At this point, David takes a deep breath and forces himself to say, "Stop thinking about Greg. You are too busy writing your own masterpiece to worry about someone else's. *You* are focused on meeting *your* word count so *you* can eventually announce your own upcoming release."

Only then, after replacing his negativity with an active affirmation that redirects his focus to where it should be, is David able to clear his negative thoughts long enough to complete his work. Eventually, as he uses these methods, he becomes more aware of what behaviors are triggering his negative headspace. Once he is aware of his triggers, he can make a conscious effort to avoid such emotional landmines by establishing boundaries.

Boundaries are a crucial part of the healing process when it comes to shifting mindset. Protecting our thoughts sometimes requires mental and physical boundaries. In David's case, it might not be a bad idea to "unfollow" Greg for a while, no matter how much he likes and admires him.

Sometimes, we have to choose self-preservation over admiration, especially if what started out as innocent curiosity leads us to a headspace that proves counterproductive.

One of the kindest settings social media has given us, is the option to "hide" accounts from our feed. The fact that this option exists at all, goes to prove how common these toxic triggers have become, even within our own personal biosphere of friends and colleagues, so don't be ashamed to use such tools if available.

Rachel is in a trickier situation than David. She shares a social media group with six other authors. It started as a virtual mastermind group, but lately the climate has become overly negative. Rather than celebrating the success of others, the group's first response to news of an outside author's achievement is usually bitterness.

The animosity of the group has now infected other parts of Rachel's life, and she has lost her motivation. As Rachel waits for a solution to present itself, the toxicity of the group continues to fester, further infecting her headspace.

In situations like Rachel's, when rot has begun to set in, there is no choice but to amputate. Rachel must remove herself from the group, as the group no longer serves the intended purpose of helping her grow.

Rachel does not like the bitter person she has become. And while she genuinely likes the friends she's made in the group, she's also made a promise to keep herself as her first priority, so she detoxifies the negative influences and relationships in her life.

In time, Rachel branches out and connects with a new mastermind group that is better suited for her goals and aligned with her desired headspace.

The point of both scenarios is, we are what we eat. If you surround yourself with negative people, your mind is constantly digesting negative thoughts. If you really want to see a difference in your thinking, you may have to distance some people from your inner circle. This includes friends, acquaintances, and even family at times.

If there is someone in your life who stirs a feeling of negativity, avoid them for a while. Chances are, your mental health will improve.

Low self-esteem has been linked to approximately sixty percent of people using social media. Stay aware of your virtual surroundings and the actual impact it is having on you.

Watch, learn, and move on. Do not stay focused on another person's success for too long or you will lose sight of your own. Remember, *awareness, intent,* and *reflection.*

It's fine to glance briefly at what others are doing. But if you're spending your journey rubbernecking, you're more likely to end up off the road, stuck in a ditch.

Eyes on the goal—*your* goal. Other people's goals are none of your business.

The Universe is Not Conspiring Against You!

To recap the lessons learned thus far, success depends on knowledge, planning, and hard work. Balance, a centering of the mind, body, and spirit, is a part of the plan, which is found through *awareness*, *intent*, and *reflection*. Positivity is key. But so is accountability.

Authors trapped in a negative headspace sometimes believe their struggles are linked to some sort of karma. It's not uncommon to find an author blaming Lady Luck for others' accomplishments, or crediting *bad luck* for their difficulties. If that sounds like you, I'm here to tell you that is a bunch of horse shit.

Your job has difficulties because you chose a challenging field. While some authors may make it look easy—and yes, privilege definitely can create some incongruent advantages among the competition—*luck* is never completely to blame.

By crediting luck, we devalue all the hard work so many of us have done. So, let's agree to keep the accountability right where it belongs, on the shoulders of each individual author. That way, when you do succeed, you know you've accomplished something remarkable and are deserving of all the wonderful praise.

The universe is not conspiring against you. It's that sort of groundless thinking that shackles the mindset to negative headspace.

Mindfulness

Mindfulness, a technique in which one focuses their attention fully on the present, a state of being aware of thoughts, feelings, and sensations but not judging them, is a great tool for combatting habits of procrastination and diminishing stress.

While mindfulness might seem like a newer buzzword, the practice is actually more than 2,500 years old. Over the last decade, businesses have started teaching employees this strategy, because many believe productivity increases when stress levels decrease.

Being mindful of our emotional state allows us to process our emotions without criticism. To do this, we must establish that as humans we are perfectly imperfect.

Mindfulness celebrates the idea of living in the present moment, but people often struggle to fully understand what that means, so let's put it into terms most will understand. Have you ever felt depressed? How about anxious?

Depression is a state of dejection beyond what is typically warranted by an event that impacts functional activity. When not triggered by a chemical imbalance, depression can often be caused by a sense of regret.

Humans have an incredible ability to replay events in their heads until reality is lost to a sort of karmic torture where their mind embeds in the past. When we are depressed, we live in the past, so we cannot possibly exist in the present.

Anxiety is a state of mental distress or uneasiness due to a fear of upcoming misfortune or danger. When we are anxious, we live in the future, fearing what might come and obsessing over ways to avoid the unwanted. If we suffer chronic anxiety, we cannot live in the present.

While some might struggle to grasp the idea of "being present," most people can relate to feelings of depression or anxiety and a desire to avoid both. When we feel sensations linked to depression or anxiety, we know we are not existing in the present moment, because we are either in the future or the past, and we cannot be two places at once.

Sometimes, simply being aware of the location of our thoughts can relieve anxiety or depression, especially if we use tools to practice mindfulness and redirect our thoughts to the present.

Picture a gauge to help yourself become more aware of your state of mind. We are most centered and balanced when we exist in the present moment.

If we are dwelling on past events, our gauge is pointed toward the past. If we are worried and distracted about upcoming events, our gauge is pointed toward the future. Only when we are engaged with the present, are we completely self-aware. Keep that needle balanced nicely in the center to be the most productive at any given moment.

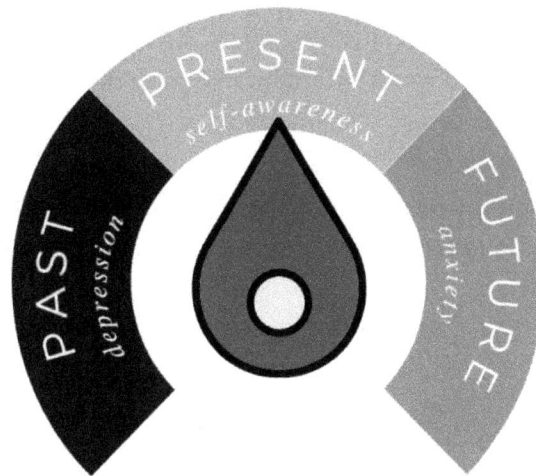

If your thoughts are tied up in the past, you might be struggling with depression. If you're constantly worried about the future, so much so that you struggle to move, you might suffer from anxiety. Knowing the label can often help us find proper treatment.

Depression often stems from regret. Many people misunderstand the meaning of karma. Karma is not a cosmic punishment seeking vengeance. It's the repetitive loop we play in our mind. The only way to stop the repetition is to fully process past events and accept that history cannot be rewritten and we can only move forward from the past.

If you have a regret so deeply engrained in your mind that it has you stuck in a karmic loop, preventing you from being present and inhibiting your productivity at work, you might take a time out and try to process your emotions.

This is why forgiveness is a key part of recovery. For addicts, it's step nine, and while it sometimes requires people to forgive others, the most life-altering part of healing comes from a person's ability to forgive him- or herself. Many times, it's our own expectations freezing our progress, not others' expectations of us.

If anxiety and depression are both signs that we are not present then, to become present, we must first deal with our emotions. We must identify our feelings and make it a priority to process them. Therapy can be a great resource during this process, especially if a person is trying to work through the effects of a past trauma.

Mindfulness is simply finding meaning in each present moment. Even when we are doing something we don't enjoy, if we can identify the purpose of the moment and embrace it, we are unconsciously combatting other emotional obstacles that could slow us down.

Anxiety is merely excitement without breath, so if you are feeling anxious, be still and practice breathing for a moment. Oxygen has amazing calming properties, and it's highly underrated as one of our greatest sources of life.

When we take a deep breath, the oxygen sends a message to the brain, telling it to relax, and the brain then transmits a message to the body that it should calm down. Ancient yogic breathing techniques have been helping people for thousands of years.

Pranayama, or controlled breathing meditation, is a quick method to center the mind. To practice pranayama, inhale a deep breath for 4 seconds. Be sure you are breathing into your belly not your chest. Hold the breath for 7 seconds. Then exhale, pushing all of the breath out while exhaling for 8 seconds. Do this 3 to 7 times and your body and mind will naturally calm down and be mindful of your thoughts and emotions.

Breath counting is a great way to combat anxiety. The practice can also be experienced by breathing through one nostril at a time in a back and forth pattern of breath in through the left nostril, breath out through the right, inhale into the right, exhale out through the left.

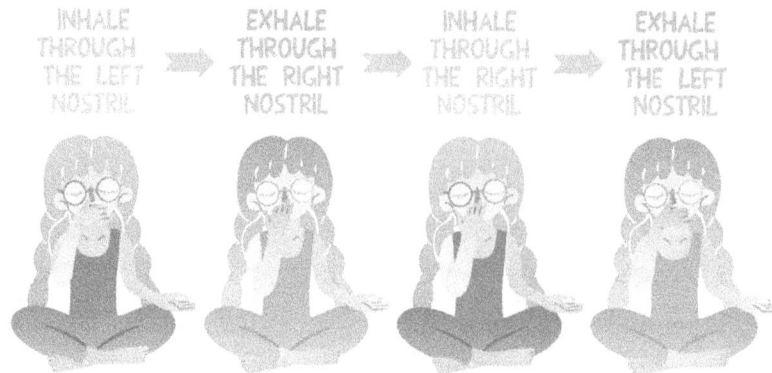

INHALE THROUGH THE LEFT NOSTRIL ➔ EXHALE THROUGH THE RIGHT NOSTRIL ➔ INHALE THROUGH THE RIGHT NOSTRIL ➔ EXHALE THROUGH THE LEFT NOSTRIL

Obviously, the more mindful we are the lower our stress levels get and the more productive we become, but does mindfulness actually benefit our creativity? The answer is yes!

Built up emotions cause an increase in cortisol. Over time, too much cortisol can cause a decrease in focus, creativity, and short term memory. Mindfulness is the opposite of brain fog, so, as authors, it's worth practicing if you want to unleash your prolific potential.

Progress Takes Time

The dangers of sitting for too long are no longer news. Yet, there remains a prevailing fear among authors that any disruption could spoil a story, and they are literally risking their lives to get the words down on paper. The cost to their health often cannot be calculated, until it's too late.

Health concerns are a prominent worry among seasoned authors, and also one of the most ignored issues in our field. A colleague once admitted that out of concern for her health, her spouse gave her a smart watch set to buzz every hour with reminders to move. She took it off after one day, because the vibrations disrupted her writing. The device was operating correctly, but its success was its downfall.

Stories like this prove authors know what they should be doing, and that the tools for success exist. But, in most cases, excuses win.

Aside from basic fatigue, excuses not to move often overrule common sense because of an imbalance in the author's value system that works in a constant debt. Desperation feeds the need to keep going the longer we exist in a state of outstanding emotional, physical, and mental debt, always trying to publish that bestseller that lets us break even.

The presumed reward of long-duration writing is finishing a book sooner, and for a large group of authors, that outcome is more valuable than health—even when the financial result fails to meet a standard hourly wage.

But what if doing something for your health, like taking short, frequent movement breaks, could actually increase your prolificacy? What if it could improve the quality of your writing and make your thoughts that much more poignant? What if the benefits of chopping up your schedule far outweighed the cost?

At the peak of my burnout, movement of any sort was exhausting and painful. I'd put on an extraordinary amount of weight, lost most of my muscle mass, suffered multiple deficiencies, and my immune system was running in constant overdrive.

I felt like I was dying, because I basically was. My body was broken from neglect. And while I, at one time, could run four miles, I could hardly hobble one. So, I understand plenty about excuses. I also understand that control is a choice.

If authors want more control over their lives and careers, they must make the choice to reclaim the control they lost. We've discussed methods for controlling mindset and detoxifying negativity, but what about the physical damages overworking has created?

When I decided to take those first steps toward physically healing myself, I was stunned to find how difficult getting healthy would be. Furious that I could not even walk a mile on a treadmill at the slowest possible stroll, I began running as hard as I could, punishing my body for betraying me and cursing the position I found my physical and mental self in.

After only a minute or two, my erratic heart felt ready to beat out of my chest and my lungs were on fire. I coughed and gasped and people stared as I fell apart, too distraught in the madness I created to even process self-preservation or shame.

When I got home and peeled off my socks, they were pink with blood. In a fit of anger, I'd only hurt myself more.

I didn't want to be patient. I couldn't justify sparing time to heal. But time was what it would take. Taking time was the only solution I had if I truly wanted to make a change, if I truly wanted to give my creative soul exactly what it needed to heal.

Synching the Mind, Body, & Spirit

One of the easiest ways to reset and form a noticeable connection between the mind, body, and spirit is through movement. Bringing movement into your workday will help speed up the process of restoring balance to your life. The balance found through simple actions—such as taking sporadic walks during the day—will overflow into other areas, such as creativity, health, gratitude, and even inspiration.

After only a short time of incorporating more movement into my life, people took notice of the ways my vibe was improving. I'm not speaking of physical improvements, though there were many positive ones. I'm speaking of a change in the energy surrounding me. It was as if my aura began radiating positivity.

My mood shifted, and a delightful sort of magnetism surrounded me. This change became noticeable after only a few days of simply taking short walks and getting out of the office.

Once I began actively turning my focus toward restoring the balance I had lost, by altering my behaviors and thinking patterns, I was able to actively begin detoxifying the negativity infecting my life.

By making subtle changes to my days, my verve drastically improved. I was so focused on pampering my mind, body, and spirit, that I became irrevocably aware of how linked this holy trinity of the soul actually is.

The side effect of actively changing behaviors to restore balance will reverberate in every component of your life. Simply put, if toxicity is the poisoning of mind, body, and spirit that throws us off balance, and too many imbalances can lead us down a life-threatening path, then restoring said balance by detoxifying all physical, mental, and emotional poisons creates a resurrection of self.

If toxins are poisons, and some poisons are lethal, then let us assume negativity represents death. But balance *is* life!

If I took time to recharge for my mental health, my spirit also got recharged. If I took a walk for my physical health, my mind enjoyed a jolt of creativity. And if I practiced affirmations to lift my spirits, I found myself energized and eager to get outdoors, which, in turn, released a wave of endorphins that channeled more positivity inside of me.

The longer we apply ourselves to this way of living, the more momentum we build. Synchronizing the mind, body, and spirit is not a complication we have to think about because, by design, these parts of us are already intrinsically linked.

Strangers took notice long before I even realized I was outwardly changing. People told me I radiated happiness. The truth was, I had struggled for years with depression, and I still felt rather fragile after suffering burnout, but I sensed what they saw and it was enough to motivate me to keep going.

My once imbalanced, sickly, chaotic norm had shifted into a state of such harmony I could hardly fathom the simplicity of change. I was accomplishing more than I had in years by choosing to do less (insert mind-blown emoji here).

Remember when I said taking time away from work was one of the most terrifying choices I ever made in my career? I'd been so emotionally and physically burned-out that, while I assumed there would be negative consequences, I no longer cared. Not once did I think the consequence would be positive and bring about an abundance of happiness, clear-headedness, or creative inspiration. All I could imagine was a loss of relevancy and income. Spoiler alert, neither happened.

The moment my world returned to its axis and I felt balanced again, I was ready to write! The words and ideas poured from me.

I was practicing *awareness*, focusing on my #1 Objective, following my custom designed road to success, and taking breaks to reflect and adjust my plan along the way.

Now that I understood the root of my stress and the cause it had on my physical and mental state, I was able to come up with proactive coping mechanisms and self-advocate. I knew my triggers, and I took time to think of positive ways to avoid them.

For the first time in my adult life, I was putting myself first. I had designed boundaries, the first being that I would no longer work in a state of imbalance. This, in accordance with actively taking steps to detoxify my life and my basic skillset of how to craft a quality story arc, unleashed my prolific potential.

The moment I returned to work, I rediscovered my joy and my confidence, and my inspiration truly soared. I was working less but benefiting more than ever before on an emotional level that replenished my author soul in countless ways. I was shifting the balance of my world and in turn, creating a complete physical and psychological change within myself.

It was the perfect storm. Focusing on the trifecta of mind, body, and spirit redefined who I was. It repaired the parts of my life I'd been neglecting and helped me understand that I was not solely "author." In the end, including *all* of me in the journey proved the absolute most effective way to move forward.

I share my personal experience and revelations with you in hopes that they inspire you to brave the steps ahead and make the needed changes in your own life, no matter how scary they might seem. Make it a point to find balance in everything you do. If you sense you're overdoing something, put it away for a while and do something else. I assure you, it will wait, and when you return, you will be better off for it.

When I divided this book into three sections, it had been in a basic attempt to deliver information in the most sensible way I could manage. But if you consider the parts of *Health & Wellness, Business,* and *Craft,* they are essentially mirroring the trifecta of Mind, Body, and Spirit.

Health & Wellness belongs to the body. *Business* belongs to the mind. And *Craft,* our creativity and art, lives within our spirit. These three parts make the soul of any author.

To reach our prolific potential is to harmonize the three major parts of the author's soul—mind, body, and spirit. It is where the journey of the successful author should begin.

Chapter Eight
Putting a Plan into Motion

"An early-morning walk is a blessing for the whole day."

Henry David Thoreau, Walden, 1854

The Heming-Way

Ernest Hemingway, celebrated author whose prose forever altered the style of English literature, was so much more than an author. His chronicled life depicts an audacious existence punctuated by artistic work, but also the marked effects of balance versus imbalance in terms of mental and physical health.

Hemingway was an irrefutable man of adventure. A seaman, a soldier, a husband, a whore, a drunk, and a delightfully dark soul, there wasn't much Hemingway avoided. Depictions of his life in France, Cuba, and America always revolve around the same swarthy essence that is so entirely masculine, I find it difficult not to shiver at the artistic completeness of his character.

Having the vantage of an outsider and the ability to study his life as a whole, allows us to see where extremes can sometimes lead to demise. But with Hemingway, we also see where balanced variety can fuel an artistic career.

Hemingway's brilliance, like any author's, can be disputed, but the impact of his stories on the book industry will never be refuted. Perhaps he captured life so precisely on paper because he lived an indulgent one without hesitation or regrets in his earlier years. When he stopped *living* a full life, that liveliness was lost, and eventually so was he.

In his letters to friends and other writers, he speaks of the craft so eloquently, often referring to an author's skill as both a poison and a curse, a perspective that is shared by many. Hemingway understood the empathetic turmoil many of us face when writing tortured heroes.

"Writers are forged in injustice as a sword is forged," he once said.

The yo-yo of emotional ups and downs experienced by authors living thousands of fictional lives can take a toll, especially when we do not allow our creative minds time to come up for air. Mentally, we need that emotional reprieve, that chance to exist as only ourselves and experience the simple joys of life.

Story arcs follow a formulaic progression of conflict and struggle. When we become so lost in our fictional work that we transcend to the mindset of our characters, our physical self cannot differentiate the emotional stress of a fictional character from the emotional stress we might face in our personal life. Our characters' pain becomes our own, even if on a cognitive level we recognize their pain is not ours, our body reads it as ours and responds accordingly with natural stress neutralizers.

Hemingway often described the dark mindset authors must enter to accurately capture a character's strife and pain, hinting at the precarious emotional state that, possibly, included his own struggles with mental health.

In his earlier years, Hemingway wasted no time or apology for wanting to live rather than write, because he was a man of indulgence and variety for most of his life, and that richness of experience showed in the texture of his work. But in his later years, when physical limitations also limited the variety of living, he suffered the consequences of imbalance.

We can learn from Ernest Hemingway's life—both positive and negative lessons. By living a robust life when we are not writing, we celebrate variety. Our personal experiences that invite opportunities for joy outside of our career, repair the taxing toll of surviving the emotional struggles of our characters.

Hemingway's work reflected a great satisfaction with life, and his stories exemplify firsthand accounts of the human condition, because Hemingway was an author who, by his own example, savored life and wrung every drop from each experience offered. But in the end, his physical limitations deprived him of such outlets, and he struggled to accept that which he could not control. This is why it's imperative for us, as authors, to practice a variety of strategies that keep us balanced, so that we may always exist in a state of acceptance and never fall to extremes.

Authors must take time to live—and live well—if they want to write relatable, good quality stories about life. But living well is more than taking a vacation or a few days off after each book release. Consistency is necessary. Living well should take place every day, no matter what.

If an author lives as a hermit, never interacting with other people or new settings, their stories will fall flat. The characters will lack dimension and the dialogue will turn wooden. You, the author, will suffer as well. Human interaction is a necessary part of living a healthy, balanced life.

While virtual interactions are not equal to physical face-to-face ones, they are an acceptable supplement at times, especially during a global pandemic or times when you cannot be in the same physical place as friends. Try supplementing with a virtual meet and having a "happy hour" with friends or perhaps scheduling a "mastermind meet" through a chat or even a video call with an acquaintance. Never underestimate the power of eye-contact or its effect on the human soul.

Authors must breathe life into fictional worlds by taking a breath of reality several times a day. "Experts" are always telling authors to sit down and write, but what about the proven greats, the experienced writers, the celebrated artists—like Hemingway, Dickens, Woolf, or King? The recorded behavior of those "experts" suggest, by example and actual measurable success, that we must get up and move.

Balance and variety are requirements in life, or our work will dull. We must feed the author soul—mind, body, and spirit—to avoid the long-term physical and mental damages that can occur when a human body is neglected.

In the beginning of this book, I claimed authors write because the act of writing is our calling. For me, writing was my soul mate, and it felt like my soul mate had betrayed me. But when I calmed down, I realized writing hadn't betrayed me. I betrayed writing.

We have bastardized this beautiful art into a modern-day business. Chances are, no matter where you are on your journey, you will always love writing. A soul mate is a spiritual connection that cannot be undone by distance or time.

But publishing… that's the whore we tolerate in the background of the seemingly perfect marriage between writing and author. It's the attention stealer, the time thief, the energy drainer, the one that can often leave partners emotionally bankrupt and resentful in the end.

Authors of the past didn't have to juggle the duties many writers face today. And while publishing remains a necessary evil, especially for the indie author, it does not have to be the high maintenance, demanding mistress we've allowed it to become.

We have handed over authority, but the author is actually in the superior position and maintains the ability to take back control at any time. Restoring balance means dialing back the unnecessary tasks of the job and focusing on what matters most.

If writing is your soul mate, your calling, your passion, addiction, obsession, your therapy, your release, your breath, or your calm, then make it the priority it deserves to be and stop getting so turned on by its sister.

Writing is about creating art. Publishing is about producing products. One is shiny and one is messy. Which are you, the artist or the publisher? It's fine to be both, but our relationship with writing often suffers when we dote on the publishing parts of the job rather than putting our medium first.

I am first a writer. Publishing is only a method for me to share my art with the world. My loyalty is to my art. I can live without publishing. I cannot live without the freedom to write.

My poor health and overwhelming obligations to be an "author" had stolen my time to write, which added to the sense that I was dying inside. I'd been thrust into a reality I could no longer deny, and I finally accepted the damage I'd done and the effort it would take to heal.

In a story arc, this point is often referred to as 'the point of no return'. It's the moment when the main character finally accepts his or her reality and understands there's no going back to the way things were. He or she can only move forward.

Visually, this is the steep, upward slope of the arc, marking a mountain that will be challenging to climb. At any point, the character can backslide or fail. But if victorious, he or she will rise, grow, learn, and be stronger for the struggle in the end.

After much reflection, I eventually woke, a little more humble, a little more patient, and a lot more forgiving of my limits, and I tried again. When I returned to the gym and climbed back on the treadmill, I walked slowly and only a short distance, but meeting that small goal was the first success to register in my heart in a long time.

I understood my motivation wouldn't come in heaps but scraps. Physically and emotionally depleted, I was starved for inspiration and bankrupt of time, so I made do with any shred I could find and finally hit pause on all the unnecessary distractions holding me back.

The reality was, I couldn't even wear laced sneakers because the simple act of bending over to tie my shoes would sap away the little energy I had. I learned to take slow strolls and show gratitude for the short distances I could manage.

For more than a year, I had existed in pain. Standing, sitting, walking, sleeping, my body was in a constant ache. But the more I patiently pushed myself to heal, the more I noticed the pain receding.

Aside from the physical trauma I'd caused, my imagination had turned to sludge. At the peak of my burnout, I literally felt my brain working slower than ever before. Toxic negativity annihilated my creative drive, and I was desperate to restore the motivation I'd lost.

The road to redemption is long and lonely, but I was determined to repair the damage I'd done. I took the needed time off and focused solely on myself, something I hadn't done in over a decade. I've already spoiled the ending and confessed this was the wisest decision I'd ever made for my career, but it's important that others facing similar situations truly understand why.

Success is never about how many books one produces in a year or how many words an author can write in a day. It's about how we feel inside and out.

When the body is getting out in the sunshine and moving frequently, there are multiple benefits that actually enhance performance. I've restored variety where there wasn't any. I balanced my life around healthy goals, movement, nutrition, and joy.

And while, at first, I'd thought I had no time to spare, it turned out I had plenty. My initial successes were small and personal, but as time went on and my commitment to heal grew more cemented in my mind, the outward effects took shape and outsiders noticed.

The glow I radiated came from a once dark place that I'd smashed open like an atom, releasing a burst of energy so immeasurable it would be impossible to contain or hide. My health improved, my thinking detoxified, my motivation repaired, and an adventurous spirit emerged.

Last September, I literally paused for a moment and found myself floating on the slow rocking waves of the Atlantic Ocean, miles from the coast, hovering in the absolute stillness of time, and I laughed at the overwhelming sense of gratitude flowing through me. The sun was on my face, the sweetness of a sipped cocktail still on my tongue, and I could breathe easily, knowing I'd already put in a day's work.

I had hit my word count with sunlight to spare. My skin wore the tint of time spent playing outside. My joints sung from healthy, daily use, and no matter what anyone else saw, I knew I was alive and beautiful and living my best life. I was happy.

How did I get there?

One step at a time.

The process I took to find my joy again has been detailed in the chapters that led you here. You can follow the trail I left and find your joy, too.

I accepted reality, detoxified my life, set a #1 Objective, and surrendered to the circumstances outside of my control. I stopped depositing pieces of myself into investments that showed no return. I placed higher value on my health and time, figuring out how to manage both better than I'd been. I became more proactive and prepared for unforeseen setbacks as best I could, maintaining my personal boundaries and reminding myself that some failures are actually lessons that lead to greater success. I stopped listening to nonexperts and started taking better care of me.

Do I still have bad days? Of course! As a matter of fact, I keep a screaming goat on my desk and press the button whenever I start feeling overwhelmed. And on the days hearing the goat's scream isn't enough to calm me down, I have a glass of wine or four.

The point is, I've learned to take the job and life a lot less seriously. I've learned to appreciate the long journey, because if I truly want to endure and make it as an author, I need to accept that there are very few shortcuts on the path ahead.

Maybe at one point I wanted to play the prima donna, but I later discovered, in this story, I'd rather be the hero. Heroes must face adversity. If they don't, their lives wouldn't be interesting enough to qualify them as anything more than a side character.

Learning the necessity of hardship—*really* letting that lesson sink in—humbled me to a degree that I no longer cared about playing the fancy celebrity author. I only wanted to play myself and make real-life connections with others so that I could depict people and reality more accurately in my writing. And *that* was a liberating lesson to learn.

There had been one person, someone I loved very much, who had proven to be a great source of toxicity in my life—a villain, if you will. She often took advantage of my time and stole a lot of my energy. While I lived to please her, she grew more critical by the day. Our relationship had become nonreciprocal, but I couldn't cut her out because this villain was *me*.

I was the most abusive source in my life and that needed to change if I wanted to succeed. I needed to respect my own boundaries, which was another profound lesson I needed to learn.

In the business chapters ahead, we will address time management and ways to define healthy limits between life and work. For now, you only need to understand that the less you live the less alive you will be.

If we learn one thing from Hemingway, let it be a lesson on living. By taking a page from his book and embracing life for the abrupt—and often chaotic—bouts of adventure it offers, we remember we are alive. Then we begin to live again. No matter how much you learn from this book, let the Hemingway lesson be one you remember. Living a full life will be your ultimate salvation—in all things. Snuffing out that liveliness will be our demise.

And when it comes to the business of publishing, that demanding whore we must often answer to, remind yourself that even Hemingway knew time was key to creating a masterpiece, even he put himself first.

"The longer I can stay away before I have to get it to you the better it will be as that gives me a whole new chance to see it cold and plug any gaps and amplify where there is any need," Hemingway wrote to his publisher Charles Scribner in 1949.

Four years later, he published *The Old Man in the Sea,* the book most credited as his greatest work and legacy. After that letter to his publisher, effectively pointing out that better work requires personal time, he went on to win the Nobel Prize in Literature and the Pulitzer Prize.

I often wonder, had he not maintained such boundaries and lived a life of variety, if we would even know his name.

10K in a Day

How do you set your new plan to live a healthy and wholesome author life into motion? One step at a time.

During the preliminary detoxification stage, I suggested consuming the daily recommended amount of water to start flushing your system of impurities. Remember, the human body is mostly water, and our thoughts and feelings can have a molecular impact on the water sustaining us. But what else can we do to *move* things along?

There is very little we can do to avoid the sedentary conditions of being a full-time writer. While I recommend a standing desk and own one, standing is not enough to reverse the negative health effects of a sedentary job. We *must* move.

But how will we find time to move *and* increase our word count? Once again, many of you are likely assuming the health section of this book will completely contradict the craft and business sections advocating high word counts, but the truth is, movement boosts creativity.

Moving regularly and getting the recommended 10k steps a day creates a surplus of energy many sedentary workers are missing. Movement clears away brain fog and boosts cheerfulness, creating a more optimistic mindset.

Improving your author soul—mind, body, and spirit—and increasing your word count requires a lot of planning and hard work, but the greatest improvements will come from following one simple rule: match your steps to your word count every day.

Meaning, if you are writing 2k, you had better be walking it as well. Writing 4k a day? You're going to have to walk 2 miles. As you work up your word count, you will also work up your steps, and both will become easier and improve with time. Once you're hitting that 10k word count a day, you're not only prolific, you're walking more than 5 miles on the days you're writing—and the days you're not writing, if you're really committed. This strategy not only keeps your goals in check, it matches your career goals with healthy ones.

Based on the popular recommendation of daily steps needed to boost overall health, and for the simplicity of this strategy, we are going to agree that 10 thousand steps a day is a good and healthy goal.

Guess how many steps sedentary authors with full-time writing jobs are taking a day? It's not good. Most full-time authors barely move, which is why so many are in a health crisis and feel as if they are literally atrophying at their desks.

To those stuck in a routine devoid of movement breaks or exercise, the idea of adding such a task to an already jam-packed schedule probably feels counterproductive. But I'm going to disprove that argument—and so are you.

Not only can I write 10k in a day, I can write it by three in the afternoon *and* get my steps in. I'm an early riser, but I never work more than eight hours a day, so while each person's schedule will be uniquely tailored to their life, word count should never be the result of overtime. On the contrary, it's a matter of structured time, which we will get into in the next section.

By incorporating movement breaks, the day becomes more structured. Less time is wasted on *busyness* and more time is spent being *productive*. This 10k structure creates pockets of time, leaving me with plenty of extra moments for family, friends, and fun.

For success to claim any sort of formula, the methods used must be sustainable. There must be balance as well as variety on your journey. The greatest way to stimulate change is to not only form a plan, but have the courage to take those first steps toward your goals. Setting a movement goal is the perfect place to start.

We must, once and for all, accept the connectivity between the mind, body, and spirit, which encompasses the author's soul. 10K in a day isn't simply a writing theme. It's a lifestyle theme, and it's going to change your life—as a writer, an entrepreneur, a person, and anything else you dream.

Consider the health benefits alone. Ten thousand steps a day burns anywhere between 2,000 and 3,500 calories each week. It just so happens that 3,500 calories is the equivalent of one pound of fat. And while I celebrate a body positive mindset, it's an indisputable fact that too much body fat can lead to deadly health complications. So, if hitting those ten thousand steps every day leads to healthy weight loss or added muscle mass, it's all the more reason to try.

Keep in mind, some goals take time. The ones that do are usually the most valuable. When I began this journey, I was standing in a very damaged place and I could hardly manage a thousand steps in a day, but I kept at it and my perseverance paid off in a big way.

Don't let your limits discourage you. Every step, no matter how big or small, will get you closer to your goals.

Let's look at the numbers. 4,400 steps a day is considered "beneficial." 7,500 steps a day is associated with "reduction." Once a person consistently walks 10k in a day, the body actively reaps the physical, mental, *and* emotional benefits.

Consistency Over Intensity

My personal mantra for success is "consistency over intensity." This applies to so much more than exercise, but in terms of our needed daily movement, it hits the nail right on the head.

We must stop thinking that getting the daily recommended amount of movement requires a complete restructuring of our lives. Yes, this is a lifestyle change, but it's nothing dramatic. In actuality, incorporating movement breaks into your daily life is so basic, the simplicity of the act will debunk every excuse you try.

You don't need high quality running shoes or a gym membership or a meal plan. You just need to get your ass out of that chair intermittently throughout the day. If you can get outside, even better. I don't care if you live on a highway and have to pace your living room to get those steps in, you have no excuse but to try.

Not only do I have systemic lupus, I also suffer from a condition called Raynaud's phenomenon, a painful disorder that constricts blood flow to the hands and feet, triggered by stress and cold climates. When this condition is triggered, it's impossible to type because my hands go completely numb.

In the winter months, this is especially problematic. However, in favor of my overall health, I've invested in gloves, hand warmers, and often follow a walk with a warm beverage in a hot mug.

We all have excuses not to get out and walk. Progress happens when we stop making excuses and start finding solutions, so start thinking around the obstacles in your way because obstacles can only truly block your progress if you allow them.

Here are some of the tools available to increase the likelihood of successfully hitting 10k steps a day. First, grab your shoes.

In 2020 the majority of the world experienced working from home, and it was no surprise that so many people discovered the joy of living in the coziness of pajamas and not having to wear a bra to work. I'm all for barefoot and braless creativity, but a solid day's work requires shoes.

Studies show that sitting barefoot at your desk can boost creativeness, but sometimes not knowing where our shoes are or the mere laziness of not feeling like putting them on, can absolutely derail your 10k a day.

Step one is putting your shoes on your feet or at least keeping a pair of shoes by your desk. That way, when it's time for a movement break, you have all the equipment you need.

Another great tool is a pedometer. These handy little devices have become so popular that they can even be purchased for under a dollar—that means even someone living on a beginning author salary can afford one. If you have a smart phone, it probably has an app installed with the factory settings to clock your steps for free.

No matter what kind of pedometer you own, be it a smart watch or something from the dollar store, a pedometer is proven to increase accountability and enhance a person's likelihood of success. However, it is not necessary, and the absence of one in your life should never prevent you from moving.

If you are truly set on clocking your distance but don't own a pedometer, set your odometer and drive around for one mile. Remember your route. One mile is roughly 2k steps. Walk that route every time you write 2k.

The next helpful tool is a timer. My favorite is the Amazon Echo smart speakers I have throughout my home, but any timer will work. Use your oven clock, cellphone, alarm clock, or anything else that can alert you of when it's time to take a break from sitting.

As simple as these tools seem, the absence of them in my life created more obstacles than I could handle. So, I hope these simple recommendations help you.

Remind yourself, movement does not require the intensity of a cardio class, although something as simple as a casual walk can enhance our cardiovascular health by gradually raising the heart rate. Getting up and moving is merely meant to awaken the mind, body, and spirit so that the author's soul remains balanced and healthy.

Do not let the idea of walking overwhelm you. Walking is nothing complicated, but the benefits are substantial and far outweigh the inconveniences.

When I started walking, I set a timer every hour. When the timer buzzed, I saved my work and walked around my block, which is a rather small block (only 500 steps).

I was in extremely bad shape and worked myself into a sweat. But the next time my timer went off, I got up and pushed myself around the block again.

Within one week of slowly strolling around my little block, I felt confident enough to try the big block (2,000 steps). Soon I had my paths clocked between 10 and 20 minutes, so neither required a massive chunk of time to accomplish.

Walks were a time for me to think about gratitude and focus on my goals, and they eventually became my greatest form of meditation. I learned to take shorter walks during the colder months, but when summer came, I had regained so much stamina I often started my day with 12k steps before breakfast, and those were the days my creativity really soared. No matter how I break up my steps each day, I make a point not to sit for longer than an hour.

Movement is an ultimate balancing tool. Walking is one of the fastest steps you can take toward correcting imbalances and recovering from burnout. But you don't have to suffer from burnout to experience the benefits of walking. Daily activity can greatly diminish the troublesome signs of neurosis, long before dangerous symptoms of burnout set in.

Still skeptical? Try taking a ten-minute walk right now to reflect on what you've read so far. Don't make an excuse, just start. Right now. This book will be here when you get back in ten minutes. Or you can download the audiobook and take it with you!

You should feel the calming, balancing effects of movement right away. And they will only get more evident with practice.

Once you start walking on a regular basis, you may find yourself anticipating those peaceful moments to collect your thoughts and step away. You could become such a reflective person that your stress levels noticeably drop and others start to see you as remarkably Zen.

All of the above happened for me after only a couple weeks of incorporating gratitude walks into my day, which is really just a trendy term for slow-ass strolls around the neighborhood. I went from an incredibly discouraged, unhealthy, and negative place, where I was overworked, overstressed, and constantly exhausted, to a place that was light, productive, and indisputably joyful.

Survival

Think back to that iceberg scene I described in Chapter Five. Remember the chaos? The more Zen I became, the higher my subconscious-self rose and the lighter I felt. It was as if I were floating away from the chaos, holding onto a rescue rope as a helicopter swept me to safety.

I no longer felt like I was about to drown. On the contrary, I felt the complete opposite. I felt happy and hopeful. And I wanted to share those feelings with my colleagues.

I spoke to my author friends and told them I had some theories about the likelihood of our success. I explained my assumption that we were burning through our nonrenewable resources, like time and energy, and that the way we were trying to succeed might not be sustainable in the end.

I got a lot of *"but, but but…"* responses and excuses about why they could not afford to take time away from work and try my approach. Some weren't at my level of burnout, so they saw no reason to pause. Others were emotionally fried to a crisp, but too afraid that time away would cost them the delicate success they held. The idea of cutting ties with readers for even a day in favor of self-care and balance wasn't a risk many were willing to take.

If I lose my relevancy, I lose everything…

My followers expect me to be present…

I'll take a break after I hit my deadline…

All of the above are examples of some of my colleagues' famous last words.

When I was a teenager, I watched some of my peers dabble with dangerous situations, substances, and people. My father sat me down and gave me a bit of advice. He said, "Imagine you're standing outside of a pool and you see a friend drowning. She's in the water, drenched, and heavy. You bend down to try to save her, but she isn't helping you as you struggle to lift her out. Are you more likely to rescue her, or is she more likely to pull you under?"

I still remember thinking to myself, my father was way more cutthroat and colder than I could ever be. He's also indisputably successful. I could write out his accolades, assets, and accomplishments, but your time is precious and so is mine. The point is, he was on to something.

My father always had big goals. He made himself available to others but knew exactly when it was time to cut ties in order to survive. He's a bit of a badass tycoon like that, and his ruthlessness actually makes him the perfectly flawed sort of character readers love. His vulnerability lies in the reality that whenever he had to leave friends behind, he left them with a bit of his heart as well.

It's not easy to follow our instincts when those we trust, admire, or love are doing something very different. How do we know who is correct, when the majority of our trusted peers argue that they can't leave a situation, but something deep inside our soul insists it's time we move on?

Business sometimes requires a person to act ruthlessly, even when there are no guarantees. Big risks come with big rewards. And if you have big goals, you have some big choices ahead.

That was what my dad was trying to teach me that day. And as an adult, I now understand he isn't cold at all. He's merely a realist, something—at the peak of my burnout—I realized I needed to be.

If I wanted to move on, I had to go. I couldn't pull peers out of the chaos if they were insistent on staying. I would only waste more energy and risk falling back in.

Escaping alone made my journey all the more terrifying. Leaving my colleagues behind and going a different route only pronounced how far off the beaten path I would have to travel by myself. And there was no guarantee that my assumptions would lead me where I hoped to go. But I had to trust my instincts, so I became ruthlessly set on seeing my theory through.

While writing this book and conducting my own experiments to enhance my success and quality of life, I've observed several peers stepping closer to that burned-out point of no return. Some have even crossed it. It's for them, and others like them, that I find myself writing this now.

It's challenging to expose our true fears, knowing outsiders may judge us for mistakes or criticize the fragile victories we hold so dear. But by allowing ourselves to be vulnerable, by exposing the truth behind the polished lies we propagate on social media in airbrushed, over-branded pictures playing into the illusion of extreme success, we open up countless dialogues that can help others grow.

Survival—true survival—comes down to sincere actuality. The ego is only an anchor around the neck. It is what holds us to a place of denial and false security. But if you want actual security in terms of measurable success, you must have the courage to stand completely exposed and address the problems at hand.

This book began on the premise that success begins with *awareness* and acceptance. I warned the reader of a choice ahead. I warned change would require surrender.

When you reach that precipice of escape, do not let the fear of surrender scare you. Shed the ego and let go. Let go of everything that's been holding you back or holding you down.

Be courageous and strong, be ruthless when needed, but most of all, be a survivor. Live your life to the fullest. Your best life will be your salvation in the end. Trust me on this.

And if you're not ready to turn your back on the familiar, that's fine. This is where we part, for now.

For those of you, who are ready to try something new, grab the rope. It's time for you to move out of the chaos and into the long-awaited successful mindset.

PART TWO

THE BUSINESS OF WRITING

Chapter Nine
The Company We Keep

"I will not follow where the path may lead, but I will go where there is no path, and I will leave a trail."

Muriel Strode, Wind-Wafted Wildflowers, 1903
(NOT Ralph Waldo Emerson, who was later falsely credited with the quote in 1992)

The Mission

Mission statements clarify a purpose. On the first page of any successful company's website, you will usually find a *mission statement*, defining the company's overall focus, the products and/or services it will provide, and a concise summary of the company's values. Every author should have a mission statement for their brand as a whole, one that captures their purpose, presence, voice, and vibe.

There is so much to cover in the field of *authorpreneurship*. Deciding which business elements should be included in *Write 10k in a Day* and which should be excluded, when everything had a way of feeling crucial, made the final call a difficult one.

Giving this book a mission statement relieved a lot of arduous decision-making. Having one for this book helped me clarify what would be included in the sections ahead. Let's review the intention of this book now, so that we are reminded of its purpose.

> ***Write 10K in a Day*** **teaches methods that help authors balance the demands between life and writing, so that they may achieve sustainable success and unleash their prolific potential while avoiding burnout.**

Reviewing the mission statement of this book should indicate what sort of business input lies ahead. I say input, because while I do not consider myself an expert or authority of trade, I am a hardworking, assertive, ambitious business woman with ample experience as a hybrid author who has many helpful strategies to share. Any advice offered is merely a suggestion, not creed, so feel free to filter as you go.

My purpose is not to teach writers how to become "authors." My purpose is to teach authors methods that continue to unleash their prolific potential and maintain balance, so that they do not burn out. Keep in mind, "author" is whatever you define it to be once you've entered the business of publishing books for profit.

In the chapters ahead, we will examine practices specifically relevant to the book industry and the responsibilities of authors acting as entrepreneurs, or *authorpreneurs*. Skills that assist with balance and productivity will be heavily examined, so that each unique author can apply effective strategies to their unique process.

Moving forward, this business section will take a comprehensive look at the *authorpreneur* job and the mechanics of running a successful company. It will examine various strategies that avoid wasting time, so that authors can better prioritize their responsibilities, leaving more time to focus on writing.

We will discuss methods for setting up support systems within an isolated career, strategies that should minimize job stress, proactive approaches to meet social expectations without losing too much time, and scheduling techniques to run an efficient business that provides ample time to write.

Once such business strategies are addressed, authors will be ready to dive into the secrets of the craft. By the end of the book, you will have a balanced grasp of strategies relating to the health, business, and craft of writing. These strategies are crucial for you, as an author, to develop your own unique writing routine in a way that directly adapts to your multifaceted life. Once those strategies are put into play, you will be on your way to writing 10K in a day.

Boss, HR, and Staff

Without the three temples working in collaboration—mind, body, and spirit—a person's quality of work ultimately suffers. But when these three temples are functioning harmoniously, an ease awakens within and a sense of connectivity shared with the outside world develops.

Having read Part One: *The Health & Wellness of a Writer,* authors should possess a firm understanding that there is no true success without embracing the wholeness of the author soul. If one temple is neglected, you will never meet your maximum potential. We must feed all parts of the soul if we wish to truly thrive.

But how does this holistic approach transition into the structural guidelines needed in the business of writing? We must first break down the engineering of an author to understand.

As an author, especially those who are strictly indie, you occupy multiple positions. You are the boss (mind), the staff (body), and the HR department (spirit). Your company relies on all three of these important roles, because without them, the company would capsize.

After taking the time to jot down a mission statement for your company, you should have a better grasp of the goals, values, and intention of your business. This statement will guide your choices in relation to how you decide to run your private company.

Working under the assumption that everyone has had a job they loved and a job they did not, and everyone wants their current job to be a dream job, let's consider how we got started as authors.

The act of writing a manuscript is a preliminary part of the creative experience. The production of the work, the editing and formatting are considered subsequent steps. The business of publishing, getting your work out to the world, is a part of the preparatory stage.

While all of these steps are part of the book writing process, this section focuses mostly on the actual occupation of an author, be it part-time or full-time, traditional, hybrid, or indie.

Part one prepared us for a journey. In part two we are shifting gears to examine the actual mechanics of the vehicle used to reach the right destination.

Usually, with most positions, an interview takes place before any commitment is made. Not only does the employer ask the job candidate questions about his or her qualifications, the candidate also has the opportunity to ask the interviewer about the job. This usually has to do with expectations, benefits, and policy.

When you became an author, did you consider the pay or benefits? Maybe you thought about the notoriety and dreamed of seeing your name on a list. But did you actually take the time to formalize what you considered "fair" in terms of compensation for your work? This is, perhaps, the first place authors make a wrong turn, so let's backtrack.

You are interviewing for your dream job as "author" (this is different from your old job working at *Modern Authors Are Miserable, LLC*). Before you arrive at your interview, you make a list for your own personal reference.

Your list may have the following questions:
What is the hourly rate?
Will regular breaks be offered?
Is there paid vacation?
Are there health benefits?
What is the company policy for sick days?
…and so on.

You, as the interviewee, will also need to supply acceptable answers for these questions, so you aren't misled during the interview process. This basic provision is the equivalent of preparing a shopping list to take to the grocery store, because we all know how simple it is to arrive somewhere and forget our purpose.

Your purpose is your #1 Objective. Never forget that. In the case of my #1 Objective—*happiness*—I would want to ask myself, *will this job make me happy?* And I would want to remind myself how valuable happiness is to me.

As the boss and HR rep, you will need to know the actual answers to these common concerns. You should offer a competitive package that motivates people to work for you—a safe and happy work environment full of job incentives—otherwise you might lose your job candidate's interest.

Note that these perks keep employees *happy*. Even low paying jobs come with incentives.

Cheyenne might work at a bookshop in a dead strip mall five days a week making only minimum wage, but the perk is that she gets to screw around on her phone all day and read whenever she wants. The pay is low, but according to her, the job freedom and low stress makes it worth it.

Doug, on the other hand, is earning about two dollars an hour and working eighty hours a week as a self-published author. He's working twice as much as Cheyenne and making less than half her salary. Something is wrong with this picture. The only way Doug could justify his underpaid efforts is if other benefits of value are in play.

This then introduces the delicate balance of part-time author, someone who devotes limited time to writing professionally and supplements income elsewhere to survive. The low yielding job of "author" is then justified, because it's only taking up six hours a week versus Doug's draining eighty hours.

Our time is valuable and should never be taken for granted. As an author, you must fulfill all of the roles in the company. You must be a decent boss, but you also should know your worth as an employee. Make sure you are getting compensated properly for your time and devotion. Don't settle for less than you deserve, and know when you've earned a bonus!

A start-up will always require more time and effort than an established company, but often times, companies offer founding employees stake in the company's growth. As an author, you will have shares in the company, but be sure to appraise those dividends accurately. Don't get swindled by empty promises. Until the company generates actual profits, those shares are worthless.

As the boss, you will have more passion motivating you because you have the most to gain from the company's success. You have the most shares. But you also have to supply the cost of starting the business, as well as any freelancer fees and employee salaries. Be careful not to overextend your resources. Success requires you to be absolutely realistic about your company's profits, which can only be measured after all losses are deducted.

As the interviewee, you must do your research and possess a comprehensive knowledge about the industry, the success rate of similar start-ups, and returns. Having stake in a company's success is only valuable if the company succeeds, and there are no such guarantees in publishing, so be careful what you invest and how much value you place on the job incentives.

As an employee expected to report to work regularly and perform a number of duties, you should be earning a competitive salary. Only you can determine what that is. Be serious about your desires and write them down.

As the boss, ask yourself who is paid first out of the company's profits, the employees, the PR freelancers, the cover artists, the travel concierge, or the company itself. If profits neglect the employees, only to roll over into the business's overhead, employees will be undercompensated and dangerous resentments will develop. Ethically, it's clear that every person must be paid, but authors frequently work themselves to the bone on slave wages.

Maybe your company needs a union rep to come in and remind everyone about labor laws, rest breaks, and fair compensation. Add that to the list of positions an author must fill.

You're also the head of the HR department. It's your duty to think of ways to improve the company's morale. It's your job to build incentives into the schedule. Perhaps you offer a reward incentive that states after each new release the author earns a monetary bonus. If that's not in the company's budget, supplement with vacation time. It's the responsibility of the company to figure out ways to adapt and juggle such fluctuations to keep the staff motivated and rejuvenated.

Hold on. The company accountant just chimed in with a look of concern. Did I mention that you're also the senior accountant? The boss might determine the wages and promotions, but you're the ever present reality check that makes sure things are mathematically feasible.

A lot of authors prefer to work with words over numbers, so they outsource the job of accounting and hire a financial planner. That, of course, comes with a fee, so until you can afford one, you had better dust off your calculator and gather some realistic estimates of what your profits will be.

Authors wear countless hats on the job, especially in the early years of a start-up when the lack of overhead might require them to act as publicist, editor, graphic designer, media specialist, inventory foreman, clerk, business manager, literary agent, publisher, publicist, and so on. But the three most basic hats are those of the boss, HR rep, and staff. Without these three branches working cohesively together, things will start to fall apart.

It pays to plan ahead and avoid inviting dysfunction into the company whenever possible. If you didn't start with a list of expectations and acceptable answers to all your questions about the position of "author," go back and think these things through now. Better late than never.

You may discover your boss is a bit of a selfish prick. And the HR rep would rather get lost in a social media black hole than think about the company's problems. No wonder why the #1 employee is so burned-out. The lead author's been taken for granted and underappreciated for too long.

Sounds like the perfect time to make a list of demands and ask for a raise. Either that, or it's time to tell the boss you'll be cutting back your hours, since your duties have somehow far exceeded your pay grade. Whatever you, the lead author, choose to do, you should definitely stop giving away your time for free, because that's the most valuable commodity you have. Time literally translates to life, and we only get one.

As the boss, now staring down at this list of demands your #1 employee just delivered, you have some choices to make. Has your business been operating outside of its means? How can you keep your employee happy without jeopardizing the company's efficiency and growth? Sounds like it's time to audit the list of expectations and make some cuts.

While you're at it, you should set up a meeting with HR and see about generating some new incentives to restore the motivation that's been lost. Maybe flexible scheduling that offers summer hours or a bonus. It doesn't have to be huge, but it has to make the employee feel their hard work is appreciated and rewarded.

At the risk of sounding like a broken record, to run a successful business, there must be balance. Effort should always be equal to reward. If there is an imbalance, deficits and resentments will develop, and over time, those discrepancies will lead to burnout.

If an author is outputting time and effort far beyond the pay, the boss must change the job expectations. Hours must be cut, because working more does not always equal more profits in this industry. It's time to get realistic about the actual value of the employee's time and cut them some slack based on what the company is able to pay.

But employees don't always like having their hours cut. Sure, there are unpleasant parts of any job, but there are also parts of most jobs that employees love—namely, in the business of being an author, writing. A healthy compromise might be to review time-on-task responsibilities and see where cuts can be made.

If certain operation expenses aren't producing revenue or are putting the company in debt before employees are compensated, then those practices should be put on hold immediately. A profit and loss statement should be completed, and only profitable practices should be permissible for the time being.

To Make a Profit and Loss Statement:

1. List all sources of revenue and calculate each revenue on a uniform timetable (e.g. monthly or annually).
2. The sum of all revenues will be your gross profit.
3. List and calculate all production costs and operating expenses using the same time measurement as above (Don't forget your wages!).
4. Deduct the sum of all business expenses from your gross profit.
5. This will give you the net profit of your company and tell you a lot about the overall health of your business.

The one thing we know for sure about publishing is that a book is always the product. While some books will sell better than others and there are various marketing techniques that can manipulate a product's success, without books there is no product. Meaning, without a book, there can be no marketing, but without marketing, there can still be a book.

If a business is running in the red, all accounts should temporarily freeze while an audit takes place. Any unnecessary costs must be cut. Books should continue to be written, and as the company's product line increases so will the budget for other business expenses.

In the past ten years, I've watched authors get very creative about income. Recognizing that being an *authorpreneur* requires some diversification and passive income, authors have really learned to hustle. Some host signings, others freelance as editors or cover artists, some teach workshops, many sell subscription boxes, some even ghostwrite.

There is nothing wrong with finding additional sources of income as long as we recognize that additional work inevitably encroaches on writing time. Many authors have turned their nose up at the idea of working a second job, because they dream of being a full-time writer. However, with outside employment, there is more financial security than there is for an authorpreneur who opens a new sister start-up.

Let's say Ellen is an author who writes 20 hours a week. She also works at the local daycare 18 hours a week. She doesn't make a lot at either job, but she knows the daycare cuts paychecks on Thursday, and every Friday the same dependable income shows up in her account.

Tara is a full-time writer. She doesn't make a lot of money, so she is expanding her brand and investing in selling subscription boxes. It should be easy, as she has a plan, a network of wholesalers, and diversifying her product line will expand her overall brand and platform. But she has underestimated the time and effort successfully expanding her business will take, the amount of stress it will add to her job, and the unforeseen fires she will have to put out.

Tara is not guaranteed a specific amount of supplemental income every Thursday like Ellen. Tara has overhead expenses and Ellen does not. Tara's upfront costs have added to her business debt, but *if* her investment pays off, she will be back in the black.

Tara has way more stress than Ellen because if her investments don't pay off, she's wasted more time and money, and she has *not* been able to focus on her writing the way she used to, so her main source of income, her primary product line—books—is behind schedule.

There are good investments and bad investments. Sometimes an investment's success comes down to the time an investor can invest. If authors are already short on time (and money), the simpler solution might be finding a more reliable source of income for a bit, rather than spreading themselves thin through a new business venture that could cost their company in the end.

There is nothing wrong with having a second job and writing part-time. It's a wonderful feeling to be able to write full-time, but only if your business is capable of sustaining itself and you. Otherwise, being a full-time author can feel the opposite of wonderful. It can be stressful, nerve-racking, and quickly lead to burnout.

Be aware of when it's the right time to go full-time and when it's not. Math doesn't lie. Use your profit and loss statements to help you decide. And never let anyone shame you into feeling like you are any less of an author for doing what is best for your business. It's your business, not theirs!

Successful business owners know exactly where their business stands. The company's expenses, beyond what the IRS forgives, should always be justified by the revenue and profits. Otherwise, a company will find itself operating outside of its means and on the verge of collapse.

As with any start-up, there is always the option of taking a business loan. As the borrower, your company will need to provide ample data about the current financial health of your business. A lender will want to see your company's spending history, any outstanding debts, a profit and loss statement, as well as projected estimates for how the loan will be put to use and when the debt will be repaid.

Authors considering funding their start-up with seed money from a family account, should treat the investment as a business loan. They will be more likely to succeed if they collect the required data beforehand, as it will force them to appraise the situation realistically and think through a functional plan. This is better than just dipping into the savings with no clue when or how or if the money will ever get paid back.

Over the years, I have witnessed authors falling into incredible debt. I've even been the victim of other authors' mistakes. When the small presses began to collapse during the last decade, companies filed for Chapter 11 and royalties were forever lost. Copyrights were under dispute, cover art was stripped away, editors weren't paid, and books were withheld. Simply put, it was a nightmare, and many talented authors lost their careers due to other people's careless oversights.

I've seen authors remortgage their homes to finance their businesses. Some of those authors took that investment and climbed right to the top, while others are still living the horror story of their investment not paying off.

I've also watched authors back their businesses on credit, accumulating debts into the fifty-thousand-dollar range—in one month. Some make the money back through robust ad campaigns, while others are in a hole still trying to pay off multiple credit cards.

Business loans, personal loans, dipping into savings or credit cards, there are countless places we can find money, but as long as it's a loan, the money will eventually have to be returned, most likely with interest. The safest way to build a company without incurring unstable debt is to rely on the company's gains.

Let's pause for a quick vocabulary lesson in business economics. *Revenue* is the entire income before deductions are made. *Gain* is the amount by which the revenue of a business exceeds its cost of operating, so the first impression of a profit. *Net profit* is what remains after all deductions. In other words, it's easy to look at royalties and see money coming in, but a lot of money went out to earn that income. Only the net profit counts as actual profit. Everything else must be paid out or paid back.

If authors want to operate a low-risk company in the green, they should rely on as little outside help as possible. There are countless free resources to help authors, which is one massive reason why authors rely so heavily on social media.

The authors that invest patience and utilize free resources will produce the least debt. But they also may produce substantially less sales than authors who invest $40,000 a month on advertising. Which authors are going to have the higher *net profit* in the end?

The truth is, they will sometimes see an even *net profit*, though the authors with hardier marketing will grow a larger audience faster and eventually lap the other authors—usually. However, at the end of the month, heavily marketed authors must show a *gain* beyond $40,000 (if that's what was invested) to see an actual profit.

At first glance, this seems incredibly impressive. If authors are making back more than $40,000 a month, they must be making six figures a year, right? Wrong.

It's possible that heavily marketed authors have a *revenue* in the six figures, but the actual *net profit,* after all expenses and deductions are made, is much lower.

Now, let's assume low-marketed authors rely mostly on social media and word of mouth. They have very shallow overhead. They make their own covers, do their own graphic design, and only spend money from the business account—money accrued by the business.

At the end of the year, the low-marketed authors have made a modest income, but it's almost all profit. The heavily marketed authors have a very complicated appointment with their accountants where they review lengthy profit and loss statements to determine what expenses are deductible and what is not. The result is still rather modest, but there is notable growth from the prior year. The low-marketed authors also show a modest growth.

As long as the authors continue to produce books, their companies and followings grow. The only difference is the heavily marketed authors are on a faster track. There is no cheating the track, because success is still a drawn out process in this business.

If the low-marketed authors are patient and continue to write and produce new products that will generate revenue with little expense, they will continue to see gains and profits. And if the heavily-marketed authors continue to write and produce products that generate revenue, they will continue to see gains, only, in their case, the more products they have to advertise the more expensive their marketing budgets will get, so they will have more deductions from their growing profit each year.

This can sometimes regulate the average author income despite the varied business practices authors use. Many times, both writers will recognize that the author business is not a lucrative one, but it is a draining one—more so for the author giving additional time and energy to areas of the job outside of writing.

Every author is entitled to one or two flops in their career, but for the most part, authors will continue to improve their craft with each book they write. The more books authors publish, the better writer they should be. And one thing we know about the publishing industry is that readers want well-written books, so the better an author's books become, the more readers will want to read their work.

The more time authors devote to other areas of the job, the less time they will have to write and improve their craft. When I was at the peak of my burnout, I would estimate I was only writing 10% of the time. I was working insane hours, suffering health complications from neglecting my needs, spending 90% of my time on the job doing anything anyone said would help my books sell, and I was absolutely miserable.

In this business, revenues will fluctuate. We are selling art. Classics are hinted by the industry but ultimately determined by the masses. Many authors are surprised by their bestsellers and shocked that their favorite works sometimes sell fewer copies than their less-loved stories. But that's just the way the cookie crumbles.

When it comes down to income, we can look at our taxes and see what we are making in the end, once that final number after deductions is declared, but no one will ever know what that dollar amount cost us in terms of energy and non-refundable time.

What did we pay in hours away from our family and friends? What moments did we sacrifice that we will never get back? What has the job stolen from our youth and health? What has it robbed from our happiness and ultimate quality of life? What emotional and physical debts has it produced?

If an author is severely burned-out, there is a debt. There is a dent in their mental well-being and physical health, as well as an immeasurable effect on their art. There is no action without a reaction. Is it worth it?

Let's go back to our two examples of authors. The low-marketed author worked 20 hours a week at her writing career. She produced two new books last year. She generated a modest net profit of $10,000, after deductions. That comes out to a little over $9.60 an hour.

The heavily-marketed author worked an average of 80 hours a week to accommodate all the responsibilities of the job outside of writing and still produce new books. She produced four new books last year and generated revenue of $540,000.00, but after deductions, her net profit dropped to $48,000.00. This averages out to about $11.50 an hour.

Let's just take a moment to recognize that in 2021 the federal government is pushing to set minimum wage at $15 an hour and neither of these authors are clearing that. The heavily-marketed author is completely fried after a decade of steadily adding to her job responsibilities, and the only incentive she's seen is a slight pay increase of a few dollars. Her health is suffering, she's severely depressed, and she has lost faith that she can sustain this way of making a living for much longer.

Who is the happier author? Who is the more successful entrepreneur?

The takeaway is that we all have a choice when it comes to running our business. We start with a mission, an intention or goal, and we plan how we will achieve that goal. We can so easily take our most important employee for granted and overlook the actual value of time.

It's fine to take a loan, put a business expense on credit, take a chance on a pricey marketing campaign, but only if we monitor the progress and measure every outcome. Our success should never come down to dollars alone.

Success is a state of being. What state have your business choices left you in?

Yes, the journey of the low-marketed author will be longer, but maybe that's okay. Maybe she will enjoy the ride more in the end.

I can't tell you how to invest in your company, because every author's situation is different. Some authors start in a privileged place with some capitol to spare while others grow up on skid row, have a family to support on their income alone, and no savings account as security in case they fail. Some authors are just natural mavericks who knock it out of the park with a bestseller on their first try while the majority strive their entire lives to make it onto a list.

We all have our cross to bear. It's your job to look at yourself as honestly as possible—strengths, weaknesses, flaws, and gifts—and determine how much you're willing to carry and how far you want to haul that load.

Don't feel ashamed if you want to put down a few things and lighten your burden. When we realistically look at the expectations, the pay, the profit, the cost—to us as a whole—you might rethink all the time and money you want to invest. But that's a decision only you can make, because it's a commitment only you will have to carry out.

The Office

Now that we've addressed the *WHO* of author business, let's move on to the *WHERE*. Laptops have liberated the industry, giving writers the freedom to create in their office, on their couch, in a car, at a coffee shop, or anywhere in between. But part of running an effective business requires a company to have a headquarters. For authors, that HQ is usually a home office.

We've spent some time considering what being an author might mean to you. Now it's time to consider *WHERE* you want to work. Think beyond the office. *HOW* do you want to feel about the place you go every day? *WHAT* kind of atmosphere fuels your creativity, confidence, and productivity?

Don't go with that Pinterest post you saw of so and so's perfectly minimalistic space. Think about you, and all your proclivities. *WHAT* is *your* perfect creative space? Get weird with it.

If I had my druthers, I'd want to work at a super Zen place that invests in state of mind. I'd want it to be inviting, so I never dread returning to work. We are living in an out of the box time when business owners can redefine professionalism, so don't be afraid to get weird with your creative space. Take your imagination as far as it can go.

Authors need a lot of space, because being an author no longer relies on writing alone. A functional office should be both aesthetically pleasing and deliberate. My advice to those hoping to sustain a career is don't underestimate the space you will eventually need when your business grows.

My office, which I still find too small on most days, includes built-in book cases, a file system, wrap around desks—yes, I said desks in the plural form—closet space, and a glass door. Having more than one desk is extremely effective because, as authors, we perform more than one job. One desk is completely free of clutter. This is my *writing desk*. It holds paper, pens, an hourglass, and little else.

The corner desk houses my desktop computer, which I need for graphic design and general backup. This is my sound studio and marketing zone. It's also where I keep incoming mail, open files, shipping materials, pre-orders, and all that other business stuff that has very little to do with the actual art of creating. To be honest, I don't like sitting at this desk very much, which is probably why I stuck it in the corner.

A standing desk is highly recommended. Mine is a simple, collapsible one I purchased for under $50.00. Authors should stand whenever possible for obvious health reasons.

Shelves are necessary to store overstock. They can also create an inviting backdrop for social media videos and footage. Being an author comes with a lot of storage issues, so a built-in closet with shelving for office supplies and inventory is something to consider.

I prefer to store my books in banker boxes, as I find that to be the most functional storage for travel. Each book or series gets its own box. If I have a "low performing" title, I will combine it in a box with another "low performing" title. That works until that "low performer" is suddenly your bestseller at a signing and you have no clue why. For this reason, I recommend giving each title its own box.

I have published more than 35 novels in my career. My office is overwhelmed by boxes, so I, along with many others, dream of warehouse-inspired storage for my inventory. Give yourself room to grow. Chances are, you'll eventually need it.

When people ask what my favorite part of my office is, it's never the beautiful floors, or the desks, or the built-in bookcases. It's the door.

My door is a glass pane door with my logo at the top. Of all the improvements I've made to my creative space over the years, nothing was more of a game changer than this door.

You see, I'm a recovering workaholic. And when I'm writing, I hate to be disturbed. However, I can easily lose track of time.

Well, that's not true. Time moves fast when I'm writing, but I'm always somewhat aware of it slipping by. It's more accurate to say I can easily fall into old, unhealthy habits and ignore my needs and the needs of my family by overworking. Having a glass door establishes a boundary, but also gives me a lens into reality.

A closed door is the same as a DO NOT DISTURB sign. I don't need to take my eyes off my work to sense someone standing there, but my family knows not to open that door without an invitation. If I'm on a roll and truly can't be disturbed, they walk away after waiting a few minutes and try back in a little bit.

This sort of respect for my job took years to establish. It's amazing how many relatives and friends assume that because you work from home they can call or pop in whenever the inclination to do so strikes.

Certain relatives are notorious for stopping by mid-day without an invitation and completely derailing my deadlines. Having a professional door, that can shut and even lock, has greatly lowered the frequency of unwanted interruptions.

On the flip side, it has also made me more accountable to the other parts of my life. When the people in my home start appearing at my door, looking hungry and dejected, I know it's time to wind down for the day.

Having a glass door creates a barrier of respect that had been lacking before. And when my notorious pop-in relatives stop by on weekends, they can see through the door. They see desks and paperwork and what is, in fact, a very functional office. This, too, establishes respect for the job.

I suspect, as we move forward from 2020, a year when many people experienced working remotely from home, that there will be an increase of respect for those who work from home on a regular basis. The general public has learned that working from home is, truly, work.

Unfortunately, there may always be those who disrespect the hours of your workday and disrupt your creative time unannounced, no matter how much you communicate that you are working. For those interrupters, you will likely need to take a more stern, direct approach—and invest in a deadbolt on your door.

I highly recommend investing in a glass door. And if a door is not an option, a partition can establish a temporary boundary when needed, a silent "do not disturb" others should recognize.

But what if you're an author short on quiet spaces? Perhaps you lost your home to an act of God and now you're living out of a small, temporary studio or trailer. There's barely room to breathe and you share this small place with family, pets, possessions, and so on. The living room runs directly into the kitchenette, so when the television is on, everyone is exposed to the sound. How do you write?

For many authors, this is the struggle. Life is chaotic and as if focusing isn't hard enough, there are always new distractions interrupting our creative time. We must be our best advocate.

If you are an author short on time or quiet, make a point to find an isolated place to work. Living through a pandemic makes shared spaces more challenging than usual, but eventually coffee shops and libraries will go back to normal.

Another option is to write in your car. Drive somewhere quiet and safe, park and then get to it. Or, if you're the passenger on a road trip, pop in some ear plugs and zone out.

A third option, and my favorite suggestion, is to write when the house is asleep. My greatest work is created between 4 and 7am.

Be creative! After surveying authors about where they write, here is a short list of suggestions for options you might not have considered:

1. Coffee shop
2. Museum
3. Library
4. Park
5. Aquarium
6. Shopping mall
7. Bus or train station
8. Friend's house (If they're at work, offer to check in on the dog and stay a while!)
9. Outside on your porch or yard
10. Local college campuses
11. She-shed or Man Cave
12. A bar
13. Grandma's house
14. A diner
15. A hotel lobby

The key to a home office is functionality. I love pretty things, so aesthetics are important to me, but it isn't a necessity. When I can accomplish both and find useful, attractive office supplies, I feel like I've won the lottery!

For basic office supplies and the thrifty author, I recommend first investigating your local dollar store. They have a surprising selection of essentials. For instance, scissors at a popular office supply chain lists between $3 and $19. Where, at a dollar store, you can find a perfectly fine pair of scissors for $1. Same goes for name brand tape, staples, pens, and other desk must haves.

I also recommend shopping the Amazon Basics line. This is a generic line that offers everything from paper to printers and the in between. Amazon has really upped its game in covering the basics for office supplies here, and they focus on underselling their competitors. You can view my favorite *author-related* Amazon office and lifestyle products by visiting my Amazon storefront, which is different from my Amazon author page that features my books.

For the traveling author, the author who hops from desk, to counter, to table, to couch, and even leaves the house to work on occasion, it's wise to invest in a decent box, bag, or briefcase. I have two homes and I bounce back and forth, so I had a box I shoved all my projects in—plotting notes, marketing lists, calendar, and so on.

Originally, I used a sad cardboard box. One day we were watching the *Crown* and I saw the queen's red despatcher box and my eyes lit up. I wanted such a box. Something with a handle and compartments and a lock so I could take it wherever I needed to go.

Turns out, since I'm not royalty and those sorts of boxes are quite rare and expensive, a briefcase suited my needs better. It's basically a leather box.

Although I work from home, I've learned to keep my "current items" in the briefcase. This way, I can decide my work location with a moment's notice and everything is right there at my fingertips. If I'm working at my desk, it sits by my feet. I unload the essentials and jump in.

This is a time saver, because it creates a sort of mental repetition that is familiar. Changing locations can often jack up an author's vibe and cost hours as they try to settle in and find their groove. But having a box or briefcase establishes a routine that alerts the brain that it's time to work, no matter where the routine is taking place.

So while I feel a little silly carrying a briefcase around my house, having one has proven to be a wise investment that boosts my productivity. And while briefcases are typically in bag form now and often referred to as computer cases, I prefer the boxy openness of the traditionally styled briefcase, as it doubles as a mobile workstation more than any bag could.

Regardless of how you design your office, make sure you establish it as your personal space, especially in the beginning of your career. If you are planning to turn writing into a producing business, it deserves the respect of a professional company, even a fledgling one.

Establish that your work space is for work. If, in the beginning, you're working out of a closet or from a corner in the dining room, set ground rules with outsiders so that creative space is protected.

As with everything else, you are your first and best advocate. If you don't establish boundaries, you can't expect others to respect them.

Clocking In & Clocking Out

Every person is unique, and while some people are morning people and others are night owls, there is some science behind the best time to write. Knowing when those creative juices are naturally flowing and what hours of the day are the most effective for hitting your desired word count, will help you reach your prolific potential.

However, in this day and age, people lead busy lives, lives that sometimes work around odd shifts and sleep patterns, so there are exceptions to every rule. What is right for most may turn out to be wrong for you. Always go with what works best for your life, and take time to develop a personal routine that complements your creativity rather than constricts it.

If your goal is identifying a time of day when you are most prolific, experiment and base your decision on measurable results. Your study should revolve around one subject—you. Base your conclusions on your performance alone, because *you* are the person you're trying to activate. Treat what works best for others as a mere suggestion, and remain judicious about what works best for you.

But if you are interested in the general consensus, morning time is the most effective time for artists to create. This is usually because there are fewer distractions early in the day, but also because people tend to have higher levels of optimism after sleep, which enhances overall performance. Adults are typically more productive during the early hours of the morning while teens tend to perform better in the afternoons.[6]

However, due to the varying shifts we keep, some people may sleep during the day and wake at night. The waking hours at 4 pm might contain a lot more distractions than the waking hours of a person rising at 4 am. Quiet depends on the setting, but the optimism is highest directly after we rise.

Remember when we discussed the *Law of Attraction*? Working with an elevated sense of optimism convinces the brain that more is possible. That belief enhances a person's mood. During the day, a person encounters multiple interruptions and mood shifts, many caused by the overwhelming marketing targeted at us. Some marketing focuses on stirring feelings of inadequacy.

To optimize your optimism, avoid social media as long as possible when you start your day. Optimism is in its purest form first thing in the morning.

This is also why productivity coaches tell clients to avoid picking up their phone first thing in the morning. Social media vaporizes our sense of optimism.

Higher optimism and elevated moods work together to increase a person's willpower. Willpower is the driving source that pushes us to accomplish our goals, but willpower naturally dwindles throughout the day. It tends to be highest at the onset of a new day.

Scientifically, the prefrontal cortex houses the *creative brain*[7]. The *creative brain* is the most useful part of the brain for writing. This part of the brain is most active directly after sleep, so it makes sense to utilize it while it's active and ready to play.

The brain also has what's called a *focus brain*. This part of the brain is best for editing. The *focus brain* and *creative brain* are not easily interchangeable.

We've already established that time is a valuable, non-renewable resource. As authors, we must use time effectively if we want to unleash our prolific potential. This means understanding how the brain functions and framing our tasks in a way that helps the brain perform at optimal levels.

In other words, you should not be writing and editing at the same time, as this will engage two different parts of the brain and ultimately slow down your word count. Writers should use their morning time specifically to create content and get the words onto the page. Later in the day, they should turn to their *focus brain* and work on revisions or other tasks that require decision-making.

There is an entire chapter dedicated to time management in this section, but understanding the basics of *when* most authors are prolific speaks specifically to the writing parts of the job.

My advice is to get one hour of writing done first thing in the morning. This will ensure that your most important duty is done at the end of each day and also that you conquered this task at the most effective time. The more you practice that one hour sprint, the sooner it will regulate into your routine. What starts as 200 words could quickly grow to 2k or more as you practice.

---

[6] Knight M, Mather M. *Look out-it's your off-peak time of day! Time of day matters more for alerting than for orienting or executive attention.* Exp Aging Res. 2013;39(3):305-321. doi:10.1080/0361073X.2013.779197

[7] Cruz de Souza, Leonardo & Guimarães, Henrique & Teixeira, Antônio & Caramelli, Paulo & Levy, Richard & Dubois, Bruno & Volle, Emmanuelle. (2014). Frontal lobe neurology and the creative mind. Frontiers in psychology. 5. 761. 10.3389/fpsyg.2014.00761.

As an example, my day typically starts between 4 am and 6 am, depending on when I naturally rise. I don't expect or suggest others wake this early. This is simply the result of my internal clock, which likes to rattle before the chickens, when the sinners are still at play.

I rise, make coffee, and take care of the pets. The house is blissfully silent at this hour, which is why this is probably my favorite part of the day—it's solely mine.

I take my coffee to my office, shut the door, and tell Alexa to play my Pandora. This ensures I'm getting a dose of music I like as I warm up and start my day. If I'm feeling extra granola and Zen, I'll do a few yoga moves before sitting down.

I allow myself 15 minutes to wake up. I glance at my calendar to refresh my memory about the events of the day. I filter my email—very different from *checking* my email, as I'm *only* deleting spam. This gives me an idea of what's waiting for me, but I won't open it until it's "email time." Then I make sure my work area is tidy and free of distractive clutter, which it should be if I concluded my day in my usual tidy up fashion.

I do not go on social media. And I do not open or respond to emails. This is not work time. It's me time.

Once I've had a few sips of coffee and I'm settled in, I tell Alexa to be quiet, ask her to set a timer for one hour, open up my WIP (work in progress), and begin.

There is always a comment on my WIP from the day before, reminding me where I left off and what my objective should be when I pick up. Leaving yourself clues in the comment section of the margin is a great strategy to help workaholics pull themselves away from work and jump back into work with little wasted time.

When the one hour timer goes off I get out of my seat and move. This can be taking the dogs out back for a few minutes, or if the sun is up, grabbing their leashes and taking a morning walk. If the family is awake, it can also mean just standing in another room and saying good morning. The point is I'm out of my chair and moving.

In the summer months, I tend to take much longer walks in the mornings. This invigorates me and provides longer lasting energy throughout the day. But in the colder months (I'm in the frigid Northeast), I tend to break up my movement and take shorter, more frequent walks throughout the day.

Depending on the day, if it's a writing day or a work day, my goals will dictate what happens when I return to my desk. If it is a writing day, I sit back down and write for another hour.

If, however, it is not a writing day, and I have other work that needs to be done, such as marketing, graphic design, accounting, research, content creation, and so on, I switch gears and focus on those tasks. I will start with my froggiest task, which I will explain in more detail in the time management chapter. For now, know that a *frog* represents the task we want to do the least. Do it, but save it for *after* you've done your one hour of daily writing.

Think of that daily hour of writing as an exercise for your brain. It's not necessarily a part of your workday, but more a part of your routine just before your day begins. That way, no matter what sort of day you have planned—marketing, accounting, correspondence, pitching, design, research, or family/second job obligations—you know you're always getting at least one hour of writing in.

Worry about dressing for the day *after* that hour of writing. Do not think about obligations or appointments. Only think about your beautiful words. This preliminary hour belongs solely to you.

For writers, this is often a pleasant time to be with their muse, so make it enjoyable and sip your coffee or tea and let go. Do not edit, as that will involve the wrong part of your brain and slow your process.

No matter what my goals, I always aim to work smarter rather than harder. That means having a basic understanding of how the human brain functions and utilizing automated apps that make my business operate without me having to micromanage every move.

By thinking through the most effective approaches to everything that needs to get done, there's less of a chance for poor work habits to build. Allow yourself time to think—is there a more effective time or way to accomplish _____?

Parents of young children might not find 5 am a peaceful time in their home. Also, adults with a lively social life might be a little foggy first thing in the morning, especially if they were out late and consuming alcohol the night before. It's each individual writer's duty to identify a peaceful part of the day when they are least likely to be distracted. Finding that uninterrupted hour is more important than *when* the hour actually occurs.

As stated in the *Health & Wellness* section of this book, I no longer work more than forty hours a week—sometimes I even work less than thirty. I'm still a full-time author, actively maintaining a sustainable writing career. But my hours depend on my work obligations, as well as my needs as a human, mother, wife, daughter, author, and friend.

I take deadlines extremely seriously. However, my job is only a small part of who I am, and my first priority is my #1 Objective, but achieving any #1 Objective long-term will always require a person to maintain balance in life.

If I start my day at 4 am, I am either taking a few hours off in the middle of the day or clocking out by noon. I try to never work more than 8 hours in a shift. By establishing and respecting this boundary, I have actually enhanced my performance. That is the result of working smarter rather than harder.

And if you didn't notice, by starting early I effectively finish early. Over the summer this was especially helpful, as I love the beach and try to get there as often as possible.

To outsiders, it sometimes appears that I'm living a life of indulgence. That's because I am. But I'm also running my own business and putting in the time.

By restricting hours, we have no choice but to figure out ways to effectively accomplish more in less time. There has to be a healthy ecosystem built and balanced around reciprocal give and take.

If you are a night owl who wants to convert to an early bird, have no fear. Change is possible, as long as you allow yourself the required time to adjust and build new habits (roughly between 18 and 245 days).

To train your mind and body to wake earlier, simply tick back your alarm five minutes at a time. Every few days, adjust the time you're waking, and your internal clock will eventually catch on.

But remember, if you're waking earlier in the day to work, you should also be clocking out earlier and retiring to bed earlier. Do not skimp out on rest. Sleep is a crucial part of keeping a well-balanced mind, body, and spirit.

Effective Work Habits

As stated, this book is particularly interested in the business methods of a prolific author who wants to avoid burnout. We reviewed *what* an author does, *who* they are, *where* they work, and *why* they do it (their #1 Objective). In examining *when* an author will be most productive, we must also look at *how* they run their business, which ultimately comes down to each individual's preferences.

Whether you use them or not, I intend to leave every reader with some useful tips to make the *how* a little easier. So much of an author's success comes down to effective, healthy work habits and methods of accomplishing tasks in a way that also preserves as much energy as possible.

Balance in life, as a whole, is the foundation of success. But what about finding balance within the aspects of the actual job?

By setting your intentions toward finding more effective and healthier work habits, you will create a chain reaction of rewards in your overall life. Think about how you define success, remembering that it's a relative term and your definition of success does not have to remotely resemble mine.

But also keep in mind that in order to reach success, however it's defined, one must actively maintain that healthy balance. By practicing healthy work habits, we become more effective in other areas. And when we become more effective, we enhance the likelihood of achieving our desired results. When we achieve our desired results—whatever they might be—we achieve success.

Below is a list of healthy work habits. Before you read my list, take a moment to create your own. You may think of things I left out.

Brainstorm healthy habits you can incorporate into your day, simple tips and strategies to keep you on track and functioning at peak effectiveness.

Think of both short-term and long-term habits that will decrease the threat of burnout. Keep your #1 Objective in mind. No item should ever inhibit or contradict that #1 Objective. Once you've made your list, come back and compare your list to mine. Feel free to adapt my personal strategies and make them your own.

Healthy Work Habits that Enhance Effectiveness:

- **Morning Sprint:** Write for one hour every morning.
- **Take Time to Make Time:** Use planning tools such as calendars, block scheduling, and benchmarking (more on this in the chapters ahead).
- **Set Work Hours and Stick to Them.** If you are working overtime, you had better be earning time and a half or double time. If not, you might need to speak to your boss.
- **Schedule According to Task:** divide your schedule into writing, editing, marketing, personal time, etc.
- **Take Meal Breaks**: *Do not skip meals!* So much thought goes into conserving energy, yet we misunderstand the basic science behind eating. Calories are, by definition, heat and fuel that convert into energy. Stop robbing yourself of energy when you're trying so

hard to preserve it! This is like trying to empty a flooding boat with a leaky cup when there's a gaping hole.

- **Invest in Ergonomic Work Equipment:** Yoga balls, standing desks, cozy chairs, foot stools, etc.
- **Set Timers for Movement Breaks** *and don't ignore them!* Hang a graphic of basic yoga poses in eyeshot and run through them during one of your breaks.
- **Schedule Personal Time:** Days off, half days, self-care appointments, vacation time, social calls, yoga classes, etc. Make weekends your own. Fully unplug for a while. The average American worker gets 10 paid vacation days a year, but the average European worker receives 20 days paid vacation and, in some countries, workers have up to 30 paid vacation days. If you feel guilty for taking a weekend off or a few days off midweek, you shouldn't.
- **Meditate:** Walk, sit quietly, play music for a few minutes, etc. You don't have to be a monk to disconnect and practice mindfulness. You just have to practice being present in a moment.
- **Walk!** 10k steps a day. Take frequent walks throughout the day or one long walk every day as well as regular movement breaks.
- **Clear Away Clutter:** Use the last 30 minutes of every day to clear away clutter and prepare your work space for the next workday, leaving clues that point to exactly where you left off and where you should pick up.
- **Have a Catchall:** Use a basket, box, briefcase, or bag to store your "current projects." By putting projects away, we achieve a sense of completion and establish a starting point for the next day.
- **Sleep:** 7 to 9 hours a night.
- **Stay hydrated!**
- **Get fresh air in your lungs and sun on your face every day!**
- **Listen to Your Body**: Take time off when feeling overwhelmed.
- **Use the Word "No":** If you say yes to everything, you will have no time left to meet your essential needs and obligations.
- **Set Boundaries!** Avoid working overtime. If you finish work at 5pm on Friday and don't work over the weekend, but an email from a freelancer hits your notifications, ignore it until Monday. Learn that you do not have to respond to everyone immediately. Others will only learn to respect your boundaries if you actually honor them. Utilize your away messages.
- **Keep it Functional:** Make your office a joyful and functional place of tranquility and creativity.
- **Live with Mindfulness:** Gratitude, purpose, intention, awareness
- **Have Another Hobby:** Invest 2 to 4 hours a week into a hobby that is not work related. Make it a goal to find something you love as much as writing.
- **Read:** Rediscover reading for pleasure and allow time for it every week.
- **Volunteer:** Do charity work. It will feed your soul.

- **Resuscitate Your Social Life:** Keep social engagements, try new restaurants, entertain, join clubs, talk to strangers, share a bottle of wine with a neighbor, and so on.
- **Find Joy in Cooking:** Food can either nurture the soul or infect it. It's best to start viewing cooking as another act of self-care and stop resenting it as a chore. Nutrition leads to balance.
- **Learn from Others:** Build an effective, likeminded mastermind group.
- **Celebrate:** professional accomplishments and life's random victories.
- **Regularly Evaluate Your Team:** the more successful an author becomes, the more they delegate. Don't micromanage, but definitely conduct regular reviews of the freelance service providers you pay. Your employees should be working as effectively as you and bringing a noticeable ROI.
- **Limit Screen Time:** Stay mindful of social media screen time and the affect it has on you.

The list above started as my ten commandments and grew over time. Hanging them on my wall, and pausing every once in a while to review them, provides a grounding sense of steadiness that's sometimes lost in the chaos. I suggest using my list as a starting point to build your own.

You will notice that at no point did I suggest authors attend X number of virtual events or Y number book signings or even release a book every Z weeks. Here at *Healthy Author Headquarters*, we don't give a rat's ass what Peter Paperback is doing. We care only about maintaining healthy foundations and building our business through sensible and effective practices that match our personal definition of success.

We do not compare ourselves to Betty Bigshot. Nor do we compete with Wendy Works-a-lot. A healthy business model is based on returns. It's balanced and fair. It will always value quality over quantity, which we will get into more detail about later. But trust me when I say, quality work begins with taking quality care of the creator.

It's very easy to backslide into bad habits when an author focuses on the competition, which is why this book started by describing how crucial it was that authors maintain a realistic perception. *Awareness* of the industry's complexities and shortcomings should act as a steady reminder of what most authors are facing in present day.

Regardless of how put together the competition appears, very few are actually making a killer living. Yes, many are sustaining, but there are countless other jobs that require less work, cause less stress, and pay a lot more by the hour.

Just because someone makes it look easy, does not mean that they are not struggling. And even if someone appears successful, their definition of success might be very different from yours. For all we know, they're a hundred thousand dollars in debt and about to lose their book deal because they missed the deadline again.

Other authors are not your competition. You are only competing with the person you were yesterday. Look there. Assess. Move on. Grow. That is how we make healthy progress and use our time effectively.

Chapter Ten
Productivity

"Amateurs sit and wait for inspiration, the rest of us just get up and go to work."

Stephen King, On Writing: A Memoir of the Craft, 2000

Organizing the Unseen

The problem with time lies in its intangible slipperiness. We can't see, feel, or hold time, but it can run through our fingers and leave tracks on our face all the same. And the problem with responsibility is that we're only off the hook when we're senile or dead. No one ever knows for sure how many responsibilities we have, but we feel them weighing on us with every breath.

The weightlessness of destructive, slippery time and the heaviness of invisible responsibility is the teetering tug-of-war between time and productivity. These two concepts are so magnetized that they can push apart as easily as they can pull together.

Nothing feels better than a productive day when we have plenty of time. On the contrary, nothing feels worse than an unproductive day full of wasted time. Managing the two comes down to—you guessed it—*balance!*

In terms of helping authors unleash their prolific potential, productive practices are critical. The chapters ahead will address theory, methodology, and strategy to help authors get a handle on both and better organize the unseen obstacles of the job.

There are countless life hacks for saving time, but I've chosen the ones that are most likely to save energy, because our energy is the greatest tool we have when it comes to manipulating time.

Your sanity will thank you for using the energy preserving tips in this chapter, as many are the methods most likely to save you from burning out. And avoiding burnout is how we meet our #1 Objective and continue our journey toward that of a successful author.

Your energy is your attitude. It's your vibe, your chi, your essence. It's the empowering pep talk the coach gives before the game that invigorates the team and leads to a win. So let's get pumped, let's get on our feet, and let's kick some writing ass!

Planning for Prolific Writing

There are many elements that go into prolific writing, and all require a degree of planning. Meeting word count is not the only skill required to be a prolific author. An author, traditionally published or otherwise, is running a business, so there are other responsibilities on the job. Prolific writing requires planning for the job by using the most productive habits available.

If an author is productive in every area of the job, they will preserve energy and time for other areas of life. And by wasting no time on unnecessary work habits, an author collects more time to write, which, after surveying hundreds of authors, seems to be the universally favored part of the job.

Before we address the many ways you can plan for success and the possible pitfalls you should avoid, let's cover some basic areas to start.

1. Know your craft! Continue educating yourself with books, workshops, peer groups, and master classes.
2. Design your company's mission statement and identify your #1 Objective.
3. Create the perfect workflow environment and design couture writing tools -- such as checklists, graphic organizers, and basic guides—to suit your personal process.
4. Set measurable goals with clear intentions.
5. Write! Write! Write!
6. Frequently perform company health checks to audit how time is being spent and where energy can be saved as well as what practices are creating the most profits or losses.
7. Plan time off.
8. Limit anything that does not produce a measurable benefit for your business.
9. Confront sources of stress before they cannibalize your author soul.
10. Celebrate your achievements!

"Great!" you might say. But how do we do all of the above? The answers are in the sections ahead. It's your duty to personalize the methods and make them your own. As you can see, there's a lot to cover, so let's keep moving.

Busyness Versus Productivity

Picture a busy day, a day when you hardly get a moment's rest and you are pulled from one task to the next without ever pausing long enough to celebrate any sense of accomplishment. A busy day is not necessarily a productive day. A productive day, a day when time spent on task is truly benefiting your business in measurable results, can be extremely rewarding. The difference between a busy day and a productive day lies in a person's control.

Your time is precious and nonrefundable. There is nothing worse than wasting our own time on inefficient practices that make us busy but not as productive as we could be. Prolific writing is all about knowing when and how you are the most productive.

Burnout results from constant busyness with little sense of accomplishment. When we lack a sense of accomplishment for too long, we inevitably suffer a joy deficiency. That continued sense of inefficiency leads to a sense of inadequacy, which quickly mutates into a muddled sense of failure.

Keeping busy means working harder instead of working smarter. The aim of *Write 10K in a Day* is the opposite. The theories ahead are designed to free up your time, get you functioning at the most effective and productive level, thus, unleashing your prolific potential.

Too many authors have become so busy trying to succeed, they are exhausted on a regular basis. And many wonder, if they've been working nonstop, why they aren't seeing more positive results. It is a misconception that time spent "at work" ultimately results in profit—monetary or otherwise.

Busyness is not productivity. Say it again: busyness is not productivity.

Crossing off items on a *To Do* list does not guarantee a profit, so how should an author decide which tasks are necessary and which will have little impact on the grand plan? Most authors became authors because they were either considered an expert in a field and had important information to share or, in the case of genre fiction writers, they had a gift for storytelling. Being a good storyteller does not automatically come with good business sense.

To survive in such an oversaturated market, many authors are forced to also become entrepreneurs. However, some of the most masterful writers struggle to navigate the business side of an author occupation, which did not require such a high level of business acumen from authors thirty years ago.

Being an *authorpreneur,* an entrepreneurial author who takes part in his or her own publicity, marketing, production of merchandise, and publishing beyond that of authors of the past, requires authors to take interest in more than writing or selling books. They must build a brand, often times with subsequent product lines relating to books in order to supplement the needed income to survive. This is why so many authors attend conventions, sell merchandise like clothing or mugs, or market subscription boxes.

Again, return your focus to the #1 Objective theory. Having that key purpose will assist in steering your attention toward the necessary goals created to achieve *your* definition of author. It will help you avoid the minutia. Authors that get lost in the weeds of all the minor things authors can do—the fluff— tend to fall behind on the actual writing of books.

Busy authors are not always productive authors, and the busiest authors can also carry the largest debts at times—financial debts, emotional debts, word count debts, and so on. Guard your time well. Spend time being productive, don't waste time being busy.

Perfectionism

A *perfectionist* is a person who believes in perfectionism or a state of being perfect. *Perfectionism* is a personal doctrine that holds that being *perfect* is attainable. It is a personal philosophy that demands precise flawlessness and rejects anything less.

Perfect, however, implies something is flawless. Without flaws, there would be little to no room for growth or development. Life—your story—is a journey. Every story arc ultimately revolves around a character's rise over adversity. Without imperfections we would have no reason to continuously improve or move from where we are. Perfection invites stillness, and stillness is dull.

Perfection can be a goal, an end point, but never a baseline. We must maintain a constant awareness that we have room to grow and improve. Otherwise, the incentive to improve is removed, and we become stagnant.

Every main character should begin a journey in an imperfect world so that they can rise with the challenges, progressively growing with the obstacles. Without that evolution of self, we, and our stories, are hollow.

If a character triumphs over a challenge, they grow. If they fail, they grow. Growth is inevitable. It's what keeps the reader interested. Perfection is boring and exactly why we love characters facing adversity more than living a perfect life.

In fiction and in real life, people are naturally drawn to the process of development. Development keeps content fresh.

Striving for perfection is natural, but the assumption that one will continuously achieve perfection—one hundred percent of the time—can cause an emotional or social negative impact. Setting healthy, realistic goals is a great way to challenge yourself. It's ambitious to aim for perfection, but expecting it with every outcome can quickly become maladaptive. We must accept that less than perfect can still measure as a notable accomplishment in many cases.

When we agonize over every detail, we fear making mistakes. But by removing that fear and risking mistakes, we increase our productivity.

Perfectionism can become more harmful than helpful. It often inhibits prolific writing. A first draft should not be perfect. It only needs to be complete. Polishing and perfecting the manuscript comes later, thus the saying "write drunk and edit sober."

Perfectionism can not only slow writing, it can halt it all together. The fear of not achieving a perfect outcome can often paralyze a person from trying at all.

By not trying, there is zero chance of success. It's failing before you begin. So which is worse, not trying, or trying and performing less than perfect?

Perfectionists are also at a higher risk for depression because they experience intense feelings of isolation, which is often self-induced and caused by a fear of rejection and a deep desire for social connection. The idea that perfection must be achieved often causes perfectionists to enter seclusion until they've achieved their goal by their standard of perfect.

To better examine the many facets of time and productivity, we are going to look at two siblings who manage energy and expectation in vastly different ways. Their story will serve as an example for many sections ahead.

Anushka is a high energy person. She's traveling for twelve months. Every day she wakes up at dawn, brews a cup of her favorite tea, and practices yoga as the sun rises. She is typically dressed and out the door by 8 o'clock every morning, after journaling and skimming her favorite periodicals.

Anushka is a blogger, and part of her job is gathering content, so she spends her mornings adventuring to various places she likes to write about. By noon, she's back at her desk, and by three, she has a rough draft of her next article finished.

So much of her day is directed by pleasure. She ends each day with a glass of wine and whatever friends join her for supper. If her friends are busy, she uses her meal time to savor a book.

In the evenings, she winds down with typical leisure activities, practices a little self-care, and emotionally prepares for the days ahead.

Amol is Anushka's brother. He has recently purchased a house and plans to remodel it while his sister is traveling abroad for the year. He has collected a variety of eccentric pieces of furniture and stores each one in what will, eventually, be his living room and dining room. As the pile grows, he becomes more overwhelmed and unsure where to start.

Anushka returns after months abroad only to find her brother's home cluttered and dysfunctional. He tells her all his plans, and he seems motivated to begin.

More time passes, and Anushka travels to Asia for six months. When she returns, Amol's house is much the same, if not worse. Her brother has accumulated an abundance of furniture and decorations to make his house nice, but he's created an almost unlivable environment in the process.

Ten years eventually pass, and Amol's once new house is no longer new. His hair has receded, his eyes are tired, he's put on weight, and he feels twenty years older than he actually is. He doesn't feel joy when he walks into his home, only stress. His depleted mood leaves him in a constant state of low energy. He's depressed or anxious, and always searching for distractions, like television, to take his mind off the unsatisfying pressures of his life.

Anushka looks younger than she did a decade ago. Her vivacious spirit leaves her full of energy, and she has lived a thousand lifetimes in only one. She exists in a state of optimism, living only in the present moment and savoring every second as a gift.

Both Anushka and Amol had the same amount of time, but used their time differently. Amol often wishes he could be more like his spirited sister. She has such verve and energy, where he has always been a little more sluggish. Some might even call him lazy. Neither is true.

Amol's constant complaint that there isn't enough time in the day is an excuse repeated to avoid accountability or change. Amol does not have a time problem. He has a problem with prioritizing his life. He is genuinely overwhelmed, which has led to a deficiency of energy. In order to change his energy, he must prioritize his goals. He must learn to manage his own behaviors, because time cannot be controlled.

When we think of Amol and his cluttered house, we realize he had an idea of perfect, but his failure to achieve that level of perfection filled him with an overwhelming sense of failure and shame, causing him to isolate and withdraw from social interactions. Amol likely lived this way his entire life, missing the best parts, solely focused on *the end*.

Anushka, however, lived a full and rich life, because she wasn't worried about failure. She accepted that life isn't always perfect.

Who had the better life in the end? Clearly, Anushka, but neither she nor Amol achieved perfection. Amol, however, was so focused on a flawless result, he failed before ever beginning.

Perfectionism can cause people to agonize over the simplest tasks. It eats up time we will never get back. It is the duty of each individual to practice self-awareness and recognize the difference between "normal" and "neurotic" when it comes to the perfectionist trap.

If perfectionism is having a negative impact on your productivity, it's time for a reality check. Perfect is a mostly unreachable standard, and nothing is achieved without the freedom to fail. We must come to a place of acceptance and forgiveness, reminding ourselves that if we mess up or create something less than perfect, it is still, most likely, better than nothing.

Get those words on the page. You can clean them up later.

This also brings us to the finality of publishing. A *draft* is a design, a preliminary intention, composed, but subject to revision. Writing a book requires multiple drafts. Every time an author or editor revises a manuscript it becomes a new draft. Nothing is final until the book is published, and even then, in some cases, changes can still be made.

Some authors are trigger-shy when it comes to publishing a manuscript, because it can always be better. It's wise to establish limits. Establish the appropriate amount of editing cycles for your work and stick to it, otherwise perfectionist authors can become dangerously obsessive.

The beauty of writing is that we can continuously come back and revise. Editors exist to provide needed perspective and input. Betas are another free source of outside opinions to help authors navigate the waters of their inner critic. But at some point we have to declare a novel *finished*.

For me, I generally follow the same production formula, though each book reserves the right to completely redefine my old habits. Meaning some projects are just more important to me than others, so I might invest more in certain parts of the process than I did with prior works.

My general timeline follows the list below. I keep it on a working grid that I mark up throughout the year, giving a column to each WIP so I can track where I am on any project at any time.

1. Write
2. Proof (1st Read)
3. Developmental Edits (Editor #1)
4. Revisions & Line Edits (Author)
5. Beta Read
6. Beta Revisions (Author)
7. Cover Art (eBook, Print, Audio)*
8. Write Blurb
9. Assign ISBN (eBook, Print, Audio)*
10. List Book Details for Pre-Order (All Sales Platforms) *
11. List on Reader Networks (BookBub, Goodreads)
12. Hire PR Company & Schedule Promotions*
13. Open Auditions for Audiobook*
14. Proofreader (Editor #2)
15. Revisions (Author)
16. Final Read (Author)
17. Pitch (Traditional)
18. Format*
19. Audiobook Production*
20. Upload Final Manuscript to all Platforms*
21. Distribute Advance Reviewer Copies*
22. Verify all short links are active
23. Approve Audiobook*
24. RELEASE!

Steps marked with an Asterisk do not apply to traditional publishing, as the publisher typically handles those responsibilities.

Using a list, like the one above, allows me to set limits on my work and establish healthy boundaries that prevent maladaptive habits, like perfectionism, which can lead to delays. While a more challenging project might require more than one round of developmental edits, such a guide keeps me from getting carried away. It forces me to keep moving and eventually detach from a manuscript and make room for newer works.

Negative perfectionism, the counterproductive effect of striving for perfection, can present itself in forms of avoidance. When perfectionism produces a paralyzing sense of doubt in a person, they can be overwhelmed by a sense of expectation.

While perfectionism might, at first glance, seem like the stance of someone in a power seat, it actually is borne in a place of fear. Too often, standards are set by what we think others deem as meaningful when we should be devoted to the philosophy that we are all unique. Therefore, our success must be uniquely measured.

Maybe you didn't make that bestseller list, but your book can still be a great success. Don't discredit yourself or your work for not meeting one standard when there are many ways to measure success. This is why it is so important to take time to celebrate the small victories as much as the big ones.

When a person learns to rely on their own validation through self-awareness, the need for perfection becomes less powerful, because they learn that success is not a bullseye but a spectrum, and there are big and small pockets of achievement open at every angle. Do not think of the book industry as a dart board with one target. Think of it as a pool table where objects are in constant motion, ricocheting and setting other objects in motion, and pockets to score points are everywhere.

Do not let a narrow scope of expectation blind you to the less obvious possibilities for success. Zeroing in on only one target will only devalue all your other accomplishments. And eventually, leave you discouraged.

Discouragement and fear frequently lead to avoidance, which triggers an artificial sense of control when success feels incontrollable. This false sense of control created by avoidance is called *procrastination*.

Procrastination

Procrastination is the act of delaying or postponing something that requires attention. People who tend to procrastinate do not possess faulty "time management" skills, they merely lack the energy needed to complete a task. This energy shortage comes from feeling overwhelmed. We become overwhelmed when we fear failure or the ability to effectively manage emotions.

When we feel overwhelmed, we trigger disproportionately large responses to circumstances. These waves of oversized emotions strike like a tsunami in the shape of panic, fatigue, anxiety, and more complex health problems over time. It's important to learn how to self-soothe and cope with overwhelming feelings before they knock us down.

One of the greatest "time management" tools comes from understanding and respecting time's fleeting presence. Time is motion. When life is moving too fast, *stillness* can be a great coping mechanism to slow down the overwhelming sense that we've lost control.

This is why people meditate and practice calming strategies, like *earthing* or controlled breathing. It's also why pausing life and walking away for a bit can repair severe burnout. By maintaining a calm, grounded presence, we are rooted in our certainty that despite future challenges, our evolving philosophies will protect us.

The more aware and accepting of your reality you are, the less you will tend to procrastinate. Proactive planning is a fantastic coping mechanism, which is why we discussed anticipating unexpected setbacks in the *Health & Wellness* section of this book. We now know how to self-advocate.

Being grounded in the present leaves less opportunities to fear the future. When you feel like a tsunami of chaos is coming for you, step back, take a breath, get mindful and grounded in the present moment, and the waves will recede.

When your emotions deflate and the panic subsides, maintain some distance from the situation long enough to think through a logical plan. If it helps, write down the plan to maintain a feeling of control and sensibility. Stay mindful, present, and conquer the overwhelming task one step at a time.

Negative perfectionism leads to avoidance or procrastination, which stems from fears of failure. This sort of performance anxiety is an indicator that a person may be a perfectionist living outside of the present moment. They are too focused on the future and that misdirected focus is causing them to hesitate and miss great opportunities.

If procrastination is the counterpoint of perfectionism, and procrastination is an attempt to exercise control, then a perfectionist *chooses* to do nothing because, by doing nothing, they cannot fail and they maintain control. The catch is that they also can't succeed at anything because they're not getting anything done.

Procrastination is an emotionally imposed state. It's an emotional urge we feed through physical abandonment of our duties. And while the best solution is to find the root cause of our baggage, some suffer from years of trauma that couldn't possibly get resolved before the next deadline.

So how do we overcome procrastination quickly? Let's go back to Amol.

Every day after work, Amol returns home and is bombarded with unfinished business he needs to handle. His dining room and living room are packed with items and he doesn't have a clue where to begin organizing the mess.

The chaotic vision hits like a physical pressure and he's anxious that others might see how he lives. He's also depressed because he's failed to achieve the aesthetic he wanted in his house. In his mind, so long as the mess remains, he's failing. Rather than focus on the overwhelming source of stress, he zones out in front of the TV and procrastinates.

Amol needs a strategy, but first he needs to get out of his funk. Often, when we lack the coping mechanisms for stress, we detach and try to find a place of existence that is numb or distracting enough to push our uncomfortable emotions to the back of our mind. We turn on television or play a game on our phone or fall into a social media hole.

While I'm a firm believer that enjoyed time is never wasted, in order to be productive and prolific authors, we must be responsible and use our time constructively. Once it's gone, there is no retrieving it.

If we allow mindless activities to syphon away our opportunities that could have improved our life, like Amol, we're not dealing with a writer's block issue or a furniture/clutter issue or even, in my case, a health issue. We are dealing with an emotional issue.

Paradoxically, one of the fastest ways to jolt ourselves out of these *emotional* procrastination holes is to make a *physical* change. Rather than vegging out and disconnecting, try moving. Straighten up a room, take a shower, go for a walk, or sort a drawer.

While stillness helps overcome the emotional sense of feeling overwhelmed, small actions can also help jolt us past the physical and mental black hole known as procrastination. Do not fall into a syphon of time. Breathe through the overwhelming thoughts cluttering your mind, then stand up and push through an obstacle physically. In cases of overcoming procrastination traps, sometimes moving a few pebbles can be as effective as moving a mountain. It's the sense of accomplishment that saves us in the end, even if the physical action is unrelated to our ultimate goal. It all comes down to feeling productive.

Procrastination is an active process, meaning you are actively choosing one behavior over another. The *Law of Motion* states that a body at rest will stay at rest until compelled to do otherwise. You can see how passive activities, like zoning out on your phone, could put you in a mental black hole. Whereas forcing yourself to move prevents that from happening.

You might not accomplish the task you've been putting off, but you prevent yourself from further derailing and losing more time to fruitless activities. By physically doing something, even if it's something arbitrary, you create a sense of accomplishment, which breeds a deeper desire for more accomplishments.

Control comes down to taking an active role in our lives. We can actively surrender to wasteful behaviors or channel our energy into something productive.

Remember, you are the main character of your story, and your goal is not perfection but development. Acknowledging that we are lifetime learners opens us up for improvement in a way that the narrow scope of perfectionism cannot. It's the difference between staring through a peephole and a window, one is incredibly constricting while the other provides a wide open perspective.

Hyper focusing on only one outcome robs us of countless opportunities. The simplicity of the #1 Objective is that it should encompass all areas of life. It opens us up to more possibilities, rather than constricting the view to a singular possibility.

We must channel our energy toward achievable goals, but never assume we know the shape and form of our exact outcome. When we assume the outcome before it arrives, we close ourselves off to possibilities. We shut out unknown, possibly greater, opportunities.

Do not turn yourself off. It's better to redirect energy. It's natural to feel overwhelmed when responsibilities amass. It's also natural to avoid unpleasantness. Self-care is a great way to defeat overwhelming emotions, as long as we choose the right method of self-care.

While a manicure might ease your stress, therapy might prove a more effective use of your time with more impactful, long-term benefits. If you don't have the means for therapy, self-advocating practices, like mindfulness and journaling, are a great start to the healing process. And don't underestimate the power of taking small actions, like organizing a cabinet or raking out a garden. Motion begets motion.

The next time you find yourself procrastinating, look deeper into the actual cause. Maybe you aren't writing, not because you can't think of the ending but because you're afraid you might disappoint readers.

Or perhaps you're hung up on a poor review you read that morning and your thoughts have created a karmic loop of distraction that's preventing you from focusing on anything else. One links to anxiety while the other links to depression, neither scenario depicts the present state of mind needed to be productive.

Take a moment to reflect while doing something active with your physical body. Work through your emotions and try to let go of the past. Forgive yourself for whatever regret you might harbor. If you're suffering from doubt, give yourself a pep talk or call a friend who is known for boosting your confidence.

Whatever you do, don't bury your feelings under mind-numbing distractions, because if our only go-to defense is zoning out the world and tuning out our emotions, they will eventually accumulate and overwhelm us. And if we have not practiced the skills needed to sort through our feelings, we will be unprepared when the tsunami comes. That is how people eventually shut down completely and look back on their lives as empty passages of time they somehow forgot to fill.

Eat the Frog

Mark Twain once said, "If it's your job to eat a frog, it's best to do it first thing in the morning. And if it's your job to eat two frogs, it's best to eat the biggest one first."

The *Eat the Frog* theory has been analyzed and reproduced numerous times in motivational speeches, books, and articles. It's a proven way to decrease procrastination and increase productivity, so a person can go through the rest of the day knowing the worst is behind them.

For me, the frog is accounting. As a business owner, bookkeeping is a necessary evil, but I absolutely loathe doing it. When I have to process quarterly royalty payments on a co-authored project every three months, I find myself constantly bumping the task from one to do list to the next. Until it can be avoided no more.

To make a frog go down a little easier, it's sometimes wise to prepare it the night before. When I must eat the frog—do those royalty statements—I clear my desk and sit the file right on top for the next morning. And when I return to work, after my usual warmup activities, I jump right into those dreaded statements.

If I avoid this rather slimy task, it costs me. I hear it croaking from my to-do list, distracting me with guilty emotions, and I'm disappointed in myself for putting it off. If I simply choked down the frog, it would be over in less than an hour, but instead, I let it distract me all week.

Don't let this happen to you. When you have a dreaded task—a frog—get it off your plate as soon as possible. By swallowing down that frog first thing, we can move on with our usual day, guilt free and proud of our choices rather than disappointed in our avoidance.

If you have several frogs, try eating one every morning, between a specific, designated block of time, most likely directly following your early morning sprint. This will free up your focus for other, more important tasks.

If there is a complex, giant frog on your plate, try cutting it into manageable pieces to make it more palatable, and nip away at a little each day during your designated frog meal time. Plan which parts you should eat first, and keep gnawing each day until it's gone. Removing this lost time from your schedule—once your frog plate is clean—will be a reward in itself.

The *Eat the Frog* technique is successful because it forces us to shut out distractions and intensely focus on one task with the full intention of seeing it through. The motivation is that when we're done, we're done, and we can walk away knowing we cleared our plate. In essence, it sets you up to win because you can then rest easy, knowing the most pressing priority of the day has been handled.

Tidy Up

A messy workspace can jeopardize productivity. An easy trick for increasing productivity is to tidy up your desk or work space at the end of each day. By making this a part of your regular routine, your office will be less likely to get overwhelmed by clutter.

When we arrive at work to a tidied desk, less time is wasted getting to work. Part of tidying up our desk means physically prioritizing our materials. If I am planning to write tomorrow, I will leave that book's file on top of my laptop in the center of my desk. But if I have a frog to eat, I might find my accounting files waiting for me.

Common sense tells us that by not having to search for files or materials we will ultimately save time. But having an uncluttered work space can also improve mental health, as it lowers stress levels, and physical health, as it reduces bacteria. Never forget that the typical keyboard is 400 times dirtier than a toilet seat[8]. If you can't afford to miss work, clean your workspace every day.

Creativity, however, is messy, so don't stress if your desk looks like a warzone when you're working. The key is starting the day at a well-organized work station and ending the day by tidying up. The benefits of the practice are simple but meaningful.

The trick is to diminish distractions. To tidy a desk, every object must have a home. Use a tray, basket, or box for your "catch all" of current projects for the week—for me this is my briefcase. Have a place for other supplies. Anything that you are not using tomorrow should get put away so you know where to find it.

Success starts with proper planning, and planning for productivity is no different. If your intentions are clear and thoughtful, your process will be the same. Yes, there are always unforeseen obstacles on every journey, but simple methods of approach can arm us with methodical ways to overcome or get around any bump in the road.

Plan for a productive day, week, month, year, and even decade by acting now. Minimizing the stress and chaos in your future will save you from wasting energy, and produce more of what so many authors spend years wishing for—*time*.

---

[8] National Center for Health Research

Chapter Eleven
Time

"Life was not to be sitting in hot amorphic leisure in my backyard idly writing or not writing, as the spirit moved me. It was, instead, running madly, in a crowded schedule, in a squirrel cage of busy people. Working, living, dancing, dreaming, talking, kissing — singing, laughing, learning. The responsibility, the awful responsibility of managing (profitably) 12 hours a day for 10 weeks is rather overwhelming when there is nothing, no one, to insert an exact routine into the large unfenced acres of time — which it is so easy to let drift by in soporific idling and luxurious relaxing."

Sylvia Plath, The Unabridged Journals of Sylvia Plath, 2000

A Priceless Commodity

The wealthiest people alive have often admitted *time* is the one thing they cannot buy. We are all running out of time. It is the greatest non-renewable resource, because time is, in essence, life. We get what we get, and when it's gone, it's gone, which is why, in terms of value, our time is priceless. Therefore, we must use it well.

For many, this will be the most useful chapter, because we have been trained to believe that time management is a game changer in productivity. But what if I told you there is no such thing as "time management?" If we could control time, it would not be as valuable. Time cannot be managed. We can only manage ourselves, our energy, and how we intend to *use* the limited time we have.

While the term *time management* might slip in here and there, what I'm actually referring to is energy management. Once a person figures out how to utilize their energy, they establish a sense of control where the perception of time is manipulated. But time remains the same.

A minute is sixty seconds no matter how you spend it, and there can only be twenty-four hours in a day. We are at the mercy of time, so a *sense* of control is the best we can hope for. If we manage our energy effectively, the perception that we have more time or an abundance of time can occur.

Ever wonder why some days lag and feel like they drag on forever, while others rush by in a blink of an eye? Yet, each day is the same length of time. Time has not changed, your energy has, and that is what effectively alters our perception.

Remember the story of Amol and Anushka? Anushka perceived the passing years with such energy, her time burst with experiences and invigorated her on a daily basis. Her brother, Amol, however, had very little energy due to the pressure of unrealistic expectations and his crippling perfectionism. He perceived the same amount of time as rapid, overwhelming, and gone before he had a chance to savor any opportunities.

Energy impacts our accomplishments, so we must preserve it where we can and utilize it on our highest priority. This is how effective people manage to accomplish—in one year—what takes some people ten years. They do not have more time. They have merely figured out the best way to utilize their energy.

In this chapter, we will address various approaches to "time management," but what we are really seeking are ways to target our energy effectively so that we might become the most productive versions of ourselves. Because our time is limited and there is much to cover, I will address each point in its own subsection to be as efficient and direct as possible.

Just as we are all on a unique journey, we all travel with a diverse set of weaknesses and strengths. You may be a person who prides herself on always being punctual. Or you may be the notoriously late friend who punctual people lie to about when events actually start. Or maybe you're the obsessive planner who compulsively maps out every detail and arrives thirty minutes early.

Because we are all facing different challenges, this chapter will include a myriad of strategies. Play with the methods and see if one helps or hinders your productivity. Advancement sometimes requires a little experimentation, so be your own guinea pig, but keep a judicious point of view so you don't get trapped on a wheel that leads you nowhere and only wastes your precious time.

Conducting a Time Audit

Authors are forever married to an ever-evolving schedule of writing, editing, promoting, releasing, and doing it all over again, regardless of the kind of author they are—indie, traditional, or hybrid. Hopefully, after reading the *Health & Wellness* chapters of this book, you've decided there will be no more sacrificing health for the fragile hope of wealth. But you still need a job, so how exactly is this going to work?

Almost every author I meet voices a wish for more time. But what if I told you doing less could actually produce more?

It's true. When we do things in the most productive way, and we remove the excess so we can stop wasting time on fruitless practices, we begin to work smarter rather than working harder. We learn to work with time instead of against it.

We have the time. What we lack is efficiency.

As you apply the following strategies, you will become more aware of hidden pockets of time you overlooked. You will also spot time leaks in your schedule. The trick to not wasting time is in really paying attention to how and where it is being spent. But because time can't technically be managed, we're also looking for moments when we might be able to preserve some energy.

Energy is precious. It's how we manipulate the perception of time.

Use the following time audit to analyze where your energy and hours are going.

Time Audit

STEP ONE

1. Make a list of everything your job entails on any given day. Include items like bookkeeping, even if you only do this task once a month. If it's a part of your job, put it on the list.

2. Assign each task a number. The higher the number the higher its significance. Remember, the most significant parts of the job should come with the greatest measurable return on

investment. Adjust the numbers until the sum of all numbers on the list equals 100. No less, no more. The total must be 100, as this will show you what percent of time on the job you hope to allocate to each task throughout the day/month/year.

3. Write out a schedule of your ideal day. This should be twenty-four hours long and show everything from personal care, family time, rest, and work. Exclude nothing, and indulge in the fantasy of the perfect day. Be sure to leave some time for miscellaneous activities, like that pesky bookkeeping that sneaks up once a month.

4. Now, put everything from STEP ONE away. You are not allowed to look at it again until you reach STEP THREE.

STEP TWO

1. Keep a running record of your day from the moment you rise to the moment you go to bed. Document every task by simply marking down the start time. You can track your day for several days to achieve varied results.

2. The following day, calculate your times into minutes spent within one 24 hour cycle. If you tracked multiple days, use the average minutes spent on the task. Do not waste time making the list fancy. So long as it's legible, it's fine. You can rewrite it tomorrow if needed.

3. For each task, divide the total minutes by 1440 (the total minutes in a 24 hour day). For example, if you wrote from 9:00am to 11:00am, that's two hours, which converts to 120 minutes. $120 \div 1140 = 0.10$, which means you spent 10% of your time writing. Repeat this step until you've given every number/task a score.

STEP THREE

1. Compare your ideal day with your actual day. Does it look different? Where are the most major discrepancies? Where do you see obvious chunks of wasted time? Did you complete tasks that weren't even included in your ideal day?

2. Highlight anything that can be removed from your schedule and on a Post-it write "I will no longer waste time on…" fill in the blank. Put this where you will see it every day.

3. Next, look at the job list you created in STEP ONE. How does it compare to the actual scores you earned? Perhaps you believed in STEP ONE that writing should account for at least 80% of your job, but in actuality, you're only giving it 10% of your time.

4. Add a column next to your ideal percentages of time and write in your actual time score. Sticking with the writing example, if you truly want to change, then you need to find an extra 70% of time spent elsewhere to relocate and fill your writing time deficit. And it's not an option to borrow from the time we need to sleep.

Conducting a time management audit is not an exact science. Different days bring about different, unexpected circumstances. If you want a more in-depth audit of your time, consider doing this for a full week and averaging your time scores before comparing the scores to your ideal list.

You can also practice clocking your time weekly, monthly, or annually to perform a time management checkup and see how you've improved with time. The idea here is to make you more aware of how your minutes are being spent. Much like keeping a food journal, we are mostly unaware of how much we actually consume until we write it down. A time management audit will increase productivity simply by making you more aware and accountable for your time.

Authors should love what they do. It's why most of us got into the business. But the pressures on the job often steal the joy. I've been doing this for a long time, and there is no author fairy godmother coming to bless us with a refund on lost joy.

Do yourself a favor and honor the fine line between love and obligation. Don't let other people define the line for you. And don't let toxic practices block your view of the end goal.

Burnout is the fastest way to destroy a talented author's success. For even in poverty, a writer will write. But once that spark is extinguished, the mind is a very dark place to live, so use your time both wisely and well.

Priorities

The word *priority* implies something of the highest importance or rank. The term came into existence in the English language during the 1400's. It was not pluralized into *priorities* until the middle of the 1900's. Technically, a person can only have one priority at a time, as the word contradicts having multiple conditions valued as *the most important* needing immediate attention.

We must determine *one* item of highest importance at a time. Focusing on too many "priorities" at once is a fast road to burnout. We should never have more than *one* priority—rather, we should learn how to *prioritize*.

Increased production is not always better. There is always a consequence, some negative and some positive. Awareness requires us to measure the cost against the value to determine what's worth doing and what requires more consideration.

Compiling multiple "priorities" can form mountains that obstruct the view of the future. Doing too much at once often causes people to lose sight of the long-term damage such overzealous approaches can have.

By definition, the word *priorities* should not exist, as it contradicts everything a *priority* should be. Based on its etymology, the word *priority* was conceived to convey the first or prime task needing completion. To assume that a person could have multiple priorities invites trouble.

The expectation that we must do more, *more, MORE* has only grown with time. A recent study in Harvard Business Review surveyed 1,800 global executives and found that conflicting priorities were actually slowing down productivity. 81% of executives found that growth initiatives lead to waste.[9]

Growth initiatives take place in every progressive business. For authors, a growth initiative might simply come from studying others' patterns of success and collecting what seems like fruitful habits.

---

[9] Harvard Business Review; *Stop Chasing Too Many Priorities;* Paul Leinwand and Cesare Mainardi 2011

How can I make more money and grow my brand? Wendy Writes-a-lot is selling subscription boxes. I should do that, too. Tammy Typist posts on each social media site six times a day. I need to up my game.

These seem like intelligent ways to drive more business and grow brand awareness, but with every added priority, you are actually conflicting your first priority as a writer, which is to write quality books.

Focusing on one priority, also known as taking a coherent initiative in business, remains a hallmark in good business practices. Focusing on one priority has proven to be three times more likely to increase a company's revenue.

Many businesses are overreaching in an attempt to outperform the competition. Diversification seems wise, but if it hinders our focus from our top priority, splitting our attention and taking time away from the most crucial area of importance, it is actually the opposite of wise.

The overwhelming abundance of demands we live with has had a ripple effect on our society's psychological health as a whole. Our culture is trembling with the reverberation of all we try to do.

Is it worth it?

A great way to avoid compiling *priorities* is to simply reject the word. There can only be **one** *priority*, one task labeled time sensitive and critical. Identifying a priority requires practice at prioritizing objectives and possibly delegating to others.

There can only be one concern that is the most important concern, shortly followed by a second concern and possibly a third, fourth, and so on. But only one concern can occupy the first place and wear the label *priority*.

By adding a plural definition of the word priority, we illogically assume we can handle multiple concerns *first,* but in reality, each item will need to fall in some sort of prioritized order, because our brains are not designed to focus on more than one task of importance at once. There is always a *priority*, and there can only ever be one.

The Danger of Multitasking

Multitasking is a lie. The word originated in an IBM report during the mid 1960's, shortly after the term *priorities* arrived. When the brain focuses on multiple tasks, the transition time required to alternate focus can be up to a minute, so the amount of additional time required to switch mental gears can accumulate rapidly and cost a multitasker a substantial amount of extra time rather than saving them time.

In essence, the multitasker *looks* busy, but they are actually wasting more time than someone singularly focused on one task—someone with a sole *priority*, rather than multiple *priorities*.

Cognitively, humans are not designed to multitask efficiently. Quality of work suffers when a person multitasks because they are relying on various parts of the brain.

When we edit, we use our focus brain, but when we write, we tap into our prefrontal cortex. Because we rely on two separate areas of the brain for these two common tasks, authors who multitask writing with editing will automatically waste more time during the creation process than authors who only focus on one task at a time.

For those still not convinced that multitasking actually costs us time, do the following exercise:

1. Count out loud to 26.

2. Now, say the alphabet.
3. Now, say the alphabet and count, alternating numbers and letters (e.g., 1A, 2B, 3C, 4D, and so on.)

You should have noticed your brain struggling and your speed notably slowing down. We can typically count to 26 and recite the 26 letters of the alphabet in approximately 30 seconds. But when we combine the task, alternating from letters to numbers, our brain slows down and works harder, therefore tires out faster. This is the fault of multitasking.

Rather than multitask the creative process, authors will save time and prove much more productive if they write without pausing for grammar, syntax, word choice, or punctuation. Only when they finish writing a scene, chapter, or even an entire book, should they go back and revise. This removes any wasted transition time. And by accessing one area of the brain at once, the work will feel more cohesive in the end because there were less interruptions and less chances for distraction.

Our brains are not designed to multitask, which is a big reason why we often wind up exhausted or feel overwhelmed or bombarded by *priorities.* Instead of constantly wishing for more hours in the day or scouring the web for better "time management" strategies, we should be simplifying our responsibilities and dialing back the pressing demands we lack the brain function to conquer simultaneously and flawlessly.

You have a higher chance of success, and will save more time, when you approach tasks one at a time. Multitasking increases the likelihood of mistakes. It can also have a negative effect on your memory, according to a study done by the University of California in 2011, which could explain why a lot of busy people suffer from fogginess.

On top of cognitive sluggishness, multitasking can also increase anxiety. But the mere "icky factor" of anxiety isn't the reason why anxiety should deter you from multitasking.

Anxiety has always been a consequence of environmental circumstance because it serves a very specific purpose. Anxiety is the body's alarm system meant to help us survive.

Think of your caveman self. You're walking along a plateau, and thunder rumbles in the distance. You look up, and the horizon is bruised with dark clouds. A bolt of lightning flickers in the distance, and you suffer a spike of anxiety.

The body registers this jolt of anxiety as a warning, and you focus on the danger, deciding to seek shelter. You locate a cave and wait out the storm.

When the rain stops and the sky clears, your anxiety subsides. You have survived oncoming danger, and your anxiety has successfully served its purpose.

When we suffer from anxiety, our brains sense danger and, therefore, accesses our primitive brain function, meant to keep us safe. Picture a crowd of people at a loud concert. You spot a man with a gun. Suddenly, you don't hear the music because your focus has narrowed on the threat. That is the result of properly functioning anxiety. That is our natural survival reflexes hard at work.

In writing, transitioning between tasks, or multitasking, produces the same anxiety response in the body, and the mind reflexively shuts out distractions, even though there is no realistic threat approaching. Multitasking between editing and writing cuts off our access to the frontal lobe where creativity flows. Authors, especially, should avoid multitasking if they want to increase the quality of their writing.

If you read a scene back and it feels wooden or flat, chances are you were thinking about something else and writing with the wrong part of the brain. For the highest quality writing, authors should limit their focus to one area at a time.

Mono-tasking is scientifically proven to be more effective than multitasking. Productivity is not about working harder. It's about working smarter, so think carefully about how you choose to work.

One Hour Intervals

Improper "time management," or more accurately "energy management," can be one of the greatest impediments to an author's health and lead them directly to burnout. Authors tend to stay stuck in their chair because with so many distractions it's difficult to focus, and once we achieve focus, we don't want to lose it. But by not taking movement breaks, we are putting our health at great risk and creating negative, long-term productivity issues and inviting symptoms of burnout into our lives.

Using timed focus strategies can increase productivity if measured properly. Based on the need for movement breaks established in the *Health & Wellness* chapters, and the evidence that walking actually increases creativity, I recommend writing for one hour intervals, followed by a 10-30 minute walking break.

Not only will this help authors match their word count with their steps, it will revive their mind, energize their spirit, and counter a lot of the health risks associated with sedentary jobs. But for this section particularly, it will help them focus and manage their time and energy more effectively.

For other author tasks, such as updating social media, responding to email, monitoring sales, and so on, shorter intervals might suffice. Whatever you choose, try to avoid sitting for longer than an hour. And when your timer alerts you that it's time for a break, do not take that break working on something else.

A break must be a break, so choose something completely unrelated to work like fixing a snack, doing some yoga stretches, switching the laundry, or taking a walk. When you return to your desk, set another timer and focus on work again. To avoid unwanted distractions, use your setting preferences on your phone and computer to shut off notifications.

These timed focus techniques are especially helpful when trying to conquer tasks that are especially known for sucking up an author's time. While many authors like to blame technology for eating up their time, studies have proven most distractions are self-inflicted. We all know how one social media post or one email can quickly snowball into an hour of lost time.

Never forget, time is our most valuable, non-renewable resource. Time is life. Use it well. When we manage our energy with techniques that access pockets of time, we maintain better control of our days and reduce the likelihood of losing track of time.

While you might have one unproductive hour, it's only an hour and, after your break, you can start again, fresh. Intervals help us monitor our productivity in manageable chunks. They keep us aware, focused, and present plenty of opportunities to meet our needs in between.

Put in the Hours

While it's comforting to believe that we can incorporate countless strategies into our work and somehow tap into extra, unused time, that simply isn't how time or business works. Anything worth doing will require focus, commitment, and a certain amount of time. If we practice too many shortcuts, we will wind up shortchanged in the end.

As stated in the beginning of this chapter, time cannot be managed, but our energy can. Success often comes down to sustainability, and we are more likely to sustain a career if we use smart strategies to maintain our energy.

Maintaining energy means never wasting it. Yes, it will be challenging. Yes, you will have good days and bad. Yes, you will sometimes feel exhausted from the strain. But if you are maintaining balance, you will regenerate the energy you've lost and be able to continue on your journey long-term.

Success will always rely heavily on sustainability.

There are no shortcuts without consequence. If writing is your second job or if you have other obligations that are a priority in your life, you will not have as much time as a full-time author. It's simple math, and math does not lie.

But what you can have is a better handle on your energy. By taking better care of yourself, you will be able to accomplish more in a day. And there's a caveat there as well, because taking care of ourselves takes work.

We must outgrow the "do it all" mentality and stop heaping *priorities* onto our plate. The answer is not more, it's less. By simplifying we are clarifying. When we aren't trying to conquer multiple tasks at once, we can clearly focus on one task and meet it with our highest potential.

Success takes time. If it were easy, it would be commonplace and less desirable. The challenge is what will shape you in the end.

We are all dealing with an unknown, but limited, amount of time. The choices we make and the energy we generate will decide if our time on this earth was pleasant or miserable, so don't let anyone waste your time twice. Even you.

Be gentle with your limits, forgiving of your towering expectations, and realistic about the time it will take to reach your goals.

To the workaholic, remember, an addict is always an addict, even when they're recovered. You will likely always be a workaholic, even when you learn healthier habits. Make it part of your job to self-advocate and stay self-aware.

For the perfectionist, remember that your need for perfection will likely always linger inside of you, but establishing boundaries and altering expectations can greatly help you keep the symptoms of negative perfectionism away.

Overall, time management is not about the time we have. It's about the discipline we choose. The methods and tools that produce measurable success will be your safest strategies to get where you want to go.

Like any story arc, the journey is the experience, so rather than rush to the end, learn to savor each twist and turn and enjoy the ride. We only get to travel this road once. This is your story, so you might as well savor it.

Chapter Twelve
Scheduling

"A schedule defends from chaos and whim. It is a net for catching days. It is a scaffolding on which a worker can stand and labor with both hands at sections of time."

Annie Dillard, The Writing Life, 1989

Parkinson's Law

By utilizing timers in our workday, we enhance our productivity by default. This is proven by *Parkinson's Law,* which states that work will expand to fill any available time. By limiting the time on task, we naturally cut away waste and reduce the likelihood of procrastination.

Authors typically witness *Parkinson's Law* taking place when they're given a deadline. If the deadline is two weeks, the author requires all of the two weeks and finishes just before the deadline. But if the author is given one week or three weeks, they will still finish their work, turning it in just in time. We use the time allotted, so to be more productive, it sometimes helps to limit the time assigned to any given task.

There is nothing wrong with taking the full time assigned for revisions. But it helps to be aware that this law exists, as we sometimes have more than one deadline at once. By limiting our time on task, we can sometimes get more accomplished in less time and turn our focus to the next *priority* in line.

Of course, if you're a procrastinator, this law will not apply to you, nor will this section because you're probably rewatching *The Office* and disrupting other people's workdays with TikToks and text messages about how adulting is overrated. I'll gently refer you back to Chapter Ten, PRODUCTIVITY, while the rest of us carry on…

Scheduling Tools

A schedule is a blueprint for a successful life. Simple scheduling tools can make goals more achievable, save on business expenses, keep you and your "team" organized and on the same page, avoid unforeseen setbacks, and help you track your progress—all of these benefits link to avoiding burnout.

While I accept that everyone has their own style and some of us claim to work best in a bit of chaos, where others need complete order and functional practicality, I strongly advocate scheduling tools to all authors. The right tools will increase your productivity. The trick is discovering which tools are right for you.

Scheduling tools can come in the form of calendars, day planners, lists, apps, and more. There is such a variety of options available, and experience has taught me that trial and error is sometimes necessary. If a scheduling tool is hindering more than it's helping, you might want to call it a failure, learn from it, and move on.

I'm a sucker for day planners. Before iPhones, when these little leather bound life holders really took off, I found the process of owning one almost titillating. I'd spend days filling in every little detail, and I'd invest in a purse big enough to take it everywhere. But over time, I found the task of updating the overwhelming number of pages and parts so tedious, it became a source of stress.

And without my handy planner, I was off the grid and running rogue, usually in a tailspin toward missed obligations and belated birthday wishes. So I definitely benefit from organization, but it has to be the right kind.

As a prior teacher, my brain works best with the style of boxy, lesson plan scheduling. Day planners are too detailed, and weekly planners don't give me the bird's eye view I prefer, so I generally stick with monthly calendars.

I love the idea of a big desk blotter where I have plenty of room to write out my months ahead, but they don't travel well. And a pocket calendar is too small. Digital calendars, like the one on a smart phone, make my dyslexic brain hurt, and I throw a complete hissy fit whenever the app updates and looks slightly different.

All of these proclivities took me years—more than a decade—to figure out. And because I'm especially high maintenance, I'm not satisfied with just a monthly calendar. I also need a weekly list. This, for a long time, took shape in a specific notebook—and yes, I had all sorts of rules and preferences about the spine and page size.

The lesson is to accept that general tools might not be enough for your needs, and it's perfectly fine to obsess over finding the right ones. Once you do, your job will be that much easier to manage.

Your preferences will not be identical to mine, but in case they are close, I've developed an Author Planner as an accompaniment to this book. Some of the design elements are explained in the sections ahead. But it also includes satisfying checkboxes for water intake, movement breaks, and other helpful tips discussed.

Explore and experiment with scheduling tools. Remain self-aware of what's working and what's not. Eventually, you'll find your groove, and when you do, you'll see an immediate uptick in productivity, energy, and extra time.

However, you also need to know *how* to use tools. Owning a hammer does not make someone a carpenter. There is a necessary skill required for even the simplest tools. The following sections will enlighten you to some great scheduling strategies you might not have known existed.

Task Batching

Task Batching groups similar activities in a way that increases focus and productivity, but avoids multitasking. This efficient method of organizing the work day requires a person to be self-aware and monitor which parts of the day they are most focused and which parts of the day they are least focused.

By batching similar tasks, we are spending less time switching focus, which is the downfall of multitasking. When we frequently switch tasks, activating opposing sides of the brain, we lose time, risk accuracy, and increase mental strain.

Many people complain of suffering from an afternoon lag. Task batching is a good way to combat this lag. Rather than try to wring out another thousand words when your brain is tired, try switching gears to tasks that require less focus. Make a phone call, respond to an email, tidy the office, or something else that could be considered a passive activity.

Passive Activities are activities that require minimal focus. Playing football would be considered an *active activity*, whereas walking would be considered a *passive activity*. In business, there are varying levels of focus required for various activities.

Avoid grouping *active activities*, as this would be the same as multitasking and would be counterproductive. But *passive activities* can often be grouped. An example of grouping *passive activities* might be taking a walk while returning a phone call.

By grouping *passive activities*, especially during that afternoon lag, you give your brain a break and redirect your energy. Overall, you are using time wisely and collectively becoming more productive throughout the week.

Another example of task batching is when we sprint first thing in the morning. We've established that our brains are most creative and efficient directly after waking, which is why we batch our daily sprint to the morning time. We also dine on our dreaded frogs during this time because we are in such an efficient headspace we will likely eat the frog faster than we would at, say, 3pm when we're fighting a lag.

A tip for task batching is to color code your schedule list. Authors might highlight writing time in orange, promo time in blue, daily office maintenance in gray, dreaded frog tasks in green, and so on. By categorizing your tasks, you will see opportunities for batching within your schedule.

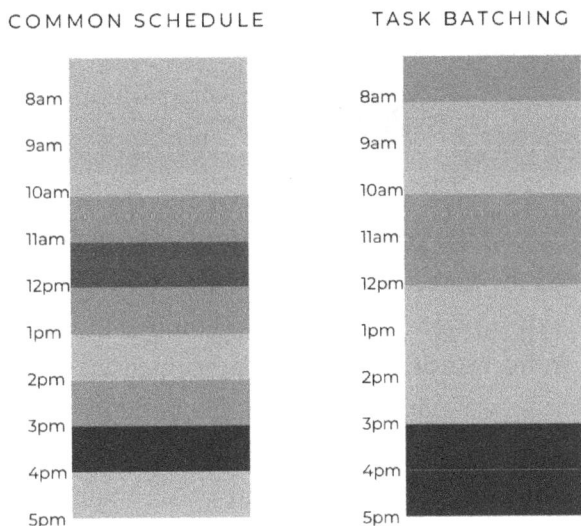

COMMON SCHEDULE   TASK BATCHING

8am   8am
9am   9am
10am   10am
11am   11am
12pm   12pm
1pm   1pm
2pm   2pm
3pm   3pm
4pm   4pm
5pm   5pm

It's less productive to bounce back and forth between promo and writing throughout the day and more effective to batch those tasks into two separate days or parts of the day.

You will note, in the graphic above, the task-batched day starts with an hour of writing (orange), which is followed by a frog task (green), and then it's back to writing (orange). This is the one exception to the rule, based on my personal rules, as I start every day with an hour sprint. I don't count that writing time as part of my day, but rather see it as a preliminary brain exercise.

If I have a nasty frog that needs eating, I place that as a top priority and it's, technically, the first thing I do. In the example above, I batch my frog, then I batch my writing, followed by some batched promo, and lastly, my batched office maintenance. However, I prefer even less transitions in my day, so I tend to batch my week.

My Typical Work Days Tend to Batch as Follows:

- Mostly writing
- All things non-writing (marketing, promo, graphic design, pitch development, etc.)
- Rest (only passive activities scheduled to give my brain a break)
- Editing

I prefer weekly batching or day batching because I find it has the least amount of lost transition time, but it also gives me the necessary opportunities to check in on what needs attention daily. It breaks up my week without disrupting my days, because each day serves a specific purpose.

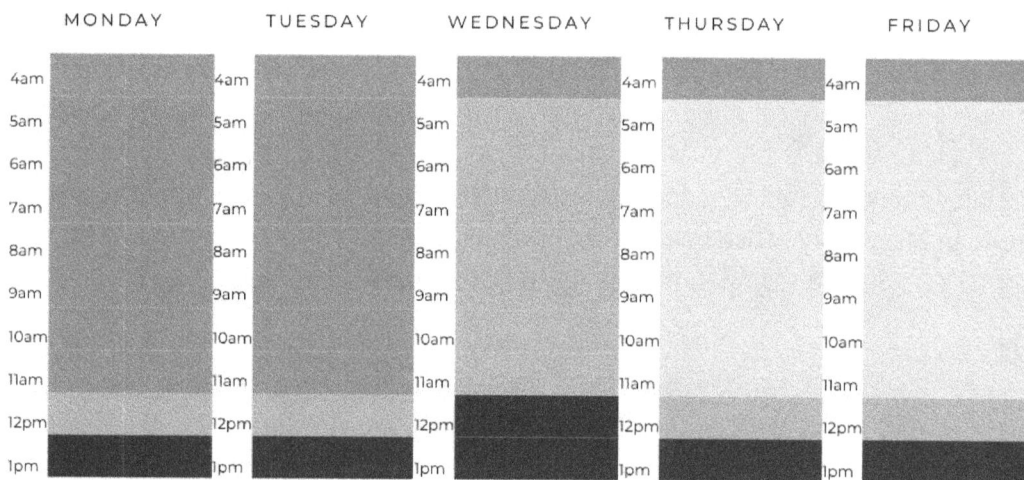

There are a few things to note in the graphic above. First, I have batched my work days so the last two focus on editing (yellow) and the first two focus on writing (orange). My Wednesday begins with eating my weekly frog (a person of stronger willpower might move this to first thing Monday morning, but we all pick our battles). Then the rest of my Wednesday is focused on promo (blue), which happens to be a rather restful activity for me, so I consider Wednesday both my day of frog eating and my day of rest—it's a cost reward thing.

Each day ends with a social media check in and some office maintenance. And, finally, you may have noticed the times have changed. That's because I typically rise around 4am, so I designed this to represent something close to my usual batched work week.

However, the guide above is only one example of how I group my tasks. I find my approach literally changes with the weather. In the warmer months, I attempt to enjoy the sunshine as much as possible, where in the colder months I'm more likely to stay inside. My life absolutely influences how I spend my work days, as should yours.

Maintain control of your time. The moment we become reactive rather than proactive, our performance becomes less effective.

I'd also like to mention that in addition to typically working less than forty hours—a benefit of allocating my energy properly and scheduling effectively—I sometimes take the midafternoon off. Because I like writing early in the morning, I'm sometimes tired midday. Rather than work eight hours, I might give myself the option to clock out and have a little *me time*, then come back once I'm energized again.

Allow flexibility in your schedule so that you can shuffle tasks to other time slots if needed. Life comes with surprises, but more importantly, we should never underestimate the power of self-care when it comes to productivity.

I take a substantial number of breaks throughout the day, some long, some short. In the end, I never work more than 6 to 8 hours in a typical work day.

Allowing myself breaks has greatly increased my productivity. Regardless of it being a 30 or 40 hour work week, I'm accomplishing more and better work than I accomplished years ago when I kept a grueling schedule of 60 plus hours a week, because I'm being kinder to my personal needs.

No matter what kind of day I have planned, I typically batch my time to start with a sprint, then a frog if there's one croaking at me, then my big batch focus of the day, and finally my "housekeeping." When I say housekeeping, I'm referring to the daily office tasks that require attention such as email responses, phone calls, cross-promotion posts, and so on.

There is always the chance of unforeseen setbacks, but I find batching my tasks helps me keep a diverse rotation without getting author whiplash. There are some weeks where I'm batching almost all writing days, but I'm always taking those movement breaks, practicing mindfulness, and using interval techniques to break up my schedule as well.

Time Blocking & Time Boxing

Meet *Task Batching's* lovely sisters, *Time Blocking* and *Time Boxing*. Similar to task batching, *time blocking* increases productivity by limiting chances for interruptions. *Time boxing* achieves the same but uses self-imposed deadlines. Similar to interval techniques, task batching, Parkinson's Law, and good old-fashioned organization, these are two more great tools every author should keep in their bag of tricks.

Time boxing boxes out a specific time to work on a task and achieve a measurable result. For an author, this might sound something like, "I will write 1k every morning by 9am." The author imposes the time limit and measurable outcome on him or herself. Working with a self-imposed time box forces us to work as efficiently as possible.

Time blocking, on the other hand, sets aside or blocks out a chunk of time dedicated to focusing on a certain task, but places less emphasis on the expected outcome. For an author, this might sound something like, "Every night, between seven and eight, I will work on my novel."

Time blocking feels less constraining because it is. It's also less productive, but if you are okay with working without a deadline and want that sort of ease, use *time blocking*.

Time blocking is great for establishing a ritual, much like some will try to establish by writing first thing each morning. We know this is *time blocking* because it's less about what we write and more about the actual ritual of writing during that blocked out hour.

If an author has an approaching deadline and wants to accomplish a goal each day, *time boxing* will produce faster results. An author might keep their blocked out, one-hour sprint as a warm up, but they might switch to *time boxing* in the early afternoon, setting a measurable goal, such as finishing a chapter or scene within a certain time.

I start my morning with a time block of writing. But when I write later in the day, it is closer to time boxing, as I have a goal in mind—*Write 10K in a Day.*

Time blocking and boxing are especially effective when it comes to accomplishing active work that requires intense focus. By chunking your schedule, more work will be completed in less time. By organizing tasks with grouping strategies, we achieve more in less time because we remove the cost of transitions.

As an author, I'm more partial to *time boxing,* because it deters habits of perfectionism. By boxing my days according to tasks like writing and editing—separate of course—I force myself to get the words down. I don't hesitate over language or grammar. It's a stream of consciousness, a rapid execution. When I reach my measurable goal at the end of the day, I feel accomplished and satisfied.

At the end of the week, when I have an editing day, I might box it out with the goal of cleaning up one chapter, even though on my writing day I wrote five chapters. Different tasks take different amounts of time. As a dyslexic author, I can write much faster than I can read, so I edit slower than I compose. The point is to be realistic and not overbook your schedule.

I find it helpful to keep that first writing hour of each day as a block rather than a box, because it's not only about the ritual of writing every day, it's about enjoying the process. Keeping the hour loose allows me to shake things up. This opening hour is also a great time for authors to write blogs or magazine articles if that's a part of their job. And on those days that life seems a bit overwhelming, sometimes it's best to simply use that hour block for personal journaling.

There is more freedom in time blocking because the only goal is to focus on a specific activity. In the case of the morning hour, that activity is writing. There is no endpoint or objective you must meet. For writing, blocking is a very liberating practice. But for authoring, boxing gets the most done.

For authors just learning this technique, I recommend using the *Write 10k in a Day Author Planner*. This accompaniment book can be found on my Amazon author page or website. It's an easy to use, customizable, time-saving tool specially designed for authors.

Regardless of which method you prefer, time blocking or boxing, both are intended to trim away any fat. Those pesky shifts of focus that cost us time are minimized, and we save energy by eliminating time-wasting transitions.

Automated Technology

Anyone born in the last century likely complained about automation at some point. Us older folks remember a time when humans answered customer service lines and there was no listening to instructions or pressing buttons to navigate a call menu. Those days are long gone.

Automation technology includes tools that allow a system to run automatically. Today, we typically call such technologies *apps*. While some apps are strictly for entertainment, many are developed to increase productivity. Some even act as automated technology and help independent business owners, like authors, get more done.

When we *automate* our work, we convert the process so that it can operate automatically. By setting up automated technology in our business, we are effectively saving time and increasing our productivity. In a sense, we are delegating responsibilities to machines or bots, much like a business owner might delegate to other employees.

Automated technology comes in the form of task/project management, sales and marketing, email bots, messenger bots, scheduling tools, and more. The automation tools available today are only improving with time.

That being said, technology is one of the most transient mediums we use. While I'd love to recommend and plug my favorite apps, I fear doing so will only date the book and send you searching for a possibly obsolete tool when more advanced ones have been invented.

However, I invite you to ask me about my favorite tools through social media any day, because at least then my answer will be relevant and given in real time. But keep in mind, I might change my answer as soon as something better comes along.

A great way to educate yourself on automation tools that help authors is to simply ask around. Find out what others are using, request a tutorial, ask what the pros are and what the limits are. You can also do your own research with a simple search for "automated tools that boost productivity."

I will say this, one that I cannot live without is a social media scheduler. I typically schedule a few batch days a year, directly focused on designing and scheduling promo. I spend approximately 1 to 2 days on this every 6 months.

By using an automated scheduling tool, I'm able to plan posts across all my social media platforms months in advance. Therefore, I only have to post social media content twice a year, but I must schedule that planned posting time into my routine, or I'm back to manually posting content on a regular basis, which eats up a lot of time.

Not having to manually post promo content greatly limits my time on social media and has an incredible effect on my productivity and healthy mind space. Social media, which we will discuss more in the chapters ahead, is one of the greatest distractions authors complain about. And while many platforms allow authors to schedule within their program, doing so can be a risky distraction in itself. This is why many prefer to use independent apps to schedule posts without ever having to visit actual social sites.

As a former workaholic and perfectionist, I understand the desire for control and the temptation to do everything ourselves to ensure things are done properly. But as technology continues to advance, the likelihood for sloppy mistakes through automation decreases.

The more we do, the more *priorities* we put on our plate, the more the likelihood for human error increases. While new technology takes time to work out its bugs, once regulated, there is very little error compared to that of human error.

There's little harm in trying something new. If you don't like it, you can always go back to doing things the time-consuming way. But if you're like me, you might find yourself wishing you started using automated technology years ago because while it delegates some control, it also frees up an incredible amount of time for writing. In the end, it comes down to deciding what your writing time is worth to you.

Chapter Thirteen
The Social Author

"When given the choice, people will always spend their time around people they like."

Gary Vaynerchuk, Thank You Economy, 2010

Social Presence

During the dawn of eBooks, when I signed my first book contract, I was amazed by the social requirements. I needed to have a website—fair enough. I needed to have a Twitter account—I knew it existed. I needed to post frequently on my blog—I didn't have a blog or a definition for this word. And—now I really date myself—I had to join the author chatroom. Suffice it to say, all of this social expectation was unexpected.

To be clear, I was the last of all my friends to get WiFi, so whenever I had to go to any of these social settings, I first needed to wait for my dial-up internet to jump online. The point is, if you were not born into the digital age, you had to survive the revolution, and for some of us, we will always be operating a little behind the curve.

Early in the new millennium, some of my friends were using something called MySpace and Twitter, but I didn't get it. A younger friend set me up with both accounts, and before I figured either out, something called Facebook came along.

But when Facebook came along, Twitter didn't disappear. Then I heard about Tumblr and a few others, and my list of virtual social obligations grew.

Authors are told they must have a social presence. Publishers often express desires to see their authors on every platform. And readers expect to have access to authors through content and private messaging. It can quickly become an intrusive, overshadowing part of the job.

These social expectations were rather disappointing because I wanted to be the author in the bulky fisherman sweater writing in a secluded cottage on the French countryside. There were very few people in my author fantasy. It was basically me, Hemingway, Fitzgerald, and Stein pounding the keys by day and drinking like thirsty fish by night. Nothing so nostalgic or glamorous ever came into play.

As a rule follower, I signed up for the numerous platforms, took a few courses on web development, designed my first website, which had a blog, and I logged into the author chatroom.

After a few weeks, my publisher reached out to remind me that I needed to actually interact. It was then I learned that lurking in the virtual shadows wouldn't cut it. But when I witnessed authors interacting, some behaved badly. Some troublesome authors were excoriated for their missteps while others organized cliques and tried turning the author chatrooms into high school cafeterias.

I didn't see the benefit or appeal. I remained unconvinced that my writing career should somehow force me to exploit my private life by sharing it with strangers, especially in such a harsh and often judgmental climate.

The chatrooms weren't for me, but I still had to post content on the public social sites. Keep in mind, I was still texting by pressing "44-33-555-555-666" to text "hello," so all of these new digital advancements were quite overwhelming.

What the hell could I possibly have to say to the world each day? I was just a clueless writer.

Cue a picture of a monkey typing and a generic "Good morning, friends!"

Ugh, my content was trite, painful, and pointless, but exactly what we authors were instructed to do. And to this day, I'm irritated because I can't say it was completely ineffective. Relationships were formed and books were read—my books—which led to book discussions. And we all know, nothing sells books better than genuine word of mouth.

As social media caught on, readers grew more entitled to the details of authors' personal lives. The pressure to perform and post interesting content was a very real stressor, especially to a new writer trying to carve out their niche on the social scene while penning their next novel.

I heard pets generated social media traffic, so I adopted a kitten. Then another. For years, I relied on pictures of my animals to hide the fact that I wanted to share nothing of my personal life.

I watched authors get too comfortable and accidentally say the wrong thing, only to be lambasted, blacklisted, and have their careers destroyed all because of social media drama.

It was like living naked in the great wide open. We were forced to be exposed, told to act interesting, and judged for every word we said. A digital paper trail established a sense of permanency. Places like Facebook might resemble a storefront, but there was no penalty for vandals who wanted to egg the display.

Authors who used the virtual soapbox in their early career, loudly vocalizing whatever controversial thought that crossed their mind, aren't really around anymore. That in and of itself says a world about professionalism.

Then there were the chatty, confident, self-promoting authors, those who glided into the public light and showed no hesitation about endorsing their work. There was something vivacious and magnetic about them, something that lured others in. These authors operated on the edge of over the top without ever tipping over into that scummy, egotistical self-promoting zone.

Watching authors self-promote created a new pressure to learn graphic design and take some courses on building a brand—one more thing to subtract from writing time. Self-promoting without sounding self-centered or arrogant was an art form many struggled to master and many failed. Using graphics and quotes from books helped create content while removing the focus from the author.

At this time, social media was still very new. Many thought it would be a passing fad. I don't think anyone expected it to become as ingrained in our world as it is today.

For authors like me, it was a great source of stress. I didn't trust it, felt silly using it, developed anxiety over fears of one day having to retract a public *faux pas*, and wanted nothing to do with it, yet I sensed myself becoming addicted to it all the same.

Flash forward, more than a decade later, and my business is still reliant on it—more than anyone ever predicted. Our personal views of social media are irrelevant when measuring its worth. Social media is one of the greatest tools authors have to connect with readers and build exposure.

But how much is enough? The list of social media sites is endless. Do we honestly need to be active on Facebook, Instagram, Twitter, Snapchat, Tumblr, TikTok, personal blogs, Pinterest, Goodreads, and so on? And those are just the most popular ones at this moment. More are sure to come.

Go ahead and exhale, because the answer is no, we do not *need* to be active on every platform. But there is a caveat.

Social media serves a purpose. It has benefits but also has just as many drawbacks. Before we delve into the worrisome downsides, let's look at 15 positive business benefits associated with using social media.

15 Benefits of Social Media in Business

1. Social media increases brand awareness.
2. Social media helps humanize companies.
3. Social media provides opportunities for brand leadership. For authors, this can be by using the platform to establish yourself as an expert in your field, as many have done.
4. Social media makes companies less forgettable by frequently posting content.
5. The right social media can direct website traffic through "call to action" content and live links.
6. Social media can help businesses generate leads through paid advertising or manual correspondence.
7. Social media allows opportunities for new-age customer service and "social selling," which focuses less on closing a deal and more on building trust and familiarity with the customer. Studies show that the more a brand interacts with customers and offers help through social media, the more money and time customers are willing to spend with brands.
8. Social media allows easy access for partnering with other brands, working with brand ambassadors, and hiring influencers.
9. In addition to ads, social media allows users to boost content through quick promotions. This is a simple way to get new eyes on a brand's content and products.
10. Social media has the potential to make a post go viral.
11. Social media is social, meaning it's interactive. Brands can interact with customers and gain feedback about products, host contests, and more.
12. Social media allows rapid communication during a crisis.
13. Social media allows businesses to listen to and observe the customer in social interactions. This helps brands gauge the sentiment around a specific product.
14. This one is both a positive and negative. Social media allows brands to watch the competition.
15. Social media allows targeted advertisements and analytics to measure an ad's performance.

Authors often have a love-hate relationship with social media due to the undeniable benefits it offers and the time it demands—time that encroaches on writing. Every business should have social accounts at this point, but businesses aren't running these accounts—people are. And when you are a sole proprietor, like an author, maintaining one, two, or ten social accounts can become a full-time job.

A downfall of social media, especially for authors, is the amount of time it wastes. I rarely peruse social media as any sort of entertainment, but it remains one of my greatest time sucks, because despite automation, maintaining a social presence takes an abundance of time.

In this book, we made a vow to assess the actual reality of the job, so we will, unfortunately, have to expose social media for exactly what it is. Aside from the emotional side effects addressed in the *Health & Wellness* section, it basically boils down to this: social media platforms are forged by self-absorption.

The entire point of social media is to share a snapshot into your life or company or world. So we snap selfies and show our food and share our adventures and open up this lens into our private lives which generates a sense of acceptance—or rejection.

The more propagated these practices become the more plagued by feelings of inadequacy audiences grow. And as friends watch their *friends'* lives go by on a carousel of doctored images, they begin to worry they are missing out, and those hints of inadequacy infect the psyche on a deeper, personal level.

The response is often to isolate or retaliate, so users are either going to post tit-for-tat and feed the self-absorption monster, or they are going to retreat and feel sad.

Remember when we discussed anxiety and depression, anxiety being a future headspace and depression being a past headspace? Social media injects us into other people's worlds, so we are not present in our own moment. We become focused on a possible, future response to our content or dwell on something we saw in the past. Our gauge is teetering rather than centered, which is why we often feel off balance after too much exposure to social media.

The trick is managing social media with balance. Are you sensing a theme?

Putting yourself first means cutting off any activity that threatens your well-being. Book contracts typically have a clause addressing social expectations, and to many, this might seem the least important paragraph in a book deal, but perhaps it deserves a second read. Do not let anyone dictate your social media practices beyond what you are certain you can handle.

Yes, having a presence is necessary. A website is a no-brainer. But as far as social platforms go, you should always retain autonomy and control over how frequently you post and what you post. Never let anyone else decide these things for you.

The publishing industry is no longer a private club. It is a split scene, divided between traditionally published authors and independently published authors. This shared territory has had an effect on the rules and expectations.

Indie authors have so much autonomy, they can follow the lead of the traditional market, but in the end, they decide exactly what and how they want to run their business. And since they account for such a large percentage of published writers, they've somewhat bent the curve of what's expected.

While publishers might pressure authors to be socially active on every platform, it's a lot to manage for the author and a source of emotional upheaval. Indie authors are more likely to pick their favorite networks and move on, thus proving authors do *not* need to be on every platform ever made.

I suggest authors have a favorite where they are most active but also maintain a presence on a few others. And I really mean a few—three or less.

Hit the major networks and automate your settings so that your organic posts on your favorite network automatically upload to your feed on the others. This will require you to only be active on your favorite platform. Your content will repost to the other platforms, so you appear active to all audiences, when in actuality you are only posting to one place. If you don't know how to do this, check YouTube. There is a tutorial for everything.

And if you're like me and want to put even more distance between your real existence and your social presence without harming your brand relevancy, invest in automation apps that schedule your content without ever requiring you to sign in to an actual social media app. These scheduling apps exist and are extremely user friendly.

The Social Goal

The goal of social media for authors should be to bridge the gap between authors and readers. There is merit to the claim that authors should have a social presence—more so at the start of their careers than any other time. But how much is enough, and what is too little?

First, it has to be within the realm of what you can emotionally handle. Second, it must be authentic, otherwise it's just a waste of time. If readers feel like they are getting a glimpse into your mind and life, they will stay engaged. If they feel like they are only seeing fabricated brand posts that could be from anyone, you've lost them.

The word *presence* relates to proximity. For your social presence to be functional, you will have to actually get close to the customer and interact. When we examine the paradox between physically socializing and digitally socializing, research claims the difference is in the eye contact. Studies prove that sharing eye contact with someone who cares about you can effectively reduce stress and boost moods. Think about that for a moment.

Authors genuinely care about their readers on some level. If we look at them, show them our eyes, they will sense our concern for their well-being. They will engage. This can't happen with pre-fabricated, cold, branded content.

The way we present ourselves matters. Branding is great and important, but nothing will ever beat true human interaction. If this is beyond your comfort zone, that's okay. For a long time, it was beyond mine. But after burning out and running myself into the ground with social expectations on the job, I decided I would give less, however, the little I gave would be so much more.

My audience finally gets to see my authentic self. I don't talk about my personal life in great detail with them. But I do share my excitement about upcoming books, my rediscovered love for life, the affirmations that keep me motivated, and my adventures. And those things are more my brand than any cold logo or color pallet ever could be.

Posting stale content is a waste of time. Pre-made graphics that lack thoughtful captions might convey branding, but they can appear cold and too clean to sustain a sense of connection, to the point that viewers aren't interested anymore because everything starts to look robotic and the same.

Keep your content organic. Use pre-made posts for filler, but don't solely rely on those impersonal graphics.

Consistency is key in terms of social relevancy, and for that, there are apps to help you generate and schedule relevant content. But real connections happen when we share the real us.

There is no master rule that decides how often you should share yourself, but there are endless theories. Here at *Healthy & Happy Authors, LLC*, you guessed it, we advocate choosing for yourself. Content doesn't have to be premeditated or staged. Your audience will adapt like Pavlov's dogs. They will get the notification, hear the bell, and pay attention when you appear. As long as you feed them authenticity, you've got them.

Social media is not a comfortable atmosphere for many, but we see its value in business and want the benefits, so we do our best to accept it into our lives. But having a social presence should never teeter into a business hindrance. If social media is distracting you from work or altering your mood in a negative manner, the risk has proven greater than the reward, and all that advice about social presence goes away for a while.

Truly reaping the benefits of social media comes down to proper management. Social media is meant to be social and entertaining for *them*. While it's fine to enjoy this aspect of the job, never forget it's part of your job. Be responsible with your time, tone, intentions, and image, because the bottom line will be your sales, and if you're losing sales or lagging on production because of poor social media management, you're doing it wrong.

Once embraced, maintaining a social media presence can quickly become a distraction and even an addiction. If you don't control it, it will control you. This is where scheduling these work-related tasks comes in handy.

Maintain a manageable social presence, automate it wherever you can, use time blocking for maintenance and stick to a schedule, try your best to be authentic, and get back to writing. Do not give social media more than it gives you.

The Social Scene

Every time I swing by Twitter it reminds me of the original Cantina scene from the 1977 Star Wars movie, *A New Hope.* Everything looks foreign, everyone else seems at home, but I don't belong, things are moving fast, too many conversations are going on in languages I don't fully understand, some seem happy but untrustworthy, others appear hostile, and there's a hint of a bullying undertone.

To some, Twitter is a "guard your six" sort of social media, and they may not be cut out for its pacing. However, it remains the preferred method of access to editors and agents. It is the home of digital events like PITMAD, a pitch war event that solicits book pitches from authors and often leads to hard-to-come-by book deals. Twitter definitely has a place in the book world, but it's not the end of the world if it's not your preferred watering hole.

The original chatroom—thought of like a corner pub—was a great invention, until I tried to talk shop with the other authors and realized I'd wandered into a rather unwelcoming hole-in-the-wall social spot. Unlike the authors of today, these writers were especially protective of their trade secrets and didn't want to share their tips with just anyone. This cold atmosphere simply wasn't for me.

However, chatrooms have since been replaced by Facebook groups—a more franchised sort of social spot. In these groups, you usually know what you're getting from the moment you enter, and you're free to leave at any time.

As an author, I belong to an almost unmanageable number of digital groups for readers, authors, bloggers, and more. Luckily, we can adjust our notification so the alerts about new posts and tags don't become overwhelming. Groups are a great way around shadow banning algorithms, *if* members have their notifications set to "on."

From a business standpoint, it's very helpful to belong to a few "author-only" groups, but only if the atmosphere is friendly and of a shared knowledge mindset where members are happy to impart what they know to help others succeed. If you sense even a hint of crab mentality or hostility, abort. But if you find a healthy author-only group, introduce yourself, participate by sharing what you know, and learn as much as you can from others.

This is digital social networking. Just keep a judicious mind when accepting advice and never forget your journey is unique. What works for some might not work for you.

Blogging is a personal platform that really allows authors to express themselves, but if we lack time to post content on social media, chances are we don't have time to write articles. I love the space and freedom of blogging when I have something of importance to share, but without social media my blog would get very little traffic. Blogging is most effective when we share the link to a blog post through social media, so the two go hand in hand.

In terms of the social scene, I view blogs as high-end cuisine. Blogs are ethnic and full of culture and flavor. You really get a full experience when a blog article is done right, but in this busy day and age, not everyone has time to sit down for a full meal, so courses are often abbreviated with bulleted information like *Three Failproof Ways to...* (you fill in the blank).

Author blogs that only announce upcoming books or describe characters and plots are what I consider the chain restaurants. They really aren't serving unique content, but if people are in the mood for their genre, they might pop in for a quick bite and check it out.

Newsletters are takeout. A newsletter is basically a blog on the move. The most crucial element of any newsletter or blog is to make sure links and images are as clickable as possible. Showing a picture and a blurb of an upcoming book with a broken link is the equivalent of grabbing fast food for dinner and realizing they forgot part of your meal when you get home. Make sure everything is included before you send it on its way!

And remember, too much fast food is never good. Newsletters that keep subscribers on a constant diet of junk mail will turn into overkill, and customers will eventually unsubscribe and move on. Be mindful of frequency. Serve something often enough to be appreciated, but don't overdo it.

Facebook is the food court of social scenes. It literally has everything, but the enthusiasm wears after you've eaten there a few hundred times. People figure out what they like and what they don't. As creatures of habit, they generally stick to the same corners and form patterns, and sooner or later everything starts tasting mass produced and stale.

But hey, it's storefront and user friendly. It's a cookie-cutter virtual identity for authors and a free resource to snag new shoppers.

Sometimes we have to be the guy wearing the weenie suit with the tray full of hot dogs on toothpicks soliciting new customers, because sometimes something so simple, simply works. But for those of you who don't want to suit up and perform, you can at least provide information to point readers to your store and post tempting promotions about your products.

Facebook was new and sexy at one time, until its hot little sister, Instagram, came around. Instagram is a hipster bar on the rooftop overlooking a chill city scene. It's all about the aesthetic and vibe. Seriously, too much talking and you will get dirty looks. Content takes a much more visual approach on The Gram, which might be why I prefer it to all the others.

The greatest drawback of Instagram for authors at this time, is the limitation to link content. And I warn that this detail may be outdated by the time you read this. Presently, if you have an Instagram profile, you can only include one link in your bio. All posted links in comments and content will show as text only and be unclickable. For this reason, it is imperative you have a landing page on your website or through a menu app that lists all your links in one place. That way, when you post, you can still have a "call to action" by pointing your audience to the link in the bio.

Tumblr is one of the more risqué hot spots. Their loose filters really allow for some spicy content.

Snapchat is the arcade sort of eatery—full of games and pool tables and fun. It's more about the entertainment than any lasting content. They have all the silly filters and you will definitely find younger generations running around there.

Pinterest is a catchall for bloggers. It can lead users to any outside source be it a store, Instagram, a website, or a random article online. It's very visually based, putting images first and language second.

Many authors use Pinterest to create digital vision boards for their book settings and character casts. I often use Pinterest to help me visualize a place or outfit I'm trying to describe. I find Pinterest to be a useful resource behind the scenes and tend to rely on it in a tool aspect more than a promotional one used to connect with readers, though I do have some book content circulating there.

Sites like Goodreads are similar to country clubs, meaning they serve members only. In this case, members are those belonging to the book industry, including readers, authors, publishers, agents, editors, and publicists. Do not underestimate the power of a social site custom developed for your industry. Make it a priority to know what they offer and think critically about how their membership can serve your business.

Then there is the old classic, LinkedIn. LinkedIn is the reserved business atmosphere where quiet midday needs are met. It's not really a place for socializing as much as it's a place for finding sustenance on the job. LinkedIn hosts an educated clientele. More than 40% of users claim an annual income above the national median. It's not flashy because it doesn't have to be. Its elite users know what they need, and they're only there to meet a need and get back to business.

And then there is TikTok, the new kid on the block that has somehow managed to establish itself in the obscure, under visited territories of cyber society and avoid most of the toxic backwash filtering through other platforms. TikTok is still so new, I don't expect it to remain untouched by social media toxicity, but for now, their algorithms are so pure and finite, it's doing something the others no longer do.

I see TikTok as the Jetson's Kitchen. It's futuristic, completely customized to each person's specific tastes. It's fast and satisfying and manages to feed a part of the soul other platforms have only managed to steal from.

This perception is so transient and delicate, it shouldn't exist, but I think it tells a lot about the mutation and evolution of incoming social platforms. Even my least loved social networks were fun at one time, but eventually the experience changed.

What changes? Is it us or them? Have we overindulged and grown tired of the selection? Or is it inflation and monetization? Perhaps it's because we've now seen "how the food is made" and know we are all being worked into calculations and tracked and spoon fed information. Perhaps we always return to that natural desire for something organic.

TikTok is currently more organic than its predecessors, but its survival depends on mass production. Like all the others, it will create methods for monetization and alter the natural selection of content to something more targeted, and the newness will wear away.

Then another social scene will appear and the cycle will continue. It's an unending process of development, so when I hear of a new platform and authors ask me if I plan to sign up, I ultimately say no.

If I visited every social scene available I'd never get any work done. I prefer to wait and watch. Every site seems to proclaim it's the next best thing, but only a few achieve that high ranking status of the conglomerate platforms listed above.

For now, I have my favorites, selected simply because of their unintrusive ease, where I visit often. I keep a select few in my peripheral vision, since I have an automated presence there. And the others, well, I might stop by on occasion, but they aren't part of my usual routine.

This lean diet of social media grazing isn't what was suggested to me when I first became a signed author, and it isn't what my colleagues universally do, but it's what works for me. I treat social media as a means to an end. I only visit to meet my needs, and once said needs are met, I leave. Just like a restaurant, just like a bar, the kitchen's gotta close and we don't always have to hang out until last call.

Initially, social media was such a new way to interact, there was very little to compare to it. YouTube, Facebook, Twitter, and all the rest that followed were not initially expected to last, yet, here we are, more than a decade later, and this is the social world we live in.

Social media is not the only way to generate sales. As a matter of fact, very few authors see an equal profit compared to the amount of time invested on social networks. But it is definitely useful in terms of networking and generating leads.

Never forget, it's a social element, a business lunch, a cocktail after five. Do not forget you're on the job, but also don't make it into a second job, unless you plan to actually give up writing and shift careers into that of a media personality.

While social media can be satisfying in small increments, too much can wind up costing you money instead of making it for you. As authors, your first loyalty should be to yourself and your second to the readers. Readers love seeing authors online, but ultimately, they want books more.

The Social Following

Having a social presence as an author also comes with a social following. While the need for a social presence can be seen as both a blessing and a curse, our following is mostly a source of positivity—unless we're struggling to grow one.

Click farms, fake followers, giveaway whores, and creepers are not what anyone considers a genuine "follower." For a follower to be genuine, they should identify with your messaging, brand, or product line. Your social presence should resonate with them enough that they interact with your feed.

Followers that fill a space like a corpse in a morgue are basically dead weight. They're just a number, not a sale. And if they aren't buying your books or your vibe, then they really aren't any use at all. And yet, we all place immense value on watching our following grow.

Once again, it comes down to the illusion of fame versus the reality of success. My following has been grown from pure organic material. I have loved and nurtured it over time, and it is incredibly loyal to me, as I only feed it the best of myself and avoid stuffing it full of bullshit preservatives.

If I share something with my following, they know it is real. I don't allow paid ads from outsiders on my page, I don't endorse unfamiliar brands, and I've learned to stop recruiting followers through arbitrary methods. Meaning, if someone only signs up for my newsletter or follows me on Instagram to enter in a giveaway for a gift card, chances are they don't care about my content and won't read my newsletters.

Numbers aren't everything. Yes, the size of your following counts for something, as it establishes social influence, but in the book industry, our capital should come from book sales, and if your following has no interest in purchasing books, they aren't the kind of followers you need.

There are countless books and classes that advise business owners how to grow a following, but they all end on the same note—an organically grown following is the most valuable, and the best way to achieve that is to be your authentic self.

Followers want to be entertained, educated, or inspired. They do not want to be sold to, and if they sense they are, then they will tune you out.

For the longest time, I made the mistake of looking at what I could get from my following, when in actuality, we get the most by first thinking of what we can *give* them. I'm not talking about gift cards and giveaways. I'm talking about intangible, emotional connection.

Human connection is the most genuine gift we have to offer in this life, and when it's real, it doesn't matter how it's dressed or if it's wearing makeup, or what it drives. Good business stems from the ideal that listening and appreciating the customer will bring about a return.

By watering down all the glamourous expectation and simply being ourselves, by offering authentic interactions with meaningful conversation, we remove a great deal of the social anxiety associated with *looking* a certain way or *filling* a specific mold.

When we try to entertain, we naturally come off less authentic. The truth is, we are most entertaining when we're behaving as our true selves. That is what the outside world wants to see and what your followers want to know—you. So keep being you.

You are diverse. You are multifaceted. You are not merely "author." You might be a hot mess on most days, but so is most of the world. Let that be the reason you're so relatable if that's the real you.

Figuring out *who* I am has been an ongoing process, spurred by my desire to market myself as a brand. When I started, I wanted to be all luxury and high quality. I wanted to represent professionalism and poise. I achieved that, but I was hiding so much.

When I wrote Calamity Rayne, my first romantic comedy, my editor advised me to write something strictly for the fun of writing, and Calamity was born. She's more like me than any other character I've ever written.

At the end of Calamity Rayne, in the *About the Author* section, I would typically paste my stuffy bio talking about where I live and what accolades my books have earned, but instead, I wrote a little confession about the real me.

I told the reader Lydia Michaels was a loud-mouthed introvert who likes to pretend she's one of those people that does yoga and eats kale every day, but that would be a lie. I confessed to being a scattered disaster most days and sixteen at heart. It felt so good to share my truth, I went right to the front of the book and dedicated the story to me—the real me—a dorky, hypochondriac, who traded in her chalk for a quill and jumped into a new career with a half-ass parachute.

To this day, I'm choked up by the emotional liberation that book brought. And my readers adore it. They love the flawed depiction of an adult woman fumbling through life trying to make sense of it all, because who isn't doing that?

It's a terrifying thing, sharing our true self with the world. We're fragile and no one likes feeling especially vulnerable. But vulnerability is relatable. We need to give trust to get it. And love is a by-product of love. At some point, if we're seeking something real in return, we have to give something real of ourselves.

We have the tools to frame ourselves in the best light, share the best parts of our journey, and build our brand as big and shiny as we please. But don't get so wrapped up in the image that you lose sight of your natural beauty as a perfectly flawed human being.

In regard to growing a social following, social media can be an enormous undertaking. It is the whale and you are the fisherman. You may conquer it, but just as easily it could swallow you. Stay in control, above the surface, and keep a little distance.

Do not equate the size of your following to your worth as a person. Your rank on social media is not an accurate measurement of your talent as a writer. Be patient. Be true. And your readers will eventually find you.

Choosing the Right Platform

Every genre has a demographic. Just as some followers will want to interact with you socially, others may only take interest in your stories. And while some might want to follow you on one social site, others will wish you were on another.

The more exposure you want, the wider the platform you desire, the thinner you will have to spread yourself. It's helpful to automate your content so it repeats on as many networks as possible.

Loyal Facebook users, the ones who love the platform and are most at home there, may not bother with its sister sight, Instagram. And Instagrammers who jumped onto social media after the Facebook wave, might see Facebook as The Gram's older, less cool sister. If you study the audiences, you will learn there's typically a dominant generation and climate for each site.

Millennials tend to dominate Instagram, followed by converted Gen X's and incoming Gen Z's. Facebook was first a Gen X playground until everyone's parents showed up. Now it's dominated by baby boomers. Twitter, well, Twitter is for any generation so long as they know how to speak in 280 glyphs or less.

Then there are the sites like Pinterest, where I believe bloggers and moms mostly play. Tumblr is for the frisky sorts. And Snapchat is for the younger crowd.

Yes, I just threw out some wildly stereotypical assumptions. To be clear, no social media group is fully occupied by one demographic alone, but there is definitely a fluidity and vibe that can only be learned through experience and time. To save time, I've shared my overall impression based on the year this book was released. Again, anything associated with technology will always be transient, so do your own research and don't rely on my observations alone.

It's helpful to know the demographic of various platforms, especially if you are using social media for business. If you are targeting Young Adult readers, knowing where the younger social users are hanging out might really help your sales. Ask others where they think your demographic is and check it out. It might not be a platform you'd first choose, but if it's where your readers are hiding, you could really benefit from belonging.

For instance, if I published a cookbook, I would definitely become more active on Pinterest, as Pinterest is the first place I look for recipes when I have my mom pants on. But if I wrote a novel about a gamer, I might consider becoming more active on YouTube, Discord, or Twitch. It all comes down to the audience you're after and what you're trying to sell.

Your demographic may include all or some of the above, which is why your following should be a diverse collection from multiple platforms. Don't alter your personality, just distribute content evenly through integration tools.

Consistency is in the messaging and the vibe, as well as the posting schedule. More time will allow you more freedom to custom tailor posts for each platform, but here in the real world, where authors are hardly compensated for their time, we try to preserve as much energy as possible and work as efficiently as possible so we can get back to what matters most—writing.

No one is going to report you for recycling a Facebook post on Twitter. You know why? Because most Facebook users aren't on Twitter. Just create relevant content, post it where your relevant audience will see, and move on.

Do that and your platform will organically grow.

Social Supplements

Everyone wants to survive on a healthy diet of organic matter, but most days we're all navigating some level of a shit show, so it comes down to whatever will keep us alive—for now. This is why there are supplements. *Supplements* are used to supply a deficiency or reinforce a whole. They are parts, fractions, toppings. There is supplemental income, vitamin supplements, and even social supplements.

Because you've read part one and are now living a stunning example of a well-balanced author life, we'll assume your need for social supplements is not due to burnout but due to circumstances outside of your control. Let's assume your Nanna broke her hip and you're her caretaker for the next two months. Poor Nanna.

Nanna is not an easy patient. While you are able to write a few words each day, you have little time for anything else. Between doctor visits, physical therapy, meal prep, and personal care, your time is completely monopolized by Nanna. Had you worked outside the house, your family circumstances might have demanded you to take personal leave. But you work for you, so there isn't someone who can cover for you in your absence.

Rather than trying to do it all, you might fall onto some quick and dirty shortcuts. Let's make a rule right out of the gate that a shortcut should never be a long-term solution or your norm. The norm is a natural approach. It's holistic and organic and grown from love and time. But right now, you need something fast. You need a way to connect with readers, give your following a little boost and get back to Nanna.

If you want a jolt in numbers, there are countless methods for stimulating new followers. Just don't expect them to be as genuine or satisfying as the real thing—the reader who read your book and loved your skill and shared an actual human interaction with you on social media.

Quick and Dirty Social Supplements:

1. Host a contest or giveaway
2. Participate in a Hop
3. Hire a PA to manage your social accounts
4. Share others' content
5. Pay for advertising

Of course, as soon as Nanna is back on her own and you're back to work, you will ease off the impersonal supplements and go back to the organic method of posting and marketing, which will benefit your brand's overall health long-term.

Organic Practices that Nourish a Brand Over Time:

1. Include a visual with every post
2. Share more videos
3. Interact with the community through comments and likes
4. Follow others
5. Customize your content
6. Always include a call to action and a reason why people should follow you
7. Use relevant hashtags
8. Tag others and encourage them to tag you
9. Promote popular posts through paid ads with targeting

Physically Socializing

Author events are a great way to meet readers, industry professionals, and other authors. However, they are not a great way to produce instant revenue. Think of author events as long-term social investments.

In the *Health & Wellness* sections we addressed the cost of these events, establishing that beyond the expensive entry ticket, fees for travel and lodging, and inventory overhead, there is also the expense of time and health. And while some authors do sell out their inventory, the expense of these events typically far outweighs the profit.

In terms of book signings and other author events, I advise writers to consider the ROI and ROJ, return on investment and return on joy. These networking events will draw new readers, some more than others. They also create fantastic networking opportunities for professionals. And sometimes they are just plain fun.

So how do you get the most out of an author event? Once again, it comes down to disruptive content. You want to catch the attention of your audience and make them stop in their tracks at your station. Some authors really go over-the-top and treat signings like conventions, but this is a lot of work that requires a lot of planning and equipment.

Other authors sell items at their table, which lures shoppers. Shoppers do not always equal readers. A shopper that purchases merchandise may not return to your product line again. They are a one and done customer, where a reader who purchases a book could return and read your work for years, as well as create new sales through word of mouth.

Your goal should be to sell books and expand your network to other readers. To sell books you need to be identifiable as a "good author." You do not want to be identified as the author who "has really cool shirts and bags." Your books need to be your breadwinning product or you're doing your company a disservice.

Books are a renewable source of income. The life of a book can outlive the author. If we write quality stories, they will eventually sell themselves. But if we rely on meaningless merchandise, we create an ongoing need to continuously update the exports. Inevitably, by doing so, we've wasted time designing novelty items rather than books.

Save your energy. Work on books. Sell books. Books will produce sustainable revenue for authors long-term, even if it doesn't seem like it at first.

Novelty merchandise cannot perpetuate the emotional satisfaction for a customer the way a book can. Customers are more likely to love your story than your novelty mug. One sale will lead to another because one product holds their heart while the other just holds a forgettable cup of coffee.

But how do we sell books to readers when we're attending events with a hundred other authors? If we aren't hocking merch or tempting readers to our table with shiny things, how do we successfully stand out? How do we get them close enough to interact on a personal level and build that feeling of trust that leads to a sale?

If an author event features a large group of authors, you might think about investing in a sponsorship. Reach out to the hosts and take a meeting to discuss sponsorship opportunities. They will likely have a generic package, but don't be afraid to think outside of the box. Before your meeting, think about how you can make your brand as prominent as possible, so readers instantly identify you as an author worth checking out.

Make a list of possible promotional options to discuss. Try to get a banner into a prominent area where it can make a first impression and doesn't have to compete with all the other banners. Have an idea of what you're willing to spend, and remember, everything is negotiable.

I recommend that authors avoid disposable swag, meaning if it isn't something of value, it will likely land in the trash. Authors have filled landfills with business cards, bookmarks, and other paper merchandise. At most events, swag is in such abundance it devalues the instant the goody bags are filled. When a reader rummages through a bag stuffed to the gills with branded paper products, their hand is most likely going to stop on the more substantial items like pens, notebooks, compact mirrors, headphones, novels, and so on.

My suggestion is, if an author wants to contribute swag, buckle down and invest in something that could lead to a book sale. The best option is most likely a free book.

I know. Books are expensive. Even at the discounted author price, they are several dollars. And if the event has a few hundred attendees, that's quite a bit of books. But they won't throw them away. Most will eventually read it, and if they like it, they could end up buying your other stories. How likely is it that a pen with your logo can do the same?

Always be thinking about your ROI. Just because something is affordable does not mean it is useful. Invest in merchandise that will not only be useful, but will also lead to a sale.

Events typically offer many opportunities to socialize. Beyond the signing, there can be boardrooms to visit, banquets, award shows, theme parties, excursions, and so on. This is where authors often cash in on their ROJ, but when they do that, they're missing a massive ROI they might not have considered, so I'm going to spell it out for you.

The parties are for the readers. There, I said it. The event hosts will hate me for saying this, but authors need to realize what isn't openly advertised.

When signings offer after-parties, the majority of the time they are for the readers. However, the event hosts are dependent on the authors also attending so they can meet their quota and sell enough tickets to make a profit. And yes, it's typical for authors to require a ticket, whether it's a complimentary one or a purchased one.

The author-reader after-parties are usually a fun time. There are cocktails and music and familiar faces. They are definitely worth a walk through. But as an author, you won't want to linger.

You will find a bigger ROI at the hotel bar. It doesn't matter if you drink or not, the opportunities are there, in that laidback lounge where only a few people are sitting at the start of the night. Eventually more will come.

If you are sitting at the bar, set a book out so you have something to keep you busy but also a red flag that says "I'm a book person." Other book people will arrive and you could find yourself sharing a book chat and cocktail with your idol. Or, better yet, a literary agent or publisher.

You have a higher chance of making an authentic connection one-on-one in that bar than you do in a ballroom with a hundred other people and music blasting. The exception to this rule is, of course, author only events, which tend to be low key and more conducive for networking.

So before you buy that after-party ticket, decide if you are after a ROJ or an ROI. I can't count how many times I learned of a book deal coming from a connection made at a bar.

That being said, this is a great time to remind you that authors live in the fictional world of pseudonyms. Never say a negative thing about anyone at a business event. Just because you're speaking to Pepper Penmanship doesn't mean she doesn't go by another name. For all you know, she could have six other pen names. She could also work as an editor for the publishing house you've been dying to write for—and yes, she would likely use a different name there. Always be on your best, professional behavior because you never know who is watching or listening.

Author events are exciting and it's easy to get carried away, which is why your purpose should always return to the ROI or ROJ. Attending an event simply because it's fun, is fine, so long as you can justify the cost.

Maybe the event is in England and you turn it into an opportunity for a family vacation. Or maybe your idol author is attending and you want to meet her. But if there is not an ROJ, it will always come down to ROI.

At signings, the ROI should result in either book sales or a book deal, which will eventually lead to more book sales. It seems simple, but the amount of additional expenses pitched to and bought by authors as "promo opportunities" has surpassed that of measurable returns. Never take your eye off the profit.

Mini-events that require authors to purchase yet another ticket, contribute prizes and more merchandise, plus donate a substantial amount of their time before and during the event, quickly accumulate into a business expense with little to no return. You are a salesperson, but so is the event host. In the case of the event host, both authors *and* the readers are fair game. Be aware of when you are being sold to and be judicious about how and where you invest your money!

Opt in to events that put you in a prime position to speak about your books to an audience that wants to learn about your books. The presence of a big name anchor author is a great way to attract readers, but you don't want too many authors or you won't find a decent spotlight.

The sweet spot is usually 3 to 7 authors, as long as there is a draw for readers. You might need a larger crowd to create that draw in your earlier career.

If you buy into a mini-event with only a few other authors, you're on the right track. However, if the event is a ho-down and the whole theme is ho-down bingo and hay bales and line dancing, will you actually get a chance to talk about your books? Will the audience be readers interested in purchasing and reading books? Or will the audience be party-goers who wanted an excuse to wear denim jackets, boots, and a cute hat?

The host of any event, especially an event you paid to join, should advertise the authors more than the theme because, the bottom line is, you won't sell as many books at a ho-down or a biker bar or a masquerade as you would at a simple no frills author speaking event.

The best author events are still the ones hosted by a conglomerate bookstore willing to feature you as the main event or you and a few others. This scenario is great for authors because the bookstore handles the advertising, overhead, and they supply a well-established audience that follows their company for one purpose, to buy books.

If you want to sign at a bookstore but you are not traditionally published, there are a few things you can do to enhance your chances. First, purchase your ISBNs—don't accept free ones! This helps your books land in brick-and-mortar stores.

Second, get to know the bookstores in your local area. Speak to the staff and managers and make a lasting impression. Don't forget to leave them with a card and perhaps a complimentary book so they don't forget you.

Third, cold call bookstores and introduce yourself. Ask about possible event opportunities. It might not be a signing, but speaking in front of a book club interested in your genre will still lead to sales. Plus, the bookstore will stock your titles ahead of time, so you know you're already getting paid.

In terms of physical events, you want to avoid practices that feed into the illusion of success. Stay aware of how you're spending your energy and what your choices are actually costing you on a whole, especially where time is concerned.

Do not waste energy on practices that counteract a consumer's incentive to buy. If a book signing looks more like a craft show, and writers are selling more novelty merchandise and tchotchkes than books, or autographing free swag without making many book sales, it is not your audience, and the event host has failed to deliver their part of the bargain. Save your time, money, and energy for events that promise a return.

The Social Impact

Ultimately, the goal of any socialization is to form a connection and leave a lasting impression. Whether you do that virtually or physically will be up to you. Your strengths are someone else's weaknesses and vice versa. Learn from others, but rely heaviest on what best suits you.

There are endless ways *authorpreneurs* can diversify their brand in this industry, but this book advocates the benefits of working smarter to create quality stories first and mastering the art of salesmanship second. The beauty of social marketing is that it takes a natural approach to socializing. The moment we realize that and stop trying to shove our products down everyone's throats, it becomes a lot easier to manage.

Authorpreneurs tend to repeat business behaviors with little to no ROI because—wait for it—it's what authors do. This is a simple excuse of justifying poor practices because they are bulk practices. The majority is not always correct. Do not follow patterns with little to no measurable proof of profit.

Quality products lead to measurable sales and return customers. Producing fresh products will grow your audience in a way that sustains your business long-term, whereas advertising, or relying solely on social practices, can only take a brand so far and ultimately wanes the moment an author's efforts stop.

Authors must write. It's that simple.

Too often, the same reoccurring author names appear on event lists, and many of those authors are peddling the same two titles they released five years prior. Their growth has stagnated, because the focus they place on marketing and slow-profiting social practices has dominated their business habits and produced a deficit in their writing time.

While it's important to recognize how people consume information in modern times and know how to adapt your business accordingly, selling books will always require the act of writing books more than any sort of personable, sunny disposition.

Don't overthink the social expectations. Recognize the benefits, but remember it's only a snapshot, a highlight reel, a glimpse into a bigger picture.

Social media is a peephole. It offers an extremely limited glimpse into the worlds of others. Networking is a door. But the foundation on which you stand is formed from time, ink, and paper (or a screen in this day and age).

Without books, we have nothing to stand on as authors. The greatest impact your career leaves on this world should ultimately come from your words, so write them and write them well.

Chapter Fourteen
Social Monetization

"An entrepreneur with strong network makes money even when he is asleep."

Amit Kalantri, Wealth of Words

The Social Salesperson

Without monetizing your social following, chances are it's not as lucrative as you'd like to believe. The slow burn benefits of sustaining an active audience on social media often demand a large commitment of authors. Just as water will always find its level, an author's baseline tends to settle at his or her greatest supporters and superfans—those who one-click without even knowing what the book is about.

In an attempt to grab the attention of new customers, authors have fallen into snake oil salesman practices, doing whatever possible to get people's attention while spending as little as possible. Here's what I know. If you are catching followers with carrots, you're likely catching fools, and readers are far from foolish.

We are not selling candy or clothing or novelty toys. We are selling books—literature—and the clientele, by nature, is sophisticated. Desperate author promotional behavior will come off desperate. And what do we do when we sense someone desperate hitting on us? We run in the opposite direction.

Putting up a large gift card giveaway or participating in hops might give your numbers a boost, but how many of those new followers are genuine? How many were obtained with an authentic interest in *your* work? How many will stay? How many plan to actually *read* a book this month? How many do you honestly expect to put food on your table in a month or a year?

The only thing an author gains from these types of investments are placeholders, higher numbers that might persuade an authentic reader to also follow due to popularity. But unauthentic place holders are not loyal readers, and they do not equate to sales.

So why do authors waste so much time worrying about acquiring dead space followers? Because larger audiences garner greater access to opportunity. While your audience may not be forged of readers, if it's large enough, it can throw around its weight to open new doors and draw readers in.

Some social sites offer incentives to users with larger audiences. You might gain access to "Swipe Up" options on stories or earn that fancy blue check that authenticates your account or find new options to sell through your platform. These are all excellent tools that can lead to more book sales but only if an author knows how to use them.

However, the best audience will always be an authentic one. For authors, that is an audience of readers, as readers will always be our most likely customers.

Authors have an obligation to study each social platform's audience if they want to adapt good business habits. If they want to do the bare minimum, then perhaps simply having a presence is enough.

But if they want to really optimize their social media ROI (return on investment), they will have to get savvy about how they use apps.

What social media is to readers is not what it will be to authors. The unfortunate outcome of using social media for business is that it, inevitably, loses its luster. From the business end of the looking glass, we don't always see the relaxing, entertainment general users enjoy. But general users aren't making money from the app, and you are—if you're savvy.

Be truthful of what activities actually provide an ROI and which do not. Then cut the fat.

As a business owner and brand, you should position yourself as an expert in your field. You can be low key or trendy or high energy, just as long as you're professional and authentic to your brand. By no way does professional have to equate to stuffy or cliché appearances. Figure out what *your* professionalism looks like and embrace that.

Carve out your niche. Followers generally want to be inspired, educated, or entertained. As an author, you provide a service. Your products—books—help readers achieve *what*? Fill in the blank. You determine who you are and what your books do. What is the problem you solve?

Be clear about your content! While it's okay to post a picture of your pet or your favorite cocktail to add a little variety to your feed, never forget what you're selling. No matter how off the grid your photograph might be, the text should point the user back to your brand, and vice versa.

What are you selling? Think of your messaging. We're all selling books, but what else? What's your messaging?

On my page, I'm selling books, optimism, inspiration, and feminism. That's my brand, my flavor, my general messaging that comes through my vibe and products. It reflects my desire to lead a joyful life, my devotion to hard work and following one's dreams, and my romantic spirit. Sometimes this shows in food posts that nurture the soul or a picture from a gratitude walk that morning or an inspiring quote from a woman of power, but all of that relates back to my writing and the characters I craft.

Navigate your audience's journey from a position of expertise and think of yourself as the guide. Know where your audience is and where they want to go. Help them travel from A to B.

In a story arc, the guide is an important side character. And while we are all the main characters of our own stories, as the salesperson on social media, you will have to step back and let the customer play the lead role.

If that doesn't make sense, think of Yoda. Even non *Star Wars* fans should have a concept of this little philosophical green guy. Another Yoda would be Mr. Miyagi from *The Karate Kid*. If you're unfamiliar with both of those roles, think of Cinderella's fairy godmother.

While none of those characters are the "main characters" they are all crucial to the story and extremely memorable. This archetype role is commonly known as the "helper" or "guide" in a story arc, and their purpose is to lead the main character where they need to go.

The salesperson is the "helper" and there to gently lead, but never steal the customer's thunder. You should always appear more interested in their story than yours. Be the Sam to their Frodo, the Jacob to their Bella, the Robin to their Batman, or the Dr. Watson to their Sherlock Holmes.

With your subtle guidance, you can lead them to a place of confidence. That feeling of confidence comes the moment you help them meet their needs. Their need, if you're working with the right sort of audience, is a book. Good thing you have many fine crafted ones to offer!

This might happen by identifying a popular book that's been trending in your genre or field area, sharing the reader experience with them, and then subtly directing their attention back to your products which relate.

The art of closing a deal rests in the imperceptibility of the sale. This is achieved through non-intrusive engagement and trust. By framing yourself as their reliable guide, you're more interested in listening to them than speaking to them. Your interaction is not a traditional sales pitch in that you are not actively selling. You are merely engaging in an atmosphere where the backdrop is a display of your product line.

At this point, you should truly grasp the "virtual storefront" theory. You've created a social profile and filled it with branded background, but those branded graphics are only your signage and displays. You're about people first and products second. Your friendly interactions and genuine interest keeps people in your store or at least keeps them coming back.

You do not say "buy this" or "try that," you merely position them in a place where they can naturally notice what you offer. Your products hide in the wallpaper, silently influencing through exposure. Your interactions have nothing to do with selling and everything to do with human connection, which is exactly why it's called *social* media.

The consumer, ultimately, has to connect the dots and decide for themselves to feel that surge of connection and confidence, the gratification of knowing their needs have been met. Their needs create a problem and your products are the solution.

People do not remember words as much as they remember the emotions associated with something said. By giving followers pleasant feelings of good conversation and having their needs satisfied, we create a trigger that then associates us and our brand with positive feelings of success in their minds, and that is the hidden magic of a master salesperson.

Brand Transparency

Trust is a major selling point in today's social climate. There are too many competitive options out there for consumers to choose, so we must give as much as we get. Offer free advice to bridge the gap between their needs and your services. If they are looking for books, host interesting book chats with your brand in the backdrop.

The ultimate goal is to convert non-buyers into consumers of your brand. We want to ultimately turn all of our followers into customers. If you use vanity metrics, numbers gained by gimmicks like "follow unfollow" or arbitrary giveaways that attract the wrong followers, the conversion won't be easy. Ideally, you want a warm audience—in the case of authors—people who, at least, read books.

Make sure that your brand is completely clear. Use the options permitted in the bio section of every platform. Use keywords so that algorithms can find you. Authors often clarify their brand with a single link that branches to many links and possibly an introduction video that welcomes new clients. Your bio is your generic greeting to shoppers as they pass through your store.

Your display—content—should be disruptive yet somewhat anticipated. Meaning, followers like consistency and should know what to expect from your page.

Don't over brand your content to the point that your feed appears plastic. You want that raw, organic vibe even if your image is sleek luxury. Unique content will pop off the page, but everything should feel like it's relevant and belongs.

Know your brand. Know your preferred fonts, your codes for your brand's color schemes, and your messaging. These details should be at your fingertips at all times if you want a cohesive display.

Do not be the predatory salesman. Be genuine. Engage with people, not just on your feed, but on other people's feeds. Do this for the human connection, not the sale. The sale is a natural consequence of the connection, so you don't need to force it.

Think of an author you admire, someone who has really enjoyed success in a niche similar to yours. Interact with their content, not as a self-promoting prick, but as someone who enjoys their brand and the company of others enjoying their brand. Be the consumer for a change. Other consumers will see you as an ally and connections will form. Connections lead to followers and followers should ultimately lead to consumers.

Just be sure to never talk about your own work in someone else's store. Posting on someone else's feed without permission is the lowest of lows in terms of tacky salesmanship. Behaving this way will not end well.

Do not poach other author's audiences without permission. If you have permission, it will be discussed ahead of time as a collaboration project or cross-promotion. Violating this protocol and jumping in with your own sales pitch uninvited is the equivalent of crashing a private dinner party, whipping out your private parts during the main course, and screaming look at me! It's just bad.

It looks bad to the host. It looks bad to the guests. But most of all, *you* look bad, rude, unbalanced, and completely unprofessional, so zip it up and wait your turn.

Don't butt in where you're not invited, but do open a dialogue to cross-promote if you're looking for an invitation. It's okay to pitch to a fellow author behind the scenes, as long as it's away from the customer's view.

Once you've cultivated an authentic audience—quality over quantity—you will have a better idea of your demographic. Use the analytic tools to review the provided details about the gender, age, location, and lifestyles of those following you closely. You might be surprised who your content is resonating with most, and you might want to change your language or content to reach other demographics you didn't realize you were missing.

I understand analytics can often read like stereo instructions, but as a business owner, you should at least explore the stats offered. Over time, the format will become more familiar. Dedicate ten to thirty minutes to glance at your analytics every week or so, and soon, the data will become familiar and help you navigate your audience and brand more accurately.

If your data shows that your presence is resonating with a specific and active demographic and a big brand wants to tap that demographic, they may team up with you to run a cross-promotion. Collaboration projects are great ways to hit new audiences and lure in fresh readers.

For authors, this might come in the form of co-authoring a biography with a celebrity or pairing products with books in a way that spotlights a specific brand you enjoy. Collaborations are the hidden spine that keeps social media standing.

You can open yourself up to collaboration projects by supporting other brands that share your niche. Highlight products and strategically place them in the background or foreground of your content.

Tag the other brand. The tag will trigger their notifications, and if they like what you've posted, they might repost it and tag you, thereby triggering their followers to notice and possibly follow you back.

Ultimately, your goal is to monetize. If that comes in the form of audience growth and consequential revenue, great! But it can also come in the form of paid collaboration projects. Just keep in mind that your brand is that of an author. But never forget you are a person first.

You're not just selling books, you're selling a specific mindset and vibe. Branded, flat content that shows no sign of life or energy is not vibe.

Speak from the heart. Be thoughtful with your words. Stop trying to sell and start listening. Be humble, open, and personable. The right content will attract the right audience. The goal of healthy growth is longevity.

The law of success states that sales are most likely to happen when you surrender your personality to adapt the personality traits of the customer. This only works for authors if your customer has the necessary qualifications of a reader. Don't play the chameleon to a non-reading follower who only found you because you were giving away gift cards.

Most business models advise not to expect a profit during the first year, so establishing a social presence during that time is an acceptable loss that will have benefits later. Desperate behaviors will only slow you down.

Your product line should be the background. You, the helper, are who the customer has come to see. The experience is designed to subtly highlight you, but it works best if you make it primarily about them.

If your schedule only allows you to be present once a month, then so be it. But make it count. Don't waste that moment with plastic gimmicks or sales pitches. Use it in a way that will leave a resounding impression with your followers and stir positive emotions.

Socializing, digitally or otherwise, generates leads only. Writing is your fastest path to dependable revenue.

Completed projects *are* proven to have a direct link to increased revenue. The entire purpose of unleashing your prolific potential is to produce high quality products—books—you can sell. New books lead to new content. Write the books so you have something fresh to market.

Book merchandise is a supplemental product and should not be your breadwinner. And gimmicks should not be your hook. Ask yourself, are you selling a subscription to your social life or are you selling well written, highly entertaining books? The answer is both, but only one yields a true royalty, so prioritize well.

Without a decent, productive product line, your inventory will suffer. Without fresh inventory, sales will falter. Direct your brain power where there is the greatest chance of a lucrative return.

Social Sustainability

The trick to making it in any business is sustainability. Your money maker is your product line, so nurture that following, but devote the majority of your time to writing high quality books.

Most authors could dial their social time back 90% and see no shift in sales. Keep in mind that once a reader becomes your customer, you have them. If they like you, they will buy your next book, but they can't repurchase something they already own. Your job is to keep them informed while attracting new customers.

The definition of *customer* is a person who purchases goods or services. Continue to create goods, and offer your services—literary entertainment—to your existing customers by writing books.

If you aren't steadily attracting new customers, your following will stagnate. A lively following should be willing to shop when a new product is revealed.

A business is an ecosystem and there is a delicate balance that must be maintained for it to function properly. Your author platforms are, first and foremost, platforms for interacting with readers. They are social. They are happy hours after the workday and you are there for business, but as a master salesperson, you're savvy enough to keep business out of the dialogue.

To the customer, this sort of networking should always feel fun. And good salesmanship will always stem from the way we make others feel. But most of all, once we find a sustainable way to manage social media while making money, this sort of work can become a fun part of the job for us as well.

Social Engineers

The days of the luddite author, those opposed to new technology or change, are gone. If your audience is so enormous you feel you're above social media, then this book is not for you. For most businesses who want to stay competitive with comparable brands, social media is a necessity.

However, when we are a sole proprietor of a company and responsible for production, marketing, inventory, accounting, and all the other areas that need managing, it's important that we monitor our time carefully and always keep an eye on the ROI.

Social media has infuriated much of the public with their intrusive data collection, but for brands, they've done us a great favor. As an author, you are your own brand. You might also be a customer, but first you are always a brand, so you should have at least a slight grasp of how data collection can benefit your business.

There are literally addiction engineers hard at work convincing users to come back and stay longer. Every interaction might seem accidental, but it's not. Each user, including you, is a calculation, a part of an algorithm, and while we can get up in arms about the sense of privacy violation this creates, I assure you there is no crime in accepting another's surrender.

Social media is a choice. Users choose to allow access to their privacy the moment they join. They can also choose to leave at any time and keep their private life private. But if you're a business owner, rather than leave, why not learn how to channel those algorithms in your favor?

There are countless documentaries doing exposes on the extreme socio-emotional impact of social media. The information gathering and engagement tactics seem endless, but should not come as a surprise. And while our first instinct might be to scream injustice, tech companies haven't taken anything without our permission, and they are doing so to create a smoother user experience, so they haven't violated our rights at all.

I don't want to see ads about duck hunting as I have no interest in such things. Ads for books, kitchen accents, or theme parties would please my brain much more, so I appreciate the personality-matched aesthetic if the advertisements are a must. And advertising is an inescapable part of our culture, so yes, they are a must.

Every social media platform starts with a consent form. Clicking *I Agree* means something, regardless of our personal belief system. If a person does not agree, they should not click or consent. At that point they no longer have the right to use or reap the benefits of that platform. It's that simple.

As a businesswoman, I *want* social media to study its users because they are saving me a job. When I pay for advertising, I can target my ads to people who are most likely to take interest in my products and make a purchase.

Data collection and ad targeting is very similar to buying leads in prior decades. Algorithms are simply modernized leads, and as a merchant, I want those leads to have a higher probability of selling my products.

Advertising Through Social Media

According to Hootsuite, 4.2 billion people use social media, and an average of 15.5 users join social media every second. Studies show more than 50% of consumers will follow a brand to stay up to date on new products. 89% of followers will visit a company's website.

The most common reason a customer unfollows a brand is due to low quality products, poor customer interactions, irrelevant content, or too many ads. More than 65% of customers claim to prefer video content[10]. While we want to alert our established customers of new products, we don't want to over advertise. They are already a member and part of your elite clientele. Save your ads for customers who have never heard of you before.

Paid advertising, or sponsored content, is an effective way to generate traffic or leads. Paid advertising is different from organic leads.

When content is sponsored by a brand, e.g. you, the sponsor is allowed to target the ad to a specific viewer, someone who identifies as a likely customer for their product line. For authors, this might be followers of a similar author, readers of a specific book, or members of a literary club.

The benefit of social media advertising is the measurable analytics generated by the ad provider. However, a good ad requires the right formula. Language, imagery, and targeting are all important, and if one is off, the ad could fail to deliver the desired results.

High performing ads can also go stale. Some ads cost more while others cost less but don't generate a decent CTR (click through rate).

Marketing is a job within itself, and social media allows businesses the ability to monetize and market through their platforms, but doing so requires time, money, and patience if you want to get it right.

For authors that do not want to invest that time, they can hire an SEO Consultant Firm to develop and manage their ads. But do not give an outsider access to your account or money simply because they "know how to run ads." There is an acquired skill to social advertising, and any PR firm you hire should

---

[10] GoodFirms

generate and show a measurable ROI. If they can't, you've been had. Don't pay an amateur when you're in need of a master.

If you prefer to run and monitor your own ads, I once again point you to YouTube, where countless tutorials exist. Just remember, at the end of the day, sponsored content is not organic content, and that is what the people want. To grow an organic audience, refer back to *The Social Salesperson* section.

If you choose to simply use social media for its free benefits, that's perfectly acceptable. Your business will grow at its own pace and your audience will be genuine.

Despite targeted advertising and the ability to sponsor paid content, there are very few reliable shortcuts to growing an authentic following in social media. The most you can do is collect leads and drive them to your platform, but it's always up to you to close the sale.

Unfortunately, throwing money at a problem doesn't always make it go away. I suggest experimenting with low-risk ads to get more familiar with the process. The beauty of social media ads is that you can set your budget and shut them off instantly if they're not performing properly. Just be sure to monitor the process as you go.

And while analytics are wonderful tools, if you do not know how to translate them, you could be losing money and not realizing it. Calculating your CPC (cost per click) is a matter of understanding the cost you, the advertiser, are paying per viewer click. Clicks are not necessarily sales.

If your book retails for $4.99 with a royalty rate of $2.70 and your CPC (cost per click) is $0.20, you have to deduct the CPC from every sale. So if you are selling 30 copies of a title each month without advertising, at a $2.70 royalty rate per sale, you're roughly making $81.00 a month on that title.

But if you're advertising, your sales should go up. Let's say they increase from 30 sales per month to 400 sales per month and your CPC is $0.20. Your $2.70 royalty drops to $2.50, but your book sales increases to $1,000.00 over one month's time. That's an increase in revenue of $919.00, and all profit, right? Wrong.

Just because someone clicks on your ad does not mean they make a purchase. You still have to pay for the clicks that don't end in sales.

While you've sold 400 copies of the advertised title, you might have paid for 2,500 clicks. At $0.20 a click, that comes out to $500.00 spent on running your ad.

If we sold 400 copies at $2.70 per copy, we should have a royalty of $1,080.00. To calculate the ROI, we must deduct the total cost of the ad ($500.00). Subtracting the monthly cost of the ad ($500.00) from the monthly royalty ($1,080.00) reveals the true profit of $580.00.

So what have we gained? Well, money, for one thing. Rather than make $81.00 in a month, you've made $580.00. That's practically a $500 increase in sales. Well done! But that's not where an author stops measuring profits.

The most profitable investment for authors is an investment that shows a return in exposure, especially when your products are being exposed to the proper customers. Exposure is the most needed ingredient of an author's survival.

Rather than 30 readers in possession of our product, we've put it in the hands of 400, calculated by the number of copies actually sold. This is clearly measurable progress.

However, all of us have purchased a book and failed to read it, so don't assume every purchase leads to instant consumption. Maybe only 300 of the people who purchased your book actually open it. And of those 300 readers, only 200 like it enough to become a return customer.

Authors rely on customer enthusiasm to sell more books, because nothing sells better than word of mouth. Word of mouth can come in the form of social exchanges or product reviews. To draw out those social exchanges, we interact with established customers on social media. New, curious readers see the interaction and are then influenced by the established customer's excitement.

Running ads is never just about one sale. It's always about the return customer. This is why many authors drop the price of some books to $0.99 or free. Advertising books that are free or marked down, creates an almost impossible to ignore enticement, causing a higher probability that their ad will get clicked.

But if an author is paying $200.00 on an ad for a free book, where is the ROI? If there is no profit through immediate royalty, as the retail price is zero dollars with a royalty of zero, then how do authors justify the cost of advertising? It's a loss, right? Wrong.

The return rests in the quality of the product. If the free book is high quality and the reader enjoys it, they will become a return customer and, hopefully, binge the author's backlist. All the other books are marked at regular retail price, so while the author hooked the customer with a free product, they profited by building a relationship based on service and trust.

The service was literary entertainment, which the author delivered to the customer's satisfaction. Trust in the author's brand has now been established, and as long as the author continues to deliver that sense of satisfaction, the customer will return, again and again, as they believe they will get their money's worth.

The sale never ends with the ad campaign. The ad lasted thirty days, but the sale potential of just one click, if it's the right click, can multiply into immeasurable sales and generate revenues for years to come.

So, yes, paid promotions create measurable returns, but there is always a gray area where the ROI blurs into the immeasurable. This can go both ways, resulting in an abundance of untraceable profit or an inexplicable loss of profit. It all comes down to how the masses ultimately consume and digest your product line.

If you market books that are disappointing, poorly edited, frustrating, or hard to follow, the customer likely won't return. Ultimately, the key to successful advertising relies heavily on a brand's product quality, which is why the craft section of this book is so important.

If authors want to see a profit and establish return customers, they must sell quality products. Writing a quality book is the foundation of every author's success. Without a decent product line, advertising can only get you so far.

Once you've established your product line, experiment with advertising. Remember to always have a clear call to action. The less hoops a consumer has to jump through, the better, meaning when paying for clicks, the less clicks required to make a sale, the better it is for your budget in the end.

But be warned, advertising is not a guarantee to success. There are no guarantees in this business.

Even a phenomenally well written story can sometimes fail to sell. Some ads simply don't pay off because the language is off or the image isn't as eye-catching as intended or the targeted audience isn't the right audience. This is why, if an author chooses to pay for advertising, they should have a decent understanding of the analytics.

An outrageous CTC (click through cost) is a red flag that something isn't right. Clicks with no correlating sales is another sign that something's fishy. Experimenting can be a costly endeavor, but to successfully run ads, one has to be willing to test the waters.

Start small, set your budget low, and get comfortable with the platform. Fair warning, just when you think you have it figured out, the platform will likely change and you'll have to learn the process all over again.

Why? Because technology is an always-improving fickle bitch. But if we want to benefit from all it offers, we have to be committed to continuing our education and understanding its capabilities so that we ultimately expand our own.

Social Balance

An author socializes virtually and physically. Virtual interactions are far more commonplace. Physical interactions are rarer, but require much more time and attention to prepare. Both subtract from writing time on the job, yet both are part of the job, so how do we determine what is enough and what is too little?

The key is balance and moderation. To avoid the negative impact of social media, experts recommend not opening social apps first thing in the morning. I, personally, suggest pushing social media off until the very end of your work day. That way, you will only have a concise time to get caught up before you leave the office, which will limit your exposure to possible toxicity.

Some authors go as far as removing the apps from their phones if they do not want the negative effects of over exposure seeping into their life outside of work hours. If you aren't comfortable being that disconnected, you might consider silencing your notifications so they aren't distracting you throughout the day.

Most phones have a screen-time monitoring system that will cut you off after a predetermined amount of time on a specific app. You can adjust such settings to your personal preferences, as well as ignore them when you don't feel like behaving, so it comes down to self-control.

Automation apps free up our time, but they are no substitute for human interaction. Authors should check in on a daily basis, but avoid spending all day checking in. Interact for a few minutes and sign out until tomorrow.

Having a constant presence on social media will not impact the return until the content is consistently engaging and diverse, until that genuine relationship and trust is formed. That's a very difficult standard to achieve, and being a frequent poster is not always the same as being a smart one.

What you post and how you interact will always matter more than the frequency of your posts, so do yourself a favor and save some of your precious time by creating thoughtful posts rather than incessant content that leaves followers cold.

Interact at your own, natural pace. Think about your mission statement, brand, and messaging. Develop a cohesive look and create reusable content for your backdrop. Rely on scheduling tools and plan ahead, but also show up on occasion to post something real and from the heart. Do that, and your following will stay engaged and grow.

But remember, to post news, you have to make news, so keep writing books and creating fresh new products. You'll have more time to write now that you've cut back the time dedicated to all that white-noise-nonsense you're no longer uploading to social media. By avoiding stale content and over advertising, your authentic self will pop and your vibe will shine. That's the healthy, less draining, organic way to manage a social feed and maintain a social balance.

Correspondence

I prefer not to conduct business deals through social media. Authors will frequently reach out to me via private messenger, and while I understand this seems convenient, it is not an efficient way for me to conduct business.

Authors typically open their email at a computer, at a desk. Social media interactions are often managed on the go, sitting on the couch, waiting for an appointment, or—dare I say—sitting on a toilet.

If you are trying to schedule a collaboration or pitch a cross-promotion, the author will need their schedule handy. Not all authors rely solely on the calendar app on their phone, so while they might mean well and say, "Sure, I'd love to help you," if you've caught them at a bad time, they might unintentionally forget.

If you want to be taken seriously and don't want to get inadvertently ghosted by a colleague, contact them at the office. The "office" is where they read their emails. The bathroom is not their office, and hey, it's a proven fact that bathroom time more than doubled since the invention of the smart phone, so don't act like you're above working from the throne.

If contacted through a social messenger, I will request they follow up with an email. If they do not, our business is done. If they repeatedly ignore my preferred method of contact, I feel less and less obligated to respond.

The exception to this rule, of course, would be if the person I want to work with prefers to converse via private messenger. In that case, I will make an exception to the rule.

I prefer to keep my social interactions light and manageable, another reason why I don't use social media as a direct means for making business deals. Aside from fifteen minutes at the end of each work day, I might schedule an hour to create content each week or run an ad. I don't invest a lot of time because time spent on social media does not always equate to a measurable ROI.

There is a skill to monetizing, as we've discussed. Any other time spent on social media, outside of purposeful monetization, should be solely about listening, engaging, and meeting the consumer's needs, not serving our own and not conducting business deals.

Mastermind Groups

One of the greatest resources I have as an author is the access to other authors. In an industry growing as rapidly as the book market, technology and strategy is changing faster than ever before, and collaboration is queen. *Mastermind groups*, or accountability groups, are peer-to-peer groups that focus on problem solving through discussion and are great ways to socialize and grow your knowledge as a professional.

When we share our thought process with other intellectuals, we become exponentially more informed because we can share experiences and backgrounds. This collective approach to expanding one's knowledge in a field is a great social way to enhance an author's career.

Mastermind groups can come in the form of conferences, symposiums, writing retreats, private digital groups located on social media, round table talks at coffee houses, or casual discussions with likeminded peers over a bottle of wine in a living room. As long as the premise remains the same and professionals are gathering to talk shop and grow their knowledge base, the result is a peer group.

Mastermind groups are so valuable for many reasons. When we collaborate with others, we share our knowledge. A colleague might have taken a $400 workshop. If they are a trusted peer, they may share their notes and knowledge and save everyone else the expense. Mastermind groups also create opportunities for networking, cross-promoting, and emotional support from likeminded colleagues who share your struggles.

To form an author mastermind group, define the purpose. A mastermind group could focus only on the craft, or it could venture into areas like marketing and querying publishers. Be sure to clearly identify these areas of focus for your members.

Next, determine the size group you want and set rules. Masterminds can often go sour when authors get discouraged and fall into a bitter headspace. Help authors cope with challenges by sharing experiences if they lead to advice, but do not allow this sort of negativity to infect your group. Set boundaries about attitude, respect, appropriate and inappropriate topics, and make sure that all members feel they're in a safe space to share.

Successful masterminds require a level of vulnerability. There should absolutely be a sacred rule of trust understood by all members. There is no room for narcissism or ego trips in a functioning group.

You will gain the most from a mastermind group if your team is diverse with similar beliefs and goals. You will want an eclectic group of backgrounds and experiences but also a shared objective.

Your group should feel comfortable interacting organically but should also convene on a formal schedule, be it once a year at a retreat or monthly at a coffee shop. Not all members will be able to make every meeting, and if your group only permits so many members, you may want to establish rules about attendance. Members should never take from a group without giving. For the group to function well, all members need to be present and actively participate in discussions.

Outlining the policies of the group will help start a group on the right footing. Think carefully about those you include. You will want to invite the right people who work well with others, are happy to share pieces of themselves, do not come off abrasive, and have a decent amount of experience in your field.

It also helps to plan the structure of meetings. Retreats will require daily schedules, and shorter meetings will require objectives. Allow members time to get comfortable. Sometimes, inviting a guest speaker to share helps others to open up and ask questions.

There are large, established groups like the RWA, Romance Writers of America, that host chapter meetings, which are essentially mastermind groups with speakers. You can make your mastermind as formal or as casual as you'd like. You can charge for memberships to help cover any meeting expenses or you can run your group free of charge.

The options are endless. Get creative. I host an annual author retreat every winter at my family's coastal home. There are usually a dozen authors in attendance, many of them repeat guests who have come for years.

Every year, I welcome the authors with a customized gift bag of their favorite writing goodies and some kind of merchandise to commemorate that year's retreat. The authors pay a fee for their meals and we do the cooking and cleaning as a community. We have quiet hours and social hours, and our nights are reserved for cocktails and shop talk.

This event has become one of my favorite things. The authors who have attended claim it deeply motivates and helps them as professionals. To know that I am a part of something with such a powerful effect is humbling, to say the least. But the most valuable thing I've gained from this experience is by far the friendships.

Being an author is an isolated profession, but it does not have to be a lonely one. Your people are out there. Take a leadership role, form a mastermind group of your own, and find them.

25 Takeaways of Social Media for Business

1. The majority of people using social media are on phones. Choose a recognizable profile picture that is easily identifiable as your brand. Think of the bullseye for Target, rather than the word Target, or the swish for Nike. Keep it simple and clear and use it on all platforms so your brand is uniform.

2. Remind yourself of your goal. Why are you on social media? The answer should be to create an author presence. If you said socializing, you should have two separate accounts—one for business and one for pleasure. You can socialize on your author account—it's encouraged—but never forget you're there for business. Business equals sales, so if the "socializing" isn't necessarily generating clicks or interest, you could be wasting time.

3. Brand your business! You should have easily accessible content with your logo. You should also have a digital logo you can slap on any graphic to brand it as yours. Branding is simply distinctive promotional material marked by a company's name or icon. This subtle formality alerts people that you're a public figure—especially if your account has yet to earn a verified symbol.

4. Learn basic graphic design! As a branded business, your promo should have a professional presence. It doesn't matter if your vibe is punk, prepster, or earthy, your graphics should have clean lines and legible messaging that resonates with the aesthetic you're after. There are great, *free* programs out there to get you started (my go-to's are Canva and iPiccy).

5. Do not infringe on copyrights! Just because a picture shows up on Google does not mean it's free. To create content with pictures you do not take, you will need to license photos for your promo. If you violate a copyright, your content will be taken down and you could wind up with your account suspended or worse. Authors are anti-pirate, so don't practice piracy with other people's art! Pay for your photos or use royalty-free photography from public domain sites.

6. Identify your audience and start recruiting. Interact with authors who write similar books to you and then interact with their fans.

7. Be a likeable person. Gimmicks will only get you so far. Be kind, gracious, thoughtful, and humble. But most of all, be your authentic self. I don't care if you're the kink-keeper of a dungeon or someone obsessed with cats to an unhealthy degree, be polite. The world is too big for us to waste time on mean people.

8. Be human. If your presence is too branded and calculated, you will come off like a robot. Remember, you're interacting with actual people so be one. Post some real pictures and talk to your followers as if you're speaking to a friend.

9. Quality over quantity! Genuine followers are more valuable than non-responsive numbers. Meaning 100 followers who actually care what you have to say and interact with your page, will always be more valuable than 1,000,000 followers who are simply place holding a number. To make sure your audience grows with genuine followers, be patient and seek relationships—not followers—when you interact. That means answering questions, responding to comments, reposting other people's content, and tagging others.

10. Use a scheduling tool, whether it's an actual calendar or automated technology, your feed should produce consistent content. Because this is not a personal account, but a business account, you must keep it active. Plan ahead, but don't over-automate or your presence will feel fake and insincere. If people doubt that they are getting the real you, if your post looks like a bot is setting it up or a PR service, then they stop watching and interacting. A great way to think of content is to theme your posts around holidays and current events.

11. Give, don't take! You should be focused on helping rather than selling. The moment people feel they are being sold to they shut off. The trick is to constantly give them something they want. Be inspirational, educational, or entertaining.

12. Optimize! The term *SEO* simply means Search Engine Optimization. If you're not techy, don't freak out. I'm going to break it down. Simply put, to optimize your presence, you need to provide all the right information. This means filling out your bio, making sure your profile names are recognizable and not something like SnuggleBug22, post relevant content so that people can understand what your brand represents in one quick glance, and use the right keywords in content. All of these things will help search engines (robots and algorithms) put you in a category and recommend you to the right people. If you are an author and you only post about your dogs on social media, the SEO will direct you to dog people rather than readers. Many readers like dogs, so they might enjoy this content, but you have to leave a breadcrumb trail so the bots and algorithms can help you. Hashtags are virtual breadcrumbs. Also, interacting with similar accounts and tagging people in your industry is a great way to hint about what you do without stuffing it down followers' throats.

13. A picture is worth a thousand words! Photos and videos are queen in the social media game, so keep your content visually enticing and you'll lighten the load immensely. A great, eye-catching photo (disruptive content) and a few clever hashtags, and boom, you've got your lure and metadata done—perfect for the average "entertaining" post.

14. Don't overthink it! As someone building a social presence, try to capture content whenever possible, but don't feel pressured to post it right away. As long as it's posted at a relevant time, you're fine. And don't invest in expensive equipment or go broke having a

photoshoot. If you have the means, invest in a phone with a good camera with lots of memory and your content will shine! Try a few photo editing apps and get fancy with your content as you gain experience. It's never the polished pictures that grab the audience, it's the authentic ones, the shots that make followers feel like they share an intimate connection with you and your world. People love an intimate glance into your world, which is why cellphones are perfect cameras. That classic shot of an author's coffee in hand, cute shoes, and a work station ready to go is a snapshot of the life that readers love to see.

15. Cross-promote! If you only ever entertain in your own living room in front of the same group of friends, your guest list will never grow. You have to attend other social settings. Pop in on friends by sharing their post in your story or announcing their book release. Visit their pages and make small talk with their guests. This is virtual networking. Think of it as merely stopping by someone else's party for a quick round and getting back on your way. Keep in mind, I'm referring to random week days, not scheduled virtual events. Do not—I repeat, *DO NOT*—post content on someone else's platform without permission. This is the equivalent of a busted wedding crasher. Security will haul your ass out of there the moment you're spotted, and you will be blacklisted from all future events. It's just rude, unprofessional, and desperate.

16. Hitch a ride with a big brand! Remember, generosity begets generosity, so when you do this, do not do it with any expectation other than you are helping someone else. If a brand (relevant to yours) is trending or an idol of yours has some big news, post about it. Through tags, their audience will lean into your post and some might even stick. If the brand sees what you've done, you could form a relationship and get a shout-out, but do it for the pleasure of sharing, not what you could get in return. This is more powerful than any sort of self-promotion, because you are actually "educating" others about what's trending.

17. Invest where there's an ROI! The impression that social media was once free is long gone. We're all being watched, studied, absorbed, computed, and impacted with such purpose there is nothing accidental about what we see anymore. And while I'd love to be one of the outraged people furious about the privacy violation, I'd rather be the businesswoman who's smart enough to make lemons out of lemonade. Social media, no matter what platform, is a choice and they make the rules. If we don't like the rules, we don't have to use their service. But if we use their service for business, we might as well learn how to monetize. Your SEO is only going to get you so far. To supercharge your reach, run ads. Ads basically give you access to all the leads collected through the bots and algorithms watching everyone. Most social ads allow targeted audiences, so if you're looking for a specific genre reader, you can direct your ads to them. There is no shame in doing this, and you do not need to wait for a big event to advertise your business. Ads are a great way to extend your reach and let others know you exist.

18. Know your ROI! Most sites offer analytics. If you are running a business, especially if you are investing time and money, you should learn how to read your performance stats. This will show you what posts are most successful so you can adapt and grow. Don't repeat behavior that produces little or no fruit.

19. Create disruptive content! You want content that will stop readers in their tracks. Be creative, be bold, and be real!

20. Ready your links! Have your social media links gathered and shortened in one, easy-to-find place, then share them everywhere, including in your newsletter so your audience knows where you're active. This will grow your audience across platforms by co-mingling your existing fans. Share your links every few months so the new followers know what other platforms you're using.

21. Keep self-promotion in the background. Authors often have to self-promote, especially in the beginning of their career when their advertising budget is low, but authors never want an obnoxious presence. Going back to the party metaphor, consider the over-self-promoter, the jerk at the party who only ever wants to talk about himself. Don't let that jerk be you. Think of your self-promotion as background. Schedule it, keep it informative but unobtrusive, and fill the majority of your space with actual content that "educates," "inspires," or "entertains."

22. Know your audience's needs. If you are, in fact, an author and the purpose of your social presence is to help your business, you want an audience that likes books—preferably yours. Never lose sight of your audience's needs. Your content should fit their needs, so make sure you're giving them something of value. If you give them a reason to follow you, they will.

23. Include your social links in the signature of your email.

24. Host Q&A's so your audience can learn new things about you, and you can learn what they're interested in.

25. Offer *occasional* incentives. This one comes with a caveat, and it's a big one. Giveaways are a great way to interact with your followers and show your appreciation. They also attract new followers. Be very careful about the followers you're collecting. If they are only there for your giveaways and take no interest in your brand or products, then they are only a follower. Yes, they will amass and make you look popular, but this falls back on the "illusion of success" we discussed in part one. Be sure to giveaway products relevant to your brand, products that could hook new readers. Gift cards are not necessarily going to get spent on books. Also, if your audience is founded on giveaways, they may become dependent and expectant of frequent, new giveaways. This is an expensive and less authentic sort of audience to maintain. My advice is to gear any sort of incentive as a "thank you" not a "hook," though it should inevitably work as both. The label you use will affect how enslaved you wind up to the process. But if you're just looking to grow your following and don't care if they're hot or cold, feel free to host an arbitrary giveaway every day.

Chapter Fifteen
The Publishing Industry

"Publishing is a business. Writing may be art, but publishing, when all is said and done, comes down to dollars."

Nicholas Sparks, Advice for Writers

Quality Counts

Quality should be a cornerstone of every author's foundation. Quality products promote customer satisfaction, establish a strong and positive author reputation, and should meet or exceed industry standard. Inadequate products increase risk and thereby increase cost to the creator.

Selling a book—selling it enough to sustain a livable income—is one of the hardest, most frustrating, unscientific challenges authors ever face. Practice makes perfect, hard work delivers measurable results, effort pays off, such clichés are often lies in the publishing industry, which is why so many authors burnout trying to survive.

There is no failproof formula, and many times one person's hard work can result in, well, their hard work and little else. While another person's minimal work can turn into the cushy deal of a lifetime, where the writer hardly has to lift a finger, except to type the next book, and an in-house editor and PR department handles the rest. They become an instant sensation, and the writing community sits around wondering what they put in the secret sauce.

There's no secret. It was simply their time, their moment. Their success negates nothing from yours. They were simply discovered by the right person at the right time with the right product on hand.

There will always be students who ace a test without studying, just as there are those who studied for days on end and it still wasn't enough to pass the final exam. Quality cannot be determined by time or effort because we are starting from different positions and facing different obstacles. And while we can bitch and moan that it isn't fair because the challenge isn't equal for all authors, doing so will not make success more likely for anyone. Only writing will.

Write. Revise. Improve. Learn. And write some more. Do it again and again, until the book you once loved and viewed as a masterpiece suddenly reads as the scribbles of a novice writer. Grow. Never stop growing. And prepare to sell, because this is not a hobby or a game, this is a business, and it's a challenging one.

If you want your moment to come, you must be prepared. You prepare by having a quality book on hand. Not a replica of what's been done, but something unique and strong, something that will make the right agent or editor say, "Yes, I want that!"

Quality is measured in many different ways, and every author faces different challenges throughout the creative process. Your stylistic preference and unique relationship with words will determine your creative process. Regardless of your prose, grasp of language, or the witty way you write dialogue, the ultimate success of any book rests mostly in the overall quality of the story, which starts with strong characterization and a powerful arc.

Quality is everything. It overrides word choice, style, and form every time. Quality is the overall superior health and completeness of a novel. It's measured in a fully developed plot with evolving, dimensional, fully humanized characters, spiking conflicts and sloping obstacles that either defeat or drive the plot to an ultimately satisfying end.

Quality story tellers is what the book industry wants to find above all else. They seek authors who know how to write a well-developed story every time. Regardless of the subject matter. Regardless of the style. They want the experience of being hooked from the first page and held to the very end.

The Industry

Authors must know their craft to master quality writing, but if they want to sell it, they must know the industry. The term *industry* refers to the manufacturing within a particular field, often named after its primary product. In the case of literature, our primary products are books, so we work in the book industry.

But an author does not produce a book alone. Sure, they imagine it and write it and it starts as their creative property, but the actual production of a book involves many people. To manufacture a book, turn it into a grossing product, we must rely on the industry.

Starting at the top, like branches of government, there are three primary branches of publishing: traditional, hybrid, and self-publishing. Depending on the direction an author chooses, they may need others to reach this level.

Traditional publishing requires an author to sign over the copyright to the publishing house so that they can sell the book on the author's behalf. The publisher then collects a royalty for their services, and yes, it's generally larger than the average 35% earned by the author because the publisher assumes all the production costs.

A *small press* is considered traditional, but it operates on a much lesser scale. Its base of writers is smaller, its budget is smaller, its staff is smaller, and its reach is smaller, but the personal connection shared with a small press can sometimes be huge in comparison to the relationships formed with a larger publishing house.

With both a large house and small press, an author should never pay for editing or production costs. A *vanity press*, however, will charge the author a fee for publishing services.

Vanity presses sometimes slip into the mix like a hooker might slip into a sophisticated social event. They really don't belong, especially when independent publishing and fancy big houses are there giving away the same opportunities with no money down. But sometimes people prefer to pay and not have to stress over the details or worry about rejection.

For the right price, which can be obscenely overpriced, a vanity press will accept any client, but they still lack the platform and reach of larger traditional presses. So once a client's hour is up, they're basically tossed out of bed and back on the streets—book in hand but no clue how to sell it.

Independent publishing, self-publishing, or indie publishing all refers to the act of publishing one's own book without the help of traditional means. Indie publishing is free upfront, as there is no charge to list a book in retail, but it's also costly, as all production expenses fall to the author. And while listing a book may be free, selling through a retail site absolutely comes with a cost.

Authors list books on various retail platforms to access the reach of conglomerate markets like Amazon and other retail leaders supplying literature. The use of their platform is collected in the form of a royalty once sales are made.

Authors typically earn between a 30% and 70% royalty from a direct retailer, which seems higher than the royalty of a traditionally published book, but keep in mind, production costs are heaped on the author up front, so the author likely started with a manufacturing debt. That includes editing, cover design, and publicity. It's a top-heavy model, placing the risk on the author rather than the publisher.

A *hybrid author* is a combination author who is published both traditionally and independently. To look at the numbers and make a snap decision about which publishing model is best would be a mistake. Each model comes with perks and drawbacks. While they might be of the same species, I assure you, they are all very different animals.

Indie authors generally keep more of the money earned, but they start with a production debt. Indie authors appear to have more autonomy, but they are also limited by retail platforms, which dictate price points, royalty rates, subscription and loaning rights, and so on.

A traditionally published author with a large publishing house will have access to that large house's publicity team, network, platform, and connections. Signing with a large house is a great credential when working with bookstores and planning author events, but an author might not have as much autonomy in terms of cover art, distribution, content and style, and so on. A publisher might only be willing to take a title to digital, which could stunt a book's potential.

Many authors favor the traditional model because it keeps the author writing and lets the industry pros focus on all of the other details. Some argue no one can ever love a book like its creator, but that's not true. If a book is packaged and marketed successfully, its readers should love it more.

Traditional publishers, collectively, have the most experience and largest budget when it comes to exposure. But an author has to trust them to properly represent, manufacture, and sell their book before they sign over the rights.

POD, print on demand, is a newer term that saves both indie authors and publishers overhead cost. Thanks to technology, books can now be produced within minutes. All that's required are the digital specs and materials. When a customer orders an out of stock print book, and there is no hidden inventory, the book is POD. When readers purchase books produced by indie authors from Amazon or major bookstores that list the book online but not on the shelves, the books are produced through POD and printed the moment the order is placed.

Small presses, in an attempt to save their small budget, typically print on demand. Large presses, however, do not.

Traditional publishers prefer to keep inventory in supply. They use their network to market shipments of books to retailers when the title becomes what's considered "active record." They use a collection of data about consumer habits, popular similar works, and market trends, to estimate how the book might perform, and they then gauge their budget and publicity on those stats.

If a traditional publisher likes a book and wants to produce it, but they are unsure of how it will perform, they might place it in a *digital first* imprint, meaning the title will become available digitally with a possibility of going to print but no real guarantee. This removes some of the cost risk to the publisher and creates more opportunities for authors to get signed with big houses, because, without the expense of print, publishers can test drive new authors through digital, low risk investments.

If authors choose to work with other industry professionals, the expense typically comes out of their royalties. So, if an author is signed with a literary agent who charges 15%, their commission will be deducted from the author's royalty percentage before the author gets paid. And if an author is only making 30% from a publisher, the agent just took half of that.

Despite the cost, agents serve a purpose. It's not easy to reach the top. And while you might be able to climb there, some publishers won't deal with authors directly. They require authors to send an agent.

Why? Because an agent is one more stage in the vetting process. An agent will tell a writer if their book is up to par or needs work. An agent understands the market and current industry standards. Agents have a network of publishers, editors, and publicists. They know what's hot and who wants what. Basically, agents are connected and authors pay them for their connections.

Literary agencies also typically have a legal department with literary attorneys who specialize in contract negotiations. Having an agent can take your book deal from digital first to a mass market paperback on an endcap display between genre giants like Sylvia Day and E.L. James (that might have happened to me).

Signing with an agent can be just as challenging as signing with the publisher. There is a pitch process and selection process and very specific guidelines for submitting any work.

Some agents will work with an author's foreign rights or audio rights but not the author's general literary rights, meaning the author must navigate the digital and print waters alone, possibly publish their work independently, handle all the PR and retain all the due royalties, but forward any audio or foreign interest to the specializing agent, who would then broker a deal and collect a commissioned salary.

Publishing is not cheap. No matter who handles the costs, it all adds up. Editors charge by the word, so try to imagine what a hundred thousand word novel might cost, especially when novels typically run through a few rounds of editing.

A traditional editing cycle will include developmental editing, line editing or copy editing, and proofreading.

Traditionally published work typically requires less energy and brain power to edit. There are few revisions and the process is very much at the authority of the editor. Authors can always question a suggestion, but the decision-making relies heavily on the editor's expertise. Plus, there is the added bonus of the publishing house footing the bill and managing the entire process. The author needs only to meet his or her deadlines.

When a book is independently published, the author must vet and hire an editor. They can either commission the freelance editor and pay them a royalty, or more common, they will pay them upfront based on the editor's private rates. Being that the editor is selected and hired by the author, their skill level is based on assumption and credentials. This places more pressure on the author in terms of final decision-making during the revision process. Autonomy is freeing, but it is also stressful.

Some authors choose to hire a freelance editor before submitting to a traditional publisher to make sure the manuscript is cohesive and polished. This is especially wise for inexperienced writers.

The incurred costs for formatting, cover art, and publicity when outsourced, weighs heavily on indie authors, which is why many have learned to handle these departments on their own. In such a temperamental market, where sustainable income is difficult to find, it's always wise to be as self-sufficient as possible. It's like the old proverb, give a man a fish and he will eat for a night, teach a man to fish and he will eat for the rest of his life.

This is usually where burnout starts to rear its ugly head. Independent authors are competing with publishing giants, and therefore, they have to bring their A game. They are working with a small business budget and a staff of one. Any freelancers hired will save time but cost money. And money's an elusive commodity for authors.

Production also includes packaging. This requires digitally mastered cover art for all formats, book descriptions, ISBN registration, sizing and spine design, pricing and barcode details, binding and material selection, paper quality and color, finish, SEO and metadata information, and galleys.

Yes, it would be nice to have complete creative control in the design, but it's also nice to have a publisher handle it for you. Some authors want more control over the production process, and that's why independent publishing is perfect for them. Some want more time to write, so they are happy to pass the chore of production to others. This can be achieved by outsourcing production or signing with a publisher that offers such in-house services. Authors who want varying levels of control for different books, might choose to become hybrid and practice both methods.

I've had the unfortunate dilemma of receiving an offer with a signing bonus from one of the world's largest publishing houses on the contingency that I replace the main character's main conflict with a less distressful obstacle. The character was battling health issues and the publisher thought the reader would prefer the story without that struggle.

To me, this conflict shaped the character. The protagonist's triumph through acceptance over what she could not control was everything that moved her development forward. I turned down the deal.

In the end, my book did well, but probably would have sold more copies with the large publishing house. However, the story is exactly what I wanted it to be, which holds value of its own.

Having so many publishing models to choose from is a beautiful thing. But when authors only want traditional and they keep getting rejected, the choice is taken out of their hands. Some authors are indie but dream of one day going fully traditional. Hopefully, books like this will help bring that dream to fruition.

Once the production is underway, authors or publishers—must decide if any other formats will be sought. Audiobooks are a great source of income for authors nowadays, but like everything else, there is a cost.

Authors typically earn a 40% royalty on an audiobook—yes, still less than half. The distributor will take a cut, of course, but what about the narrator?

A producer, or narrator, will typically get paid one of two ways. They can either get paid for their time upfront, usually *PFH*, per finished hour, or they can collect a royalty share from the sales. That royalty share comes from the author's portion.

If an author is producing an audiobook and using a royalty share model, their 40% royalty just got lobbed in half. Think it's better to pay upfront? Narrators typically range between $50 and $400 per finished hour and audiobooks can be anywhere from 2 to 40 hours long.

If an author has a 10 hour audiobook and a narrator who works for $300 PFH, they just created a debt of $3,000.00 before selling a single audiobook. And if an audiobook sells for $18 and the author collects a 40% royalty, they earn $7.20 per sale, overlooking any additional fees the retailer might tack on. In this case, the author would have to sell over 400 copies of their audiobook to clear the production debt and start making a profit.

It's doable, but probably not without a robust promotional campaign. There goes more of the author's time and money.

All of these upfront costs are perfect examples of why authors must understand where they will see an ROI. Publishing has a lot of upfront costs, and someone has to pay the bill.

It is for this exact reason that when a new author enters the scene—bright eyed and bushy tailed—so full of hopes and dreams, the veteran authors wish them the best.

Sometime later, that new author isn't quite as energized or shiny, but they still haven't grasped the laws of industry. They claim they *write for themselves* or that it's *a labor of love*. That's cute.

Seasoned authors smile and move on, respecting the still-green author's right to make it whatever they want. But when those new authors have finally accepted the reality and are willing to admit it might be a little about the money, they are ready to move from author to *authorpreneur*.

Writing is a hobby. To qualify as an author, a writer requires only one published work. Publishing is a business. Authors that want to have sustainable incomes from their writing careers had better be willing to do business.

To the authors that only "labor for love," feel free to experiment with that in real life. Try buying groceries with smiles or paying a mortgage in hugs. Let us know how you make out.

Come on, people! This is not a hobby. It's too damn hard to be something we do just for fun! You're allowed to enjoy it, but this is a job. You are an independent business owner the moment you entertain the possibility of writing to earn an income and start expending energy toward that goal.

If you want to succeed, then you must know how to run a successful business. Not the illusion of success—no, no. Illusions pay the bills as good as hugs. Seriously, next time a plumber fixes an issue in your house and wants to get paid, ask him if he prefers illusions or hugs (if he accepts either, call the police).

Money is a requirement for survival in our society. There is no shame in wanting some.

We all have our passion projects, but work is called work because the effort and skill required is laborious. Not every book can be as fun and fulfilling as your first. Sometimes, if you want to make money, you have to write for the market, not yourself.

In many cases, an author's greatest work is their lowest performing title. It typically has nothing to do with the quality of work and everything to do with the delivery. If a book is not marketed properly, it will not get discovered.

Visibility

Visibility is a must in the book industry. If an author is not visible to the reader, they're unlikely to get discovered. If readers can't find an author's work, they will never talk about it. Without word of mouth, an author will have to rely solely on marketing. Authors who aren't selling books have very little income, so if they aren't making money, they don't have much of an advertising budget. To market effectively, low-earning authors have to get creative if they want to be seen.

I return you to the Titanic analogy. Picture it again. The ship's gone down, people are desperate and panicking, hoping one of the lifeboats full of industry professionals and readers notices them. Survival does not look good.

So they shout. They splash and scream and do whatever they can to get noticed. Let's say a reader sees them. But the drowning author looks exactly like the frantic author to their left, right, and back. The decision's too hard, so the reader either turns away or makes a random choice. Things are too chaotic to decipher why one author was selected and not another.

Desperation is everywhere in this industry. Authors need to calm down and retain their energy.

Think of Rose Dewitt Bukater, played by Kate Winslet. After the Titanic sinks, Rose is shivering on her back, looking at stars, singing *Come Josephine My Flying Machine,* while everyone else panics around her.

Sweet Jack didn't make it. Poor Jack.

Now, flash to reality. In author world, this chaotic sinking and panic might represent a year or so after an author dives into the industry. We can either burn out, screaming for attention in a storm of pandemonium, or gather our strength and prepare for the right opportunity by using our time wisely to write something brilliant. But we must be prepared when our moment arrives, or the opportunity might pass us by.

Back in the water, Rose is preserving her energy, lying stiff and still, thinking up stories, and blocking out the chaos around her. She saves her strength until the right opportunity—a lifeboat—appears, and then she calls out to get noticed. She's ready to rock and roll.

Rose is swept up by the boatful of publishers and readers. She is rescued and, while her life no longer looks as it once did or how she dreamed it might pan out, it's a happy, sustainable life. The experience of getting there has changed her for the better. She's stronger, tougher, and wiser.

Surviving the industry will toughen and educate authors if they truly want to make it. But we have to make ourselves visible. Blowing whistles and screaming look at me will only land like a whisper in a hurricane if it's exactly what a thousand other people are doing at exactly the same time.

Visibility is relative to the situation. It is an unobstructed view. The book market is so saturated with authors at the moment, obstructions are everywhere, and the probability of being seen by the right person—an agent or editor or publisher—is slim to none. But they're out there, so be ready in case one happens to pass you by.

In the meantime, authors will do everything in their power to attract the attention of readers. Readers can sometimes create a current toward a specific book that lures the attention of publishers and agents like a riptide. This is how indie books turn into mass market paperback deals.

Authors have to be smart. They have to stay visible but not burn out or slow down production. Books keep authors afloat, but even a multi-published author will sink if they burn out. This is why we must always keep a pulse on our expended energy and the return.

Authors should only spend money where they will see the greatest return, where they are most likely to get noticed and stand out within the crowd. Sometimes they have to wait out an opportunity, so there is no shame in idling to focus solely on writing for a bit. A good book is a great way to make a big splash.

Visibility leads to discoverability. But you don't want to get discovered empty-handed. Authors must time their journey so that when they are discovered, they are prepared. Being prepared means having a high quality, well-written, polished novel ready for the right audience.

Discoverability is an elevator pitch on the tip of your tongue. It's a mission statement you're eager to share with an agent. It's an upcoming project you want to sell, and a resume full of performing titles in your backlist. It's an organic, active following that will encourage investors like publishing houses to buy and sell your products. It's an understanding of the market, the ability to speak about the industry from an informed position. It's a track record of analytics, a sense of capability others can feel, and the poise of a professional that invites others' interests.

Just as an author does not want a life sentence of marketing expenses, a publisher wants the same. Marketing will always be an essential part of the game, but the better the product, the more likely the product is to sell itself—once discovered. And to get discovered, it must first become visible.

Go back to Rose and picture her staring at the sky, softly singing, as people struggle and panic around her. Authors tend to panic in the stillness. Many try to bargain for survival, but there is no quick fix for success, no failproof gimmick or writing tool that solves all your problems. Discoverability depends on knowledge, hard work, talent, and *timing*. Your survival as an author absolutely requires a degree of patience many do not possess.

Know your industry. Apply yourself to becoming more educated by taking an online course every few months—or more frequently if you're just starting out. Being a lifelong learner will help your business in the long run and teach you new ways to stay visible as technology advances. But nothing will help you as much as a well-written, quality book to sell, so get writing.

Write, and write some more. Then when you're finished writing, revise and re-write what you've written. Keep improving and learning. Don't waste energy screaming into the chaos where no one can hear you. Be present but patient, and prepared for when the right opportunity comes along.

Quality products will deliver themselves. The more you apply yourself to your writing and craft, the more your product line will grow and improve.

If a product is crap, it can start with just as much fanfare, but it won't survive long without a constant stream of advertising. We have established that authors typically love the writing part of the job, but the publishing aspects are draining, especially for independently published authors trying to do it all on their own. The goal is to ultimately pull back from the performance, focus on the craft, and build a legacy that readers trust and know.

In the game of publishing and success, there are many players on the court, but quality is queen. Once you have a quality product, release it into the world. Use sensible marketing that shows a measurable return. This requires experimenting, and experimenting can be expensive.

Spend wisely, observe your results, and determine if a promotional practice is actually delivering a return. Don't worry about what everyone else is doing. In an industry where less than 1% reach measurable success and 99% of authors don't make it, 99% of those causing a ruckus around you are more likely playing into illusions than anything else.

Keep that 99% in mind when you find yourself tempted to do what everyone else is doing. Ask yourself if they're actually finding successful opportunities or burning through the last of their energy trying to make a splash and stay afloat. Will they survive the choppy waters by morning?

Those preserving their energy and sticking to the tried and true—writing quality stories—will most likely have the most strength. And when the waters finally do calm, which is statistically quite a ways off, the patient author who preserved their energy will be in a visible position with many books to keep them afloat. Their survival in such a saturated, tumultuous market will act as a testament to publishers.

Don't copy desperate "look at me" behavior. Experiment, spend wisely, measure results, review, and reject what doesn't offer a return. Then get back to writing. Understand that visibility in the book market has less to do with personal approach and everything to do with unanimous circumstance. Penetrating an oversaturated market of any sort is an incredibly challenging task.

The objective with visibility is always to be seen. Timing matters. If there are obstacles obstructing the view shared between you and readers, no amount of fanfare will remove the obstacles. However, money can move you into a better position where you are more likely to get noticed.

Larger marketing budgets can airlift an author out of chaos and plant them directly in front of readers. This is why the high grossing authors tend to stay visible. They have made the sales to justify the large marketing budget so they can afford the visibility.

Less grossing authors might have to wait it out. Or they can take a loan and hope it pays off, or put their investment on credit as discussed in earlier chapters.

Knowing the market well enough to know what is a good investment and what is not is key. If a promotion can't deliver you to the *correct* audience, the promotion isn't delivering and the visibility achieved is of little value in the end.

Authors grow a marketing budget by growing a backlist. We do that by writing books. New products naturally entice an audience, even if that audience is made up of your mother and your best friend. Eventually, that following will grow to twenty loyal readers and then a hundred and then thousands.

In an industry as challenging as the book industry, it's expected that authors will grow impatient. They will attempt the quick-fix solutions, and every book comes with different variables, so no experimental promotion will ever be the same. This is why it's crucial for authors to have ample business sense. As the boss, the staff, the creator, the HR, and the accountant, the decision-making ultimately will come down to you.

Sometimes, when we step back from the chaos, we can clearly see. Time is precious. Energy can easily get stolen. Patience can save you both. Invest in resources that prove resourceful to you.

4 Proven Ways to Penetrate a Saturated Market

1. **Branding:** Having a cohesive design identifies your promotions and products, while creating a more comprehensive impact to outsiders.
2. **Know Your Niche:** Big brands broadcast to big audiences, but smaller demographics are often overlooked. Don't underestimate untapped audiences that feel underrepresented.
3. **Bypass the Crowd:** Successful marketing takes strategizing. There is no cookie cutter approach and, often, advertising that looks the "same as everyone else's" will cost more than it earns. Think outside the box and be disruptive at the right time.
4. **Ensure Customer Satisfaction:** Quality is queen! Nothing beats word of mouth endorsements of a product. Satisfied customers talk and leave reviews. 81% of consumers trust the

recommendations of social media friends, so don't just write quality books, work on ways to keep your consumers chatting about them. Encourage reviews, posts, and testimonials.

Do not give up! Yes, an oversaturated market can be extremely intimidating, and the competition is sometimes daunting, but a market gets oversaturated because a certain kind of product is in high demand—in other words, people want books!

The customers are out there. The challenge is earning their loyalty and praise. Quality stories and proper marketing will get you there, but timing is everything. Stay present so you are visible, but don't burn out trying to shift the unmovable. You can only move yourself or wait for the waters to calm. Be patient, be smart, and be a confident badass. You've got this!

Audience

The audience is the consumer. Different genres have different audiences and different guidelines to suit each specific audience. Understanding the book industry means understanding the consumer's desires.

Who decides the genre? It's a mix. The author, editor, and publisher will determine where the book fits, but it's the masses that dictate what they want within a genre.

How does the general public relay their desires? Through dollars.

Reader behavior indicates what is profitable and what is not. Hundreds of years' worth of data translates those numbers into guidelines which publishers still rely on today. Sometimes contradicting interpretations arise, and wrong decisions are made.

In romance, there is an unwritten rule that a book has to end on a happy note and main characters should not die. Authors often debate this rule, using examples like author Nicholas Sparks, who is a formulaic writer with a reputation of killing off his main characters. Nicholas Sparks has written some of the most successful love stories to date, so he is, in fact, succeeding in the romance genre, but he appears to be breaking the rules.

The truth is, he's not. There is no rule that the main character can't die. But there is a rule that *every* story should include a satisfying ending.

It is not about a *happy ending* versus a *sad ending,* or the main character's mortality. It is only about satisfaction. Satisfy the reader (a.k.a. the audience)—no matter the fate of the characters. Do that, and you've done your job well.

While the publishing pros have their data, they aren't always the best at reading popular culture's signals. The indie author community has beyond proven that there is a reader for everything. *But*—and this is a big but—there are more readers for certain things than others. The question is, how much money do you want to make?

While there is varied experience behind an agent's, editor's, or publisher's feedback, and an author should always handle feedback with an open mind, one person's opinion of your book is not a true representation of the world's. You've all heard stories about global bestsellers getting rejected before someone took a chance on them. It happens all the time.

Herman Melville was asked if *Moby Dick* had to be about a whale, and would it not be more entertaining to have the captain chasing maidens? F. Scott Fitzgerald was told he'd have a great book if he got rid of that *Gatsby* character. Stephen King was warned his stories wouldn't sell. Dr. Suess, J.K. Rowling, and Agatha Christie have all been rejected.

Some genres are much larger and more popular than others, which leads to a higher demand and therefore more openings for writers, which we have learned causes a more saturated market. Depending on the genre, authors face varying levels of competition but all levels are fierce.

Carving out a niche, for instance, writing romance but narrowing an audience down to Christian-based sweet, small town romance, might be easier to market than an author writing for a broader audience. There are two ways to look at the equation, a niche audience will be smaller and, therefore, limited, while a broad audience is much wider and unrestrictive but behaves like an overwhelmed jungle, and the competition is everywhere. It's survival of the fittest, and anything goes in the wild.

The romance genre is the highest grossing genre, creating an impressive 1.44 billion dollar industry, an overwhelming leader when compared to the second highest grossing genre, mystery & crime, which comes in at a much lower $728 million.

In addition to genre, there is style and format to consider. Some readers prefer enormous stories that take months to read, while others desire short, bite-sized novellas. Neither is better, because they are simply different. They satisfy different audiences and meet different expectations.

All genres have a purpose, need, and a place. Some will prove more lucrative, but there is no way to value one over the other when both are required for an industry to fully function properly.

What matters most is the quality of the work. We can be whatever we wish to be, as long as we do our best.

There is a market for every book. Some readers are more obscure and harder to find, but they exist.

The caveat—of course there's a but—is that in a market as oversaturated as the book industry, even masterpieces can fail to sell. But the audience is there if you can find a way to reach them. Clever marketing can make all the difference. However, regardless of the genre or style or advertising, if your story lacks quality, it won't sell for long.

The author's goal is to connect with the right audience. That connection is made through astute marketing strategy, yes, but it's fortified and sustained through quality work. It is the writing that must resonate with the masses, thereby selling more books organically through the most powerful endorsement of all, word of mouth.

Start with branding, find your niche, and strategize ways to bypass the crowd. But, in the end, it all comes down to customer satisfaction. No audience is as valuable as a loyal one.

Marketing

Marketing is the transfer of goods from the producer to the consumer, or, in our case, it is the transfer of books to the audience, the reader. Although lucrative, advertising is a synthetic method of connection.

A wise author will always rely heavily on quality over quantity or publicity. Human connection should always be the top priority. And that connection starts at the very first step of the writing process, through words.

An author's marketing budget will only increase with success, adding more responsibility to the author's plate and taking more time away from actual writing as their backlist and reach expands. It is a misconception that the publicity gets more manageable with time and titles. Aside from a select handful who can sell anything based on their fame and name, publicity is an endless course to navigate in the publishing industry.

The trick is creating a product line of such fine quality that it publicizes itself. Think of the popular sportswear company, Nike, and their extremely simplistic *swish* logo. Nike is not only a household name, its logo is recognizable without words.

Imagine, for a moment, the kind of effort it takes to market a product without persuasive language or even the title of a brand. This is only achieved through strong initial marketing of superior products consumers can rely on.

First comes the quality product, then the consumer's trust. Repeat this pattern enough, and products begin to market themselves, the creator need only announce a new product's arrival.

When an author's work is discovered and loved by enough readers, their name becomes the selling point. This is why many powerhouse names appear larger than the actual book title, because the readers will buy the book based on its creator more than its content. Readers trust the brand, and the brand sells itself.

However, no matter how successful a brand, marketing can never subside completely. Audiences are fluid and older books will need to be highlighted if authors hope to keep their discoverability alive. This means reminding consumers of old favorites they might have missed.

Just as your time is precious, so is a reader's. New products have the advantage of newness, which is always more exciting than old, so they are often easier to market. But old products should still generate revenue, especially in the book industry.

Older books have lost a bit of their luster and require a little finessing to sell. Sometimes finesse comes in the form of new covers or a robust ad campaign or a special sale. The idea is to be creative and think outside of the box, but always keep an eye on the ROI.

Publicity grows stale the moment it occurs. Technology is continuously evolving. Readers shift social platforms. The way people consume product information is forever changing and improving as the world gets louder and more populated with competitors. What an author does to publicize their first book most likely will fall flat by their fourth or fifth book.

That means, on top of the time needed away from writing to consult with PR companies or develop ads, authors must also allow time to research which practices are profitable and which are obsolete or pay an expert to decide for them.

Rather than decrease with time, the advertising budget grows. Meaning at the start of an author's career they might put aside a budget of one hundred dollars to advertise a book. But in time, they will want a larger platform with greater exposure. As their success grows, so does that marketing budget in order to sustain and grow a broader audience.

What started as one hundred dollars for one book has now grown to ten thousand dollars for twenty books. But how much has the profit really changed? The increased profit is typically relative to the increased budget. Big risks earn big rewards, but if the investment flops and the ROI doesn't deliver, big risks come with big loss.

The end goal should always be balance. Yes, it truly comes into every aspect of success.

Take a look at the following model that shows the difference in time allocated to marketing and writing when comparing a new author to a veteran one.

VETERAN AUTHOR

WRITING TIME   BUDGET

NEW AUTHOR

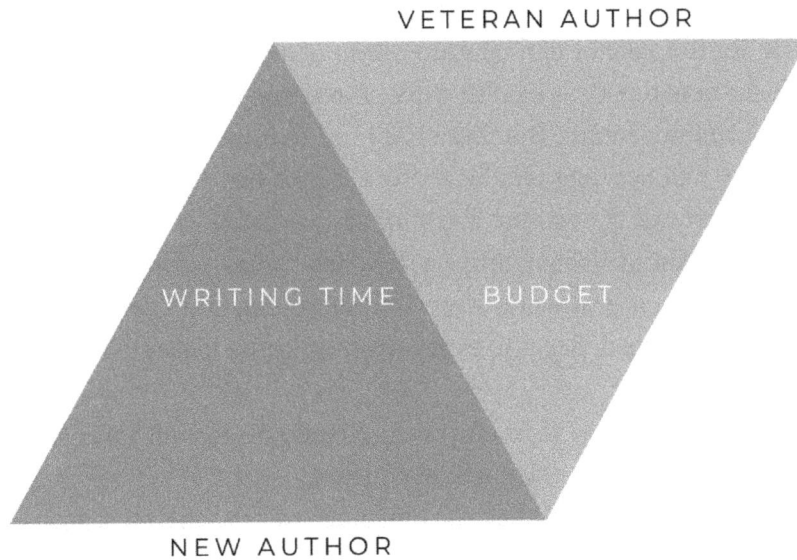

You will notice that the longer the author continues in this career the less writing time they have. Yet their budget is growing.

What's the problem?

The problem is marketing. Marketing is a full-time job and it's killing authors, literally taking a physical toll on their lives as it sends them hurtling toward burnout.

Authors need to write. Taking writing time away from an author is akin to suffocation. If you suffocate a flame long enough, what happens? The flame burns out.

Now, look at the next model. You can see when the author reaches a point of sustainable income. Just in the center of the illustration, where both triangles seem most even, the author's income has created a justified budget.

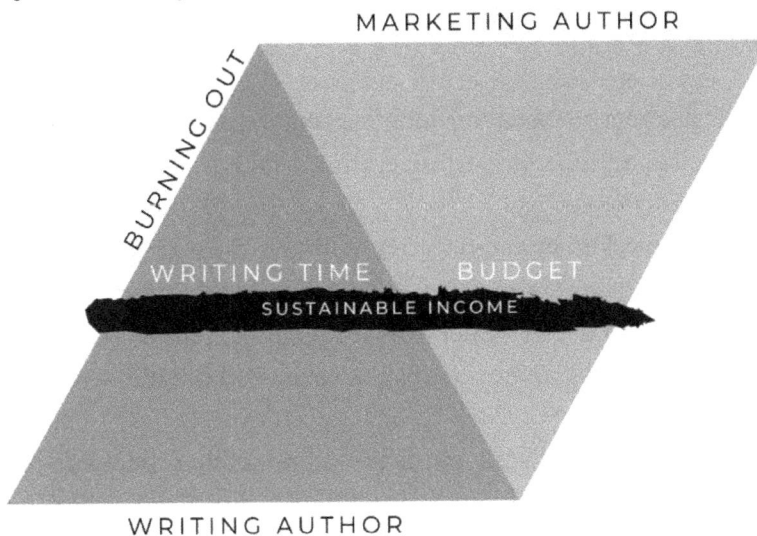

MARKETING AUTHOR

BURNING OUT

WRITING TIME   BUDGET

SUSTAINABLE INCOME

WRITING AUTHOR

This is usually the time an author leaves a second job and becomes a full-time writer. It also happens to be the point just before authors begin experiencing symptoms of burnout.

If you are reading this, you can mark your current status on the model above. You should sense the proximity of burnout based on your experience as an author and your income growth.

So how do we maintain a sustainable income, market adequately, and prevent burnout from happening? You guessed it! Balance!

The model that worked at the start of an author's career when the author is sacrificing—as many new business owners do for the sake of their startup—cannot sustain them long-term.

The lack of profit for new brands is exactly why entrepreneurs are advised to have a nest egg saved before they start a new business venture. But there is a limit to how long a new company can go without a profit, a limit to how long that nest egg will last before it runs out. Generally, around the 2 to 3 year mark, a business owner has to call the venture a failure or a success.

The goal is to reach a point of sustainability within that three-year timeframe. To do so, authors must market wisely and write their best work. Every minute spent, and calorie of energy expended, counts as much as each dollar earned, because every profit must be measured against the total cost to you as the sole investor.

When authors start to shortchange their craft in exchange for instant sales, the craft inevitably suffers. Quality suffers. And ultimately, the customer suffers.

It's more than a cycle. It's a spiral. When the customer suffers, the sales suffer and then the author suffers. Financial hardship skews perspective, and struggling authors often stop marketing wisely and start marketing desperately. It's not a difference between prudent advertising and aggressive advertising, but a difference between smart investments and foolish ones.

Financial hardship can often break an author's spirit, because they become so focused on marketing gimmicks they forget that writing a book is the best way to reinvent themselves and make a splash. When authors stop writing or minimize their writing time, an imbalance forms and they burn out. At this point, their company starts to crumble.

Many authors feel this flip around the 3 to 5 year mark of their career. They were doing well, and things looked optimistic, but then something changed.

When an audience stagnates, authors tend to act impulsively and dump more money into promotional stunts. But they're tired and creatively deprived, so they aren't thinking clearly. Their desperation and exhaustion shows in poor marketing choices, yet they continue in this pattern, hoping more money will do the trick.

When it doesn't and they stop this destructive behavior long enough to gain some much needed perspective, they usually find themselves lost in the world of marketing with hardly any time assigned to writing.

If an author spends 90% of their time marketing and only 10% of their time writing, are they still an author? Well, yes, but not a happy one. Authors are married to the business of advertising a brand. And a brand without new products is a stale brand. No matter how frequent the publicity, the audience will lose interest and grow cold. As the pulse of the audience lowers, some will die off. And sadly, once they're gone, they're gone.

A consumer does not recall the exact words you said, but they will remember the way you made them feel. An author's audience is made up of readers. Readers want books. Books give them a feeling of satisfaction. Not having books is the reader's problem. Giving them books is the solution. But they have to be *quality* books, or you will leave them unsatisfied in the end.

If a consumer buys a product, they expect a certain level of quality, especially if promotions led them to believe the product would meet their needs. If they are not satisfied, they will feel betrayed, as they trusted the brand to deliver something and the brand failed. They paid the brand their hard earned money and invested their time, which they cannot get back, and the brand didn't do what their marketing promised.

Here lies the troublesome consequence of authors overly invested in marketing at the expense of their craft. Yes, marketing will stimulate sales, but sales attached to a sense of betrayal will only damage the author in the end.

Success acquired through advertising over quality of work is only sustained through more advertising. When a profit only comparatively increases by an author's marketing attempts, it's indicative of a product imbalance and a red flag that the author needs to focus more on their craft, possibly spend time on some self-care, restore a sense of balance, maybe take a course to improve their writing, and basically rethink their position on writing versus marketing.

How can authors measure their reliance on marketing versus talent? Increase your marketing budget 50% and invest wisely, and you should see a comparable uptick in sales. Dial back the budget, and watch to see if those sales immediately drop off or continue to stimulate new readers.

If the 50% surge was successful and the quality of your work speaks for itself, your numbers will stay elevated for a period of time (but eventually taper). If they drop off *immediately* and there is no new motion in your backlist, that tells you something about the quality or audience is off. Authors must dig deeper to find the exact discrepancies.

Patterns that only fluctuate with the marketing increase indicate an imbalance. The brand has become solely reliant on marketing tactics rather than customer satisfaction, and the audience has grown cold.

The best insurance to stimulate a cold audience and grow new fans is to produce a quality, well-written book that will form an authentic connection. When authors focus too heavily on marketing old products, the audience isn't growing. It's the same audience that was there yesterday and the day before, so when the author repeatedly advertises the same products to the same audience, it's a little like crying wolf.

They are shouting, "Look at me! Look what I have here!"

The audience gets excited, expecting something they haven't seen before, only to deflate when they see the same old products the author has been peddling for years. Once again, it's less about the marketing and more about the book.

Lean too far into the wrong side of the job and authors might find themselves working in a PR field more than a creative one. For authors who love the job for the creative freedom it offers, this will inevitably lead to burnout.

At this point, authors often wonder where they went wrong or how their affection for a job they so deeply loved could have taken such a sharp turn in the opposite direction. Like the consumer who is no longer satisfied with their investment, the author feels betrayed.

They loved writing like a soul mate. How could their soul mate leave them so depleted and heartbroken after all they gave them? How could this beautiful marriage between author and muse, pen and paper, creator and art have ended so badly?

I said it before, and I'll say it again, writing was not the culprit. It's that whore, publishing, stealing everyone's attention and putting unwanted pressure on the marriage.

Writing is loyal and dependable. It will always fill that void inside an author the way nothing else can. It is never writing that betrays us. It is us that betrays writing. We take a beautiful marriage and fill it with filthy expectations.

Ideally, books should pay us, and they do. We love our books like children. We spend long nights with them like partners. We worry over them like fragile parents or babies. There are few careers out there that stir that level of devotion and affection on the job. I never met a mechanic who said, "But damn, I love this motor so much I think I might stay up all night just to look at it and hold it."

However, an author might say that about their book. And that is the expectation. That is the reward. That is the goal we hope to share with every reader we introduce to our book. It's when we start to expect more that we start to feel betrayed.

Do not blame writing for the feelings marketing has created. Blame the imbalance and stop feeding into behaviors that leave you feeling depleted and robbed. Write. Only writing will nurture your author soul and return that sense of rightness to your world. The marketing will come when you finish your next book. It doesn't have to be the main focus.

Successful writers have mastered living a balanced author life and the art of storytelling. It is statistically proven through market trends that the heavily promoted approach of quantity over quality is not an equal substitute for superior, well-crafted books.

If an author continues to improve their craft and establish brand trust based on quality products, the effort to sell should decrease in time, allowing the author more freedom to do what they love—write. You might be able to write beautiful novels at age sixty, seventy, or even into your eighties, but will you have the cognitive strength to manage all the other responsibilities? What if your book sales rely on those marketing gimmicks because that's all you've ever done to sustain your audience?

A wise professional would follow a business plan that alleviates unnecessary work while increasing profits, rather than the other way around. Why not grow your audience organically through quality stories and word of mouth recommendations? Yes, it will take longer, but I promise, a slow and steady audience will earn an author a priceless reputation. Do it well and that sort of payoff outlives a career and lifespan, creating a legacy that cannot be bought.

There is a need for advertising in any business and the book industry is certainly no exception. However, the only investment that will sustain an author long-term is an investment in one's self.

If authors hit an imbalance, they need an alignment. Sometimes this alignment is a minor adjustment and sometimes it's a complete overhaul of their business model. Take a look at the adapted model below.

By sliding the triangles together, we have overlapped our efforts on the job and inverted the way the budget will be allocated.

In prior models, the longer a writer worked as an author, the more their marketing time increased. When they achieved sustainable income, the effort shifted, allocating more time to marketing than writing, until almost no writing time remained, which eventually leads to burnout for the author.

In this model, however, the author has chosen not to simply assign their budget to marketing, but purposefully market while devoting 75% of their time to writing, always keeping their craft as the highest priority.

At the start of the author career, the budget will gradually increase. This is when a business is still considered an infant and increased marketing is suggested to help a brand's visibility. But once a sustainable income is achieved, the model must change.

Rather than continually increasing the marketing budget, the author should invest in purposeful marketing. *Purposeful Marketing* is exactly what it sounds like, marketing with a purpose.

When we market with purpose, we have a clear understanding of what our brand represents, who our audience should be, and a collection of established data that tells us where we stand and how we're performing. Brand, audience, and data must be in alignment for marketing to be purposeful.

If these three things are not aligned you will be speaking to the wrong audience. And if your brand does not speak to the right audience, your data will report a failure. But if you have reached a point of sustainable income, you can study that sweet spot and see exactly who your audience is and what demographic is resonating with your brand. Then you can point your marketing in that direction.

Purposeful marketing only targets a *hot* audience. Don't waste a single worry on trolls or haters. You're too busy crushing it to care about their bitter opinions. All a hater is telling you is that they are not your customer. Do not mistake them as your audience. Do not try to sign them up for a newsletter they won't read and do not waste your time trying to change their opinion of your work. Your brand just isn't for them, that's all. There are plenty of warm-blooded customers out there who are literally salivating for you to focus on them.

Purposeful marketing requires business skills, which is why you've been attending all those workshops to stay up-to-date on trends and technology as well as craft practices. Guessing will no longer cut it. Yes, if you fling garbage at a target, something will eventually stick to the bullseye, but this is no way to run a business. You've had years to study and learn and develop strategies. Now, it's time to use them.

Data exists for a reason. Metrics matter. Metrics should ultimately get converted into sales. Impressions, site traffic, followers, likes, comments, and shares, should all convert into sales, contacts, or leads.

Purposeful marketing points to a *hot* audience. It is not doing what your best author friend is doing or copying what your favorite writer just did. It's doing exactly what works for *your* brand and *your* audience, in accordance with the data *your* analytics show.

But that seems like a lot of work. How do we manage that and somehow create more time to write? Well, this is when you become a diva. Guys, you can be divas, too. We'll call you *divos*.

Being a diva in business means you know your shit. You've put in your time and worked hard to get where you are. Nothing about your position is by chance. Everything about your trajectory is strategized. You're informed, knowledgeable, and more of a leader than a follower from this point forward. You are, without a doubt, the greatest expert on your company to ever exist, and it's time to invest in yourself.

Rather than trade precious writing time for marketing, you delegate purposeful marketing. This requires you to know what works and what doesn't.

Authors often double dip into the same old pond of cookie-cutter, preemie PR companies. These companies have a decent reach for a new author, but when an author's audience outgrows that of the PR company's, it's time to trade up. You've moved to the next level and sticking with a limited publicist will only hold back your reach. Thank them for their service and start shopping for a larger PR firm.

Bigger firms with bigger platforms cost bigger dollars, which is why you must continue to produce new, shiny products. A renowned publicist doesn't market hand-me-down duds. They market the next hot thing, so have something irresistible to pitch.

Did I not mention that you would be pitching? Yes. Powerful publicists come with powerful connections, and therefore, they're in high demand. You will have to sell yourself to them.

An agent can help here, but as a diva or divo, I'm pretty sure you can handle the job on your own, especially when you take a meeting and show an aptitude for the market by discussing your metrics and how they convert to sales when targeting the right audience. You can also impress them by coming to the meeting prepared with a marketing plan for your next book.

The only way to delegate purposeful marketing is to understand what the purpose is. Your purpose is sales, which comes from forming connections with the right audience. Do not spend money on a PR company that will only use a cookie-cutter model and market you to a general audience. It has to be specific to *your* brand and only *you* can know for sure what that is.

There is a shortage of qualified resources out there. When we shop for effective PR, we become the consumer. We have a need and that need is "effective publicity." If a PR company cannot deliver effective publicity, they are not meeting our need and we, the consumer, will wind up betrayed.

It's very easy to build a website, structure a social following, and brand a PR business. It is not easy to publicize a unique product in an oversaturated market.

Do not go by first appearances. Do your research. Any good investment will require time. Watch how the PR company performs. Reach out to past clients and find out if they are still satisfied or why they moved on. Look at the success of the PR company's clients. Are they doing well?

Look at the interactions between publicity and readers. Is the audience cold or hot? If their content is getting the attention of the client and only two others, keep searching.

And if you want to be taken seriously, take them seriously. This is a business. If at any time they indicate that your company's well-being is not their first priority, cut ties and move on.

There is nothing more infuriating to me as a business owner than when a fellow "business owner" behaves unprofessionally at my expense. If a PR company does not follow through on a paid service, you are due a refund and an apology. This is your livelihood, and if they do not respect that, they do not deserve your business.

I once had a publicist fail to launch a campaign I paid for because she had to put down her cat a few days prior. Now, I am not an unfeeling person. I'm compassionate, and I love animals. But someone else's crisis should not be my company's consequence. If this publicist was unable to do her job, then she should have reached out to her team and still put me, the client, first. I never worked with that company again.

If we have to babysit a PR company they are not saving us time. They are an added distraction. A decent PR company should save us a job, not create one.

Yes, we have to always monitor our marketing, and a portion of marketing will always be personal and impossible to delegate, but the goal is, as a consumer and client, to invest in a company you trust. So find that company and then get back to writing.

Pitching

Once a book reaches a stage where it can be sold, an author's attention divides, partially focused on marketing and the remainder focused on writing and revising. Authors are forever attempting to sell their novels, and a sale starts with a good pitch.

The cover is an attention grabbing package meant to entice the consumer to look closer. A blurb on the back of a book is another pitch. It's the preview used to tease a reader after the cover catches their eye.

There is also the synopsis, a typically 1 to 2 page tell-all describing the events of the book, including spoilers. Synopses are not for the consumer but fellow investors, meaning traditional publishers, agents, or publicists.

Before pitching a book, the author should have a complete, polished manuscript available. Never pitch without a product. Your product is the solution to a problem. If you aren't ready to actively solve a problem you aren't ready to pitch.

At the minimum, and only in unique cases, is it acceptable for an author to have three chapters or fifty pages as a sample without a finished manuscript. These unique circumstances are mostly saved for authors working long-term with an agent or editor. A sample suffices, in this case, because the agent or editor is familiar with the author's prior work and abilities, and the sample is enough for them to make a decision.

Authors that do not have an established relationship with a traditional publisher, editor, or an agent, are advised to stick with the generic model for pitching.

First, write the book. Then, polish the book so that it is free of errors and an example of your best work. As the creator, you will have to also write the synopsis (with spoilers), a hook, and the back cover blurb. All of these accessories will help your pitch.

Many authors, who have never experienced the traditional world, fear the unknown. Or avoid it for the sake of saving time. Pitching can be a time-consuming process, but it should not be an overwhelming or draining process.

Assuming you've written and polished your book, have a blurb, and a synopsis, you're almost done. Different operations prefer different sorts of pitches, and it is critical that pitches follow the unique set of "submission guidelines" for each operation, especially if the operation took the time to spell them out.

Your query should address the precise person you want to read your submission. Be sure his or her name is spelled correctly. It's up to you to decide where your book fits and who you will pitch it to, so plan to read a lot of biographies from important players in the industry. You will mostly find these on a company's "about" page.

Do yourself a favor and block out a day or two for pitching once you have all of the preliminary work complete. Keep in mind, if you are pitching your book to traditional houses, it should not be anywhere on public domain, this includes listings like Goodreads, where authors often promote their WIPs before they're available. When you pitch, you are assuming a publisher will eventually buy the rights. They will want control over such listings.

Same goes for cover art. If you sell your book to a publisher, they will provide the cover art. They can even choose a new title, if they think the working title isn't marketable.

When it comes to indie authors pitching to traditional publishers, you can't be a little bit pregnant. You are either moving in one direction with that title or another. If traditional does not pan out, you can always backtrack and take the book indie, but it's unprofessional to start both processes at the same time.

Ultimately, the publisher wants the right to introduce the product to the public the way they see is best for the success of the product. When you take that step away from them by announcing your product too soon, you take away from a book's newness and the book deal's potential to create disruptive content. It's fine to announce that you're working on something and encouraged as a way to keep followers interested, but leave the product branding and packaging to the experts.

Pitching to traditional publishers is time consuming because it requires patience. It forces authors to have a ready to read, marketable product, and sit on it while they wait.

Discovering where to pitch isn't complicated. Searching words like "literary agency" or "call for submissions" will help compile a list. A great way to discover publishing houses is to take a field trip to a bookstore, go to the section where your book belongs, and search the copyright pages of similar books. The publisher will be listed in the front matter and sometimes on the spine.

Once you have a list, do research on those companies. Some will not accept unsolicited work and require an agent. If the majority of your favored publishers seem to follow that rule, you will need to pitch to agents first. This takes more time.

Gathering your resources means compiling your research in a functional manner. Create a grid that lists the name of a company, if they are a publisher or an agent, if they require an agent, who your point of contact will be (spelled correctly), what their interests are as far as submissions, what the exact submission guidelines require, and what the expected wait time is. You may also want to add a column for credentials to include relevant clients and books they've signed.

I recommend doing this on a spreadsheet and also leaving space at the end of each row to make notes throughout the process, such as more time requested, accepted, or rejected. Your notes will help you pitch your next book.

If a publisher is "open to submissions" be sure to read their "submission guidelines." Submission guidelines can get very particular and list specifications about font, spacing, headers, page numbers, and so on.

You want to follow each operation's specifications to a T, so expect to create a lot of versions of your book. Some will even give explicit instructions about what to include with your query, such as the first three chapters, the first ten pages, the first fifty pages, or no attachments at all. Straying from these instructions by even a small degree can land your book in the slush pile.

The *slush pile* is a collection of unsolicited, discarded manuscripts submitted to a publisher or literary agency. Slush piles are landfills where books go to die. Don't let yours end up in one!

Before you write a query and start the actual pitching process, you will want to gather your resources. Remember at the start of the book when I told you this was your personal journey and you were the hero? Well, in a story arc the "gathering of resources" usually takes place just before a climactic event. This is the moment of every story where the main character has learned and grown from their mistakes and understands what he or she needs to do to win.

Once you've gathered your resources and have a complete list of requirements organized, you're ready to start the actual querying process. Authors, unlike other careers, do not often send resumes. We send queries. A query letter is simply a specifically designed cover letter.

Keep in mind that agents and editors are reading thousands of query letters a year. They are rejecting thousands and only accepting a select few. The formality and design is important, because it saves them time when reviewing submissions. Do not try to reinvent the wheel. Stick to the traditional format or risk landing in the slush pile without a second glance.

In a professional's mind, if an author did not take the time to review their company's guidelines, they probably didn't do much research on the industry or much preliminary work on their manuscript. And if they don't know how the industry works, they will likely be a high maintenance author that requires a lot of hand holding. Agents and editors want to sign authors who require the least work and can make them the most money. A query is your first impression as a professional, and it counts.

A query letter should include a professional greeting, your book details such as genre, word count and title, the hook, a brief author bio, and a thank you. That's it. Do not talk about *why* they will like the book or what your beta team thought of it, do not use juvenile or floral fonts, and certainly do not include typos.

The seduction is in the simplicity. When they know, they know.

The *hook* is the blurb. It should accomplish three things. It should identify the main character(s), explain what they want, and why they can't have it. Later, in the craft section, we will learn more about this, as it's also sometimes referred to as the goal, motivation, and conflict. Every story has one and you must know yours.

Your hook will be the foundation of your *elevator pitch*, a 30-60 second spiel that sells your book in the time it basically takes to ride an elevator with a potential customer or investor. It should be enticing, relatable, and meet a need.

There is an unforgettable moment in the movie *The Wolf of Wall Street* when Jordan Belfort, played by Leonardo DiCaprio, asks a roomful of salesmen to sell him a pen. This goes back to an earlier scene when he's sitting at a diner having the same discussion with colleagues.

Inevitably, someone always takes the pen, examines it, and begins listing its qualities—it's sleek, lightweight, comfortable to hold, has good ink flow, and so on. This is not what Jordan considers masterful salesmanship.

Eventually, a true salesperson takes the pen and then asks Jordan to write something down. Jordan then grins and says, "I need a pen."

Now, they are ready to make a sale.

The salesperson identified a need and had the exact product on hand to meet said need. That is salesmanship. Always identify the consumer's needs before your own.

If this opportunity arises in person, you should have your elevator pitch on the tip of your tongue and a business card in hand. Know your hook by heart, speak clearly, do not ramble, identify a need, identify how your product resolves said need and solves a problem. Briefly share your skills and experience, hand over your business card, and then wrap it up. Do this in under a minute and you have an elevator pitch.

The elevator pitch is the verbal equivalent to a query letter. It's brief, informative, and persuasive because the product itself creates a solution to a problem, and the delivery is professional, so the audience understands and feels at ease.

Query letters and elevator pitches are very generic. The frills are in the product you're selling, the hint of satisfaction, relief, and possibility felt by the consumer when they imagine possessing your product. If you pitch to someone who has no need or desire for what you're selling, you're pitching to the wrong audience.

Sample Query for WAKE MY HEART:

Dear Theresa Kohler,

WAKE MY HEART is a 96k word, small town romance with series potential. I'm currently querying both agents and traditional publishing houses.

When Ryan Clooney moves to the outskirts of his small town, the last thing he expects to find is love. Cursed to always be single, he's burned-out on blind dates and pity "plus-ones." He's through waiting for The One to arrive. But when he meets Maggie, the beautiful, young widow next door, his plans change.

Maggie O'Malley is not looking for love. Since losing her husband, she has withdrawn from small-town life and prefers to be left alone. But her new neighbor doesn't seem to understand personal privacy, and the more he intrudes on her solitary life, the more she remembers how wonderful friendship can be.

Determined to reach Maggie's heart, Ryan has an awakening of his own, and learns what love is all about.

As a hybrid, award winning author previously published with Penguin Random House, I have released over thirty-five novels. I am the consecutive recipient of the Author of the Year Award (2018 and 2019) from Happenings Media and the Best Author Award from the Currier Times. My stories have earned commendations for Best Contemporary Romance and Best New Adult. I hold a Bachelor of Arts, magna cum laude, dual degree in Special Education, but now work as a full-time author.

If you would like to learn more about WAKE MY HEART, please feel free to contact me. I have attached a ten page sample and synopsis. Thank you for your time and consideration. I hope to hear from you soon.

Sincerely,

Lydia Michaels
Lydia@LydiaMichaelsBooks.com
215-555-5555
www.LydiaMichaelsBooks.com

If you break this letter down to a template it looks like this:

Dear [Agent or Editor],

[BOOK TITLE] is a [word count] [genre]. [Your purpose for contact.] [If you have a referral or met the agent/editor at an event, mention that here to jog their memory.]

[The Hook or Back Cover Blurb | Often in bold and italicized]

[A brief bio including any notable credentials, such as previously published works, accolades, notable rankings, education, relevant experience, and audience, if you have an established and notable following.]

[Mention of any attachments per specified guidelines. Thank you and a salutation.]

[Insert attachments]

Sincerely,

[Full Name]
[Professional email *(NOT: Bunnynuts22@jinx.com)*]
[Phone number]
[Website with hyperlink]

There are exceptions to every rule and the above is a very general example, nothing too exciting. The excitement should come when the editor or agent glances at your blurb and thinks, "Oh, I've been waiting for a book like this!" That will only happen if you are pitching to the right person.

When you are ready to pitch, write up a generic query letter for your book and customize it for each agency or publishing house according to their guidelines. The more places you pitch, the more files you will have to manage, so organization is your friend in the query process. Keep your files labeled clearly and group your correspondence in easy to access folders.

Once you've sent out your queries, print your chart, put it on your wall, and forget about it for a while. The query process can take anywhere from thirty days to six months. This is a great time to start writing your next book so you're ahead of the curve when an offer comes in.

If you do not receive an offer, it does not mean your book is no good. It only means it wasn't right for the people you queried. This is a good time to read it again with fresh eyes, work with betas and critique partners to see where improvements can be made, and possibly start the submission process again, or explore options for publishing the book independently. Do not get discouraged!

The book industry is one of the most challenging industries out there. It's painfully selective and more secure than Fort Knox. If everyone could get in, there would be no glory in the acceptance. The best way to improve your chances is to keep improving your craft and keep trying. Eventually, your big moment will come.

Fiction is a Service Industry

In a creative field made up of artists, one can easily get misled by emotion, but the truth is, fiction is a service business. And as such, there are proven ways to achieve success.

Hobbies live in comfort zones. Success requires authors to stretch beyond their comfort zone. That's what separates work from play. Writing can be playful, but publishing a book means making a business deal with the world. Respect it as such.

If you want to write for yourself, keep a journal. If you want to write for a living, know your audience and what sells. Like architects, authors need a blueprint if they hope to build a masterpiece.

In fiction, what exactly are we selling? Books? Thrills? Angst? Sex? Ourselves? All of the above?

We are selling escapes. A good author's skillset must include an ability to emotionally transport readers, but first you have to convince them to open the book.

Transporting a reader while they sit silently in a room a thousand miles away from where the author wrote their book several years prior is the magic of literature. But behind all magic is a spell, and what is a spell, if not a fancy word for recipe or formula?

The craft section of this book will examine the various formulas for writing fiction, but before we move on, we must be absolutely certain we understand, not only the workings of the book industry, but the fluctuation of change.

The climate of the book market is not what it was twenty years ago, nor will it look the same twenty years from now, but we can still learn from the past. That is why every successful business owner must study their industry. Forecasts, in any field, are merely predictions, educated guesses based on collected data and an understanding of patterns.

After the initial surge when mainstream print books segmented with eBooks, sales tapered and faltered, which increased publishers' cautiousness. Such prudence infected the industry, resulting in shrinking bookstores, closing publishing houses, and a select group of favored, "low-risk" authors dominating the market.

The long-term projection of the book market remains extremely flat. While digital audiobook revenue continues to grow, eBook sales appear to be decreasing. Backlist sales, sales of books published prior to the present year, are leading.

In 2015, backlist sales accounted for 58% of transactions, jumping to 64% in 2018. While frontlist sales, books published during the present year, made up only 36% of sales[11]. This means that readers are buying more books published in 2000 than books published now, despite the overwhelming amount of money plunged into marketing new releases.

What does that tell authors? More readers are interested in stories published twenty years ago than they are in what's being produced now.

To understand why these patterns are showing, we must figure out what's changed in books over the last twenty years? What is the attracting factor of old books versus new ones? Could it be quality?

---

[11] American Booksellers Association

Prior to the recent accessibility to self-publishing platforms, authors were required the approval of trained specialists. Publishers were the bridge keepers between writers and readers. And they relied on gathered data to tell them what the target audience wanted to read. If the audience wasn't there, a book was rejected, because they knew advertising undesirable products only led to loss of profit.

The market was more controlled in 2000 compared to now. But with the rise of indie publishing came a freedom for authors to write stories according to their personal creative preferences, sometimes overlooking the reader's desires completely.

There is incredible talent among those published independently. Many readers found this shift a refreshing breath of fresh air. But when anyone can publish anything with very few requirements, there is no guaranty that quality will remain a consistent goal. Frustrations emerged when readers found themselves spending hard earned money on poorly crafted, sometimes unedited work.

Today, quality control rests in the hands of each indie author who chooses to send their story out into the world, while publishing houses still retain final say about what mass market books are hitting the shelves, since they are also footing the bill of all production costs.

However, even publishers can fail to accurately read the market in such tumultuous times, which is why many presses prefer to err on the side of caution and save their money, rejecting more than 95% of books submitted or signing contracts that only offer digital first imprints. They will likely play it safe with similar practices until the industry levels out.

Independent publishing has released a tsunami in the book industry, completely restructuring the terrain of the book world and turning many businesses upside down. The industry is unrecognizable in comparison to what it once was, and many are still trying to find solid ground. Unfortunately, there are no absolutes at this time. Everyone, the indie, the traditional, the old, the new, the rich, and the poor, are all guessing at what might work.

If a strategy proves profitable, it's repeated until it's defunct. Publicity stunts are copied, and trends spread like wildfire in this industry, so the moment something is done it's already overdone. There is no finite solution for selling books.

An author, by definition, must write. Don't get too lost in the minutia. Write. Write often and write well.

Study and improve your craft. Keep it your passion. Stay educated about your industry and grow your network. Make connections with other professionals, and as you produce new products, pitch them properly. Do this, again and again, and as you improve, your network will organically grow because the quality of your work has become more advanced, and you've established yourself as a professional within your field.

It's time to get back to basics. Readers are statistically searching for stories that match the quality produced twenty years ago—before the market changed. It's time writers stopped focusing on quantity and turned their attention back to quality—quality of writing and quality of life.

Publishing is a game. Writing is a passion. Differentiating the two is what makes this a business rather than a hobby.

With the boom of eBooks and independent publishing came multiple challenges and changes that broke the mold of traditional publishing. The market is in a steady state of flux. Readers have a stronger voice than ever before, and authors can hone their stories, writing to a specific audience awaiting a specific kind of book.

Social media allows for intimate relationships between authors and readers. Not only that, once a relationship is established, the author can bounce story ideas off the sample audience, post surveys, test ads, and so on. Utilizing social media is a strategy that should never be dismissed, but in this over-saturated market, one must be more than talented and tech savvy to survive. They must be brilliant!

Only a select few have managed to land that six-figure book deal with a team of publicists eager to shout praises from the rooftops of the *"Big Six"* publishing houses in New York.

There are multiple areas of expertise required to succeed as an author, regardless of the sort of author one is—indie, traditionally published, or hybrid. An author could write the best story since *Romeo and Juliet*, but if said author doesn't possess the readership required for proper exposure to the right audience, no one will ever read it.

Signing with a traditional publisher can prove beneficial to authors because publishing houses come with an established audience and advertising budget. Traditionally published authors do not always need to sell as hard to readers, but they absolutely need to sell themselves to the publishers. No matter what kind of author you choose to be, you will need to sell in order to survive.

There is an art form to selling within the book industry. Where an author lands on the sliding scale of publishing, will influence how much time they invest in other areas of the trade. But nothing will ever influence your success as much as a quality product can.

PART THREE

THE CRAFT

WRITE 10K IN A DAY

Chapter Sixteen
The Creative Process

"In a sense, one can never read the book that the author originally wrote, and one can never read the same book twice."

Edmund Wilson; The Triple Thinkers; 1976
American Author & Editor for F. Scott Fitzgerald

The Plan

Every success story should begin with an intention, a plan, and a strategy to execute each objective. If you plan to write thousands of words a day, you must first clear the path for creativity. Your goal can be writing 10k in a day as long as you understand it takes time to develop that skill. Plans require realistic timelines, so be patient with yourself. You will get there.

The *Write 10k in a Day* plan can be broken down into three main subsections: *planning, knowledge,* and *hard work.* The first two sections of this book supplied a great deal of knowledge, but as lifelong learners, your knowledge will continue to grow. Never stop educating yourself about your craft, the business aspects of the book industry, marketing trends, and of course, strategies for living a well-balanced life.

This section—*The Craft*—will address the creative process and many elements that go into becoming a more prolific author. The information provided in this section is based on industry standards and advice from celebrated experts working in the business of writing and publishing.

Like everything else in this book, you will need to be judicious about which strategies you apply to your own personal creative process. Everyone's journey is unique, and what works for many might not fit for you. But being knowledgeable of various methods for creating and why we follow certain standards in this industry, will improve your work as a whole.

The *plan* is to apply as many helpful strategies as possible to your creative process, increase your word count, amplify your success, and enhance the quality of your overall work. Doing so will incorporate the aspects from the earlier sections about health and wellness, the business of publishing, as well as the craft of writing.

Remember, balance is key. To truly succeed, we must harmonize all parts of the author's soul—*mind, body,* and *spirit*—so don't get lost in one section over another. As you apply these strategies, remember not to overdo it. Take lunch breaks, keep your work week at forty hours or less, schedule balanced dinners with friends and/or family, take frequent movement breaks, get those steps in, enjoy your personal time, and get 6 to 8 hours of sleep on a regular basis.

But most importantly, remember to celebrate the victories, even the ones that might not announce themselves in monetary reward. You are accomplishing great things, and the value of those accomplishments are not always obvious to outsiders. But they must retain value and significance to you.

Consider all of the above your new plan! If you're recovering from burnout, give yourself the necessary time to heal. Use your recovery time to reflect and visualize the way your career is about to change for the better, and work on your plan before beginning.

Not only will your *knowledge* of the industry and its history improve your craft, it will help you establish yourself as a great resource within the book community. Be genuine and generous with your knowledge. Stingy practices lead to limited reward.

Share everything you know and your energy will invite an abundance of rewards in the form of new relationships, business connections, new knowledge, and pleasure. When we combine masterful business acumen and expertise with regard to industry standards, we unleash the secrets of writing marketable fiction.

You do not have to be a formulaic writer for this section to work for you, but there will be a lot of *recipes* you'll want to understand. If you want to serve up something delicious and satisfying, you'll need to know how the secret sauce is made.

Acceptance remains an imperative quality as we move forward in our plan, because possessing a knowledgeable grasp of the craft means recognizing and accepting that everyone's creative process is unique.

Our old friend *awareness* remains relevant as well, because we have to stay *aware* of our personal limits through this entire process. Do not try to keep pace with others. Your journey is not theirs and vice versa.

In the words of James N. Watkins, "A river cuts through rock, not because of its power, but because of its persistence." And that is where *hard work* comes in.

Writing should be an absolute joy, but achieving a successful and sustainable author career is hard work. Never forget that part of the *plan's* success will rely on your own determination, devotion, and consistent drive. Pace yourself, fall back on proven practices that help authors maintain balance and avoid burnout, and you will eventually find the success you've dreamed of achieving.

Writing is a Subjective Experience

Reading and writing are highly subjective experiences. No two readers will ever read the same story, and no two writers will ever share the same creative experience.

Every author's creative process will be influenced by writing styles and life experiences. Personal strengths and weaknesses will tailor every referenced method within your personal bank of knowledge. Other unique factors will also influence your individual interpretation of the strategies ahead.

The *Write 10k in a Day* methods supply a flexible and effective framework for writers of all levels and skillsets. Interpret the tips ahead as malleable suggestions. The craft strategies in this book are merely scaffolding for the many masterpieces you and your muse will write.

Every writer is different. The writer you are today may be nothing like the writer you become a year from now. As you become more knowledgeable of the industry and craft, your opinions may shift, so it's important to always keep an open mind, no matter what kind of writer you are at this very moment.

Some authors approach writing methodically, analyzing the craft until words group neatly into scenes or chapters, organized meticulously into a chronological timeline that travels from Point A to Point B. These writers are traditionally referred to as *plotters*.

Then there are the less organized writers who, by default, are labeled as *pantsers*, because these authors typically "fly by the seat of their pants" rather than plan. *Pantsers* typically write without plotting ahead.

The problem with labeling a writer as a *plotter* or *pantser* is that both descriptions pigeonhole authors in one extreme or another and dismiss the idea that a person's creative process could possess plot formula and spontaneity. Both terms are relatively new buzzwords, originating with the surge of early indie authors that hit the scene around 2005. Regardless of the terminology, authors have been plotting and writing spontaneous twists for hundreds of years.

Often, authors, like any group of people, take issue with blanket labels that overlook the many facets of each individual. As artists, it goes against most creators' natures to adhere to one mold, and such labels are rejected completely or adapted with comments like, "I'm generally a *pantser,* but I still plan my stories. I just don't write from a detailed outline."

Plotter, pantser, or *undefined,* there is no right or wrong way to craft a novel. But there should be a term to identify the authors who reject the limited labels and fall in the undefined gray area. Writing is an art form and, as artists, we should allow vocabulary for the undefined Picassos of our field.

As self-aware authors, we should always have the confidence to color outside of the lines when creativity calls for it, so don't get too tied up in stereotypical labels. By definition, art is the expression of beauty and beauty is one hundred percent subjective. Subjectivity pairs well with a widely diverse audience.

Celebrate the array of talent and diverse readership out there! There is a book for everyone, which would never happen if we all wrote using the exact same methods to fit only a few precise types of stories.

This book was born in the gray area of a dyslexic author's mind, so things are bound to get a little abstract at times. Embrace the fact that your process might be a little weird. Weird is where the wild beauty of creativity grows!

While authors work with the medium of words, our usage and approach ranges phenomenally, and we should never feel obligated to remain in one corner of the spectrum or repeat methods that have already been done when there are magnitudes and countless dimensions we can apply to the creative process. Constricting artists of any medium to a select set of labels narrows the scope of resources available within the creative community.

Writing should be diverse and adaptable and boundless in all genres. The moment we say an author must be either *this* or *that*, we cut off the potential for so many more possibilities to emerge. There is no right or wrong way to create. There are only tools, experiences, and advice to help you discover *your* way.

Pantsers are often stigmatized for being less professional than the ever prepared *plotters*. And *plotters* are sometimes branded as less artistic creators than those who let their muses lead. Neither stereotype is correct, and hardly ever does one author fit perfectly into one writing style over the other.

The space between these two common labels far outweighs the space occupied by those who unflinchingly adhere to one rigid style over the other. The majority of authors I've met identified somewhere in the undefined, gray area of the in-between. Let's call this majority—for the simple sake of identification—the *plan-sers*.

Plan-ser authors plan without overly plotting. They do not act spontaneously without thinking ahead in regard to plot and characters. They have a firm grasp of the character's motivation, strengths, and weaknesses, but not a chronologically detailed plot outline.

This middle ground of flexibility is a lovely place to live as a writer. This is where I would identify myself, as neither a *plotter* or a *pantser* but a *plan-ser*.

Plan-sers see the value of knowing a formula, but don't always use a formula to achieve their writing goals. The longer a writer is in the publishing business, the more experience he or she garners in the book market, and the more likely they are to develop into a *plan-ser*. *Plan-ser* authors grow less reliant on the structures needed earlier in their career once they learn to straddle the fence between *plotter* and *pantser*.

The Yellow Brick Road

In the last chapter of the previous business section, we learned that fiction is a service business. We call it such because, while writing is a creative process, there is a definite art form to selling our written work. And if we want to sell it well, we must not only understand the art of doing so, but master certain skills to meet the market's ever fluctuating needs.

As established, we are selling escapes. To properly move the reader from their living room couch to a different place and time created in a stranger's mind, we must possess skills similar to that of a master hypnotist. Just like a hypnotist, transcending occurs through the convoluted yet simplistic art of suggestion.

On a stage, we call this magic, sleight of hand, or illusion. In the world of fiction, we call them writing tricks, strategies, or hacks.

Applying strategies does not make one a formulaic writer any more than enjoying an occasional glass of wine makes someone an alcoholic. Different circumstances call for different approaches, and in an industry as oversaturated as the book industry, it's high time authors stop worrying about labels and return their focus to what matters most—writing quality stories.

The truth is simple. There is a formula to writing best-selling fiction. There are hidden patterns in every story that undeniably match plots that have come before. This is why such a thing as a *Cinderella Story* can be told a million different ways and still remain entertaining.

The diversification of words and characters keeps old stories fresh. But whether an author is writing a Cinderella story or a dark psychological thriller, there are always similarities hidden in the structure. There are repeated patterns authors use to engineer a fine functioning plot, and knowing such methods can save authors years of time.

It does not matter what "type" of author you identify as. The secrets of the craft belong to every kind of author trying to write fiction.

The current social climate is more sensitive than ever before regarding how we identify as people and professionals. We live in a society that naturally sorts people into demographics, for better or worse.

When a writer announces him or herself as an author, they are quickly filtered down to a type—fiction or non-fiction, which genre, then subgenre. And if it's a colleague asking, they will likely want to know what kind of writer you are—*plotter* or *pantser*. But such limited labels rarely give anything away about the quality of work created.

Labels, brands, and genres are secondary to the creative side of writing. Those identifiers are for the fancy Emerald City side of the curtain where the readers play. The craft side is where the gears and mechanics work, where the delightfully imaginative, sometimes frenzied, creative process takes place. It's where you, The Great and Powerful Oz, hide.

No matter what level writer you consider yourself, this book can help you. Whether you're a seasoned author, coming into this with a burned-out, jaded heart, perhaps torn by opposing theories, or perhaps a green newbie seeking a lioness courage to write without apology, or maybe you feel lost—like Dorothy—with no clue where to begin, this book can guide you closer to success.

Once an author clearly sees the path to novel writing, the "yellow brick road", they will recognize it in every book they read. There is always a plot and never an accidental outcome in *quality* stories.

Well-developed fiction is a strategized, methodical, work of art, no matter what sort of planner the author is. As long as the author has an intention, a goal, a reason for telling a story, they have a plan. How orderly that plan reveals itself will greatly influence a writer's speed.

Every author should understand the structure of a story arc and accept that there is a science to formulaic writing. Not that formulaic writing is the answer. God no. But whether an author is a plotter or not, there is a formula buried within their personal methods. Recognizing the formula will increase productivity and the quality of any author's work in immeasurable ways.

Before the *pantser* shuts this book and deems it not for them, let me explain one thing. If someone took the story arc of a classic like *The Godfather* and placed it directly over the story arc of a polar opposite classic like *Jaws*, both arcs would align. That is the identical yellow brick road that weaves through every successful plot.

Do all of my books contain this arc? Hell no. There was a time when I didn't have a clue what I was doing. But I've learned a thing or two in the process of writing over sixty novels—some that will never see the light of day. I've learned that when my characters are circling the same conflict for too many pages, I, the author, have strayed from the path.

Knowing that yellow brick road, which leads both the author and reader from beginning to end, is a lifesaver. It has saved me time, stress, health issues, and bad reviews. It's also scored book deals, new readers, and notoriety in various forms. So whether you intend to write using a detailed arc or continue on *pantser-ing* with just a thread of intentions, I promise nothing in this book will hurt your creative process.

Forget the labels. If you are a writer, this book is for you. It doesn't matter if you're approaching fourteen or seventy, the information ahead can help you write better and faster.

From this moment on, we stop thinking of writing as a linear style, tightly bracketed by right and wrong methods with opposing approaches, and start viewing it as a spectrum where *every* method is right and there are infinite roads that lead to Oz. The industry is wide, and writers tend to get lost in specific territories, obsessing over two cent advice and forgetting that this fluctuating business has continuously evolved since it first emerged in the 1400's.

On this side of the curtain, authors need to only be concerned with practices that will enhance the value of a story. Different authors will land on different areas of the spectrum, but we are all aiming to accomplish the same goal—to hook and hold a captivated audience to the end, and regardless of title, genre, or style, the basic principles of character-driven fiction novels have stood the test of time.

Various learning styles have been considered in the chapters ahead to aid in comprehension so that this book will be an asset to authors of all levels and backgrounds. Writers are encouraged to fit each strategy to their personal writing style, tightening or loosening the framework until it fits with their creative process.

Once your preferred method is identified and the strategies in this book have been adapted to meet your personal needs, incorporating a balanced approach that self-advocates a higher quality of life and quality of work, old erroneous methods for writing will disappear. Having a customized plan will streamline your creative process, help you avoid burnout, and unleash your prolific potential.

Learning Styles

There are four kinds of learning styles: *visual, auditory, verbal-linguistic,* and *kinesthetic.* People generally have one dominating learning style they are most comfortable using, but that doesn't mean they're incapable of learning other ways.

Lectures without visual aides are extremely challenging for *visual learners. Auditory learners*, not to be confused with *verbal-linguistic learners*, absorb information best when the information is spoken aloud to them. *Verbal-linguistic learners* excel when reading written words, but tend not to do well with visual aids because it's the actual words that stimulate their brain. And *kinesthetic learners* learn best through movement.

Learning styles register with different brains in different ways, but when all four methods are applied, comprehension is maximized. Why is this relevant information? Because authors come from all walks of life and possess varied styles of learning.

Some might benefit from voice-to-text technology while others might cringe at that approach to writing. Others could speed up their progress with a read-aloud function. And some might prefer to simply do things the old-fashioned way by simply writing.

Some authors might require a method approach while others can work from vision boards or blueprints. The kind of learner an author is will dictate how deep they submerge themselves in the research part of the job, and research is absolutely a part of the job, even in fiction.

Authors must learn everything there is to know about their characters, far beyond what they share with the readers. Not only do they have to know the people they are writing, they must have a clear picture of the setting and world they are creating. All of this takes a great deal of time. Knowing which type of learner you are can impact how efficiently you manage the preliminary stages of writing, such as plot, character, and setting development.

Give yourself the opportunity to learn with the best possible chance of rapid comprehension. If you are *visual*, try researching settings through Google images or YouTube. If you are *auditory*, perhaps a podcast could help. If you're *verbal-linguistic*, start reading up on your settings. And if you're *kinesthetic*, it may be time for an adventure!

Comprehension is necessary to learning, which is why I didn't think twice about putting this book in audiobook format so that *auditory learners* could benefit from it as well. Comprehension is required in order to apply information to real life situations. There is no value in what we fail to absorb.

Acknowledging the diversity among artists opens up a dialogue to teach new methods, approaches that might have been missing in previous lessons. New methods spread knowledge, and the more we know as a community, the more likely our working conditions are to improve as a whole.

When applying the strategies ahead, keep these varied learning styles in mind. You are the hero and you are the helper. Help yourself triumph by adapting approaches to your preferred style of learning. Forget what others are doing. Your success depends solely on knowing what *you* need.

The Right Brain and Left Brain

In addition to preferred learning style, each person's brain also has a dominant side. Brain dominance is simply divided by right and left. *Right-brained* people are said to be led by emotion, creativity, imagination, and memory. While *Left-brained* people are said to prefer thinking in terms of order, objectives, analytics, and rationale. People generally have one dominant side, although sometimes people are considered a mix of both.

Those who operate more frequently from the *right brain* are driven by emotions, possess a vivid imagination, and long-term memories. They tend to operate from a place of creative function more than any source of order.

Those with dominant *left brain* skills will excel at translating analytics. They typically enjoy order, having measurable objectives, and working within the bounds of a logical rationale.

Although not always the case, *right-brained* people tend to enjoy the arts such as music, literature, sculpture, paintings, and so on. *Left-brained* people are said to excel at critical thinking, reasoning, and problem solving. They do well with science and math.

You might assume all authors are *right-brained* since it takes creativity, emotion, and imagination to write a captivating story. But that's not always the case.

As an author who also happens to be dyslexic, I'm irrefutably *right-brained*, as my head literally begins to hurt when reviewing data and statistics. However, I know a colleague with a background in analytics whose brain computes data in a way mine simply cannot. She's a powerhouse of information when it comes to reading results of test ads and understanding the value of CPCs (cost per click) and CTRs (click through rate). And while we adhere to many of the same writing philosophies, our creative processes are completely opposite.

This colleague is undoubtedly *left-brained*. She outlines every series, knowing each twist and turn in the plot before writing a single word, where I—a *right-brained* author—focus mostly on the characters, placing plot second. I've tried her rigid methods only to find my muse creatively unmotivated in the end.

One could also call this colleague a *plotter,* which many *left-brained* authors tend to be. That also means that the *right-brained* group of authors could technically be labeled *pantsers.* But what about the *left-brained* writer who loves to fly by the seat of her pants, or the *right-brained* creator who absolutely needs an outline before beginning a novel? Well, there are exceptions to every rule.

Creativity needs to breathe. Writing should remain fun and fluid but also lucrative. For this reason and many others, you learn *your* process and forget everyone else's.

Writing, like reading, is personal. There are a hundred ways to write a story, and no way is any better than the other because each method works differently for different people and accomplishes different goals.

What might work for Author A, causes creative constipation for Author B, just like what works well for my colleague does not work well for me. Don't stress over what's *not* working. Focus only on what *is* working for *you.* Just because nine out of ten authors do something during the writing process, does not mean you have to. Be proud that you're the exception to the rule.

Outlining should be a productive strategy, not an oppressive one. Try the methods ahead. Whether they succeed or fail, you will learn something about yourself and your creative process. And the more we understand our process and our creative proclivities, the better we can use these gifts to our advantage.

Pricing the Menu

Since we're in a service business, a lucrative author career will require us to feed the market at times. Different readers have different appetites. Some are veracious and consume a book a day, while others prefer to savor stories, drawing them out as long as possible.

Some authors love writing and reading intense, intricate plots with word counts well into the hundred thousands, but admittedly see the challenge in selling such mammoth books. The insatiable reader who buys a new book every day might not linger over a story, but they will easily outspend the slower-paced reader who only savors one book a month.

This market trend creates advantages for authors who cater to the faster-paced customer. But these customers want quick, affordable selections. Nothing too heavy and nothing too time consuming. Marketing strategist and New York Times best-selling author, Pam Godwin, refers to this sort of book as the "dollar menu option." They are fast, inexpensive, and they serve a consumer's need.

Quick, inexpensive products often save on time, which is why places with "dollar menus" are typically labeled as "fast food." But no artisan chef wants to think of themselves as a "dollar menu" creator, nor does a masterful author want to see his or her books devalued to the point of pennies when they took years to write.

Authors writing for the "dollar menu customer" will lose money if they put the wrong book on a discounted menu. "Dollar menus" should not serve up masterful prose or qualify as literary works of art, but they do sell—often times more than the so-called masterpieces. Do not assume that because something is on a "dollar menu" it cannot qualify as a bestseller.

"Dollar menu" books can be well-written and extremely satisfying. They take less time to prepare, but are not necessarily less filling.

Think of a high quality, organic, grass fed, free-range angus burger from a high-end steakhouse. Such ingredients take time to cultivate.

Now, consider a thin, greasy patty from a drive-through window that's open 24/7. Some would say the steak is higher quality. On the other hand, sometimes people just want hot, accessible, greasy comfort food.

Filet mignon, served with fizzing champagne prose and robust, caviar characters that burst with flavor is a meal that deserves to be savored. Logically, it should be higher priced. Let's assume it is. But which serving is actually making more money, the upscale, elite restaurant serving prime cut books at five dollars and above or the fast food joint peddling dollar burger books so quickly the line never ends?

The "dollar menu" reader will continue to purchase a book a day and feed their hunger—or book habit—from the more affordable menu due to budget and endless supply. When an author—or restaurant—requires reservations, and makes customers wait months for a book or meal, they naturally need something to tide them over. It's in that time in between that customers learn both options can satisfy their hunger, even if the experience differs.

The steakhouse typically makes less money than the fast food joint because the fast food joint can feed more people faster for less of an overhead cost. Unfortunately, this leads to the down-valuing of products. In favor of luring new customers from the competition, the steakhouse drops prices and extends the hours of operation.

In debt and overworked, an imbalance has been created for the filet mignon author who invested more time into their product. A profit will be harder to turn after the costs of production are fully weighed. Whereas the "fast food" author has invested prudently and requires less of a reimbursement to break even.

Different products require different pricing, but the book market has become such an orgy of selection, readers sometimes see all books as equal, and often view the up pricing of books as audacious or arrogant author behavior, which can have yet another negative effect on sales.

The exception to this rule, however, is the sustained high pricing of products sold from well-established publishing houses. Because these suppliers form a monopoly, they can maintain a higher price point backed by years of meeting quality standards. Newer authors do not have such a record of customer satisfaction, but that does not necessarily mean their products are lower quality.

Every creative process comes with a production cost. In the business section, we broke production time into an hourly rate. But authors are often not paid fairly for their time, so how do we correct that imbalance? Why should a book that takes three years to write be priced the same as a book half its length that only took two months to write?

How do we charge for steak when we are serving steak? How do we convince the readers that one meal is worth more when they could just as easily enjoy something sort of the same for less?

The trick is efficiency. We can still produce high-end, quality books that deserve to be savored like steak but take less time to prepare if we use our time wisely. We, as creators, need to manage our energy better if we want to be reimbursed fairly for the cost of our time. Do not skimp on ingredients like editing or quality. Invest in better practices, more efficient tools, and snappier, sharper skills to increase production speed. Cut the fat not the value.

The fat in a high end restaurant might be the glitz, the music, or the centerpieces. Let the meal speak for itself. Cut the fat in the social extras, the fluff, and the pricey cover models. Let your masterpiece stand as the main event.

Price your books the way they deserve to be priced. Do not undervalue your work for fear of the competition. Market to the right reader, and prove to the world you're serving something worth trying. But to do this, authors must be honest and aware about the effort that goes into their creative process for each individual product.

Production

I grew up in the Pennsylvania suburbs located in the tri-state area, just one hour outside of Philadelphia, New York, and New Jersey. In the 1940's, just after World War II, a company called Levitt & Sons used this area to mass produce neighborhoods and homes for veterans returning from war, offering affordable housing for families, positioned exactly in the center of a triangular job market for various trades.

Each neighborhood within Levittown generally included the same elements, such as a school, a church, a playground, sidewalks, streetlamps, and paved roads. One might say these are the foundations of a community. The houses were all built the same, one kitchen, three bedrooms, one bath. The lot sizes met a standard and included one driveway and one tree.

William J. Levitt saw a story in his mind. He pictured thousands of men returning from war, hungry for home and family. He structured his vision, plotting out everything those men could possibly need to find a satisfying end, and then the baby boom was written into American history.

Levitt & Sons was not the only company to construct towns this way during the mid-nineteen hundreds. The real estate market was saturated. While expensive homes still sold, nothing sold as much as the affordable seven thousand dollar cookie-cutter suburban model during this time.

People like Levitt saw a need and fed that need. He figured out the formula to meet that need as efficiently as possible, wasting no superfluous energy in the production.

On the Levitt & Sons crew there were men who only installed doorknobs. And men whose only job was to plant trees, one lot after another. These men, with their designated jobs, would arrive in the morning, complete their installation, and move on to the next house, thereby preserving energy by avoiding multitasking, and staying focused on meeting the customer's need as quickly as possible.

If an assembly line can exist in the food industry and it can make sense at times in the real estate market, it could very well work in the book market. Sometimes survival and success isn't about creativity or originality. Sometimes it's about consistency and productivity. It's your job as the creator to decide which times call for what products. We do that by accurately reading the climate of the market.

The book market will never be a solid hunk of statistics. It's as fluid as the ocean and always moving. Authors must go with the flow and follow currents if they want to stay afloat.

But shifting methods of production should never mean sacrificing talent or skill. It only means you're temporarily applying your talents and skills differently while the waters are at their choppiest. Things will level out again, and when they do, you need to make sure you're still afloat, not buried somewhere on the bottom of the sea under all the competition.

Catering to the market is a tricky business. Authors must know when to say *when*—meaning only you can decide when it's the right time to work quickly and when you've had enough of mass production and want to dial back and create something a bit more refined or one of a kind. Feed the market, but stay flexible enough to keep food on your table, too.

Understanding the craft allows us to adjust the speed of production, becoming more prolific when needed but also allowing the option to dial back our output speed when a certain project commands more focus. The trick is flexibility and versatility. Authors able to do both—write masterful, epic, one-of-a-kind stories while also producing commercial fiction—will be more likely to enjoy all the riches the market can offer.

Whenever I write small-town romance I am writing for a "dollar menu" reader. The books are short, sweet, and follow a basic recipe.

But when I wrote the book *Hurt*, there was nothing prolific about the process. This epic undertaking was not written for rapid consumption. It was written for a slow, savory experience and demanded a slow, savory creative process.

I applied every skill I had and poured over every sentence until the book was finished. *Hurt* is a dark and twisted psychological thriller with extremely graphic content set in multiple countries across various cultures. It took three years to finish and stole a bit of my soul. And while the subject matter might not be for everyone, it is by far the most masterful story I've written to date.

And I expect every one of my small-town romances to outsell it.

Why? Because more customers order from the dollar menu in today's climate. It is rare for a reader to invest beyond the standard, and currently the majority of books are standardized at minimal price points. By basing book prices on length and time spent in production, we cut out a large portion of the market on our more masterful titles.

So when readers ask me when another book like *Hurt* will be released, a book I know will take years to complete, I divert them to my other stories available, the stories that are putting actual food on my table, because hey, an author's gotta eat!

We long ago established that this is an extremely difficult business with a very narrow escape to the top, so don't beat yourself up too much for using your knowledge and skills to sell something for the simple sake of making money. Having a moneymaker series on a "dollar menu" could finance your business for the time it takes to write that masterpiece you've been dreaming about.

The irony of pacing your efforts differently for different works, is that the formula remains the same. The process is identical, it's just moving at a different tempo. There is no difference in engineering the plot structure in a bite-sized romance versus a masterpiece. There is only a difference in time spent on production.

Use your instincts. Success is about surviving the ever-changing tides of the industry. Knowing the market means staying ahead of the trends, so rather than looking left and right at everyone else, look as far ahead as you can see and try to predict what's on the horizon.

It is possible for a market to overindulge on a certain "dish" and implode. As the saying goes, history tends to repeat itself, and there are patterns in the book market every fiction writer should be aware of before plotting their next novel.

Wants Versus Needs

In literature, *foreshadowing* is a warning or indication of something to come. It's a device used to creates a sense of unease in the reader, and often used to hint that a character's *want* might not match their *need*. Authors, as the main characters of their own stories, sometimes fail to recognize their needs and shortsightedly cater mostly to their career wants, thereby creating more struggles in the end. Knowing the craft, industry, and yourself, will better prepare you for success.

By remaining knowledgeable and continuing your education as a lifelong learner, you will be in a better position to predict market trends. Knowing the history of the book industry will help you predict the future. And if you can predict which books will sell best in the near future, you will be more likely to have a lucrative career.

Often times, authors *want* to write a certain type of book, but can't because it makes more sense to focus on the book their business *needs* at the moment. Story arcs are often based on the tug-of-war between a character's *wants* and *needs*. In your journey, you are the main character. To be the hero, you must develop. That means accepting that what you *need* will aid in your success more than satisfying your current *want*.

While the story you *want* to write would be fun and exciting, you *need* to deliver the next book promised in a series you already started. That is what your paying customers were promised. And if you don't give your customers what they want, they will meet their needs somewhere else.

Deciding what project to write next is a delicate balance between reading the market, listening to your audience, and pacifying your muse. And while I strongly advocate keeping your eyes on the road and not slowing down to look at what the person next to you is doing, I do think it's smart to use your rearview mirror and look back at the history of the market to learn from the past.

During the late 1970's, bodice rippers were all the rage in the romance genre. Instant superstars were pumping out one blockbuster after another, and the market quickly saturated at the cost of quality. The industry lowered its standards, accepting less-polished work from less-skilled writers, simply to meet the demands of the market.

Investing in disappointing products can cost a business its customers. Readers are no different.

As the quality control of bodice rippers dropped, so did the fans. Romance readers, after feeling repeatedly let down, moved on to other genres. This had a devastating toll on the romance market. Publishers suffered, authors suffered, and readers suffered.

The moment we stop putting the consumer first, everyone loses. Once an author has lost a reader, they're gone forever. Temperance is key. Flexibility is a necessary part of industry survival as is the ability to move quickly and change lanes at a glance.

Genres like mystery and crime benefitted from the loss, gaining all the displaced romance readers looking for books with quality content. But the bodice ripper phenomenon wasn't the only case of overindulgence imploding a market.

One little tremor can easily turn into a tidal wave trend. In the early 2000's, after the arrival of Twilight and Sookie Stackhouse, a deluge of vampire romances flooded the market.

Shortly after that, another trend whipped its way onto the scene. The *Fifty Shades* phenomenon left a handprint on the book industry that wasn't quick to fade. Greatly powered by the privacy readers found in eReaders, the book market heated to an unprecedented smolder. Lusty storylines, graphic erotica, and explicit kink had heroes' palms *twitching* like Mr. Grey's all around the world.

These trends were beat to death until the readers grew fatigued and bored, wanting something different and new. It's natural for the market to overindulge to the point of burnout. Your job is to never burnout! That means maintaining balance on a soul level as much as a production level.

Before indie publishing, the conglomerates of the industry were responsible for any market trends. They were the puppeteers pulling the strings.

The first eReader came out in 1997. Some people didn't even have email yet, but technology was several steps ahead. Ten years later, in 2007, Kindle debuted and Amazon changed the ease at which readers could consume books.

Many purists rejected the idea of eReaders when they first hit the scene. Us bibliophiles love the weight of a book in our hands. We love the scent of the paper and ink, the feel of the pages, and the tightness of the spine. Reading on a digital device just seemed wrong to many of us. But marketing and lower prices paired with convenience and shrinking bookshelf real estate made paperback purists consider switching.

On the author side of things, indie publishing was on the rise. "Digital first" imprints became all the rage. The digital market flooded, and if readers wanted a certain book, they needed to own an eReader device. Once reluctant readers took the plunge into the digital book age, they learned reading on a device was mostly the same and the book prices were often lower, and then they were hooked.

A cottage industry of vanity presses emerged, and while these smaller presses saved authors a lot of stress and grunt work, they didn't possess the impressive audience the *"Big Six"* publishers could claim. Small press sales were often unremarkable, and as more authors turned indie, many of the smaller companies went bankrupt. By 2015, hardly any small presses had survived.

But let's go back to 2011 when *Fifty Shades* first hit the scene and small presses were still a hot commodity. The *"Big Six"* publishers had figured out a way to avoid new author risks with digital first imprints, so emerging authors were given an incredible chance to play with the big names.

It was an exceptional and exciting time to be a writer. But the thing about any kind of bubble, be it a housing bubble or a bodice ripper bubble or even the bubble Truman found himself in in the movie *The Truman Show,* is that the main character—you—doesn't usually realize they're living in a bubble. And what is the inevitable fate of a bubble? Spoiler alert—they pop.

So everything is flush and exciting for authors. But this beautiful new book utopia is starting to get crowded. More people are showing up every day, and the competition is growing fierce.

Over on the reader side of things, life's pretty great! There are so many new books to read! Prices are competitively low, and readers don't even have to waste gas money to buy books. The world's library is at their fingertips, and best of all, reading has become more private than ever before. A world of taboo topics has become accessible, thereby amplifying the stakes and making plots more exciting than they had been in years!

Publishers benefited from the success of erotic romance and wanted more, *More, MORE*! Submission calls went out and qualified writers sent in books, but the market was so hungry for kinky romance, the publishers couldn't keep up with the demand. Just like with the bodice rippers, the hungry publishers lowered their standards. But things were a little different in the new millennium than they were in the 70's.

Books were everywhere! Both readers and writers became more knowledgeable about digital technology, and self-publishing was on the rise. The demand for faster production rose, and soon authors and publishers started cutting corners. The indie-published community was stigmatized, and many small presses suffered a loss as things began to capsize.

Bookstores, knowing a thing or two about book industry history and the dangers of betraying readers with low quality stories, didn't want to take risks, so they held blanket policies that they would only stock traditionally published books during this period. The *"Big Six"* publishers maintained the majority of power in the industry at this point in time.

Meanwhile, the romance market was growing more inundated with impersonators every day—faster than it had in the 1970's and 1980's with bodice ripper reproductions—due to the ease of self-publishing. It was a dramatic repeat of the phenomenon that derailed the industry before, but now with way more passengers aboard and no assigned conductor to slow the runaway train.

When the crash finally came, the collision knocked millions of authors down. And that train we had all been riding skipped the rails and threw countless authors off course, leaving many to panic and think for themselves. Many didn't survive.

The majority of small presses closed, many massive houses followed, being bought out and consumed by The *"Big Six"*, which is now more like "The Big Four." With the dawn of indie publishing, the book industry jumped to unforeseen heights. But over the course of the last decade, it has been stretched so thin, very few actually feel as though they're standing on solid ground.

Currently, there are 129 million books available, with an expected increase of an additional million titles added each year. Once a book is published, it remains part of the cumulative, competitive market.

What's the lesson? Where is the relevance and how can we anticipate market shifts before we write?

The lesson is that projections for the long-term book market are extremely flat but fluid. Various bubbles are imploding more and more frequently, placing the overall book industry in a sort of wild, boiling state. Nothing is stable. Trends are hot and then they pop. And authors must be more flexible and adaptable than ever before.

How is something so wild and riotous still considered flat? How does the ocean draw a perfectly straight line along the earth's horizon when beneath the surface there is a ruckus of life in constant motion? We are the motion, and the book industry will forever be the untamable ocean. We must learn from past experiences and do our best to predict the seemingly unpredictable -- by riding the waves and pulling back when dangerous patterns reappear.

During the first quarter of 2019, backlist sales made up 64% of all book sales. This means readers were buying more books published from the year 2000 or earlier than they were buying from books published in present day.

In 2018, there was significant growth in suspense/thriller fiction. And in the first quarter of 2019, there was a 45% growth in adult action and adventure.[12] The rise in such genres could be due to a decrease of interest in the reigning queen of genres, romance.

The takeaway is that history is, once again, repeating itself, and a trend can only swell so much before the wave breaks or the bubble pops. High profile titles are driving the market, and readers are relying on dependable names to get their money's worth—be it the trusted name of an author or a well-known publishing house with stringent quality control.

The fact that readers are shopping from shelves with publication dates prior to the influx of self-publishing, says they are seeking a sort of commercial nostalgia, a level of quality that seems to be missing in today's novels—not always, but enough that they no longer want to take risks on new authors.

This is a problem for all of us, so it's one hundred percent relevant to your choices moving forward. Will you be writing for the dollar menu? Or will you be serving steak? Perhaps you might want to pace yourself and try shopping your next book with a publishing house to get the backing of their trusted audience. All of these options are serving up similar, yet different dishes, so look closely at what the readers want, according to your point of destination, and what you're willing to invest of yourself.

I'm sure many of you expected the craft section to focus only on technical strategy, which it mostly does, but before beginning any project, we would be remiss not to consider all obstacles on the path. One last look around at how other books are—*realistically*—performing, will never hurt you. Making predictions, based on educated guesses and a hardy helping of industry knowledge, will only help your book become more marketable in the end.

No matter what you write, know the audience you're writing for. Publishing is absolutely a service business, and you will need to serve something that makes commercial sense on whatever menu you choose.

Time to Begin

Writing is a skill. Writing well is a talent.

Authors are first readers, therefore, they know what good literature looks and feels like. They know when they're writing rubbish and how to use the delete key.

The greatest key to writing well is writing every single day. Does that mean you should write 10k every day? No, but the strategies ahead, combined with the philosophies already addressed, will make it possible for you to work up to 10k on the days you really need to hit your word count.

I do not recommend continuously hitting high word counts day after day after day. Not only will your work eventually suffer, *you* will suffer. We must pace ourselves and remember to always live a life of balance, or we will burn out.

If you are working on one book this month, writing 10k a day can really help, but don't push for more than 5 consecutive days of writing that intensely. Your mind, body, and spirit will need a break—regardless of what you think you're capable of.

Weekends exist for a reason.

---

[12] The American Booksellers Association | *The State of the Publishing Industry Today*; published June 3, 2019

I am capable of writing well beyond 20k a day, but that doesn't mean I do it. When we push ourselves beyond a reasonable limit, we shove ourselves right into burnout. Know your limits! *Awareness* and *acceptance* must remain in play. Do not overdo it.

Authors have a lot of work to do outside of writing. We are not *always* writing a book, but we are always working on one in some manner. Save some days for the other job requirements, but never miss that one hour of writing in the morning or whenever you squeeze it in.

When you write, write without inhibitions. Don't worry about the stylistic details during the drafting stages. Think only of the characters and the story needing to be told.

Embrace the wildness of the experience. Get lost in the world you've built. Allow the essence of your characters' cultures to swallow you.

By the end of this book, you will know many secrets of the craft, and if you take the preliminary steps advised, you will learn to trust your talent and skill like never before. The chapters ahead will explain exactly how to unleash your prolific potential.

There will be no writing blocks, only inspiration and direction. You will zone out and let your fingers fly across the keys in a stream of consciousness, a beautiful surrender to your muse. And in the end, with your newly acquired knowledge, careful planning, and devotion, you will be amazed at what you discover you can do.

Let's begin.

Chapter Seventeen
Transporting the reader

"Readers are not sheep, and not every pen tempts them."

Vladimir Nabokov, Lectures on Literature, 1980

The Hook

The *hook* is the opening of a story that ensnares the reader. According to industry standard, if you don't hook a reader by the first few pages, you've lost them.

A good *hook* is the difference between a reader taking your book to the cashier or placing it back on the shelf. The hook should start on the first page, sharp and poignant, sinking into the reader, and latching on tight enough to pull them through the entire book.

A hook contains key elements. It's an instant problem. It's what the character wants and why they can't have it, all the while establishing why the reader should care. There is value to every necessary part of a novel in fiction, but very little is as valuable as a good hook.

From the first page, an author should start with action, regardless of the book's tone or genre. World building must be both strong and subtle, powerful yet unobtrusive, and done so masterfully that the reader quickly forgets they are holding a book.

The reader shouldn't have to guess where they are or what the character is doing. Build a world of pictures that evoke every sense. Give as much information about the setting while saying as little as possible. You do not want to bog down an introduction with an *information dump*.

Show the reader what they see, feel, taste, smell, and hear the moment they step into your world. Don't tell them. Rely on your senses and do the heavy lifting for the reader.

Your words are your medium. The keys are your brushes. Every stroke of your fingers should show the reader what you see in your head, and your word choice should be so precise and concise, they picture your vision exactly the way you've designed it.

This is achieved with many techniques but relies heavily on an author's skill at writing *deep point of view*, a method that silences the author's presence in a narrative and delves deeper into the characters' perception and senses, exploring emotion so intensely the reader and protagonist identify as one. Regardless of the genre or point of view, every modern novel should have a deep enough point of view that the reader is not aware of the mechanics.

Do not assume deep point of view is limited to first person narratives. Deep point of view can make any point of view read as intimately as first person.

When we drive, we don't think of the engine function or which valve is pumping fluids into what cylinder. We just turn the key and go. The reader should open a cover and *go*, transported by your brilliant engineering that is so flawless, they never question if the book will break down in the middle. It's your job to see they make it to the end.

The test drive is on the first page where you show them your skill, hooking them so completely they can't break free. That little tease of talent builds their confidence in your abilities as a strong storyteller, and off to the checkout they go.

Remember, you are the Great and Powerful Oz and the reader is on the other side of the curtain. You are the hypnotist. Blow their mind right out of the gate! Hold nothing back. The opening and climax are the two most powerful parts of any novel, so set the dial to *STUN* and make it impossible for them to walk away.

Use strong verbs and sensuous, emotion-enticing words. Never tell the reader it's about to rain. Show them the mist blanketing the horizon and the gray gossamer clouds shielding the sun. Describe the humidity, the thickness of the air, so the reader senses the density in every breath, even while sitting in a completely opposite climate. Sing through the ink until the reader feels the sultry weight of the heat and hears the lazy hum of insects nearby. Help them smell the damp trace of rain building in the air.

Give them a taste of the salt on their skin. Irritate them with a trickle of sweat skating down their spine and the daunting reminder that there's no breeze for miles. Bury them in layers of senses until there's nothing but the hot, suffocating heat, and the rumble of thunder approaching.

Do all of this, but do it efficiently enough that they don't get bored with descriptions or lose sight of the action. There should always be a sense of impending doom or danger. World building is not enough to hook a reader. Give them something to fear—even in a gushy love story.

By showing the reader what's going on through familiar imagery and vivid descriptions, you build your world around them. Yes, they're looking at inked words on a page, but you've given them a second sight in their mind's eye.

Think of all five senses: taste, touch, sight, sound, and smell. But never forget, in deep point of view there's the sixth sense of emotion that authors must awaken for the reader to be fully transported through the page and into your world.

Emotion is the most important sense, but when we speak of emotion, we never want to be *told* how to feel. We want to be *shown* circumstances and events so that our own emotions can feel them firsthand.

The author's magic should project the character's circumstances so powerfully that the reader can't escape the sense that they are in the character's shoes, and the provoked emotions are *their* feelings and they are experiencing them right there with the character. Both the reader's and the character's emotions are linked when experiencing a deep point of view story. And we say experiencing because if done masterfully, it will be recalled as an experience more than a story read.

Regardless of who picks up your book, and how good or evil the character on page one appears to be, emotions must be depicted in a relatable way. It doesn't matter if the character, John, is drowning puppies in a vat of acid, if you want the reader to eventually root for him, you must build an *empathetic link*.

Simply telling the reader that John is sad or angry will only slide into a mental file next to other inconsequential facts, like John has brown eyes or John is wearing muddy boots. But if we mention the hammering of John's heart and the crushing memory of his son's innocent eyes as his voice called out to him, *"Daddy! Don't leave me!"* Well, then we've triggered something.

That thin thread connecting the character's emotions to the reader's is called the *empathetic link*. It's the author's job to build that thread up to a rope's thickness. This is accomplished by layering strategies of deep point of view from the first scene all the way to the last. A deep point of view novel should be the most personal kind of story a reader can experience, even if the character and situations are nothing like the reader's actual life.

Let's get back to John, our current main character and the poor puppy he's about to murder. Stay with me…

Feel that coiling knot in your stomach, just behind your ribs? That's empathy.

Really picture the puppy. The scruff of its neck in John's bloody fist. It's pathetic little whimper of playful confusion as it turns its innocent eyes on you, so watchful and trusting, completely unaware of the danger it's in, yet sensing the agitation in the air. The puppy only knows love and only wants to please. It squirms and tries to figure out the situation, a look of worry flashing in its eyes.

Feel sick to your stomach yet? I do. Anyone who is an animal lover should. Why? Because empathy is a healthy human emotion, and I'm tapping into it with an extremely brutal image of an innocent puppy on the cusp of death.

John lowers the dog toward the vat—

I won't torture you much further. You get the point.

Those of you irritated by the cruel picture I just painted in your mind might feel queasy and *hate* John (or me for using such a gruesome example). You might argue that all I've done is build sympathy for an innocent animal while introducing an absolutely irredeemable asshole named John.

Wouldn't it be easier to simply give the reader a flawless character in a perfect world—one who doesn't harm innocent creatures? Maybe, but unflawed characters are boring as hell to read about, so they don't build a great hook. They're also extremely unrealistic, as every human has flaws, and we often relate through shared struggles or dysfunctions.

Also, that immediate sense of danger has you fully focused. It's a natural reflex, a survival instinct, to zone out distraction when we sense danger. Wise authors will use that natural instinct to their advantage at every opportunity by jacking up the stakes and putting characters in the absolute worst situations they can imagine.

That doesn't mean a novel has to be gory or violent. It can be as simple as a little girl losing a coin during the Great Depression when sent to buy supplies for her family. What matters is how it's told. Authors must use those punching verbs that knock the breath out of a reader and form that empathetic link, right away showing that the situation *and* the character are greatly flawed and there is so much at stake. Amp up that sense of danger and trouble!

Readers don't want to start in a cotton candy world full of rainbows and butterflies where everything is perfect. Or maybe they do, but only if the author plans to rip away the sense of security and perfection in that peaceful opening—hence *Finding Nemo* when the first scene ends with the slaughter of Nemo's mother and all his unborn siblings. Sushi anyone?

Readers want to be surprised. They want immediate action. Shock them! Stun them! Disturb them! Do whatever you can do to keep them reading!

Do not—I repeat—do *not* back off because the content scares you. If you're nervous, you're on the right track.

The point of a hook is to literally hook the reader. If you want your character to drown puppies, ready the rain barrel and find a sack, but you better have a damn good reason why he or she is doing it if you also want the reader to empathize with more than just the dog.

Forming that empathetic link is absolutely key in hooking the reader. There has to be a point connected to the lure, otherwise your catch of the day will get away.

Maybe your character is behaving horribly because their child is being held hostage. Or maybe they're being blackmailed with a career-ruining secret. Maybe there's a backstory the reader hasn't learned yet—there better be.

It is your job, as the author, to know exactly what is motivating your character in every choice and action before the first word is written. But don't give those secrets away too easily. They are the reader's greatest motivation to keep reading. The suspense will drive them further and further into the plot, until the hook is buried so deep they're tangled up in the story to the end.

In the hook, your job is to speak through action and emotion. Give the reader a tangible, relatable emotion with which they can empathize. Not knowing the kind of person the reader will be makes this especially challenging. It's best to make the emotion a general "human" source of empathy, so you don't miss your mark.

General sources of empathy might include grief, failure, feeling overwhelmed, humiliation, fear, illness, pain, suffering a broken heart, or losing a job, parent, spouse, or pet. All of these examples are situations that could make a person feel alone, but they are universally shared across all cultures and backgrounds.

They are relatable challenges we face through life, challenges almost anyone should be able to personally relate. Even if the reader has never lost a parent or pet, they have most likely loved a parental figure or animal and can picture the loss to a poignant degree.

Missing the empathy target usually sounds like this in a review, "I just couldn't get on board with the hero," or "I found the protagonist frustrating." And worst of all, "He was simply irredeemable after what he did."

The goal is to get the reader emotionally invested. Empathy is the purely humanistic ability to identify and share emotions with another. In science-fiction, *empaths* are characters who feel others' emotions intensely, sometimes unwantedly. In order to turn readers into empaths, authors must do more than describe emotions. They must bring them to life on a visceral scale.

If the character is jealous because her ex is with a beautiful woman, do not simply say the character is jealous. Describe the emotion. What does jealousy feel like? Is it slimy? Does it gnaw at her insides, twisting and coiling to a point that her hands begin to tremble? Does it sound like a scream with no escape? What does it look like? How does it present itself in human behavior?

Writing is so much more interesting when the cause of deep emotion is shown to the reader rather than reported. No one likes to be told how to feel.

Deep point of view can be interchangeably called *showing* versus *telling*. It allows the reader to participate in the journey, lets them identify the cause of such feelings and experience them firsthand with the characters.

When deep point of view is achieved flawlessly, a multisensory experience will be created for the reader. Yet the author will avoid sensory words such as *saw, heard, smelled, tasted,* and *felt*.

Let's assume your character is, in fact, drowning the puppies, and the reader is shocked and appalled, but wait, we quickly discover he's also the captive of a psychopath. Not only is the character, John, a captive, so is his innocent little child, and the psychopath is threatening to cut off the child's nose if the main character doesn't drown the puppies.

You, the reader, instantly see the moral dilemma. Is a puppy's life worth more than the pain of mutilation to an innocent child? And what if the injury causes so much blood loss John has to watch his son slowly die?

Am I making you uncomfortable? Good! That's exactly what a hook should do! A hook should rapidly submerge you in a pit of squirmy emotions. There are lots of squirmy emotions. Some are sexual, some are gory, and some are heartbreaking. All are visceral, meaning you can feel them in the deepest cavity of your gut where the most powerful emotions grow.

But back to the story. At this point, it doesn't matter what John chooses. You, the reader, have already identified the moral dilemma and comprehend how horrific such a decision would be. You know John doesn't want to hurt the puppy. He just wants to save his son.

You're so glad you don't have to make such a choice, but the character isn't so lucky and for that, you sympathize. Cue the empathy—*poor John.*

It's all about the stakes. What is motivating the character? What's the internal and external conflict? It doesn't matter how gruesome or horrific an opening scene is, as long as the reader is on the main character's side. They have to identify with their plight and want to see them succeed, at any cost.

Empathy connects the character to the human being holding the book. On a subconscious level, once empathy for the character is achieved, it tells the reader, *me and this guy, we're alike in some way.*

Let's recap. You've built the world, established empathy between the reader and character, shown off your voice and ability to wield provocative language. Now that you've achieved all of this, you've temporarily changed the overall pattern of a subjective experience, meaning you've taken control of the reader's mind and thought patterns. In other words, you've created a *state of altered consciousness.* The reader is not unconscious, yet their thoughts are dreamlike. Now it's time to transcend the reader through space and time.

Have you ever been so engrossed in a story that you don't hear someone speaking to you? That's because when we read a well-written book, the conscious mind is sedated and the subconscious mind takes control. We become more anchored in the fictional world than our actual reality.

Much like a hypnotist alters his or her speech patterns, author tone of voice is a crucial part of achieving a state of altered consciousness. In the hook, an author's voice takes on a specific cadence that sets the tempo and tone of a book, so purposefully, it controls the reader's heartbeat.

The author's presence should remain as unobtrusive as a puppeteer. If the reader sees the strings or catches your hands casting shadows, you'll destroy the imagery and interrupt the connection.

Once the tip of the hook is in, the author draws the reader deeper and deeper, until the exterior world disappears. Just as an expert fisherman knows how to keep a fish on a line, a master storyteller knows how to keep a reader hooked.

If done right, the reader won't be able to escape the lure of curiosity. They can put the book down, do a load of laundry, and take the kids to the dentist, but all the while, the book is pulling them back because the author has embedded the hook, and the reader is now attached.

We want this state of altered consciousness to happen as soon as possible. So when the industry professionals, like editors and agents, claim to want the hook on the first few pages, you should now understand why.

Our stories are up against millions of other stories. There is only a small window to hook the reader into our world and convince them to stay. Do not delay this point of absorption with too much detail and backstory that can come later. Jump right into empathy and action, because they are powerful triggers, and we need to start as strong as possible.

Your fictional world should be fully developed in your mind before you begin writing, but you don't want to weigh down the introduction with lengthy descriptions of a map. No, you want to use your skill as a writer to imply the setting. Show, don't tell. Use that powerful vocabulary to evoke all the senses.

In the style of Hemingway, say as much as possible in as few words as possible. Time is fleeting and you only have a brief instant to sink your hook. If a detail isn't moving the plot forward or providing absolutely pertinent information relevant to that exact moment in the story, leave it for later.

It's crucial that the lead character be identified in that opening scene. Understand that you, the author, must know more about your character than his or her appearance. If you aren't familiar enough with the protagonist to identify what drives him, what his greatest fears and regrets are, what he would ask a genie if he had three wishes, then you aren't ready to write.

The writing must be seamless, polished, and clear so there are no style issues interrupting the experience into a state of altered consciousness. Skilled authors understand the value of well-developed characters as much as they respect the need for a fully developed plot. Both are necessary to transport readers into your fictional world.

New authors often want to convey as much information as possible to the reader right from the start of the book so they can get on with the story, but this is poor story structure. Filling your first chapter with *info dumps* will have a negative affect on your hook.

A hook should be smooth and easy. Jagged hooks that turn and pivot to dump unnecessary information are not efficient. They overwhelm the reader before ensnaring them in a new world, and the reader often turns away, the temptation not worth the trouble.

SMOOTH HOOK   JAGGED HOOK

 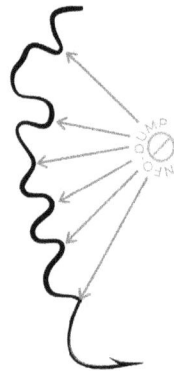

There will be time for background information later. For the hook, keep chapter one as smooth as possible, and only include the absolutely imperative information. Focus on the point.

As the author, you are the holder of all secrets. Tempt the reader with a sense of mystery.

Like an iceberg, hide the majority of what you have under the surface. Even by the end of the book, the reader will likely only ever know ten percent of a character that you've shown them. The rest of the details are for you and the development of the character's personality.

Info dumps are lazy writing. Rather than do the leg work and place the details throughout, writers are over eager to give away all the secrets. There's no excitement in info dumps. They put the reader on overload and make them work rather than relax.

Details are a part of characterization, revealed as the story unfolds. Background information is a seasoning. Pepper it throughout. Too much at once will kill the flavor.

Keep the pace moving, fizzing with possibility, and get the reader drunk on your words. Be the most powerful hypnotist you can be. And as the reader's physical world falls away and they are transported into the world you created, hook them in a way they won't be able to escape.

Do this and the reader is no longer the reader. They have identified with the plight of the protagonist on such a deep level, they have become the character. The hero's needs and desires have become the reader's, and they will think and make decisions on a subconscious level as the character would, based on the information you've provided.

Just as the volunteer on stage with a hypnotist barks like a dog, believing they have become a Saint Bernard, the reader weeps and worries, believing they have become the protagonist, and there is no other world but the one you've created for them.

This is the escape readers are paying for. Real life stressors and struggles disappear, replaced by the safety of fictional consequences and only a sense of danger. They know they are safe, but your words are so convincing, they forget for a time that what they're reading isn't real, and that transportation is the service a quality fiction writer should provide.

It's truly magical to transport a stranger through time and space as authors do. The better the writer, the more exact and precise the skill will be.

Daily distractions such as phone calls, chores, or family can disrupt a state of altered consciousness, but a good hook will keep them coming back. The author has an ongoing duty to keep a reader hooked, so don't assume chapter one is the only place a hook belongs.

A potent author knows there's always room to slip in a squirmy emotion. After all, squirmy emotions make the best bait! Just slip one on the end of another hook and lure the reader back to you.

Transporting and keeping the reader hooked comes down to all the terrible emotions we physically feel such as worry, angst, fear, and suspense. If you've properly achieved empathy, these trusty sentiments will work every time.

And why shouldn't they? You've convinced readers they are the character and all those terrible, squishy, angst-inducing things are now happening to *them*! Keep raising the stakes, ending every chapter on a cliffhanger, and keeping readers hooked until the very end.

Motion Versus Action

Authors must know the difference between motion and action. Motion is simply movement. It is not always interesting and is often boring because it describes things that an audience already knows. Authors should never confuse *motion* with *action*.

New authors often waste pages describing motion, getting lost in every grainy detail about the way a character lifted a chipped teacup to take a sip, their mouth pressing to the cool ceramic mug and the rich flavor of the earl gray hitting their tongue. Unless that teacup contained poison, or the description is necessary to *show* how the character's hand is trembling, thereby alerting the reader to the character's nervousness, such details really have nothing to do with the plot and, therefore, aren't relevant to the story.

Nor is the tedious act of making a bed or driving a car or putting away groceries. Such things are commonplace and not the details you want to waste time *showing*. These mundane motions are better left unsaid or brushed over quickly by simply *telling* the reader and moving on.

The exception would be if the bed the character was making was covered with an antique quilt that was an intrinsic part of the storyline. Or if the character putting away the groceries was an amputee missing an arm and the struggle is *shown* in the common act, reminding us, the reader, that we might take ordinary mobility for granted.

Perhaps an author wants to show the motion of driving a car because action is coming on the next page in the form of a hit and run. Maybe the character is hit by another car and loses a limb in the terrible accident. Stranded in the freezing cold on the side of the road, the character shivers and waits for help, bleeding all over the priceless quilt on the seat to her right, and later, when she makes the bed, she is reminded of the whole ordeal, which causes so much PTSD she shakes through her entire morning and needs a cup of tea to calm her nerves.

Only then would such details be somewhat relevant, because the motion is actually moving the plot forward, and therefore, it is no longer just motion. It's action.

Action propels a plot forward. Motion is the fluff that puts movement inside a static scene.

Motion is useful during lengthy dialogues. Readers would much rather follow motion tags than dialogue tags. Authors should only use dialogue tags when a tag is absolutely necessary and a motion tag is not an option.

Sample of Dialogue Tags:

"Will you be attending the wedding?" **Chester asked.**

Veronica answered, "I'd like to, but I don't have a dress."

"My sister has something you could borrow."

"We aren't the same size."

"Of course, you are!" **Chester exclaimed.** "I'm sure she has something that will fit."

Sample of Motion Tags:

"Will you be attending the wedding?" **Chester's gaze dropped to her chest then returned to her face.**

Veronica shifted in her seat, and hid a smirk behind the teacup as she took a sip. "I'd like to, but I don't have a dress."

He leaned closer. "My sister has something you could borrow."

It was a thoughtful offer, but she had to decline. "We aren't the same size." **She added another cube of sugar to the tea, her sweet tooth the likely culprit of her uncooperative waistline.**

He caught her hand, a buzz of electricity shooting up her arm. "Of course, you are! I'm sure she has something that will fit."

There isn't any real action in either scene. Just a man and a woman chatting over tea. But in the second scene, the reader can visualize the casual movements of the characters, which makes the scene feel less static.

Using motion tags breaks up the monotony of wooden dialogue. Human beings speak with more than their voices, which means that for characters to appear realistic they should use body language as well.

Eyes often share details the mouth won't say. Posture tells plenty about a person's mood. And a character's rigidness or fidgety fingers can say a world about their emotions.

By peppering dialogue with slight motions and gestures, the author adds texture to the story. Motions are great ways to flesh out characters. They are little tells that paint the larger picture. People are more a product of what they do than what they say, and motions prove that.

If an author were to write a scene about a priest speaking to a parishioner directly after mass, where he delivered a beautiful sermon, his words would likely be proper and polite, giving very little insight into his thoughts.

But, if while he spoke to the woman, the priest's motions paralleled every polite comment with an inappropriate glance at the parishioner's daughter, perhaps a tug at his constricting white collar or a trickle of sweat teasing down his back beneath his robe and a dry swallow breaking his concentration…

Well, that would paint a much more vivid picture. Readers appreciate the clues found within the subtleties. Motion tags are a straightforward, yet unobtrusive, way for a reader to read between the lines.

But motion is never a true supplement for action. It should never be the meat of a scene, and it takes a careful hand as the creator to make sure motion is not overdone.

Sample of Motion Overload:

"Will you be attending the wedding?" **Chester's gaze lowered then returned to her face. He shifted and the chair creaked under his weight. He glanced back at her chest.**

Veronica sighed. Her arm stretched across the table, reaching for her teacup. Noting the bowl of sugar cubes, she lifted the prongs and dropped two into the steaming tea. "I'd like to, but I don't have a dress." **Her spoon clinked softly as she stirred the sugar, sweetening the brew.**

His eyes perked up and he grinned. "My sister has something you could borrow."

Her thumb and index finger curled around the smooth porcelain, lifting the teacup to her lips. The gentle scent of earl gray filled her nose as she took a slow sip and swallowed. She lowered the cup to the saucer and met his glance. "We aren't the same size."

"Of course, you are! I'm sure she has something that will fit."

Yikes! That took way too long to convey nothing of great importance. An author should always be conscious of the time it takes for motions and conversations to occur in real time. Their writing should not take longer than an actual event. In this case, the act of sweetening tea and a brief dialogue is moving too slow compared to the length of time it would take to unfold in real-life.

These details of this simple back and forth have become tedious and boring. The reader is not gaining anything more than they gained from the brief motion tags above, yet the pacing has slowed down and the word count has expanded to make room for all these new words. This is *not* the sort of word count you want to accumulate.

Readers know how to drink from a cup. It's not interesting for them to read about characters doing regular things. It's too much detail. This is a perfect example of mistaking motion for action.

Not every scene can be jam-packed with action and that's fine, but authors should never invest as deeply in motion as they invest in action. Motion is a valuable writing tool that allows readers to see the characters perform in their natural habitats. Motion should allude to what a character might be hiding.

A good trick is to ask yourself when writing a static scene, "What *exactly* do I want to convey here?" Is it that Veronica sees herself as larger than Chester's sister? Is it that she has a shortage of formal attire? Or is it Chester's eagerness to see her at the wedding?

My guess is it's his eagerness, especially since the motion tags alluded to his attraction to Veronica. If that's the case, we could probably keep only the tags revealing his attraction and cut everything else out, so the scene reads more fluently.

Action, however, has nothing to do with subtleties. Action is shoved in the reader's face. Action is loud and fast paced. Action is the result of every compiling complication the author has layered onto a plot until the weight of conflict is about to buckle the story arc and destroy all chances of a happy ending.

Action will rarely be two people sipping from a teacup. However, if there's poison involved and a sense of angst is achieved, such simple motions could easily converge into action.

Remember the inconceivable moment in *The Princess Bride* when charming Westley challenges Vizzini to a battle of wits? Iocaine powder, one of the deadliest poisons known to man, with no odor or taste once it dissolves into liquid is used to poison one of two goblets of wine, thereby creating an element of suspense and turning the simple motion of drinking into action.

The dynamic of a static scene can suddenly change when stakes are raised and an element of danger and uncertainty is introduced. This often happens during a reflective lull, a quiet scene in a movie, when a conversation pauses and the character hears something suspicious approaching. That direct shift is the transition from motion into action.

Quality authors recognize the different values of both motion and action and will make eloquent use of both while writing fiction. The more experienced an author, the more seamlessly a writer will weave the two.

Motion should be used sparingly as a tool to enhance a static scene and bring it to life. Motion is a part of characterization.

Action is a plot tool. It propels the characters into predicaments, speeding up the pace and limiting the time left for strategizing solutions. Action forces the reader to judge a situation using only gut instincts, like the character must often do. This is exactly why, in a story arc, situations must get worse before they get better.

Action is hasty and messy. Mistakes can easily be made in action scenes as they move rapidly, and knee jerk responses are the first reactions.

Motion enhances characters. Action enhances the plot.

The PLOT is *what* happens. ACTION is *how* it happens.

Pacing

A good story should rise and fall like waves in the ocean, each action scene reaching higher than the last, with short lulls in between so as not to fatigue the reader.

Those waves should build and build, knocking our beloved character down, filling their lungs with water, threatening their actual life, then retreat long enough for our character to get up again. This continues until a mammoth tsunami appears and both the reader and the character stare wide-eyed and breathe a curse, wondering how the hell they're ever going to survive what's about to unfold.

Quality authors will compile the waves of action progressively as the plot carries on. This is another way to describe raising the stakes.

In the beginning, that first terrible situation was so horrific we were hooked, but since then, so many more horrific things have happened, each one worse than the one before.

The situations must get worse, because if the character survived the last several conflicts, they should naturally be stronger, at least on an emotional level. It's the author's job to write both the hero and the villain, so the author must make every incoming challenge more difficult than the last.

The reader and the character are building up an emotional callus, and in a way, becoming desensitized and shockproof. The next wave of terrible events must be progressively worse than all the waves before.

A way to amplify the effect of a wave is to restore a sense of security, which lulls the reader into assuming they are once again safe from danger. The calmer breaks in between are perfect opportunities to check in with characters.

Perhaps there has been an exciting battle and now the hero is being bandaged up by his love interest. That's a rather static scene, but dialogue will make it interesting. Give them a relevant talking point, add texture with motion details about how she might carefully tend to his wounds with limited supplies, and the plot will emotionally move forward.

Just remember, a reader doesn't need a detailed lesson in anatomy or care what color the bandage is. But they do care if the medical supplies remind them of the timeframe or lack of technology. They care if he flinches at her soft touch, trembles to disguise his pain, and then tentatively gives over to her care when he's never been able to stomach closeness before.

If the hero's internal conflict has to do with deep-seated trust issues that act as a barricade between him and others where intimacy is concerned, the author has just shown growth.

Characters must grow. Through *internal* and *external conflicts*, demonstrated by plot elements (situations) and character interactions, the characters steadily change.

These *telling* moments are critical to a story and the development of characters, but in comparison to action scenes, they can sometimes feel like lulls to the reader. Be sure to place them carefully, like waves in an ocean, back and forth, intense then peaceful, so there is an up and down tempo that gradually builds.

Uncertainty is a writer's friend in fiction. By making each climactic moment progressively more dangerous, the reader is thrown off balance. We want readers to desire a happy ending, but we also want them to doubt a happy ending is possible. It's a clever trick when an author can provide a surprising and satisfying solution that wasn't anticipated.

If lulls are placed carefully throughout the book, the reader will come to appreciate them as moments to catch their breath. Placement and content must be equally considered. Static scenes can lose a reader's interest when things get too boring and a lull lasts too long.

BASIC PACING

BETTER, FASTER PACING

POWERFUL, PROGRESSIVE PACING

HOOK LULL ACTION LULL ACTION LULL ACTION LULL ACTION

Never forget that a plot is forever in motion. It is a back-and-forth pattern that swells and retreats progressively, maintaining a balanced pace.

Authors must never stray too deep into an inner monologue or exhaust a reader by pummeling them with too much action. This can often occur in romance when a love scene carries on twice as long as it should. The potency is lost and the reader gets bored—regardless of how exciting the author intended the scene to be. Same can occur in a battle, kidnapping, or argument between characters.

Avoid too much inner monologue. Dialogue is a great way to put some white on the page and give the reader's eyes and brain a break from heavily inked paragraphs and reflective moments. Often times, when there is a quiet scene where the main character is doing something important with their hands, such as baking or sculpting, the author will introduce a side character to break up the monotony of the moment.

If it's a private moment the author doesn't want to share, perhaps the hero is constructing a bomb, there are still tricks to break up the text on the page. Maybe he cuts himself and releases an expletive.

Perhaps a cat comes along searching for food and gets in his way. He nudges it out of his space, but it comes back, hoping for a gentle stroke or a piece of the character's sandwich sitting on the table. The hero might give in and say a few nice words to the kitty, reminding the reader that although he's building a bomb and about to blow something up, he's not an entirely terrible guy.

A general rule of thumb is to never move away from the action for more than a page or two. Six pages of inner monologue is simply too much. Do not allow static scenes to carry on that long.

Another trick is to keep paragraphs short. Forget what you learned in fourth grade English class about three to five sentences in a paragraph. The goal is to keep readers reading fluently. As a courtesy to readers, keep paragraphs quick and snappy—two to three sentences should suffice, as long as they are a combination of simple and complex sentences.

Readability is a design technique achieved through pacing mechanics that the reader should never have to think about. They should simply enjoy the result. Comments like, "I read the book in one sitting!" Or "It was a real page turner!" are both examples of the effect caused by readability.

Fluency will always be less dependent on a reader's reading level than it will rely on an author's skill. Pacing techniques that manipulate the tempo and sprinkle details, rather than haphazardly dumping info and bogging down the story, can greatly improve the overall health of a novel.

A novel's fluidity is engineered by an author's strong design. Readability starts with craft and skill. It's our job to develop that skill enough so that it carries over to the reader's experience.

Building Suspense

With every complication, regardless of the genre, the character's situation should get darker, and the reader's angst should grow. However, simply piling one random catastrophe on top of another is a sign of lazy writing.

Quality writers will connect complications, forming a secret bridge of events, where one arbitrary decision causes a seemingly unrelated obstacle down the road. Writers should never base outcomes on chance or coincidence. The direct effect of an outcome should always relate back to the character's choices and behaviors. Linking conflicts in such a way makes a plot almost impossible for a reader to predict, and clever yet surprising twists are what readers love most.

Creating subtle connections between complications will keep readers engrossed in every detail, whereas random problems don't require a reader's full attention. Without connectivity, readers might be tempted to skim ahead. But if they suspect a connection, their brains will go into detective mode, and they will naturally become more invested in the plot.

Quality stories are fast paced. Avoid delays. And *never* fill pages for the simple sake of length. Every word should effectively develop your characters or move them forward in the plot.

Main characters should be intelligent. Remember, the reader will identify with the protagonist, so try not to make him or her a moron out of respect for the reader. Stupid characters that fail to communicate effectively and continuously make dumb choices will ultimately frustrate the reader and lose their respect.

Intelligent main characters think ahead. If the reader can see or predict an obstacle approaching, the character had better see it coming as well, especially if you want to keep the reader hooked and transported. The moment they feel disconnected from the character or can't relate to the character's thinking, you've lost them.

The same can be said for writing a character so advanced that the ordinary reader can't keep up. If the reader can't follow the protagonist's thought process, you risk making the reader feel unintelligent, and readers don't want to read books that make them feel less than smart *or* make them think too hard.

Your words, character development, world building, deep point of view, and empathetic link should all work together and do the heavy lifting for the reader. The reader is simply there for the ride. You've done the proper engineering to see that the ride functions correctly so they don't fall off track.

By increasing the action as the complications flourish and making each connected complication progressively worse than the last, authors keep readers on their toes and empathetically invested in the characters, even when the characters make mistakes.

Keep in mind, the hero does not have to be victorious in every conflict. There is just as much value in failure as there is value in triumph when it comes to a story arc. Win or lose, the reader only needs to understand *why* the character chose to act a certain way. They have to understand the rationale and empathize with the character's plight if you want them to continue rooting for the hero.

If you keep building the speed and momentum, the reader won't be able to hop off, nor will they want to.

A story arc should be a breeding ground for obstacles, and no solution should ever be without a consequence. When the final external conflict arrives—*the climax*—it should be so all-encompassing and jam-packed with action that the reader questions if there will be a happy ending.

That manufactured doubt and worry translates into suspense. Suspense should build from page one and never fully decline until the end of the story.

The last few pages of a well-written novel, the climactic pages just before the final conflict gets resolved, should leave the reader absolutely breathless. This is the pummeling of one bad predicament after another, the waves knocking the character down until they can hardly breathe. It is the tsunami on the horizon, barreling for the hero—and the reader—leaving no safe escape.

Suspense throughout an entire novel, from the hook to the end, is one of an author's greatest tools. This state of excitement, or feeling of anxious uncertainty about what may happen, is the catalyst that compels the reader forward.

Suspense stirs curiosity. There is an unfinished sensation that can't be ignored when suspense is built properly.

A big misconception is that only certain genres deal with suspense. This is not true. All genres require suspense. Without suspense, there's no sense of urgency.

Suspense grows with consequences that must be confronted. Non-confrontation is the death of suspense, so get those confrontations on the page directly in front of the reader.

Characters require the reader to move them forward in the book, much like Westley required Fred Savage to move him forward in *The Princess Bride*, or Atreyu needed Bastian to get him to the princess to stop The Nothing in *The Never Ending Story*. The reader must keep reading, otherwise our fictional characters remain stuck in time, pinned to one page. For conflicts to be conquered, the reader must go on, so we, the authors, must make the next page even more tempting than the last.

When authors write characters that avoid confrontations or show poor communication skills with side characters, even when opportunities for resolution present themselves, this is not so much a personality trait of the character's but a failure of the author's. Avoidance is boring. It is a page-ruining, word-wasting practice done by subpar writers.

Do not be an uninspired writer. Be a master. Force your characters into situations that require confrontation and leave no cowardly escape for them or you.

If you find yourself dragging out a confrontation, it's a sign of a plot hole. Chances are you've overlooked a part of the arc, and your writing reflects that you're guessing.

Do better. Readers expect better. As a source of income, you want a product that offers better.

Suspense is temptation. It's the *need* to know what will happen next. It's the carrot before the reader's nose, the bait on the hook, the uncomfortable sensation of unresolved business that the reader simply cannot ignore. But it is ever evolving and never based on avoidance.

Authors have a duty to layer suspense. It must exist in every plot, regardless of the genre, or the book will lack the interesting pull readers need to follow through.

What if you write sweet Christian romance for young adults, do you need suspense then? Yes! Every book. Every time.

How about children's books about kittens? Always! There is no fictional genre exempt from this rule. It doesn't matter if a book is the most wholesome, coming-of-age tale to ever hit the shelves, and a fluffy unicorn named Sven saves the day. Suspense must exist for the reader to keep reading.

Authors place cliffhangers at the end of chapters in hopes that the reader keeps going rather than setting the book down. A mistake often made by writers is telling the reader too much too soon. Disperse your secrets with a modest touch—breadcrumbs not loaves.

The reader is hunting for a solution. It's a game. Keep some of the mystery alive. Hold back some details to motivate the reader to continue with the story.

But don't be cruel. Reading should be a rewarding process, not a torturous one. The reader loves to feel successful. While an author should keep the reader guessing, they should also reward the reader's sleuth work by revealing more details.

Consider a novel a scavenger hunt of clues that leads the reader to the gratifying end. Always keep them in suspense but motivated at the same time. If the reader feels hopeless or led on with little reward, they lose their incentive to continue the book.

Storytelling is an art. There is the initial hook, accomplished through world building and empathy, then the moment of transcending the reader to a state of altered consciousness. But the true challenge is holding readers in a fictional world even when reality beckons them back to real-life.

Words are only one part of an author's tool kit. There are many intangible mediums required to form a masterpiece. Suspense is one of the most critical tools in every author's bag of tricks, yet it's also one of the most overlooked plot devices because too many times, writers assume suspense only belongs in genres like mystery, thrillers, or other suspense-ruled categories.

Not true! Suspense belongs in every novel!

Think back to the waves of complications building and swelling as details are layered and problems accumulate. Each advance introduces more impending doom, but after tense moments, the action recedes, and there is something new to discover about the character, a secret breadcrumb that is revealed in the action's wake.

Character growth hides in the recesses of action. Action is propelled through suspense. The lull is where authors reveal their secrets because it's a moment when both the reader and the character are able to catch their breath and reflect on what just happened. Lulls are for processing, repairing, learning, healing, and growing.

In movies, often after battle scenes, there is a scene showing soldiers back at camp, banged up and licking their wounds. Maybe an important character was lost at war. Perhaps the hero was gravely injured in an act of bravery.

The battle is the action, the rising wave. The reprieve after battle is the lull, the revelation of details.

These plot devices feel familiar because they work. But they are not limited to violent, action-packed plots.

Consider the movie *Pretty Woman*. Toward the end of the movie, Richard Gere's lawyer, Stuckey, shows up at the penthouse when only Julia Roberts' character, Vivian, is home. The lawyer, played by Jason Alexander, is a real slimeball. He propositions Vivian and grabs her, assaulting her roughly until Edward, Richard Gere's character, shows up and rips him off Vivian.

The next scene shows Edward holding Vivian as she ices her cheek where Stuckey hit her. The scene moves into a solemn moment when both she and Edward acknowledge their differences. He is a millionaire and she is a prostitute. They can't continue pretending they belong together.

There was action then a lull. But it's the connectivity of the two that makes this plot work. Prior to Stuckey's visit to the penthouse, he saw Vivian at a polo match—another action scene—where he discovered that she was a prostitute, something both Edward and Vivian worked hard to disguise.

Having a villain in possession of a compromising secret fills the reader and protagonist with worry. That worry creates suspense.

Just because a story carries on with lulls and rises, does not mean the reader or viewer is safe. As long as that secret is out there, our heroine is in a dangerous and vulnerable position.

Sometimes the author of a tale will purposely try to make the reader forget a detail, so when it crops up again at the end there is a feeling of cleverness, and all the puzzle pieces suddenly fit.

In the case of *Pretty Woman,* that secret Stuckey discovered came back to haunt Vivian the moment he found her alone and thought nothing of treating her like a whore.

If we dig even deeper, throughout the movie, Edward has been working on a deal, trying to buy out a family company to dismantle and turn a profit. Edward's opposition is humanized during a business dinner when Vivian charms everyone at the table.

At the polo match, before learning Vivian is a prostitute, Stuckey sees her speaking to the heir of the company they are trying to buy. Finding her behavior suspicious, he goes to Edward, questioning if she's a spy sent to seduce him by their enemy. Edward laughs at his lawyer's paranoia and to discredit his assumptions, he confesses Vivian is a hooker.

The intricacies of this seemingly simple plot are perfect examples of conflict connectivity that takes a story from basic to brilliant. In the end, Edward spoils the deal and decides to partner with the opposition rather than destroy their legacy. This climactic moment of a truce between business enemies is what leads Stuckey to the penthouse in a rage.

Stuckey wanted Edward to make the original deal so he could earn the commission, and blames Vivian for altering Edward's shrewd business sense.

As you can see, everything is connected. One complication links to another, and no obstacles are randomly dropped into the plot. Everything is relevant and related. Cause and effect. This layered webbing of a story is what makes readers rave in reviews!

However, readers can easily grow fatigued if there isn't satisfying resolutions throughout. And they will be downright angry if they follow your breadcrumbs only to be led to a disappointing conclusion in the end.

This is a great moment to remind writers that an ending does not have to be happy to be satisfying. Satisfaction comes in many forms. Sometimes it's the realization that a life had value, despite being cut short. Sometimes satisfaction hides in sacrifice. It's okay for characters to perish or lose, as long as there is a point and connection to the rest of the book.

By the end of the first quarter of a novel, the reader should understand the main character's goals and motivation. They should also understand what is creating a conflict for the character. In other words, what is stopping the character from getting what they want.

Conflicts conduct the tempo and rhythm of the story. A book should have its own cadence. Action adventure stories typically follow a faster tempo with an extreme, spiking rhythm.

A love story might create a slower tempo that burns hotter as the plot goes on, and when a climactic moment arises, the action dramatically spikes to scalding temperatures.

Mysteries might create a drowning tempo that carries on so long without pause that the reader is breathless and desperate for a break. They will get one, but the rhythm will increase the moment danger returns.

If an author isn't sure how to create suspense, they must go back to their characters. Character development is the missing puzzle piece that often gets mislabeled as writer's block. Writer's block is merely the loss of motive. To discover the motive, we must go back to the character, reexamine their goals, and consider the conflicts.

Perhaps the plot isn't challenging enough for the character we've created. Only the character can tell the author what he or she needs to ultimately succeed.

Once an author establishes the character's GMC (*Goals-Motivation-Conflict*), it's easy to decide what to write next. The GMC and suspense should work together, all parts powering each other like the seesaw mechanism of an oil pump, gelling the connective events together in the arc, exactly the way the mechanics of a story should cooperate. That's ingenious engineering.

If an author runs out of opportunities for suspense, the characters need more development. Dig a little deeper into their personalities and fears, and those opportunities will come.

Suspense is such a powerful plot device, it is a shame to lose it in a flashback. We never want to waste opportunities for suspense. Never put major events off the page by summarizing for the reader with a recap. The reader paid for the book, so they deserve to see the events first hand. Use every opportunity to create angst by planting the reader directly in each important moment.

Dreams, retellings of events, or flashbacks all rob the reader of the front and center experience of living the moment with the character, so if you want to write a flashback, you had better write it so damn well that the reader forgets they're reading a recollection. You must transport them into the memory, essentially hooking them again with a story inside a story.

Telling a reader about something exciting that happened off the page is like bragging about a good meal to someone on a diet. It's rude. But if you give them a taste, really let them share the experience, it can be appreciated.

Buying a book is essentially like buying a ticket to a show. Give the reader a show, not a review. Don't *tell* them *about* a story. *Show* them. The reader should see and feel everything happening to the character firsthand, as it's happening.

However, that doesn't mean the author should walk the reader through every bit of the character's day. Remember not to mistake motion for action.

If the important part of the plot doesn't take place until late that night, it's perfectly fine to summarize the character's usual rituals and work day in one or two sentences. Don't get lost in insignificant details.

Suspense deals specifically with action. It happens at the height of the wave, triggering fear that compiles and teeters so high it must eventually tumble down. Build. *Build! BUILD!* Leave motion and lulls out of the action scenes, because they will only steal your momentum when you need it most.

If you're unsure what type of scene you're writing, you should be able to tell by the tempo. Action scenes create a sense of urgency using quick, simple sentences with strong verbs.

Motion scenes (lulls) are where authors sometimes slip in prose. The reader is taking their time and is more attentive in those moments, so it makes sense for an author to say something a bit more flowery.

Never waste prose on action scenes. The reader is moving too fast to appreciate style. They simply want to resolve the suspense and get to the end where it's safe and they can catch their breath.

A great trick for speeding up the tempo of an action scene—and the reader's heart rate—is to write an extra-long, action-crammed sentence, piling up details until a crushing sensation is created in the reader's chest. When done properly, this should physically feel like a breath is needed and forbidden, stirring a sense of urgency to read faster so the scene will end and the reader can inhale.

Here's a Sample of Tempo Hard at Work:

Her body pierced the surface of the lake and she plunged like a bullet into the icy water, all sound cut off as her blood chilled and the air left her lungs in a muffled scream, bubbles dancing before her eyes like lost souls in the black abyss that swallowed her whole as she kicked without purchase, arms tied behind her back—useless—and her panic drowning her as much as the cold water ever could.

Run-on sentences are rare but useful, especially in moments of fast action. Any scene with an immediate consequence provides a good excuse for the author to pile on the details and overwhelm the reader with a run-on. Situations like gunfire or a car accident are perfect examples of when a lengthy run-on is useful, anything that presents an immediate consequence.

One of the worst things an author can do to kill off building suspense, is to describe an action longer than it takes to happen. If the reader is in fact the character, and a trigger is pulled on a gun, the author has a very small window to move the bullet from point A to point B.

If the author wants to describe the shot in detail as an attempt to crank up the suspense, then they should try to accomplish said description in one paragraph, preferably one sentence. Too many words will detract from the sense of urgency and tempo of the action.

In action scenes it's important to remember that less is usually more. Every blow to a character should resonate within the reader. Authors who create physical responses in readers, such as queasiness, tears, racing heartrate, or arousal, are masters of suspense.

Suspense is not a tangible object authors can turn on. It's an invisible device that, when applied properly, catapults a story into the desired forward motion by tugging the reader along.

Suspense is fluid. It moves and stretches and molds differently to various plots and characters. Suspense hides in everything from murder scenes to quiet Sunday schools. It is the faucet that unleashes the sixth sense, and every author should have their hand on the tap, ready to turn it on and crank it up at a moment's notice.

Without suspense, there would be very little emotion. Without emotion there would be no uncertainty or discomfort. And without uncertainty, there is no unresolved curiosity or incentive to continue reading. Whether the suspense is merely a pinprick of suspicion or a spike of urgency, it should accomplish the ultimate goal of driving the reader to the next page.

Characterization

Characterization encompasses the full scope of a character and is, perhaps, one of the most imperative elements to any plot because characters drive the plot. They are victims of conflict, struggles which the author creates and heightens with the powerful literary device known as suspense. Characters, plots, settings, and events are all connected and felt through suspense and other vivid emotions.

Characterization is a multifaceted literary device that includes internal and external qualities of a character. Characterization is not reserved for main characters alone. A thorough author will conduct a full characterization on every character in a book. This typically starts with physical features and then jumps directly into the GMC, the *Goal-Motivation-Conflict.*

It should be common sense for an author to know the physical appearance of a character. They will start with the basic outward identifiers such as hair color, build, eye color, skin tone, and so on, but should have a system in play to track these characteristics and maintain consistency.

Creating a *character dossier,* or character outline, can help authors consider the many aspects of a person's identity, so no detail is overlooked. Never expect to use all the details in a dossier as the reader will only ever see about 25% of what's on the character's surface. The other 75% is disguised and revealed through subtleties in behavior.

A basic character dossier should cover physical appearance details such as weight, style, age, the various traits mentioned above. But it can also cover finer details of characterization, such as voice and speech patterns, religious background, body language, past life experiences, vocational skills, other talents, sexuality, fears, passions, and dislikes.

A helpful, time-saving tip is to brainstorm appropriate descriptors during this preliminary process. If under voice and speech patterns I decide that my character has a speech impediment, I might list the following strong words in my preliminary notes:

Stammer	Yip	Fumble
Falter	Stumble	Flinch
Slur	Spastic	Consonants
Mumble	Fluent	Speechless
Stutter	Tremor	Flicker
Lisp	Jitter	Abnormal
Wabble	Hoarse	Gawk
Gait	Judder	Misfire
Echo	Grimace	Gangly
Cadence	Wince	Tremble
Tic	Stilted	Rhythmless

All of the above are words I might associate with having a speech impediment. By creating a word bank for a specific characterization that might plague my protagonist throughout the book, I'm saving time. Prior to writing, I might actually type a list and tack it to my wall as a quick reference.

It also helps to attach visualizations to a dossier. Many authors use Pinterest to help choose a character's wardrobe, the design and architecture of a setting, and so on.

For the *pantser* writers out there who cringe at such formalities as character dossiers, I suggest the simple act of brainstorming. If that feels intolerable, set a timer, and commit to brainstorming for twenty minutes. You will be amazed at what you can discover. If you're feeling brave, try an hour.

Brainstorming characterizations through webbing, listing, or writing a stream of consciousness can sometimes be just as effective as a dossier. Different authors will decide their character's in different ways. Choose the method that best fits your style.

Below is a basic example of webbing based on the beloved matriarch from my McCullough Mountain series, Maureen McCullough, who is featured in each book as well as the Jasper Falls series. Maureen is such an intricate character, her web could have been poster size, but these are the basics of who she is.

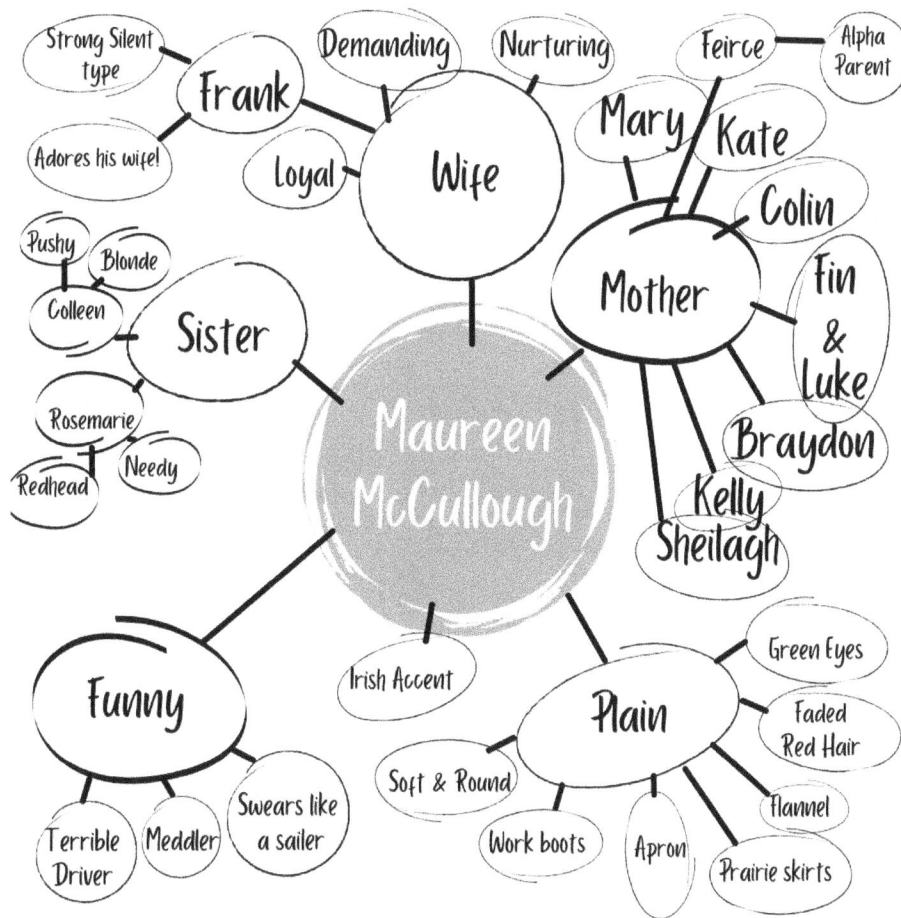

No matter which method an author uses, they should always know the character's GMC. While 75% of a character's traits will never be revealed to the reader, 100% of the GMC must be. If an author doesn't have the character's goals, motivations, and conflicts figured out before they begin, their novel is in trouble.

The GMC identifies key elements of a character's past. A story isn't finished until everything's come full circle, and the *want* of a GMC is replaced by the character's awareness of a *need,* and the acceptance that the *need* is more valuable than the initial *want*. In other words, the events of the story have enlightened the character, and they have grown and adapted their desires through an evolution of self. But before we get into all that *want* and *need* business, let's backtrack and truly define the tool GMC.

GMC

GMC, as mentioned, stands for the character's *goal-motivation-conflict*. Every character should have an *external* GMC and an *internal* GMC.

The *goal* is *what* they want. The *motivation* is *why* they want it. And the *conflict* is *why they can't* have it.

This is critical information, because characterization is perhaps one of the most imperative elements to any plot. Yes, plot and characterization are two separate animals, but in a good novel, characters should be intrinsically entwined with the plot, always driving it forward in a fundamental way.

When an author knows a character's greatest fears, they can quickly decide the worst possible thing that could happen to the character. It then becomes the author's sole job to throw that character into a situation that is basically the character's worst nightmare, thereby plunging the character into absolute turmoil.

In other words, by using a GMC to properly identify your character's deepest secrets, you will reveal exceptional plot twists you otherwise might have missed.

Remember the image of building waves, the rising stakes portrayed through action and the reflective lulls in between? Each conflict should be worse than the last, so prepare to outdo yourself as the story goes on. This is why novels get especially challenging around the 60% point, when we have to think of new ways to harm the protagonist without fully annihilating them or the story arc.

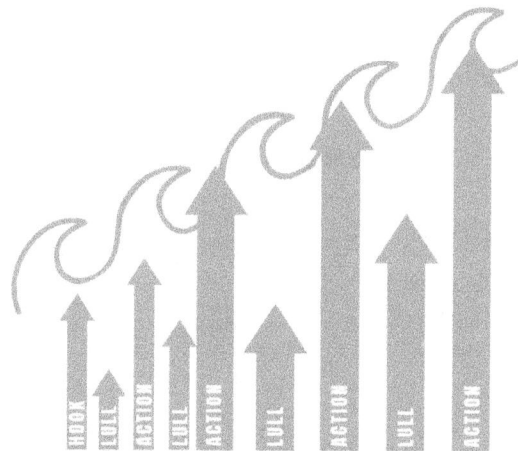

Authors are using action and motion to create opportunities that *show* the character's personality to the reader. Behavior is a powerful conveyer, which is why we use it. Actions will always speak louder than words.

The external conflicts will most likely present themselves in action scenes, while internal conflicts will be revealed during reflective moments reserved for those quiet lulls.

Remember, never bog down an action scene with too much inner monologue. Inner monologue or intimate dialogue is usually how readers discover internal GMCs. They live in the lulls of a story arc.

A very basic external GMC in the *Game of Thrones* series, written by George R. R. Martin, involved the weather as a threat. There are several exceptional villains in these stories, but winter is the first conflict we, the reader, fully accept. Right out of the gate we hear the warning that, "Winter is coming," and we understand this is an omen of troubles to come.

This is not just any winter. It's a winter that will last years and shroud the world in darkness, a winter where resources like food are scarce, a winter with enough snow to decapitate the tallest castles, a winter cold and long and miserable enough to drive the kindest soul insane.

Clearly, the *conflict* is winter. The *goal* is to prepare. The *motivation* is survival.

But this GMC affects more than just the main characters. Part of the northerners' preparations include protecting their resources. They don't want to be overrun by wildlings when winter arrives.

Who are the wildlings? They're basically wild, lawless people living on the other side of The Wall and one of the northerners' greatest enemies. Yes, we've just revealed another threat.

The connectivity of these villains is so simple, yet by the time George R. R. Martin is through layering one conflict over another, the reader feels as if they've lived a lifetime in his world. His talent is truly a magnificent and stunning example of brilliant writing.

But he's far from finished! Winter is coming and the wildlings are on the other side of The Wall. What's The Wall? The Wall is a colossal buttressing fortress that stretches three hundred miles along the northern border of the Kingdom of the North, segmenting The Realm from the wildlings' domain on the other side. It's over seven hundred feet tall, made of solid ice, and occupied by the soldiers of The Black who have vowed to give their life to protect The Realm.

A wildling's GMC might be slightly different than that of a northerner's. The *motivation* remains survival. The *goal* is to move south, away from the winter weather. But the *conflict* is the gigantic freaking wall blocking their path. And there you have the most generalized summary of one of the most intricate storylines ever written.

George R. R. Martin's characterization is what makes his epic tale so spellbinding. Regardless of the point of view, he creates an empathetic link. The reader can sympathize with opposing enemies and find themselves rooting for both parties. It's a terrible yet delightful mindfuck, and some of the most exceptional characterization to exist in modern fiction.

No matter what genre or type of character you are writing, there should always be an internal and external GMC. The goal of any story is character development. As the challenges and conflicts grow more complicated, our characters must learn and grow wiser, stronger, and braver.

A proper story arc should increase the levels of mayhem as the plot moves on, each wave growing taller and more intense than the last. And when that final conflict appears and it's the ultimate moment of truth, the moment when a character will either prove victorious or be destroyed, their true nature will finally be revealed.

To be victorious, the character must learn enough to realize that what they originally *wanted* was not what they actually *needed*. If they missed that lesson, they will fall, and the lesson becomes the reader's to learn—exemplified by the character's mistakes.

While a GMC addresses what the character wants, why they want it, and why they can't have it, you, the author, are fully in the know about what the character truly needs.

You will share the GMC subtly, with breadcrumbs, but not the *need*. The *need* takes time to develop. Only reveal the *need* to the reader at the very end, just before or during that final conflict.

Lay out your GMC before deciding anything else about your character. This will determine the character's greatest internal and external *want*, why they want it, and why they can't have it.

GMC	Internal	External
Goal	*What they want...*	*What they want...*
Motivation	*Why they want it...*	*Why they want it...*
Conflict	*Why they can't have it...*	*Why they can't have it...*
Need	*Driving Passion*	*Evolved Truth*

External conflicts will likely be a person, place, or object. Figure out why they are so motivated to possess said thing. And what obstacle is stopping them from possessing it?

These are all important characterizations that define the character's thinking and background. These are his or her *wants*. We all go through life driven by our desires, but sometimes we want unhealthy things, and it takes a lifetime of consequences to get through to us that what we *want* isn't always what we *need*.

You, the author, must step back and look at the lessons presented through the plot, figure out how your character might respond to the conflicts and what consequences might arise, creating new, bigger conflicts. Decide how long this process will go on and where the breaking point will come in. That is the moment the character truly grasps their *need*.

The *need* then becomes the driving passion. It is the evolved truth of the character. This grand revelation resolves the plot and saves the day. If the character fails to have this revelation, they lose the day and perhaps the girl or their life or whatever is at stake. But the lesson is never lost, because the reader is the character, and they can learn the lesson as well, especially if you've written the story so masterfully that it reads like a firsthand experience to them.

Texture

Plotting starts with characterization. Only when authors have a fully developed concept of who they will be writing about, should they move on to plotting the actual events of a book. But sometimes, during the plotting of events, authors discover holes that can only be filled through diligent research. This is where texture plays a key role in bringing stories to life.

No matter how intricate or basic your plotting outline, you may find some holes in your arc that need filling. Texture not only fills plot holes, it smooths out the overall reading experience.

Texture is the mood of a story. It's the intimate lens the author shares with the reader, always adjusting the focus to direct—or misdirect—the reader's attention where the author desires.

Texturizing a story will bring a setting to life. It's describing a desert in such a way that the reader feels the arid, parched earth underfoot, cracked and pocked with dried brush and cacti. They can sense the danger inhabiting the few shadows where venomous creatures lurk. They suffer fatigue from the relentless sun and can clearly picture the repetition of the towering mesas and canyons that are as inhabitable and dry as the scrubby wastelands.

Before the actual writing begins, all the research and texturization should be complete. Start by gathering as much *texture* as you can find. This might be in the form of a book soundtrack or interviewing specific people. If you can't find experts in a specific field, check YouTube.

Think of ways to experience the culture. Play with cuisine, order out from a restaurant that might be specific to the ethnicity you're trying to convey. Try new recipes. Experiment in your kitchen and take notes on every flavor and smell.

Get lost on apps like Pinterest. Really look into the style and appearance of flesh and blood people who resemble your characters. Create vision boards that include every setting, outfit, character, car, and so on.

Use Google Earth to take a trip via satellite to a direct intersection where you plan a scene. Reach out online and speak to people. Listen to their voices and try to fully capture the auditory pleasure of their accents.

Confuse your Netflix. When I was writing *Hurt,* I watched a lot of Scottish films and found a lot of differences between their general mannerisms and American humor.

The goal is to create a cocoon of data and imagery around your muse. Get inspired! Go overboard! There is no limit to the amount of inspiration you can collect. It will all enhance your novel in some way or another.

Book Bible

Plotters or *plan-sers,* a *pantser* who plans, may want more room to lay out such character details. While having a file for each series or book is advised, sometimes it helps to also keep a notebook, specifically dedicated to a unique world. As authors, we often revisit old worlds to give them a reboot. This might be in the form of a new cover, or a rewrite, or maybe a spin-off series with a *"Where Are They Now"* theme. Loose papers have a way of getting lost over time, so keep your records safe.

Intricate plots and characters require organization. Characterization notes, plot outlines, world maps, texture notes, family trees, should all be compiled into a *book bible*, a document where an author compiles detailed notes pertaining to a specific manuscript or series that tracks locations, character descriptions, timelines, and so on. Once you have your details organized and the GMC figured out, it's time to take it for a test drive.

The preliminary test of a plot often happens in the imagination of an author, but some authors like to jot down their ideas in a timeline, outline, or a synoptic overview of events. Basically, we walk through the story mentally, taking notes and marking areas where we might want to dig deeper.

The following is an example of a synoptic overview that expresses both plot twists and the thought process of the writer. While all of the details might not get written into an outline if the author is a pantser, they will most likely be considered on some level. Book bibles are great places to jot down areas for more consideration or details determined during brainstorming.

Sample of a Synoptic Overview:

Jill, the female protagonist, wants to save her family's land, which is under the threat of being redeveloped by some brute of a businessman. The brute of a businessman is, of course, the antagonist.

But wait! The brute isn't all bad. He's charming and sexy, and now Jill is getting mixed signals. But she must save her family's land!

The protagonist's external GMC is clear. She wants the land. Why does she want it? Because it represents a part of her family, and she lost her family in a terrible accident. The land is all she has left of them. What's stopping her from satisfying this want? The horrible, sexy brute of a businessman.

Is this external GMC engrossing enough to grow into a full-length novel? No, probably not. That's why characters also need an internal GMC. And if we really want to beef things up, we'll create GMCs for the antagonist as well, because hey, even brutish, corporate alpha-holes have feelings sometimes.

We must dig deeper into Jill's psyche to unravel her internal GMC. As mentioned, the land is all she has left of her family after they perished tragically. Hmmm… How did they die?

The author decides it was an avalanche and then does a little brainstorming and research on avalanches, using a page in her trusty notebook to create a word bank of avalanche related words and a graphic organizer web to demonstrate all the intricate ways this experience might have led to some post-traumatic stress issues for our protagonist. All of these extra details would fall under texture and add to the realistic feel of the book.

What these details really reveal is that Jill is lonely. Her internal goal is a *home*. Why does she want this home? Because, in her mind, home represents family. Is the businessman still the conflict? No, not really. But we'll put him in there anyway to spice things up. This will give the character room to grow.

An enlightened person would eventually understand that a piece of land, no matter how nostalgic, can't replace the love of family. What the protagonist truly needs is connection. Enter said businessman.

But, to further complicate things, let's humanize the businessman. We'll give him a name—Jack. Let's give Jack some baggage as well. He's just wrapped up a messy divorce, which consequently caused some serious commitment phobias. He's only focused on business at the moment. The last thing he wants is to get emotionally involved with a woman.

But what's this? The bratty land owner, Jill, has actually gotten under his skin and he can't stop fantasizing about her. Then she accidentally reveals a soft, vulnerable underbelly and… You can see where this is going.

The businessman's GMC reveals that he wants the land but can't have the land without crushing the woman who happens to also be the woman he wants to screw into next week. How does he screw her one way without screwing her the other? Seems like a bit of a problem.

By placing the characters in one conflict after another, quirks are unveiled and both Jack and Jill become multi-dimensional characters. Soon, the reader learns the characters' greatest fears. This most likely happens during a reflective lull directly following an intense, action-packed scene where emotions ran high and there wasn't time to think—like an almost-kiss in a board room just before the attorney walked in.

Here's what we discover in the reflective lull. Jill was in the avalanche with her family. She was trapped for hours as they slowly died. She now has a phobia of enclosed spaces.

To create suspense, the author must think of the worst thing that could possibly happen to the characters and do it. The ball is rolling where Jill's property is concerned. That's pretty bad for her, but is it enough? Meanwhile, it looks like Jack's going to get her land, but he's extremely frustrated that he's attracted to Jill when he wants nothing more than to get her out of his head. There's definitely a connecting conflict, but how can we make matters worse?

To crank up the stakes, the author has to do the worst possible thing to the characters at that time of conflict. The author decides to force the characters to spend time together by putting them in an inescapable situation. The author could put them in a courtroom or something like that, but what if the author put them in a teeny, tiny space like an elevator? No, that's just mean. Both Jack and Jill would hate that.

Exactly! Into the elevator they go. Trapped for hours in the dark, hot space. Jill's fears work her into a sweat. She's terrified, and of course neither of them have working phones to call for help. Clothing starts to come off. Things have gone from bad to absolute hell as Jack struggles to ignore the sexy, half-naked woman panting to his left.

But what's this? The animosity between them fades as he hears the panic in her voice and recognizes she's not as tough as she first appeared. Her vulnerability calls to him and he reaches through the shadows to comfort her, showing a softer side of his own, but she tenses and—

That's where the chapter ends. Boom. There's the suspense. The reader now has two choices. They can either put the book down and start making dinner or they can squeeze in one more chapter, see what happens, and order pizza, again.

The author might think of several scenarios for Jack and Jill, but she will only keep the best ones. In the end, the author should reveal the characters' needs overruled their wants—or show the consequence that accompanies a lack of growth.

Jill didn't need the land, she needed human connection and a place to belong. And Jack wasn't such a brute of a businessman. He just needed to find the courage to trust again. In a way, their evolutions resolved each other's conflicts and met the other's needs. What a perfect pair. They're clearly going to live happily ever after—on the land Jill wanted all along.

It all comes down to revealing the underlying truth. The *need*. The human condition. And the sacrifice of *wants* for *needs*, because that is the truest form of survival there is.

Knowing the secret—the character's evolved truth before the story begins—will help the author control the plot. Although a controlled plot can often spoil the fun of writing, without control, the writing can face one derailment after another, costing an author years on what could have taken months, weeks, or even days to resolve.

We need a plot. But we don't want to rely on it too much. Our faith should rest mostly on the characters' ability to lead, which is why good characterization is critical to quality story writing.

Authors must balance somewhere between plotter and pantser. They must plan their plot without constricting their muse. But, above all, they must listen to their characters and honor their established nature.

The secret to prolific writing is creating character driven plots. It's not about the arc. The arc, like a rollercoaster, is just scaffolding that supports the events so the character rolls into the right place at exactly the worst time.

We are all linked by the *human condition*, in other words, our existence—the journey from birth to death and all the challenges and desires in between. It is the anchoring point that makes us more similar to each other than different. Through our life's events, conflicts, growth, and mortality, we identify with each other, and it is that connection that gives literature the magic dust to transport people through space and time.

So, while we can construct a plot with a story arc, never forget the character is the one experiencing the ride. The conflicts are the high rises and steep, pivoting falls that keep the reader riveted in their seat and gripping the book tight. The character is the story. The plot is the framework. You, the author, are the engineer and operator.

Without a character there is no motion, just an abandoned ride in a ghostly old park. If you want to bring your story to life, you have to put your character on the ride, lock them in, pull the lever, and let them go.

Chapter Eighteen
Plot

"But my philosophy is that plot advancement is not what the experience of reading fiction is about. If all we care about is advancing the plot, why read novels? We can just read Cliffs Notes."

George R. R. Martin

Step Right Up

Let it be clear that a plot is just another device in literature. It is a cog, a gear, a wheel that motors something forward with the help of other cogs, a contraption the character rides to the end. The plot is not the be-all and end-all of a book. And it certainly should not be the sole focus of an author's preparations. The passengers, or characters, are what brings a ride to life.

Characterization will always be superior to plot. It is the character's response and performance that makes the plot entertaining. The plot, without a well-developed character, is just a bunch of points between A and Z.

The character's scream is what lures readers in and says, hey, this is an unforgettable ride. Developed characters consume the readers, so make the characters gasp hard enough and you'll have the reader sucking in a sharp breath as well.

Without getting too technical, this section will teach the absolute basics of plotting a well-developed story arc and provide a collection of knowledge and time-saving tools. There is a skill to plotting, and it is a necessary part of the creative process that cannot be skipped.

When paired with dimensional characters, a plot can be downright gripping. But a plot cannot stand alone, and without an entertaining cast of characters to vicariously share the ride, the story will fall flat.

Picture a rollercoaster. Imagine the rickety climb when the anticipation builds and a sense of unease sets in. Then picture the steep fall, just before everything lets loose and the passenger is sent barreling into what feels particularly troublesome and exciting. Think of the swooping sensations in the belly, the butterflies fluttering wildly, the gasps, the screams, the rushing wind and the sensation that everything is moving too fast to think or slow down.

Then, after what feels like a disorienting eternity spent fighting for your life, comes the jerking click, click, click as the ride slows to a stop and reality intrudes. There is that strange sense of displacement, like leaving a movie theater in broad daylight, that readers experience when they shut the cover of a good book after a satisfying end.

When we finish a good book with a captivating, gripping plot, we almost forget how to function in reality. That off-balance moment of return is proof that we were taken on a phenomenal ride because we now have to find our bearings again.

The book has changed us, perhaps even created an ache where there wasn't one, a sense of longing to return to the world the author made. Reality hits differently now, and saying goodbye is almost like losing a dear friend.

At an amusement park, an adrenaline seeker might board the same rollercoaster again and again in hopes of repeating the rush. For this same reason, readers reread their favorite books or binge an author's backlists if the writer proves an entertaining storyteller.

But what does it take to build a worthwhile ride? What goes into an entertaining plot? There is a bit of engineering every author should know before inviting riders onboard if they don't want any passengers falling off course.

The goal is to amuse, thus the term amusement park. And what are carnival folk if not amateur magicians attempting to mystify and amaze? But when hired to construct a rollercoaster, the first thing the engineer—or writer—must know is how the ride operates and how to keep the passengers safe through the twists and turns to the end of the ride.

So step right up, as the magic is about to begin. It's time we venture behind Oz's curtain and see what the gears do, which levers we should pull, and what buttons we only push in an emergency.

It doesn't matter how tall or old a person is, everyone can enjoy the ride. Whether you're selling tickets to thrill seekers, modest riders who don't want too much motion, or those who prefer things slippery when wet, every ride is constructed with the same elements. As the craftsman and lead engineer, you will decide the angles and degrees used to amuse your specific audience.

The Structure

The dramatic structure of an arc, regardless of the shape, should always include six elements.

1. Exposition (The Hook)
2. Inciting Incident (The Fork)
3. Rising Action and Complications (The Adaptation & Rising Stakes)
4. Crisis (The Low)
5. Climax (The Climax)
6. Outcome (The Aftermath)

Number three, the rising action and complications should sound familiar at this point, but we will briefly go through each critical part.

Exposition is the introduction of a world and characters to an audience. Keep it brief. No information dumps. This is a basic glimpse into the characters' world before a change. The change is the *inciting incident* that is about to happen.

The *Inciting Incident* is exactly as it sounds, it's an incident that incites, an event, a mishap, an occurrence that causes a consequence or provokes a reaction, be it positive or negative. The *inciting incident* should always be linked to the *outcome* that comes at the end.

The *rising action and complications* are the waves we discussed. They must be full of action, and each event must be progressively worse than the last, leading to the final *climax*, which is the worst of the worst complications in the plot.

The *crisis* is the moment of choice. It's when the character must make a decision that can't be put off any longer, and there is no obvious right answer. Every option comes with a sacrifice.

The *crisis* is a major dilemma for the protagonist and the reader's worry trips into doubt. Nothing seems safe anymore. There's no easy solution. How will they ever get out of this mess?

At the point of *crisis,* a character might be tempted to simply give up. That's how bad things have gotten and how far away a satisfying resolution should feel.

Life is not black and white. We do not live in a world that can easily get sorted into good or evil, joyous or miserable, and our fiction should reflect reality, so don't make it too tidy or it won't feel real.

Never resolve a *crisis* with coincidence. It's extremely frustrating to the reader and they feel cheated by the writer, because coincidence is lazy writing.

When characters are continuously saved from inescapable, dangerous situations by random rescues that are completely untethered to the layers of plot, the reader is disappointed. Coincidence is not an acceptable solution, especially at the crisis point of an arc when complications are at their absolute worst.

The *climax*, usually in the third act, is the final exam. It's the moment where the character is truly put to the test, the tsunami of all waves. If the character has not learned or developed throughout the book, he or she probably won't survive. But if they grew and adapted their ways, if they accepted that what they *want* might not be what they *need*, then they have a fighting chance.

A *climax* should be an action-packed scene, full of drama and passion, and the highest point of the arc. A climax should be earth shattering, life altering, dizzying, depleting, and leave you gasping. Bring your A game and don't fake it.

You want the reader to really remember the effect you had on them so they keep coming back for more. When you write a climax, you should leave the reader so shattered they can't wait to come again.

The *outcome* occurs directly after the climax. It's typically one or two scenes that tie up all loose ends.

It's a rookie mistake to drag out the end. When authors carry on long past the climax, the effect of the climax fades and the reader forgets. You want to leave them when they're still hot and flush with satisfaction because just as people remember first impressions, they will also hold on to last impressions.

Give them a decent mic drop and get the hell out of there. That's how you get people to leave a movie theater in amazement, eyes wide, mouths agape, as they gush over what they just saw. You want to end your story the same way, where the reader closes the cover with an expletive and suffers an instant compulsion to tell a friend they have to read the book.

Regardless of the slopes and material used to build an arc, you should be able to find these six structures in every decent work of fiction. Different schools of writing might call them by different names, but they follow the same function.

You might hear them referred to as *setup, new situation, progress, higher stakes, final push,* and *aftermath.* Or *opportunity, turning point, point of no return, major setback, climax,* and *conclusion.* Or *hook, change, response, attack, resolution, climax.* Or *goal, problem, danger, all is lost* (also known as the *black moment*), *climax,* and *assuaged curiosity.*

Regardless of the terminology, the patterns remain the same. A story arc typically has three acts imaginatively titled: Act I, Act II, and Act III. To visualize this, simply picture a fraction bar and divide it into three even sections.

Act I is where the set up happens. Worlds are built, characters are established, goals are identified, and complications have arrived.

The reader should understand what the protagonist wants, why they want it, and why they can't have it, but without the author explicitly saying these things. Remember, breadcrumbs. Show, don't tell.

Act II typically begins when a choice is made. This is the first fork in the road and the protagonist sets off on an adventure. Life is about to change. Act II is the meat of the sandwich where all the flavor hides. It's layered and revealing but also unpredictable.

Act III is sort of like biting into a delicious sandwich you've waited all week to have only to break a tooth. It's a major setback and causes a massive change of plans. Things are about to get very uncomfortable and costly. And you're unsure if the damage done can be reversed.

The third act is the most intense part of the story. Nothing is certain and it can make or break the character. It's a final push to resolve all the conflicts once and for all. No matter what the outcome, a resolution must be made.

And then there's the aftermath, the unfortunate moment of settling the bill and figuring out how much the character owes.

When we see illustrations of story arcs, they can take on different shapes. Some look like rollercoasters, some look like linear timelines, some are made of blocks, and some look like flowcharts. In this book, I will be using a rollercoaster model.

The structure of a plot is often referred to as a *beat-sheet* in the entertainment industry. A *beat-sheet* is simply a document that marks out the beats of a screenplay. Each beat represents a specific plot point, and screenwriters use this formula as a blueprint. Fiction writers often borrow this guide to write novels, but there are two issues that complicate the *beat-sheet* approach.

First, modern day fiction is typically measured in chapters not acts, so dividing a book into thirds might help an author chunk their novel into parts, but it does little to direct a more specific placement of events.

And second, *beat-sheets* are often segmented by percentages, marking each turning point and twist for the writer at specific measurements such as 10%, 25%, 50%, 75%, 90% and so on. But authors do not measure novels that way when writing. We measure by chapters or word count.

When we start a book, we typically have a goal in mind and that goal is rarely thought of in terms of percentages. *I want my book to be 65k words* and *I plan to make the book 20 chapters*.

Authors rarely think in terms of percentages, but we often place events in terms of word count or chapter measurements. *The hero needs to lose the girl by Chapter Three, which should happen within the next ten thousand words.*

Authors often have to adhere to specific story lengths. But many writers struggle to measure plot points and, therefore, lock themselves into a very redundant pattern of books that are generally the same length regardless of the market.

Experienced authors should understand the formula used to measure an arc. Knowing such a formula will enhance their skill to write quality stories at any length.

But if we do not know how long our story will be, how can we determine where 10% or 50% will fall according to word count? These are decisions experienced authors make before writing a single word, and there is a simple formula that can fit an arc neatly over any story idea, providing the much-needed scaffolding to keep an author's twists and turns in line. But first, we must fully understand what a story arc is.

The *Write 10K in a Day* Story Arc

The rollercoaster of the *Write 10K in a Day* arc can be modified to fit any genre or book length. Unlike other arcs, it includes 7 basic structure points rather than 6. For transparency, I've labeled them: *The Hook, The Fork, The Adaptation, The Rising Stakes, The Low, The Climax,* and *The Aftermath.*

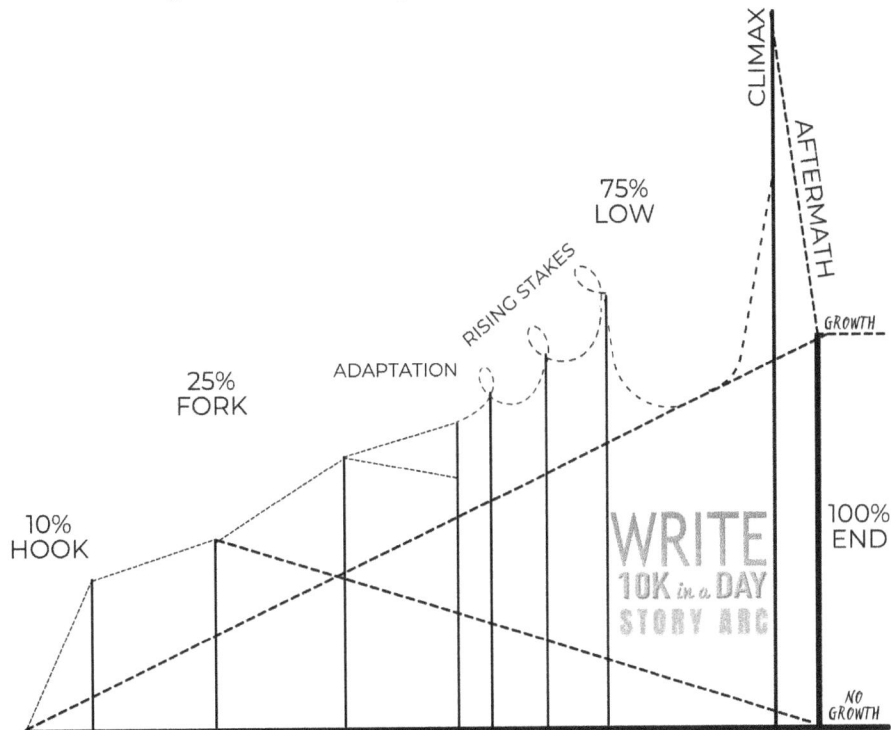

In the illustration, you will notice it looks like a rollercoaster. Like a classic rollercoaster, it starts with a rise. This tick, tick, ticking climb up a steep hill alerts the reader that the ride has begun. Whenever there is any sort of rise in the structure, there is action, so during that first 10%, otherwise known as the *hook*, you will be in an action scene.

The height off the ground alerts the reader to the tone and how high the stakes will likely get. If they're already nervous, chances are they'll be an absolute wreck by the end.

Once some height is established and the action has begun, there's a false sense of safety. The track feels almost level as we move toward 25%, but the stakes are in fact gradually rising. This is where we establish a lot of the background details we avoided in the hook.

Then comes the snap. The character reaches a fork in the road and has a choice to make. They can get off the ride, taking the lower track which leads them back to the baseline and removes any opportunity for growth and development, or they can rise with the challenge and take the risks presented on this wild adventure ahead. As authors, we want the character to accept the challenge, because without an adventure, there really is no story.

Midway through the arc, just about where Act II would fall, is a section for *adaptation*. This is where the reader, or passenger, gets a hold of their nerves, gets a little more comfortable with the predicament, and prepares to endure the ride. We call this part of the ride *adaptation* because the character's sole focus is on adapting to a new world.

During the *adaptation* the protagonist will either flounder or prove themselves a natural in their new environment. An example of a natural would be Bella Swan in *Breaking Dawn* post transitioning to a vampire. Everyone assumed she'd be a hot mess, but Bella proved to have incredible self-control and agility compared to her prior human self. She was a natural.

An example of a character floundering might be Rudy in the movie *Rudy*. After getting accepted to Notre Dame like he'd always dreamed and even making it onto the team, he spent the next several scenes getting his ass handed to him on the field. Rudy was where he *wanted* to be, but he was floundering.

Then the stakes begin to progressively rise and the challenges ahead increase with action and height, leaving a greater distance for the character to fall if they fail. Just like the illustration of the waves, the action grows until it reaches tsunami heights.

Between each spike of action, there is a reflective lull, where the author will use this pacing wisely to reveal secrets to the reader.

Around the 75% mark, roughly three quarters of the way through the book, there will be an extreme lull. This is when a wave feels like the worst to come. It knocks the character down for a spell and some major rethinking must happen before they get back up.

If you prefer the roller coaster analogy, this is the grand finale, the loop-de-loop, the peak you can spot on the horizon from miles away, the reason why park goers line up for the ride. This is the moment that makes passengers scream or worse.

If we go back to *Pretty Woman*, it's the moment when Vivian is icing her cheek and admits she and Edward would never work as a couple.

For a more dramatic example, think of *Braveheart*, just after William Wallace is captured. This is his lowest of low points and we can't imagine things getting much worse. The climax is his brutal execution. The aftermath is the lesson learned by Robert the Bruce who then takes up Wallace's cause.

Not all rising stakes end in a slaughter, but there is typically a sort of death just before the highest stake arrives. This can be a symbolic demise or an actual death. It can be the death of a relationship, the death of freedom, the death of trust, or even the death of a cactus, but something should die to signify the hero's low drop at this mark.

In the epic American tale *Dances with Wolves,* the death of John Dunbar's horse marks the start of this lowest low. By jarring the reader and knocking them down with the hero who they've been rooting for, we amplify the highest stake by giving the characters farther to rise.

Then comes the most action-packed moment of all, the *climax*. This peak, like a rollercoaster's last hurrah, should leave the passenger screaming and out of breath. Throw every obstacle you can think of in the character's path and strip away every illusion of safety the reader had. Then plunge the character into trouble and let them do their best to get out.

The aftermath is the descent back to reality. It may be a tragic piecing back together of all that was lost, or it may be a victorious celebration where the enemy is put down once and for all. The outcome will depend on your character and how much they learned during the adventure.

If the character grew and developed, they most likely will prove victorious. But if they were unteachable and ignorant to the end, they will likely come out on the losing end.

As stated before, the purpose of a story is to show growth and development, but it can also show the consequence of stagnation. Plots are fluid. Movement is necessary to make our characters grow and progress, but it's the character's emotions along the arc that keep us so thoroughly entertained.

The *Write 10K in a Day* Fiction Formula

A formula is a set procedure that follows conventional methods and fixed specifications. In the case of the *Write 10K in a Day fiction formula*, we will be solving the story arc and breaking down its components into measurable, easy-to-follow chunks so that authors may use the resulting guide to create fully developed story arcs quickly.

Before we begin, I want to once again remind authors that a plot is just scaffolding. The characters are what bring a story to life, so do not simply use the *fiction formula* and skip the characterization steps. A good book is a combination of great characterization, careful plotting, and expert writing.

When we discussed an author's success, we determined that it is usually the result of planning, knowledge, and hard work. Plotting is mostly planning, but it also requires knowledge of the industry.

Different genres and imprints will have different expectations. An author's goals will decide how long the story should be commercially and how they intend to divide it into measurable pieces. Some authors don't think of these concepts early enough and end up with a book that is either too long or too short to be considered marketable.

A formula is another word for recipe. With any recipe, measuring is important.

The industry standard for a full-length novel is 60k to 90k words. There are, of course, exceptions. Some great stories have been of epic length while others have been surprisingly concise.

A novella is typically anything under 50k words, but this is a broad range and should always be clarified. When some people say novella, they mean a 2k word story, while other people mean closer to 40k.

Different genres will permit different word counts. Extra length is usually excused if extensive world building is required, as is with dystopian novels, paranormal, and fantasy.

Novels are typically divided by chapters and scenes, but can also be broken into parts. Scenes and chapters tend to be between 1k and 2k words but, yet again, there are always exceptions to every rule.

Before applying the formula, you will need to determine your desired length in words and chapters. I will provide two examples in this section, one for a full-length novel of 60k words that is 40 chapters long and an example for a novella of 40k words and only 15 chapters. You will be able to adapt the formula to your own preferences

The Formula Equations

To solve for WPC (words per chapter) divide W (the word count) by C (the number of chapters).

Formula for Words Per Chapter:
W ÷ C = WPC

Example:
60,000 words ÷ 40 chapters = 1,500 words per chapter

To solve for the words per percent (WPP), divide the total word count (W) by 100.

Formula:
W ÷ 100 = WPP

Example:
60,000 words ÷ 100 = 600 words per 1%

To accurately measure the targeted word count of a plot point indicated by a specific percentage, multiply the WPP by the estimated percent mark (X%) in the plot.

Formula for an exact word target:

WPP x X = word target

Example:

If a writer wants to locate the *fork* plot point, typically located at the 25% mark of an arc, they would solve the following:

600 WPP x 25 = 15,000 word target

This reveals that at 15k words the author should be 25% through the story arc of a 60k word novel. This is a handy formula when identifying standard plot events such as the fork, the middle point, the lowest low, the climax, and even the 90% beginning of the end.

All of the above is based on the same 60k word novel example. Results will fluctuate depending on book length and the number of chapters used to divide the book into sections.

If an author wants to get even more specific, they can count chapters by WPC (words per chapter). If the WPC for a 60k novel was revealed as 1,500 words, then they could also calculate the book length by chapters.

EXAMPLE:

Chapter 1 located at: 1,500 words
Chapter 2 located at: 3,000 words
Chapter 3 located at: 4,500 words
And so on…

If the author aims to write a 40 chapter book, they know that Chapter 10 would mark the 25% point and Chapter 20 would mark the 50% middle point.

Keep in mind that these are only estimations. Events, or plot points, can always occur earlier than expected, but authors should avoid tardiness. If an author wants to place the fork at 15% instead of 25%, that would be acceptable, but delaying the fork until 35% might feel like things are dragging and the author then risks losing the reader's interest.

The industry relies on these general standards of percentage points to keep things moving at a crisp pace. If you find your plot is struggling to meet the necessary points at the appropriate times, then your book likely needs some editing.

The way we correct a delayed plot point is to trim away any unnecessary information such as info dumps or descriptions that got too flowery and take up too much space. Cut the fat and try to get the plot back on track. Trim enough unnecessary words and you will see the events shift and realign.

In this example of a 60k book with 40 chapters, we're dealing with fairly short chapter lengths between 3 to 5 pages, depending on page dimensions. By that measurement, Chapter 10, the designated 25% fork point, should appear somewhere between page 30 and page 50, depending on words per page—not too long of a wait for a reader to get acclimated and reach the fork.

Now, let's try the formula for a novella of 40k words and 15 chapters.

Example:

W ÷ C = WPC

40,000 W ÷ 15 C = 2,666 WPC

The chapters are longer in this scenario because we are trying to squeeze a novel 2/3 the size of the last example into only 1/3 the number of chapters. Every combination an author uses of *word count* and *chapters* will alter how their words are distributed.

Next, we must find the WPP (words per percentage) value, so we divide the total word count by 100.

Example:

W ÷ 100 = WPP

40,000W ÷ 100 = 400WPP

This means 400 words represent 1% of the story arc.

To reveal where the fork will appear, we must identify the 25% point.

Example:

400 words = 1%

1% x 25 = 25%

400 x 25 = 10,000 words

We now know the 25% fork will occur around or before the author hits 10k words.

To solve which chapter the fork will most likely appear, take the word count of the fork point, 10k, and divide it by the word count per chapter.

Example:

10,000 words (which represents the 25% fork point) ÷ 2,666 words per chapter = 3.75 chapters

This equation tells us that the 25% fork should appear in Chapter 3, close to the end, almost in Chapter 4.

You can play with this equation by plugging in your own numbers. If W is the word count and C is the number of chapters, the equation for chapter length will always be W ÷ C = WPC (words per chapter).

Percentages are only guides based on standards frequently applied in the industry. If you'd like to see these industry standards hard at work, watch three very different movies or read three very different books and keep the story arc in mind while doing so.

For example, if I chose to watch *Goonies*, *Annie*, and *The Family Stone*, all of these plot elements would occur at predictable moments. The arc is a mold, a cookie cutter device that fits over almost any plot. Some plots are much more layered and intricate than others, but for the most part, the patterns is the same and occurs at roughly the same percentage point of every plot.

Now that you know how to solve the equation for the *fiction formula*, you will be able to construct solid plotlines with a strong foothold in basic story structure engineering.

But if algebra is not your strong suit and I've only managed to overwhelm or confuse you, have no fear. As a dyslexic author and prior teacher, I like to make sure I'm meeting the needs of multiple learning styles, so I'm going to break this down another way as well.

How easy would an author's life be if they had a chapter by chapter outline of every plot element a novel should include, specifically telling them—according to industry standard—when certain plot devices should occur and what they should accomplish in the story? That would be pretty wonderful, huh?

Well, let's do it!

The Outline

Let's assume you've chosen to write a 40 chapter novel. All that means is you plan to divide your book into forty somewhat equal portions. For a smaller, twenty chapter novel, an author would simply blend the following sections, conquering more objectives in each measured out portion to make everything fit in less chapters.

Just as we learned as children that various fractions fit neatly into a whole, we learn as authors that any number of chapters can fit neatly into books. They are all just parts that divide one whole book. Adjusting how many parts we break a book into does not dramatically change the book, as long as we include everything needed to make a well-developed plot.

The following is a general outline of what should be accomplished in a fiction novel according to industry standards. Measurements can be tweaked according to each author's individual preferences for chapter and book length.

For the first example, I will provide an outline for a forty chapter novel, but feel free to drop it down to thirty, twenty, or even ten. Typically, screenplays follow 15 beats, but we are not writing beats or screenplays for that matter. We're writing books divided into chapters, so measure by whatever chapter count you prefer in your novels.

And remember, master writers complete their characterization before considering the plot. The plot is only the story structure, the turns and twists. Your characters decide the level of excitement.

Character-driven novels write themselves. Meaning once your character is thoroughly developed and ready to go, you only need to put them on the ride and pull the lever so they can go.

Your hard work and planning during the preliminary stages will tell you exactly how your character should respond to each twist and turn.

Chapter 1: The Hook

This is the beginning of the book. It shows the reader how things are "before" everything changes. The hook is one of the most critical points in a novel, so it is strongly suggested authors fully understand its purpose.

Give the reader a glimpse into the protagonist's flawed world. It should be a direct contrast to the last chapter, which, in the end, will show how much circumstances have changed and the character has grown. Chapter 1 is the hook, and it should be packed with action and accomplish everything a hook is meant to do—lure, ensnare, transport, and hold the reader to the end.

Chapter 2: The Conflict

Chapter 2 presents a "problem," otherwise known as a "conflict." Every prominent character should have an internal and external GMC, determined during the preliminary characterization. Chapter 2 is the perfect place to reveal the C or conflict the protagonist is facing. But don't give away the full GMC. Sprinkle, sprinkle, leaving a trail for the reader to follow.

INTERNAL	EXTERNAL
G	
M	
C	

Chapter 3: The Goal

Here we meet the supporting characters, and the author starts to scatter breadcrumbs for the reader by hinting at the theme. The *theme* is the truth that will be revealed at the end of the story, otherwise referred to as the character's *need* rather than their *want*. This is when the reader will learn the G or *goal* of the GMC. There should be no mistaking what the character *wants* at this point.

Chapter 4: The Motivation

A big incentive appears and motivates the character. This will say a lot about the character and reveal the M, or *motive,* of the GMC. Whatever event or new information has just been revealed cannot be undone. There is no way to unknow what is now known. This is a life altering and defining moment for the protagonist.

Chapter 5: The Options

A character should have a number of options that are progressively limited as more complications are revealed throughout the book. Eventually, a choice will have to be made. At this point, the reader senses a fork ahead but has no idea which way the protagonist will go. All options should be evaluated.

Chapter 6: The Crush of Pressure

Time is running out. There is great pressure to make a decision, but the choice is still unclear. We are now approaching the 25% point when a choice must be made. If the character chooses the easy way out and avoids the upcoming adventure, there will be no growth and the story will be over. Things will stay exactly as they are. It's the author's job to add pressure to the character so he or she always chooses the adventure. Without the adventure, there is no story, so make it a difficult choice but an inescapable one all the same. Perhaps an additional complication will help the character decide.

Chapter 7: The Reluctance to Change

The character has suffered adversity, and does not want to change but has to. Reluctance for change is a classic human trait. This is a great chapter to reveal some characterization and show the inner workings of your protagonist by forcing him or her into a predicament that is less than first choice.

Chapter 8: The Fork

Chapter 8 represents the first step onto the fork in the road. It is a commitment, a decision, probably a reluctant one, but a choice all the same.

Chapter 9: The Helper

Typically, at this stage of a story a "helper" will arrive. The archetype role of the helper is that of a "guide." Their purpose is to lead the main character where they need to go. Examples of helpers include Yoda to Luke Skywalker, Sam to Frodo, Jacob to Bella, Robin to Batman, or Dr. Watson to Sherlock Holmes.

If your subject matter is heavy, "helpers" are great at adding a little lightness and comic relief to the plot or intensity if that's what's needed. The helper knows what the protagonist *needs,* and that is the helper's priority. The helper holds little concern for what the protagonist wants.

Chapter 10: The Adaptation

This chapter is the beginning of the adaptation stage, which roughly leads to the middle of the book. Whether your character is a natural or a complete disaster in their new situation, this phase should be action-packed and full of excitement.

During this stage, the reader gets to see notable growth and determination from the hero, which will result in the reader's growing respect. The character is changing. This evolution should take a bit of time, rolling into more than one chapter, if there is space, and presenting itself in physical action.

In the movie *The Cutting Edge,* the adaptation came when the hockey player first attempted to figure skate. He was not a natural and continuously injured himself on the ice, tripping over the toe pick of his new skates. It was rather humiliating for a champion hockey player. That is what we consider floundering.

Chapter 11: The Effort

Still in the adaptation phase, we see the protagonist learning from their mistakes as much as they learn from their successes. Talent can't be faked, and some characters struggle no matter how much they want to succeed. This chapter is all about the *effort* required for success.

Drawing out this stage really makes the reader want the victory. It's where the character earns the right to triumph before actually becoming triumphant. They prove to the reader that they truly deserve to win.

There can be a lot of heartbreak during this stage, like the miscarriages in the *Time Traveler's Wife*. But if the character is a natural in their new setting, they might perform with the grace of Anastasia once she steps into the role of submissive in *Fifty Shades of Grey*. Just as Bella Swan was a natural in her new role, it was no accident that Anastasia was as well in *Fifty Shades*, as *Fifty Shades* is admittedly fan fiction inspired by *Twilight*.

Chapter 12: The Acclimation

The character slowly acclimates and the reader is given a complete glimpse into their new life and setting as they find their bearings. But there is a lingering sense of their old self. For some, this lingering sense of their prior self is a major obstacle of grief.

Consider Elaina's role in the show *Vampire Diaries*. Elaina never wanted to become a vampire but had to become one anyway. Unable to accept her fate, she clung to the idea of returning to her human self by hunting for a cure. This basically derailed the plot and left some critics wondering what would have been different if Elaina had just accepted her destiny and let everyone move on.

Chapter 13: The Progress

Progress is an important motivator that keeps the character moving toward their goals and the reader reading. This chapter often encompasses a sort of time-lapse. It's the first true sign of acceptance, when the reader sees the protagonist almost forgetting their prior circumstances and making the best of this new world.

An example would be in the story *Beauty and the Beast,* when Belle settles into the castle and befriends Beast. In the Disney film, they are shown ice skating and laughing, and she no longer appears the victim or even a captive. She's making the best of her situation.

Chapter 14: The External Setback

The author will often use this chapter as a reminder by revisiting the protagonist's external goal and announcing the conflict in a way that there is no chance of the reader misunderstanding.

This is a place of reexamination. Is the motive still as motivating? By now, the character should have grown a bit and their belief system may be slightly changing. Do they still want the same things? What limitations are they still facing?

This chapter is an update about the external complications ahead and in the character's past. Because this chapter deals with external complications, it will most likely include some action. This might even be the one opportunity where an author can get away with a well-written flashback, but only if it's written well enough not to read like one.

Chapter 15: The Internal Setback

Just as the chapter before, this one deals with setbacks as well, except now the author is reevaluating the *internal* GMC, which tells us this chapter most likely takes place in a reflective lull.

Restate the internal conflict as a reminder, revisit the goal, and reexamine the motive. Are they still relevant? Has there been a change? Don't resolve too much too fast. There should always be an issue the character has to work through until the very end.

Now is the time to establish *why*, even if circumstances feel like they're on the mend, the situation is not quite as tidy as it could be. Don't let the reader forget this is not the hero's ideal situation.

Chapter 16: The Hint of Evolution

The overall intention of this portion of the story is to show that the character is changing. This reminds the reader that it's quite human to want what we might not need and that things are not always as terrible as they first seem. The dilemma becomes our commitment to our initial goals, when to walk away and when to keep fighting.

All three chapters (14, 15, and 16) deal with the GMC and character evolution. These are critical parts of characterization, but depending on an author's writing style, they may be able to accomplish the task of reminding, revisiting, reexamining, and reflecting in one hardy chapter, as long as the end point is a hint of evolution.

In fiction this moment is typically just before the middle of the story. Consider *Pride and Prejudice* or the modernized interpretation, *Bridget Jones's Diary*. Both involve a character named Darcy, and it's at this point that both Elizabeth and Bridget realize Mr. Darcy might not be as bad or as uptight as he originally seemed. In the movie, this is established when Mark Darcy looks at Bridget and confesses he likes her just the way she is—and the world swoons.

Chapter 17: The Reality

Fun time is over and reality strikes hard. No matter what the preliminary stage was, it has now concluded and the protagonist is no longer considered "new." The shine has dulled, the honeymoon has ended, the boot camp is wrapped up, and it's now time to deal with real consequences.

In *The Great Gatsby*, this point presents itself when Daisy Buchanan makes her choice and realizes marrying a man for class and luxury might not be as satisfying as she assumed, which leads her into a mad affair with Gatsby. This is the consequence of not being self-aware enough to sort *wants* from *needs*.

Chapter 18: The False Conclusion

If it feels like things have wrapped up too soon, that's because they have. Life is messy, and fiction mimics life. While things might seem nice and neat, the author is about to unleash a shitstorm. This is simply the calm before the storm, the sense that the other shoe is about to drop.

This is a challenging chapter to navigate because it can go one of two ways. If the protagonist has been triumphant in their new world, things are about to flip over, and they're about to fail horrifically. It's the basic case of taking a situation and security for granted.

If the character has been floundering, however, they are about to experience a win—*finally*! Their seemingly endless spiraling shifts and circumstances pivot dramatically.

No matter what direction the situation turns, there is one crucial rule to this chapter—It must end on a cliffhanger!

The drastic shift of luck will be startling and so out of the ordinary, the reader is shocked. Take advantage of their shock and slap them in the face with another surprise. When you leave them with their jaws gaping, they will be completely motivated to move on to the next chapter.

You just pulled the pin and threw a grenade! They obviously can't just stop there!

Chapter 19: The Twist

Boom!

There has been an unexpected game changer in the plot, some sort of explosive reveal, and shit is everywhere. Massive cleanup on aisle five! How could this have ever happened? How did we not see it coming?

The illusion of security is lost. Or if they were floundering, the assumption that the protagonist was not meant for this world has been officially debunked.

Stakes are now much higher. Things are moving faster. A clock seems to be ticking and there is extreme pressure to act quickly before time runs out.

This chapter is all about revelations and urgency. It can be a reflective lull after a hotbed of action, but it's an extremely exciting one because the world was just shaken to its core.

Chapter 20: The Push

Now it's time for a little fanfare. This might be in the form of William Wallace's "Freedom" speech in *Braveheart,* or Katniss accepting that she's the tribute in *The Hunger Games.* No matter how this chapter plays out, the protagonist should do something to officially declare themselves an irrevocable part of the new world.

They have finally accepted that change is inevitable. They are surrendering completely to their circumstances once and for all. There will be no more excuses and no going back.

In *Game of Thrones,* a moment like this came when Jon Snow broke his vows to The Black. There was no going back for him once he gave his heart to someone else.

This chapter feels so pivotal because it is. It's the middle point of the book. The turning point that leads us home. It should feel sharp, precise, and exciting. We're moving in a new direction, and we feel almost unstoppable in our commitment to our declared objective. This is a chapter of strength and vindication.

Chapter 21: The Polar Shift

Now that things have turned around, the reader gets a peek at what this new direction looks like. The switch we felt at *The Twist* has stuck and created a new sense of normal.

The spiraling protagonist has successfully become the unstoppable protagonist on the rise. And the seemingly victorious hero is on a losing streak that seems impossible to stop. Regardless of the protagonist's good or bad luck, they're basically on a dangerous path and obstacles are everywhere.

Where the protagonist's luck and performance is concerned, the reader should be able to identify a polar shift from the first half of the book to the second half. Everything has either started to gel or unravel. It all depends on how things were going at the beginning of the adventure.

In *The Color Purple,* this moment occurs when Celie finally stands up to Mister and escapes her oppressive marriage. Her sudden backbone is startling and scares the monster in her life. Her marriage was the new adventure and she'd suffered terribly, but when she takes a stand and leaves with Shug Avery, Mister is so startled by her courage he lets her go.

Chapter 22: The Difference

This chapter should show the contrast between now and then. The difference is extreme, so this is a fairly easy chapter to accomplish.

Sticking with the example of *The Color Purple,* this is where we see Celie's life make a dramatic shift. She is finally happy and confident, while Mister's life is falling apart without her.

Chapter 23: The External Villains

Villains are awesome! They give us so many opportunities to build and express our characters' personalities by showing how they react to trouble. The stakes are about to get very high, and a tsunami is coming. But before the waves start to hit, use this moment to really emphasize how treacherous and evil the villains of your story are.

Villains do not have to be people. Sometimes they're a company or a disease or poverty or some other external or internal conflict. That's right! Your villains should reveal themselves in the GMC, and there should be an internal one and an external one.

To properly identify your story's villains, look at the conflicts the protagonist has faced. During the GMC section, we used an example of Jill and the brute businessman, Jack. Now would be a great time to show the businessman being extra brutish and possibly betraying Jill—even after she slept with him! Gasp! Treachery!

No matter how many changes the characters have gone through, there must still be a conflict to resolve. We are confronted with the nature of the beast. The external villain is still a problem and the internal conflict, well, that's still preventing the protagonist from reaching their internal goal. But what is the internal villain?

Chapter 24: The Internal Villain

The internal villain is most likely fear. Fear is an incredible motivator. Remember when we discussed the hook? Fear has the power to motivate a perfect gentleman to the point that he would drown puppies in acid! Everyone fears something. What is the protagonist's greatest fear?

You better know it, because as the stakes rise, you, the author, will have to use that fear and make it increasingly worse until it feels like that one emotion might actually kill the character.

Now is the time to beat that fear into the readers head, so that when your stakes rise in action, you won't have to waste time slowing down the pace to explain why that fear is so relevant.

Chapter 25: The Compromise

The protagonist must be put into a position that they have no choice but to compromise something valuable in order to move on—possibly his or her principles. Make it a hard choice that makes the reader squirm a little. If a situation feels real, at this point it should make everyone involved uncomfortable—including the author and especially the reader. Challenge yourself to color a little outside of the lines here, and break out of your comfort zone.

Chapter 26: The Internal Conflict

Fear rears its ugly head in an action-packed scene when the protagonist's courage and commitment to his or her goals is truly tested, but do not have him or her overcome those fears just yet. Present a way out that lets them escape the confrontation at the last second.

Chapter 27: The Problem with Non-Confrontation

By sidestepping the confrontation with the protagonist's greatest fear, a new problem has been introduced. No action is without a consequence. It's now time to pay the piper, and while the shortcut taken in the last chapter seemed like a good idea at the time, we now see that it clearly was not. Things have gotten worse.

Chapter 28: The Crisis

Internal and external conflicts collide! This is an orgy of villains in an action-packed situation that forces the protagonist into a corner. The conflicts are growing in size and consequence, and choices are limited. It should feel like there is no way out to both the protagonist and the reader.

Chapter 29: The Absolute Worst Possible Choice of All

No matter what patterns of success or failure have stood thus far, this chapter will cut your hero down. In an attempt to outwit and overcome the obstacles, they somehow worsen the circumstances.

You will note we are just about at the 75% point of the story, which starts the hero on the lowest low, but how do they get there? This is usually when something must die. It has to be a loss felt so deeply by everyone involved it leaves both the hero and reader staggering.

This shocking moment is stunning. Readers should be left in a state of disbelief, shocked by the author's audacity to take something so precious and loved away from them!

If you want to see how this is done, I dare you to read _Hurt_. I promise you'll hate me at this mark.

This, of course, will be an action chapter. It will leave little room to anticipate trouble and it will move quickly.

Chapter 30: The Fall

To reach the lowest of lows a character must fall, and we should feel that fall on a visceral level. Let the pain truly seep into every pore. The author has forced the protagonist off a cliff and the bottom is nowhere in sight.

Chapter 31: The Lowest Low

And now we enter the most extreme point of reflection where all feels lost. This lull takes the hero—and other characters on his or her side—plummeting so low it feels as if all the progress previously made has been lost.

This is more than a major setback. This is rock bottom. Unforgiving, hard, bedrock. The main character is shattered from the landing of such a fall.

Chapter 32: The Solution

After much reflection, the protagonist finally fully grasps and accepts the *theme* of the book and figures out how to solve the problem. They understand that what they *wanted* was not what they *needed*. They have learned exactly what they *need* to do in order to resolve both internal and external conflicts.

Chapter 33: The Lesson

Here the author will use motion and dialogue to spell out the lesson to the reader so there is no mistaking the *theme*. This will also prove that the protagonist truly understands the lesson this journey has taught. Win or lose, that in itself should feel like a reward, even if it's a solemn one.

Chapter 34: The Preparation

It's time to ready the troops and get this ragtag team ready for the greatest shitshow fiction has ever seen!

This is an action chapter but behind the scenes. It will not involve the enemies at play, only the good guys. Or if you're writing a romance and the alpha-hole hero is both the good guy and the villain, you will want to show him gearing up for a good grovel so the reader can cope with such duality.

Whatever the enemy, the protagonist is through underestimating the stakes and not taking any chances. It's ride or die time. They are making every preparation imaginable so there is no chance of failure. They know success will be an almost impossible outcome, but they would rather die than lose.

Preparations should be a gathering of resources. This could be weapons, knowledge, allies, food, a spaceship, children to help a hero propose to his ex-girlfriend who also happens to be a teacher, a scientist, an ex-wife who doesn't want to get involved, or anything that will help the hero win and achieve their *new* goal, which is what they *need,* no longer the misguided goal of what they originally *wanted.*

Chapter 35: The Execution of a Plan

Set your characters on the precipice of something big as they take the first step to put the plan in action. This chapter leads the reader right to the opening of the climax, then the author reveals a twist the protagonist hadn't considered, and the chapter ends on a cliffhanger. This should make the reader gasp and hunker down for the show. No way they can put the book down now!

Chapter 36: The Price of Sacrifice

The protagonist has been through hell and decided the price of sacrifice must not be in vain. What they have lost, whatever has died, be it a friend, freedom, a business deal, a relationship, it must be lost for a reason. It brought them to this moment, and their new cause is everything.

They've accepted the pain and are now using it to galvanize their purpose and courage. They've learned from loss and heartache. From the ashes, they have been forged into a true hero who has not overcome fear but understands courage is doing the right thing in spite of fear.

This is an action chapter and it should *show* the above truths. It should display the protagonist's absoluteness, their resolute commitment to the cause. They have never been more committed than they are now. This chapter should also end on a cliffhanger.

Chapter 37: The Proof

The final test has arrived and it very well could cost the protagonist his or her life. Doesn't matter. They're in it to win it. Send them charging like a maniac into the mouth of the beast. Their purpose means more than their life.

Chapter 38: The Greatest Weapon of All

When the ultimate internal conflict is *fear*, the greatest weapon of all will be courage. This is a brief reflective lull in the midst of the action. Do not get so lost that you lose the momentum, but lure the reader to a white noise part of the chaos and emotionally recap the journey for them. Keep it brief but crystal clear.

This moment is a frozen portion of time that establishes absolute commitment and strife. There is no doubt in the reader that our protagonist is absolutely a hero, because they have the sort of courage authors write books about.

This chapter, which is sometimes just a scene, is full of goosebumps, worry, and concern. In an action film, this scene might look like our hero fighting for their life surrounded by the fires of what might as well be hell, with buildings collapsing around them, black soot and smoke blinding them, burns blistering their skin, screams roaring from the depths of their soul, lost into the absolute chaos. This is where a film score might include an exquisite symphony that builds and builds and builds with the chaos.

Chapter 39: The Climax

Slam the reader back into fast-paced motion as things return to real time. It's all or nothing. The hero is battling their greatest internal and external villains at once and those villains are one thousand percent present. And then…*victory!*

But wait, I didn't say if the victor would be the hero or the villain. Your reader should be so far beyond the edge of their seat they don't have a clue who it will be either.

It's the author's choice who will be triumphant in the end. Sometimes bad guys win and the lesson belongs to the reader, not the character. But many times, the journey is a culmination of conflicts and lessons that teach the protagonist how to win, and the ending is a happy one.

Happy or sad, the ending must be satisfying. In *The Notebook,* she is lost to him at the end of each day no matter what he tries, but the win is in loving her better than anyone else ever could. His love should cost him nothing because loving her is a privilege to him. The lesson, the theme, is that it was all worth it—even if it couldn't last for more than a glimpse.

Chapter 40: The Aftermath

The struggle is over and the reader is given a glimpse into the aftermath of the adventure. This chapter should directly contrast with the first chapter. It will show extreme growth and evolution in a way that cements that feeling of satisfaction in the reader and marks this sense of conclusion as the end.

Phew! I feel like I just survived something traumatic and life changing. Probably because I did. That's what good stories are made of, life altering situations that completely redefine characters and somehow take an emotional toll on the reader.

The outline just used was extensive to show the explicit purpose of each point of measure in a story. In no way do authors have to use 40 chapters to accomplish all of these points in a book.

If authors write romance or have a love story in the background of a novel, the plot will most likely run on two tracks, sort of a parallel arc.

This can happen in two ways. The first way is to bounce back and forth between the hero and heroine's point of view, hitting each character's GMC synchronously on a parallel arc running at the same time.

If the story is not told in dual points of view, the partner's GMC should be revealed through the other partner's perspective by using plot devices such as action and dialogue.

The second way to layer a plot with a love story, or any sort of side story, is to simply split the track at some point. Secondary plots require less attention than primary plots but do a great deal to spice up the intricacies within the overall plot and keep the reader interested.

A secondary story line is a great way to make a book seem more intricate. But be sure to avoid red herrings. Red herrings are diversions that mislead the reader. Do not introduce a secondary plotline if you don't intend to see it through and resolve the conflict by the end of the book. Loose ends only frustrate readers.

Chances are, at some point while reading the summary of those forty chapters, you began picturing various familiar stories or movies in your mind. You should have been able to pinpoint exact moments in the plots that lined up with the outline.

That's because the above is an example of the most classic, linear story structure. It does not matter what kind of story we are telling, the stop points of every plot are generally the same for a screenplay or a book.

This classic linear plot structure is the most common, but there are other kinds of plot structures out there. When a plot does not reveal in the classic order of beginning, middle, and end, the reader is challenged.

Sometimes nonlinear plotlines work brilliantly and critics call it genius, while other times, nontraditional approaches are criticized for getting a little too weird and off the beaten path. But as authors, we know we can't please everyone.

Some examples of popular nonlinear plots include *Pulp Fiction, Eternal Sunshine of the Spotless Mind, The Time Traveler's Wife, Citizen Kane,* and the show *Lost.* A nonlinear plot is basically a plot where the events occur out of order in a disruptive or disjointed fashion.

Regardless of how intricate you get with the events of your plot or how many words or chapters are in your novel, fiction tends to follow the same basic design for linear narratives.

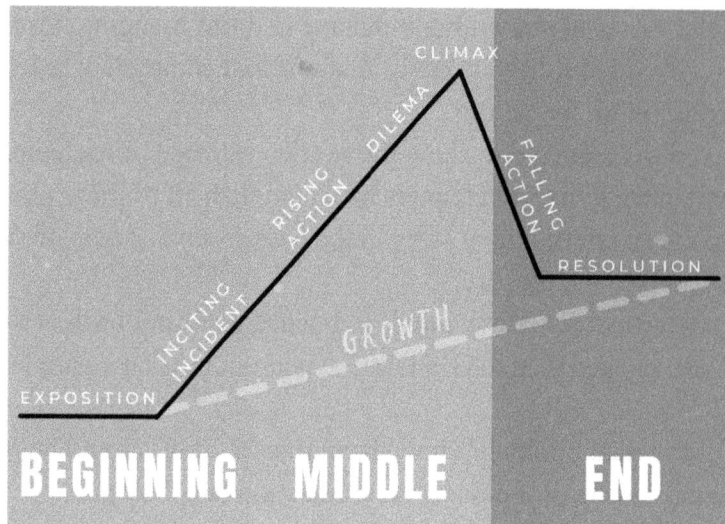

There is a beginning, middle, and end. Within the beginning, we experience the exposition and an inciting incident. From there, we move toward the middle, which is full of rising action and a pivotal dilemma that points to the ultimate climax. Finally, the intensity declines with falling action and a resolution is revealed. If done properly, we should see or feel notable growth, either in the characters or ourselves as readers.

The *Write 10K in a Day outline* is a closer, more detailed examination of traditional models, intended to save writers time by creating a sort of author cheat sheet for fiction writing.

On the next page, we will look at the outline again but in less detail.

The Plot Points of a Linear Narrative Structure

1. The Hook
2. The Conflict
3. The Goal
4. The Motivation
5. The Options
6. The Crush of Pressure
7. The Reluctance to Change
8. The Fork
9. The Helper
10. The Adaptation
11. The Effort
12. The Acclimation
13. The Progress
14. The External Setback
15. The Internal Setback
16. The Hint of Evolution
17. The Reality
18. The False Conclusion
19. The Twist
20. The Push
21. The Polar Shift
22. The Difference
23. The External Villains
24. The Internal Villain
25. The Compromise
26. The Internal Conflict
27. The Problem with Non-Confrontation
28. The Crisis
29. The Absolute Worst Possible Choice of All
30. The Fall
31. The Lowest Low
32. The Solution
33. The Lesson
34. The Preparation
35. The Execution of a Plan
36. The Price of Sacrifice
37. The Proof
38. The Greatest Weapon of All
39. The Climax
40. The Aftermath

The more familiar an author becomes with the plot points the less detail they will need in their outline. Remember in the beginning of this book when I told you this is your journey, and you are the hero of your own story? Well, consider this the pivotal twist where things shift directions.

Pantsers have become *plotters*, but the more we learn the less plotting tools we actually need. After a while, *plotters* will become *pantsers*. But they're never truly flying by the seat of their pants. There's always a plan in the background, and that plan comes from the industry knowledge they learned about plotting, strong characterization, and story structure.

The more we understand these constants, the faster we can practice them. By studying the detailed outline, authors will eventually recognize the objective of each plot point by name alone and have no trouble writing them into action.

Want to simplify things even more? Let's try blending the outline into fewer steps so that we can squeeze every part of a well-rounded story into a novella. When done well enough, readers won't realize they are reading a half-size novel without holding a much thinner paperback in their hands. Lucky for us, readers now read mostly from electronic devices.

The trick to accomplishing every part of a plot in half as many words is nothing fancy. The author is simply squishing events together as tight as possible, like a passenger might pack for a trip using only one very small suitcase. They're still going on the same adventure, but they're only packing the absolute necessities for the journey.

If we have to choose between one item and another, how do we prioritize? We, the author, will be forced to make quick and dirty decisions about what pieces of the puzzle deserve the most attention and which can be brushed over.

Folding matters too! If you can fold three or four items into one chapter to save space, do it! A great way to figure out how you'll pack everything into a novella length book is to look at the forty step outline above and group events into sets.

No matter how intricate the outline, an author should always begin with a GMC for the main characters, one for each in the case of romance novels or other genres with multiple main characters. On the next page I've provided an example of a compact outline. This is the one that I used for *The Best Man, Love Me Nots,* and *Pining for You,* which are all under 40k words and generally fifteen chapters long—give or take.

Sample of a Novella Outline

INTERNAL EXTERNAL

G
M
C

1. The Hook, Goal, and Conflict
2. The Motivation, Options, Pressure, Reluctance, and Fork
3. The Helper and Adaptation
4. The Setbacks
5. The Hint of Evolution
6. The Reality, False Conclusion, and Twist
7. The Polar Shift
8. The Villains and The Compromise
9. The Problem with Nonconfrontation
10. The Crisis
11. The Lowest Low
12. The Lesson and Preparation
13. The Sacrifice and Proof
14. The Climax
15. The Aftermath

As you can see, I've covered what I believe are the basic points of any plot, focusing mostly on what's absolutely necessary. I still included the other points, but they earned much less focus than they would get in a full-length novel.

The handy thing about an adaptable outline is that it will free up the author's time, allowing them to create more books, from start to finish, in less time if desired.

To be clear, subtracting word count is not the answer to writing faster. Book length should be irrelevant to an author's prolificacy. However, in a market as saturated as ours, where consumers will easily pay four dollars for a cup of coffee but dispute the price of a book that costs above 99 cents, it's nice to know that authors have options when it comes to adjusting the overall word counts of novels.

Rather than cutting costs for customers at the expense of the creator, why not cut creative content in exchange for a slash in price? Remember, this does not mean a story lacks quality.

While this may not always be the solution, it is an option that can restore a sense of control for struggling authors and help them produce more titles if they believe that will help their audience grow. If readers are paying less, perhaps they should get less words. A masterful writer should still be able to tell a quality story in fifteen chapters.

Don't believe me? *A Farewell to Arms* is 148 pages. *The Old Man and the Sea* is only 128 pages long. And *The Sun Also Rises* is just 98 pages. These are considered literary masterpieces and counted among the classics of literature, all written by my beloved Hemingway.

We've reached the point of the journey where you, the hero, learn that what you *want* might not be what you *need*. You do not need 100k words to complete a novel. You need to say as much as possible, as powerfully as possible, with as few words as possible. That might be 60k or 40k or 20k.

The word count isn't what makes a story epic, the characters and craftsmanship are. But how nice would it be to write 10k in a day?

Don't worry, that lesson's on its way.

Planning the Plot

Plotting comes after characterization—always. Different authors will plot in different ways. Some will jot notes in a notebook, perhaps scribbling around the framework of a story arc, others will intensely outline every scene, and some will never write a single note down and work directly from their mind. But regardless of the procedure, every good plot requires preliminary planning.

Strong characterization will go a long way as well-developed characters will drive the plot themselves. You, the author, will only need to start the ride and send them on their way. Their fully fleshed out personality will tell you how they would respond as the twists and turns appear.

This is why we always develop our characters first. But people are not the only elements of a story that require characterization. The setting of your story should feel as dynamic and alive as the flesh and blood hero.

Anything worth mentioning should feel alive! So put on your Dr. Frankenstein lab coat, and let's bring some things to life!

For those who would like to plot their narrative in detailed fashion, you now have the outline. You can glance at it, write it out before hand, fill it in as you go, or throw it away, but it now belongs to you.

You can also access the outline and many other helpful graphic organizers in the *Write 10k in a Day Workbook*.

Develop those characters, get a handle on your plot, and you are almost ready to write! But before you do, I better give you some pointers to get that word count up so you can build to writing 10k in a day.

Chapter Nineteen
The Art of Writing

"Write freely and as rapidly as possible and throw the whole thing on paper. Never correct or rewrite until the whole thing is down. Rewriting in the process is usually found to be an excuse for not going on. It interferes with flow and rhythm which can only come from a kind of unconscious association with the material."

John Steinbeck, Nobel Prize Winner and American Author of
The Grapes of Wrath and *Of Mice and Men*

Submersion Writing

Submersion is the act of submerging. Think back to the frigid water surrounding the Titanic. Now imagine going beneath that water and staying under for too long. Eventually, your energy will drain, you will run out of oxygen, and your flame will burn out.

Submersion writing is the act of disappearing into the writing cave for days on end and not coming up for air until a book is finished. Submersion writing is lethal and leads to burnout. It's also the way many authors create.

Authors fall into bad habits when a deadline looms and the work is simply not near ready. And while brief bouts of submersion writing might be excusable—meaning 1 to 2 days once in a blue moon—submersion writing should never be the basis of an author's creative process.

If you suffocate a flame, it will go out. If we suffocate ourselves, we will burn out. Writing is not meant to be a suffocating, oppressive process. It is meant to be the opposite—easy, clear, and liberating.

If, when you write, you feel a knot of tension in your back and pressure to meet a deadline tightening your muscles and focus, you are working the wrong way. This tightening cannot be sustained mentally, physically, or emotionally long term.

Submersion writing is constricting and harmful to yourself and your muse. Writing 10k in a day is about feeding the author soul, not restricting or compromising it. It's about finding long-term solutions that will work *for* you, not against you.

For authors to build their endurance, they must retain a sense of balance. That is the only way to become truly prolific. Authors must form habits that allow regular life to occur simultaneously with hard work. This is accomplished through careful planning and knowledge, not through submersion writing.

Method Writing

Method acting is a term used in the entertainment industry when actors totally immerse themselves in a role. Jack Nicholson is a method actor. Before he filmed *One Flew Over the Cuckoo's Nest,* he actually stayed in a mental hospital to prepare for the role.

Jim Carrey is another method actor who is rumored to have acquired so many of Andy Kaufman's characteristics when filming *The Man on the Moon,* he famously went full method actor during the production, refusing to answer to his real name, only interacting with other cast members as Andy.

Any kind of method training can be costly and time consuming. *Method writing*, a strategy that takes the author out of the office and into a setting that allows them to experience a book setting firsthand, can also be time consuming and costly.

Henry David Thoreau, author of *Walden,* was a method writer. While simplifying life, he actually removed himself from society and occupied a cabin in the woods on the banks of Walden Pond.

There are undeniable benefits to approaches like method writing, but also drawbacks such as expense, time away from family and regular life, and the cost of limiting one's focus to only one project at a time—a luxury many modern-day authors cannot afford.

Method writing might cause an author to travel to exotic lands, or tour a plantation, or live within a different culture for a time. This method of complete immersion is a wonderful experience, and an invaluable one, but not a realistic option for all and certainly not a creative process that is easily repeated.

While I recommend experiencing *method writing* whenever possible, it is not a prolific approach. This experimental writing process is more likely to be a rare luxury, a privilege afforded by circumstance and perfect timing. It is unlikely to be a pattern authors can repeat, especially if their goal is to produce multiple books a year. But I do encourage you to try it at least once because the experience will surely be one of the most memorable ones in your career.

Reverse Immersion Writing

Immersion writing is almost identical to *method writing* and, therefore, not easily repeated long term. *Reverse immersion writing,* however, maintains the benefits of method approaches but adapts the process with more manageable habits that most authors can replicate while maintaining a balanced, full life outside of writing.

Reverse immersion writing is similar to method writing in that it helps the author experience cultures, settings, and people, but does so without ever causing the author to travel from the office. *Write 10k in a Day* advocates *reverse immersion writing* for writers who want to unleash their prolific potential.

Immersion of any sort is an exclusive act. If a French teacher is using immersion techniques, they will only speak in French, which might not work for all students due to the diversity of learning styles.

Like *submersion writing, immersion writing* is a complete disappearance of the author from their regular life. Simple *immersion writing* is not a healthy option. Some authors have other jobs, or children, or other responsibilities that prevent them from disappearing, whether it be for a dangerous bout of *submersion writing* or an adventurous trip to experience *immersion writing*.

Reverse immersion writing deals with shorter, more manageable intervals, rather than disappearing for days on end. It allows the author to remain present in their day-to-day life, existing as other identities as well as simply "author," yet it allows writers to also get lost in the craft. It is an organic, affordable process that enhances deep point of view, a strong authentic author voice, and takes place within the author's natural environment.

Rather than send the author out into the world, *reverse immersion writing* builds the fictional world around the author. This is accomplished through technology, using research methods that did not exist thirty years ago.

Choosing a writing method happens before the actual writing begins. The *only* way I am able to write 10k in a day and avoid burnout is by using the *reverse immersion method*. Submersion is what led to my burnout in the past, among other things. *Reverse immersion* is safer, healthier, and will increase your writing speed!

Reverse immersion writing begins with preparation. Establish a work area. If you travel, this would do best as a file, briefcase, or book. But if you are stationary, you might want to clear a wall or invest in a corkboard.

Reverse immersion writing includes everything from the preliminary tools, such as your character dossiers, story arcs, and outlines, to the strange piece of fabric you found at a flea market that somehow reminded you of your heroine's great grandmother's muumuu.

Only once you've found everything you could possibly use are you finally ready to write. Set the stage by building your *reverse immersion* bubble. Alert the locals that you are preparing to write and should not be disturbed during your writing time. Make every final preparation, such as word banks, texture research, and character dossiers, before you begin to ensure a successful and speedy outcome.

Turn off notifications. Adjust your timers to alert you of when it's time to take a break. Pour a glass of water. Set out a blank notebook. Have your fully charged laptop ready and open with your plot and characterization notes on hand. Look up at the texture surrounding you. Check your arc, and begin!

Ready, Set, Write!

We're finally at the point you've been waiting for! It's time to write!

Go on. Get to it. Fingers to the keys and go.

If it feels unfamiliar, give it a minute. You're ready. You've got this. Vision board—check. Character dossiers—check. GMC—check. Arc plotted—check. Timer set so you know when to take a movement break and grab a snack—check. You've got everything an author needs and the keys are waiting. Simply start typing.

Don't overthink it. To write 10k in a day an author has to trust in their plan. The *Write 10k in a Day* method works. I know this, because I've been using it for years.

You are an author. You are an artist. You have the natural talent, and you've backed up your plan with the skills and strategies necessary for success. Trust the methods you've learned and put them into motion. Just let go and start telling your story.

The world is waiting. Set your mind free. Release your muse and let her play.

Your characters will speak to you as they go. You've built a strong structure to carry them to the end. The only thing slowing you down now is you. You must trust your preparations and let go.

Writing is meant to be a wild stream of thought. A riotous, freeing sequence of events within the mind, suspenseful enough to leave us breathless and get our hearts racing, pivotal enough to make a stranger's hair stand on end or send tears rushing to eyes we'll never stare into. It is chill-inducing magic, and you are the Great and Powerful Oz. Pull the lever, and let's get this show on the road!

Writing as a stream of consciousness is a narrative technique that naturally puts the reader directly into the character's mind. Do not overthink it.

You know your characters well enough to know exactly how they will respond and behave. Now it's time to become them.

You've planned where the plot will twist and turn. You've thought through every rise and fall. You've conjured the best possible troubles ahead. Now shove the characters off the peak and set this story in motion.

Let the words naturally flow from your mind, through your fingers, across the page. Don't hesitate or waste time thinking about prose or word choice. That comes later, during the editing process.

Remember everything we learned about using the correct part of the brain at the correct time? Right now, we're creating. Nothing more, nothing less.

When your timer goes off, stop! Get up and move around. You're on fire. Stepping away for only a few minutes will not be enough to cool your groove. Trust me, your seat and ideas will still be warm after a short walk—maybe even warmer, since movement actually boosts creativity.

Move around, refill your glass of water, grab a snack, stretch, do something completely unrelated to writing, and after a short break, get back to work.

Reset your timer—no more than an hour. Keep all distractions shut off. Your door is closed, your notifications are silenced, and your fingers are going again.

When authors wonder how I write so many words in one day, this is how. It's a matter of intervals and determination with a lot of preparation and planning in the background.

Do I write 10k every day? No, but I could if I didn't choose to do other things. I accomplish 10k easily—in a matter of only a few hours—when I want to. The goal is control and the *Write 10k in a Day* methods give the author complete control over their word count.

Not every day for an author can be a writing day, but as a devoted author, I dedicate at least 2 to 4 days a week to writing, and I always sprint at least one hour of every work day, regardless of the sort of day scheduled.

Some week days will be devoted to marketing while others are devoted to editing. The point is, on writing days an author should be the definition of prolific and know how to write quickly without sacrificing quality in the end.

You now have the knowledge to formulate your prolific plan and write 10k in a day. Build your habits into successful rituals, and your word count will naturally grow. Practice will unleash your prolific potential. Remember, it all comes down to balance, knowledge, hard work, and a good plan.

Give yourself time to improve. Practicing writing every day without distraction will increase your chances of success. By buckling down for an hour each morning to write *something*, you are creating good habits like shutting out distractions and controlling your focus.

This is all part of energy management, which is the truest form of time management we have. It's all connected. The habits we learn to keep our mind, body, and spirit balanced will fuel and nurture our author soul. A healthy author soul is bursting with creative energy.

You do not need to lock yourself away for hours on end to hit that deadline. By planning for breaks and maintaining a sense of balance, your work will be better, your health, both mental and physical, will improve, and your overall energy will rise with your word count over time.

If you take only one truth away from this lesson, let it be that sometimes less is more. We must let the air in to help that fire grow. Get up, get out, and get some fresh air—then come back to work stronger. We must revitalize the mind and keep that flame growing. The days of burnout practices are done.

But how do we ensure we're not writing absolute rubbish? We trust the process and edit as effectively as we write. Right now, just worry about getting the words down on the page. Set goals and meet them, one step at a time.

When you're ready to move on, the editing process awaits!

Chapter Twenty
The Job of Editing

"Kill your darlings, kill your darlings, even when it breaks your egocentric little scribbler's heart, kill your darlings."

Stephen King, On Writing: A Memoir of the Craft, 2000

The Stages of Editing

Every story starts as a draft. Some drafts are merely glorified outlines while others are manuscripts twice the length they need to be. The editing process can either refine a work in progress (WIP) or develop it. It all depends on the type of writer you are and what your process is.

This chapter will address the many stages of the editing process while also addressing some great editing strategies collected over the years. As with everything else in this book, use what you find useful and disregard what does not apply to your personal methodology. Be loyal to your process and needs above all else.

The writing and editing process, otherwise known as the creative process, will fluctuate depending on the author's, editors', and publisher's schedule and backlog. The more projects an author juggles at any given time, the slower their performance will be due to pitfalls associated with multitasking.

Writing a book can take days to years. I've written complete novellas in three days, full-length novels in under ten, and I have some books that I've been writing for over a decade. The less preliminary preparations made, the longer the process.

It's natural for authors to suffer the temptation to return to earlier works so that they can polish books to a higher standard, but it's often more productive and lucrative to focus on something brand new.

Correcting old projects can waste an immense amount of time and quickly burn an author out. Your earlier work might not reflect a strong grasp of story structure, GMCs, and characterizations, but that's okay. You were a beginner. We all were at one point. As tempting as it can be to go back to where we started and fix our mistakes, try not to hold up your career by rewriting less-polished manuscripts from years ago.

Ignore the inclination to go backwards. Recognize that writing is a process, and your marked improvement is proof you are growing. Be proud of the distance your work has come.

Your process, as well as your writing, is meant to become more efficient and skilled with time. As a creator, you are not monogamous to one process, so feel free to play the field and find other strategies and methods that work.

The more authors plan and research during the preliminary writing stages, the faster they will produce a first draft and the less backtracking they will need to do during the editing phase. While every author's process is different, the following is a general, but comprehensive, overview of a thorough editing cycle.

Once a manuscript is written using the *Write 10k in a Day* methods and planning, the next step is revising. Depending on book length and time available, this stage can take weeks to years.

A general rule is that a scene takes twice the time to edit as it does to write because now the author is slowing down and focusing on word choice, sentence structure, emotion, and other writing techniques.

After first revisions, an author might choose to bring in the services of an alpha reader. The alpha reader's objective is to spot major plot holes or inconsistencies. The alpha is generally only reading for the overall experience of the arc and watching for scenes or sentences that blatantly do not make sense or fit in the story.

It is not about the quality of writing or the grammar at this point. The work is still very raw and unpolished.

It's healthy for an author to take some time away from a project at this stage, so work on something unrelated, like marketing or self-care, while you allow the alpha to do their part. This will give you a fresh perspective when you pick the manuscript up again, and you will be less attached to any suggested cuts or changes.

Next, it's time for a purely mechanical proof. Throughout the writing process, the author can make hundreds of notes. At this point, the author will *scan* for comments, run a spelling and grammar check, unify formatting choices, polish word selection, hunt for overused words and phrases, reduce non-descriptive or cliché adjectives, deepen the point of view, and so on. Techniques for these strategies are ahead.

Some authors use editing programs to help with this stage. An editing program should never be the last stage, as these "time saving" programs often make mistakes. A qualified editor should be the last person to modify your book before the final—author—read through.

Once the book is ready for a professional editor, it usually starts with a developmental round. An editor will read and look for big picture issues.

This stage is all about making sure the characters are fully developed and motivated, that the inner and outer conflicts are explained clearly to the reader, the element of suspense and other mechanics are properly applied, and that the overall format of the story follows a logical arc.

Editors will keep records for inconsistencies and chronological story mapping. They will watch for structure issues, wooden dialogue, and lags in the plot, as well as any redundancies or awkward phrasing. Developmental is all about the story structure, not about the actual writing.

Experience and skill will greatly influence how many rounds of edits an author needs. No matter how talented the author, however, having your mom or best friend edit your book will never be enough. Authors should work with various editors at various stages on various projects so that they are always learning, growing, and improving their craft.

In the story arc of you, the hero, this is the point when outsiders notice obvious growth. And they absolutely love watching that evolution, so keep growing.

If an author requires a second round of developmental edits, it's usually due to massive rewrites, additions, or detractions. It isn't uncommon for WIPs (works in progress) to shift 10k or more in word count, up or down, during this stage of the process.

Copy edits can sometimes be combined with a second stage developmental edit or done as a separate round. Copy edits address grammar, punctuation, sentence structure, spelling, inconsistencies in language, overused adjectives, reduction of prose, and general texturizing of words. Weak, passive sentences will be improved with strong verbs.

Think of this stage as weeding out the flower beds, in preparation for a garden party. Company's coming. Time to tidy up the overall appearance of the yard. No stone should be left unturned.

The more eyes on a manuscript prior to publishing, the better the health of the novel in the end. After copy edits, authors often bring in a team of beta readers for any last minute suggestions or corrections.

This selection of trusted beta readers will offer feedback on the actual reading experience, the flow of the story, pacing, tempo, voice, and overall enjoyment of the book. Betas should also identify any typos missed by editors thus far and will sometimes even help authors by highlighting catchy quotes for marketing.

Authors are advised to give betas specific instructions. Different authors have different expectations, and many betas read for more than one author, so be specific and clear about what you see as the purpose and how you would like to receive feedback.

The last stage of editing is proofreading. It's suggested to hire a proofreader after the betas in case any last minute content is added, and select a proofreader who has not seen the manuscript at any previous stage to avoid the chance of overlooking typos.

Qualified proofreaders carefully review the final, polished manuscript for any missed typos. This includes front matter and back matter, headings, footers, chapter titles, and any book content, including the cover.

If an author plans to submit their manuscript to a traditional publisher, the standards will be especially high. It is suggested that the author hire freelance editors and complete the stages of editing prior to submitting.

The submission process typically takes anywhere from a few weeks to six months. If accepted by a traditional publishing house, the editing process will cycle again, this time with in-house editors at the expense of the publisher.

The publishing process with a traditional house can take months to more than a year, depending on the house's other projects slated for the near future and any possible competing works that will need to be navigated. The publisher will decide the schedule based on marketing and revisions required of the author.

Ultimately, the publisher will dictate the time needed for each deadline. Deadlines cannot be missed without breaching a contract at this point.

By the final editing stages, the manuscript will be locked by the editorial staff. Any requested changes must go through an appeal process and be approved by the lead editor and team.

Traditionally published authors will be asked for cover input. However, the publisher will have final say on the cover, as it is considered product packaging and will influence the overall marketability of a book.

At any time, the publisher retains the right to cancel a project. Never forget how difficult success is in this industry. Always place your needs first, but also try not to take for granted the needs of others, especially those working hard to help you succeed.

Galleys, or final proofs, also known as *advance reviewer copies* or ARCs, will be distributed and publicity will begin. Keep in mind that the marketing has been planned for quite some time. Nothing is ever spontaneous in the traditional book world. Everything is done with a purpose and intention.

If an author does not intend to pitch their book to traditional publishers, then they would simply upload the polished manuscript to the desired retail platforms after the final proofread. Indie authors often work with freelance reviewers. If a typo is found in an ARC, the benefit of being independently published is that it's not a massive undertaking to make a revision and upload a new file.

The same can be said for updating back matter, hyperlinks, metadata, content, book details, and covers in independently published files. In traditional publishing, any changes require much more effort and are not always approved.

As I said, not every author will follow every step of this process, as this is a rather thorough example of the stages of editing. Freelance editors are expensive and many lack appropriate credentials. It's advised for authors to request referrals and only work with those who possess years of editing experience or some sort of educational background in the field.

Typos

Authors are people, and as such, we come with a strange set of proclivities, some unintentional. For instance, many of us know that *they are* is shortened to *they're* and *they're* eating *their* dinner over *there*. But even well-educated authors can suffer brain farts from time to time. It's an editor's job to make sure the public never catches wind of such accidents. I'm dyslexic, so I have many situations like this.

Typos are rarely the result of a lack of knowledge. We know the rules. But sometimes our brains short-circuit. Sometimes we mix up *your* and *you're* in chapter seven, even though we got it right throughout the rest of the book.

And sometimes typos are simply the writing gods' way of making us giggle during moments of stress, like when we wrote that scene where the hero *pooped* the cork on the champagne! Whether it's due to clumsy fingers or some cross wiring in the brain, the editor is there to correct things.

If there are words you commonly spell wrong, words that your spell-check program might not tag as incorrect, you might want to keep a list. In romance, men often have gravelly voices. But when authors rush to get those words down, they might accidentally give him a *gravely* voice. This is so visually close to the word intended, an editor could easily miss it, hence the necessity for a proofreader.

Some words are easily mixed up, despite knowing better. If a word is confused more than once, it may need to go onto a list you reference, a list that doubles down on what general spelling and grammar checks might miss. Some of my words include: giggled and jiggled, posses and possess, sever and severe, lead and led, barrow and borrow, and halo, hollow, and hallow. Such typos have nothing to do with intelligence and everything to do with general human error.

Authors often mix up apostrophes as well. For instance, if the character is visiting her parents' house, and there is more than one parent, the author could mistakenly place that apostrophe before the S. A common mistake and one that is easily searched and corrected.

And for specific books, you might want to search names with multiple spellings. I have a Vito in my vampire series who is always causing trouble with his name spelled V-I-T-O, because Vito can also be spelled V-E-T-O. Searching names with multiple spellings will keep your work consistent and clean in the end.

Remember, if you notice a pattern with specific words, keep a list and use it as a reference at some point during the editing process. A simple *Find* using the search bar on the document can do a lot of good where simple typos are concerned.

Overused Words

Just as some authors tend to get hooked on a typo trend, they can also overuse certain words to an almost obsessive degree. I'm sure, by now, you're sick of seeing certain common words in my vocabulary. If not, the praise is owed to my editor. She usually filters my overused words before any book is published.

Common overused words will differ for each author, but there are some fairly universal ones which should be avoided.

Overused Words

a bit	get	seen
a little	got	simply
a lot	had	slightly
about	half	small
actually	has	so
all	have	somehow
almost	here	something
already	highly	sometime
always	in	somewhat
and	into	sort of
appear	just	start
approximately	kind of	such
as	knew	suddenly
basically	knowing	that
because	large	than
been	like	then
began	momentarily	there
begin	mostly	therefore
begun	must	thing
being	names	to
caused	nearly	to be
close to	notice	truly
completely	now	unbeknownst
could	only	utterly
essentially	out	very
even	practically	was
eventually	pretty	watch
exactly	quite	were
extremely	rather	within
fairly	really	would
finally	seem(s)	

Filler Words

Filler words are similar to overused words in that they should mostly be removed. We speak with a lot of extra words we don't necessarily need. Writing, and especially editing, is all about trimming the fat and saying as much as possible in the most concise fashion. Often times, filler words can be removed from a sentence without altering the meaning.

Filler Words

about	his	the
all	in	then
and	into	they
as	it	to
but	just	up
by	little	very
down	of	was
for	out	well
from	really	were
had	she	which
he	so	while
her	that	

Voice

An author's voice will modulate a scene with various tempos as discussed earlier, but there should be an overall cadence to a story, a tone the author suggests within the first chapter and holds true to—while in that point of view—until the end.

On page one, the author generally establishes certain laws that should not be broken. If the story is told in first person, it should be told by one person (this rule has become less important in the indie market where authors often write in dual points of view while using first person present or past tense). Or, if the book starts in third person, it should continue as such. Same goes with tenses.

These details should be worked out by the author before the writing process begins, otherwise they can be a nightmare to clean up after a book is fully written.

The narrator of a story, most likely you, should be confident and nonintrusive. A narrative shouldn't read like a story, it should feel like an experience. Leave your opinions out of it! The opinions will be formed by the reader. Lead them, but do not dictate or preach to them.

Writing can often get clumsy, but editing should never be. Once an author identifies the laws of a book, such as tense, point of view, genre, and voice, those laws should be upheld to the end. Books with multiple points of view will have multiple voices, but they should be fleshed out and recognizable.

The voices should follow a specific cadence that rises and falls with the tempo of the scene. The voice should come across the page so purposefully that it controls the reader's heartbeat, while staying so unobtrusive the reader forgets they're reading a book.

The goal is to keep the reader in the story and avoid anything that might pull them out. Authors are competing with millions of distractions a day. They have to be damn good if they want to win a stranger's attention for any period of time. A strong voice will help hold the reader's attention.

Shoddy, poorly edited writing often jerks the reader out of the story and reminds the reader of the author's presence. The best way to erase your presence in a book is to polish it until only the words shine. Leave nothing but carefully inked letters on a pristine page.

Head hopping is a literary misfire that distracts a reader and pulls them out of the story. It's the intrusion of the author's personal opinions over the narrative voice. This mix up in voice can easily confuse the reader. When a reader is confused, they pause and think, *Huh? What did I just read?* Thereby reminding them that they are in fact reading and disconnecting them from the character they have become.

Head hopping is exactly as it sounds. It's leaping from one character's thoughts to another's. A general rule of fiction is that an author should stick to one character's point of view per scene. If I am in Jill's point of view, I have no way of knowing what the brutish businessman is thinking. Jill can observe his body language and make assumptions, but his thoughts are private.

And if I am in a child's mind and that child believes in Santa Clause, a villain could easily dress in a red suit and convince the child he is, in fact, a right jolly old elf. The reader would know, but the character's knowledge in this instance would have to remain limited.

We must be true to the character's perspective and never give them more knowledge than they should rightfully have. Stay in one character's head during their point of view if you want to keep the reader in the story.

While some might argue that omniscient point of view—a point of view where the narrator assumes to know the thoughts and opinions of *all* characters at any given moment—breaks these rules, omniscient point of view is so dated it is now practically unheard of in modern day fiction. But there are always exceptions, so if omniscient story telling is your passion, have at it.

Deep Point of View

Writing point of view remains a skill of varying levels for authors. Writing *deep point of view* is an early sign of mastery.

Deep point of view, first recognized in the hook and established through empathetic relatability, happens when the author uses narrative techniques to create an even more intimate link between the reader and character. It is what makes a book feel like an experience rather than a story.

When written exceptionally well, deep point of view disguises the mechanics of a book and establishes a trust between the reader and author where the reader is the passenger, resigned to simply enjoy the ride, without thinking about maps or traffic or if the check engine light is on.

"Was the book written in first person?" someone might ask a fellow reader in a book chat.

316

If the book was written using deep point of view, the reader might pause for a moment and say, "You know, I can't recall…"

This is a perfect example of deep point of view hiding the mechanics from a reader's view.

Achieving a deeper point of view should always be an author's goal when writing quality fiction. So how do we do it? While reliant on each individual's skill, deep point of view often starts with mechanics, so it absolutely can be taught.

By practicing the application strategies in this section, an author will become more familiar with deep point of view patterns and eventually will naturally begin applying these strategies during the writing process when typing the first draft. The more a writer practices deep point of view writing, the more natural it will become.

If you are unfamiliar with deep point of view, this next section will walk you through some easily applied strategies. Let's assume you've just finished writing the first draft of your novel using the reverse immersion method, and now you're ready to read over your work. Before you do, try the following steps.

Use the search command to locate any filler or overused words from your personal list. You can search each word manually and review the sentences, but that's not a very prolific approach. I recommend doing an advance search and opting to highlight specific words in specific colors.

Filler words should be highlighted in red, because most of the time they're completely unnecessary and can get cut. Let red remind you to STOP using such words.

Overused words should be highlighted in yellow, because these common words often SLOW down the reader by creating a sense of repetition that can be boring.

Next, search for descriptor words. These are words that tell rather than show. You will highlight these words in green to signify that you, the author could GO deeper.

Common Descriptor Words

Feel	Saw	Taste
Felt	See	Tasted
Hear	Smell	Touch
Heard	Smelled	Touched
Look	Sound	Watch
Looked	Stared	Watched

Rather than telling the reader that the character smelled something, go deeper and use vivid words to show them.

Example 1:
Telling: The marsh felt squishy and smelled bad.
Showing: Mud squelched and gurgled under foot releasing the putrid stench of sulfur as we crept through the marsh.

Example 2:

Telling: "Stop crying!" she yelled, and Emma's tears stopped.

Showing: "Stop crying!" Her voice was a clap of thunder. Momma's image swam into focus as Emma blinked her tears away.

This example is a little different in that it doesn't rely on descriptors provided in any list, but as the author, I know there is a way to show this moment that will make it more impactful than simply telling the reader what happened. The goal is to practice noticing moments for deeper point of view and eventually your mind will learn to write in a deeper point of view during the first draft.

Always show the story unfolding in real time. Do not use words like: *started* or *began* when showing.

Example:

Telling: It *began* to rain.

Showing: Rain pelted her face.

Like many writers, I love words—actually love them to the point that they excite me. Coupling words together in poetic fashion is like letting the ink have sex on the page, right in the open, explicitly for all to see. It makes language erotic and full of body.

By highlighting, your eyes will be able to better track opportunities for deep point of view during the editing process. Adjusting sentences is all part of the line editing process.

Once you've cut out the overused and filler words, stayed loyal to your selected points of view by limiting character knowledge and honoring the proper voice, you've already gone deeper. Replacing descriptor words will help you show rather than tell.

Now, let's get rid of any wooden dialogue. Unnatural dialogue can kill the experience and pull a reader right out of a book. Remember, the goal is to keep them transported. They should forget they're reading. To achieve this, dialogue should read as naturally as possible.

Natural isn't perfect. Simple speech imperfections can often feel more organic than flawless speech. You showed the reader you're a master wordsmith in the narrative, but dialogue doesn't have to be perfect. It has to sound real—the raw fumbling and imperfections are what you, the author, must get right. It should read like a human is speaking, most likely casual and never scripted.

Human's use slang. We're sloppy with words, and we use contractions. Dialogue volleys at varied tempos.

It's a simple task to check for common words in dialogue that can be shortened into contractions by searching wooden phrases such as: *you are, I am, that is*, and so on. We typically do not speak so carefully, especially with familiar friends.

Don't get hung up on slang either. If your character is a country boy, he might say words like *gonna, gotta,* and *ain't*. This is completely permissible in dialogue as long as the speech is authentic to the character.

To keep dialogue volleying at a natural tempo, avoid slapping a dialogue tag on every single comment. And when you do need a tag, opt for an action tag over a dialogue one.

A conversation typically goes back and forth between two people. Trust the reader to know this. More tags will, of course, be needed in a dialogue with a larger group of people in a mixed setting, but when it's between two people, very few tags are needed once the back and forth pattern is established.

Example:

"Wash your hands before dinner." Alerted by the scuff of my boots entering the house, Momma's order echoed with the clatter of silverware. The inviting scent of honey-baked ham sweetened the air.

"I just washed them." A quick glance at the underside of my fingernails showed traces of mud from playing on the barge.

"Wash them again. Lord knows what germs you brought home after playin' on that old dock. And leave your shoes at the door. I don't want mud tracked all over my clean floors."

I glanced at the trail of footprints and winced. "Okay." Tugging the bandana from the pocket of my jeans, I quickly cleaned up the mud.

"What are you doing?"

Tensing, I glanced over my shoulder to find Momma scowling at me. "Sorry."

There was not a single dialogue tag in that whole exchange, yet it's established that Momma is the first to speak. Everything is identifiable by circumstances or action tags.

Savvy authors will enhance dialogue through motion. This keeps a visual alive for the reader, rather than depending on auditory cues alone in the characters' dialogue.

Flavor each character's speech patterns with personality. If you write in truly deep point of view, such patterns are even permissible in the narrative. _Hurt_ is written in such a deep point of view that the voice of the hero's narrative and inner monologue remains in a Scottish accent.

Moving on from dialogue, the final step to deepening point of view lies in avoiding a passive voice. This is a challenging one and can easily overwhelm an author if they choose to use the highlighting technique. To remove passivity from a novel, eliminate the passive voice that hides in words like: _was, were,_ and _be._

Example:

Passive: Her head _was_ under the pillow.
Active: The pillow _covered_ her head.

There's something delightfully challenging about deepening the point of view in the editing stages of a novel. Despite deliberately applying such techniques, in the end they should come off as seamlessly as if a master writer wrote the deep point of view naturally during the first draft. And eventually you will. Practice makes perfect.

Killing Your Darlings

"It was a bloodbath," I've said more than once after finishing a round of edits. Our darlings are our prose. Prose are the flowery words we sometimes get carried away with in writing. And in the words of Stephen King, we must kill them, even when it breaks our heart.

While we want to go deeper and add an incredibly intimate point of view, there is a point when things get a little too deep and become downright convoluted. A good editor will help you pinpoint if and when this happens.

A stubborn author will refuse to hack apart her babies and kill off her darlings, but a disciplined author who knows better will smudge them out of existence without hesitation. Which kind of author do you intend to be?

In the case of killing darlings, I find experience makes the heart grow colder. There will be more opportunities for darlings at other times.

It's understandable to cling to words that came from such a secret part of our soul. It can even wound us to harm them—our babies. But it's not personal. If you want to improve as a writer, you must develop a callus where editing is concerned and cut. You must shove those pretty little bitches out of the manuscript and get to the point so the story can move on.

They're not actually your babies or your darlings. They're merely weeds that have overgrown into distractions. For the overall health of the novel and your career, rip them out, close up any openings, and move on.

It's such a turn on for authors to write a novel that hits like poetry, but in modern fiction when people have such limited time as it is, show-offs are put-offs.

Never forget, fiction is a service business. Your job is to entertain the readers, not titillate your muse's ego. Too many showy prose in a book is the equivalent of masturbating in public. It's great that you *can* do it. But the general public really doesn't need to see it. Just a hint of sensuality should suffice.

Where little darlings are concerned, pick your absolute favorites, then it's off to the slaughter house for the rest of them. We kill the darlings because we don't want the reader to get lost in the descriptions, grow bored, or worse, confused and have one of those *huh?* moments that pulls them out of the book. We want to move the story forward at a quick but comfortable pace, using such explicit and meaningful language it takes as few words as possible.

Stick with strong verbs and deepen that point of view without falling into an abyss of flowery descriptions. Quality stories should be fast paced and avoid delays.

Don't "Bury the *Lede*"

A wise author wouldn't put this step last in the editing chapter, but this thought usually occurs to writers at the end of editing. Unless we are in this career to write one book and walk away, we will want to leave openings for future works. We can accomplish creating such openings by leading on the reader.

I don't want to hear that readers hate cliffhangers. So what? Cliffhangers sell more books and, if readers continue reading, they will reach the ending eventually. Maybe a story isn't meant to fit into sixty or a hundred thousand words. Maybe it needs six hundred thousand to be told to completion. There are no rules, so stop pretending there are.

Authors are drowning in this saturated market. It's so bad, sometimes marketing hardly pays for itself. Having a clearly defined lead that convinces a reader to shop from you again, is basic, brilliant salesmanship. Stop acting like it's somehow disloyal. Your loyalty is to you. If readers want you to keep writing, then you have to do so in an affordable way. Bottom line, cliffhangers sell more books!

Well-written stories will create a loyal readership. If you want to sell books, you will have to write well but also market your ass off. Establishing a lead is just another form of marketing.

In books, the "lede" can come in many forms. It can be an interesting side character who is eventually getting their own story, a spin off series, or a cliff hanger that keeps the saga going as long as your readers will tolerate being led on.

Many best-selling authors follow a formula when writing a series or trilogy, following an individual arc for each book, but also adhering to an overall series arc that ties everything together. The books are often written as one and released strategically close together once the series is finished.

Pricing and branding is all determined during the creative process to make the books as marketable as possible. The word count of each book will be fairly uniform, but the first book may be slightly shorter to justify marketing at a lower price or longer to account for world building. The final book in the series may also need extra length to accommodate tying up any loose ends.

Each book, in this type of formulized series writing, ends on a cliffhanger, except for the final novel in the series. This is done so that the author can sell more books, plain and simple.

After a year or more of being on the market, the author might drop the price of book #1 or even make it permanently free to hook new readers. The profit comes in the click through sale of the sequential books.

This is just one method of keeping readers interested and there are many more, but the point is to leave your options open. If you see an opening for subsequent profits, don't bury that "lede".

Every side character is a possible main character because everyone has a story to tell. You know this because every single one of your characters has their own GMC.

Keep this in mind during the editing process. If you buried the "lede" while writing, you still have time to dig it out and plant more seeds for other leads to grow.

The ultimate goal is to not just publish books, but publish books in such a fashion that you achieve a sustainable author career. Writing is just one small part of an author's success. Talent is another part. But what sustainable success truly comes down to is balance, knowledge, planning, and hard work.

I hope this book has helped you develop those qualities in some way. Keep applying the skills and strategies taught in this text, and you'll soon find yourself writing 10k in a day, living a happier, balanced author life, and unleashing your prolific potential.

Chapter Twenty-One
The Takeaway

"When I was a little girl, I won a gold medal for figure skating, not because I was the best competitor on the ice that day, but because I fell in the middle of my routine and immediately got up and tried again. We never truly fail as long as we continue to rise. Rising, again and again, is the only way to reach the satisfying end."

Lydia Michaels, Write 10k in a Day, 2021

We All Have a Story to Live

Writing 10k in a day has more to do with knowledge, planning, and hard work than anything else. The preparations you make today will make you a more prolific writer tomorrow.

Your devotion to the craft will fluctuate through the years. Sometimes life interrupts us in the most unexpected ways, but we only get one life and it would be a shame to miss it.

Only you can claim to be the expert of you. You are the hero of your life. You decide how you will live, and as the CEO of your company, you determine what the best practices are for your business.

This is the part of the story where the helper, me, must step away and let you, the hero, rise. Don't let fear rule your success. There is no room for timidity in writing, and the book industry takes great courage to survive.

There will be high stakes and terrifying moments ahead. But every struggle will be followed by a lull. Take the lull. Reflect and learn so you are stronger and wiser when tomorrow comes.

There will be days when you feel as if all is lost and there's no possible way to survive. That's just a damn good plot doing its job. Life would be boring as hell without some unexpected twists and turns.

You know how the arc goes. The stakes have to progressively rise, each challenge growing bigger than the last. But every day that you do better, you are better because you're surviving the course and growing from the trials. You're not giving up, no matter how difficult or intimidating the path ahead.

Your devotion is as much a part of this story as the obstacles and conflicts ahead. Be brave even when it scares you. Sometimes we're naturals and instantly triumphant on our journey, and sometimes we flounder, but we now know that no one is infallible and no spiral is eternal. A shift will eventually come.

We know this because fiction mimics real life. Just like any protagonist of a story worth reading, you will be tested. You will tremble and you will fall. That's expected. But we, the world, will be watching closely to see how you rise. Don't let us down.

Pace yourself. Don't rush to the end. The beauty is in the evolution of self, the development and growth. No matter where you are, if you're taking chances and rising to the occasion, you will continue to grow.

Look around. Your position looks much different from where you started. The journey is far from over. The view at the end will be a direct contrast from your first chapter. But you have to keep going. You have to keep learning and growing.

Set goals, stay motivated, and prepare for conflicts. Know your own GMC and stay on the lookout for those revealing truths. Listen to your needs.

In the beginning of this book, I started with a story that felt like defeat. I was as burned-out and as used-up as a person could be. At that time, my greatest worry was that my story might end too soon.

I thought my journey was over, but I was wrong. It was just a fork in the road, a difficult decision I, the main character, had to make. It wasn't the first, and it won't be the last. We all have many challenges and choices ahead.

We must confront our fears and face down whatever demons threaten our happiness. We must accept our fate and learn how to rise, even in the worst case of adversity. Do that, and you will live a story worth telling. You might even inspire others to try harder, and what a humbling thought that is.

You know the challenges ahead. Gather every resource you can find, just as our heroes have taught us to do. Commit to your goals, not because you *want* something but because you've uncovered a deeper need. Then raise your quill like a sword and go screaming into the flames, because the climax of your story has yet to come.

Don't let this mark THE END.
Make it the pivotal moment where the action truly begins…

A Note from the Author

I hope my strategies and stories have helped you. And I hope, if we ever find ourselves sitting near each other, that you say 'hello'. I'd love to hear about all the success and happiness you've found.

Let's stay in touch!
Email: Lydia@LydiaMichaelsBooks.com
Instagram: @Lydia_michaels_books
Facebook: www.Facebook.com/LydiaMichaels
TikTok: @lydiamichaels

Want More Write 10k in a Day help?
Check out the accompaniment series, which includes the
Write 10k in a Day Author Planner
Write 10k in a Day Workbook
Write 10k in a Day Audiobook

PART FOUR

REFERENCES

Glossary

Glossary

#1 Objective
a person's greatest goal in life; an ultimate priority used to navigate the path to professional and personal success

50-Minute Focus Technique
a technique used to build momentum through fifty-minute intervals of intense focus separated by physical and mental breaks

A

action
a writing technique used to speed up the story with suspense and functional movement that shows *how* the plot occurs with very little attention given to prose

action tag
a verb placed either before, after, or in between dialogue to direct the reader's attention to a specific character speaking through descriptions of motion

active activities
activities that deserve full focus to perform successfully

advanced reader copy (ARC)
a pre-published copy of a book sent to readers prior to the release date to generate feedback and publicity through word of mouth and reviews; galley; ARC

alpha reader
a preliminary reader who offers private, developmental feedback to an author after reading a portion of a raw first draft or the entire manuscript

antihero
a main character in a story who lacks conventional heroic qualities and attributes such as idealism, courage, and morality

ARC
advanced reader copy; a pre-published copy of a book sent to readers prior to the release date to generate feedback and publicity through word of mouth and reviews; galley

arc
an extended or continuing storyline in episodic storytelling that follows a dramatic plot design

auditory learner
a person who predominantly absorbs information best when the information is spoken aloud to them

authorpreneur
an author who organizes and operates a book business or businesses, taking on greater than normal financial risks in order to sell, not just books, but a specific brand and catalogue of related products through strategic marketing, skillful writing, and publicity within the publishing industry; a badass in the book business

automated technology
applications of machines used to reduce human intervention in processes after an act has been initiated by a human so that specific acts and tasks can be repeatedly performed without manual human intervention

B

beat-sheet
a precursor outline to a screenplay that identifies the important moments in an episode or feature film and measures various plot locations within an act or story arc

beta reader
a person who reads a pre-published manuscript in order to mark errors and suggest improvements, typically without receiving payment

"Big Six"
the trailblazing companies of the publishing industry in North America composed of Hachette, Macmillan, Penguin, HarperCollins, Random House, and Simon & Schuster, which wields a great deal of influence over the written word

biopsychosocial

an interdisciplinary model that looks at the interconnection between biology, psychology, and socio-environmental factors that influence mental health and well-being

book bible

a document where an author compiles detailed notes pertaining to a specific manuscript or series that tracks locations, characterization, timelines, and other plot-specific details

booklandia

the many virtual locations where authors, bloggers, and readers interact on social media, which has established a sense of community since the rise of the digital age

burnout

a reduction in speed and productivity that, without intervention, inevitably leads to physical or mental collapse caused by overwork, personal neglect, or compiling stress

C

call to action

a refence to the next step a marketer wants its audience or reader to take, triggered by stimulus to achieve an aim

character development

the craft of giving a character a personality, depth, and motivations that propel them through plot circumstances and events in a manner that shows measurable personal growth and an evolving belief system

characterization

a narrative technique used by authors which relies on the behavior, speech, and appearance of a character, as well as the opinions of other characters, to imply personality traits of specific characters to the reader

click through rate (CTR)

a metric that measures the number of clicks digital advertisers receive on their ads per number of impressions; CTR

climax
a literary element that marks the turning point of a narrative at its highest point of tension when the action should reveal a possible solution

commodity
a useful, valuable thing

complication
a circumstance that complicates matters; a difficulty

conglomerate
a large corporation formed by the merging of separate and diverse firms

cost per click (CPC)
the amount paid for each click on a pay per click digital ad

cottage industry
a small-scale, decentralized manufacturing business often operated out of a home rather than a purpose-built facility

CPC
cost per click; the amount paid for each click on a pay per click digital ad

craft
the art of writing, through the author's intentional use of figurative language, imagery, and details to achieve a desired impact on various readers

creative brain
the part of the brain that directs creative thought

crisis
a time of intense difficulty, trouble, or danger

CTR
click through rate; a metric that measures the number of clicks digital advertisers receive on their ads per number of impressions

D

deep point of view
a writing technique that uses third-person-limited, and silences the narrative voice while providing the reader with intimate knowledge of a character's thoughts through internal monologue and descriptive, private emotion

dialogue tag
a small phrase either before, after, or in between dialogue which indicates who is speaking or how the line is spoken

digital first
the theory that publishers should release content into new media channels prior to older, non-digital media outlets to tap a fresher audience and save on production costs

disruptive content
an innovative tactic which changes traditional marketing methodology by creating an unusual proposition that engages customers on a deeper level and creates brand awareness through interactive stories that connect with consumers on a personal level

dossier
a collection of documents about a particular person, event, or subject

draft
a preliminary version of a piece of writing

Dunning-Kruger effect
coined by the psychologists David Dunning and Justin Kruger in 1999, the study is based on a hypothetical cognitive bias that people with low ability at a task overestimate their ability

E

eat the frog
coined by Nicolas Chamfort and later linked to Mark Twain postmortem, the frog represents an undesirable task on a to-do list that stirs no motivation to complete, hence "eating the frog" means to just do it, otherwise suffer the consequences associated with procrastination

edit
prepare (written material) for publication by correcting, condensing, or otherwise modifying it

empathetic link

a technique used to invest a reader's interest in a story by forming an emotional connection between the reader and main character

energy management

utilizing energy to establish a sense of control that manipulates the perception of time

exposition

a comprehensive description and explanation of an idea or theory

F

final proof

the stage in production when all revisions have been made and the formatting is complete, but the manuscript awaits the final approval of the publisher prior to going to press

first person

a literary style in which the narrative is told from the perspective of a narrator speaking directly about himself or herself; first person point of view

focus brain

the analytical part of the brain best used for tasks such as editing, and not easily interchangeable with the creative brain

foreshadowing

a warning or indication of a future event

formula

a method, statement, or procedure for achieving something

G

gain

the amount by which the revenue of a business exceeds its cost of operating; the first impression of a profit

galley

a final proof of a book before it goes into production, created primarily for editors, proofreaders, and authors to do a final review to catch any mistakes before publication; an ARC; advanced reader copy

GMC

goal-motivation-conflict, what the character wants, why they want it, and why they can't have it

Goal-Motivation-Conflict (GMC)

what the character wants, why they want it, and why they can't have it

H

head hopping

private thoughts and feelings of side characters conveyed in a main character's voice through reports of an omniscient narrator when point of view should restrict an omniscient view

health

a person's mental or physical condition

hook

a literary technique for creating an enticing beginning that ensnares and transports the reader

human resources (HR)

the department of a business or organization that deals with the hiring, administration, and training of personnel; HR

HR

human resources; the department of a business or organization that deals with the hiring, administration, and training of personnel; HR

hybrid author

a writer both independently and traditionally published

I

immersion writing

the complete disappearance of the author from their regular life into the culture and setting inspiring a work in progress; method writing

inciting incident

the event that sets the main character or characters on the journey that will occupy them throughout the narrative

industry
economic activity concerned with the processing of raw materials and manufacture of goods in factories;
a group of businesses that provide a particular product or service

information dumps
an overwhelming amount of background information supplied at once in a narrative

investment

the act of investing money for profit

J

judicious
having, exercising, or characterized by sound judgment

K

Kinesthetic
relating to a person's awareness of the position and movement of the parts of the body by means of sensory organs (proprioceptors) in the muscles and joints

kinesthetic learner
a tactile learning style that requires touch or manipulated materials to learn

L

Law of Attraction
a pseudoscience belief that positive or negative thoughts bring positive or negative experiences into a person's life

lead
a potential customer

lede

an introductory intended to entice the reader to read the full story or subsequent stories relating to the character or subject matter

left brain

the left-hand side of the human brain, which is believed to be associated with linear and analytical thought

Let-Down effect

a condition that leads to illness or symptoms following stressful events, such as conflict, time pressured work projects, or school exams

Luddite

a person opposed to new technology

M

mastermind groups

coined in 1925 by author Napoleon Hill in his book *The Law of Success* as a peer-to-peer mentoring group used to help members solve their problems with input and advice from the other group members willing to share life experiences

method acting

an acting technique in which an actor aspires to completely identify as a character through emotion-oriented practices rather than the traditional techniques primarily based in action

method writing

a technique in which an author identifies emotionally with a character in the story and assumes that character's persona in the telling

mindfulness

a mental state achieved by focusing one's awareness on the present moment while calmly acknowledging and accepting one's feelings, thoughts, and bodily sensations

mono-tasking

the practice of dedicating oneself to a given task and minimizing potential interruptions until the task is completed or a significant period of time has elapsed

motion

process of moving or of changing place or position (not action)

motive
a reason for doing something, especially one that is hidden or not obvious

multitasking
the performance of more than one task at the same time

N

narrator
a person or character who recounts the events of a novel or narrative poem

negative perfectionism
an unremitting and compulsive behavior that slows or halts productivity in the process of striving to meet one's goals due to overwhelming doubts, concerns, and pressure to achieve a perfect outcome while fearing any outcome that might be less than perfect

net profit
the actual profit after working expenses not included in the calculation of gross profit have been paid

O

omniscient
all knowing

omniscient point of view
an all-seeing and all-knowing narrator who scrutinizes the characters, and narrates the story in a way that shows the readers that s/he has more knowledge about the characters than they have about themselves

optimism
hopefulness or confidence about the future or the successful outcome of something

P

pantser
a writer who likes to fly by the seat of their pants and write without an outline or roadmap for their plot

Parkinson's Law
coined by Cyril Northcote Parkinson, the theory that work expands to fill any allotted time

passive activities
activities that require minimal focus

past tense
a tense expressing an action that has happened or a state that previously existed

per finished hour (PFH)
when a narrator is only paid for the final, "finished" hour(s) of audio

perfect
having all the required or desirable elements, qualities, or characteristics; as good as it is possible to be; absolute; complete

perfectionism
refusal to accept any standard short of perfection

perfectionist
a person who refuses to accept any standard short of perfection

PFH
when a narrator is only paid for the final, "finished" hour(s) of audio; per finished hour

plan-ser
an author who plans without overly plotting or acting spontaneously in regard to plot and characters; an author with a firm grasp of the character's motivation, strengths, and weaknesses, but not a chronologically detailed plot outline; the combination of a *plotter* and *pantser*

plotter
an author who meticulously plans and outlines before they writing

POD
a printing technology and business process in which book copies are not printed until the manufacturing company receives an order, allowing prints of single or small quantities with little to no upfront costs to the publisher; print on demand

PR
public relations; the practice of deliberately managing the release and spread of information between an individual or an organization and the public in order to affect the public perception; the professional maintenance of a favorable public image

present tense
events of a narrative told in real time

print on demand (POD)
a printing technology and business process in which book copies are not printed until the manufacturing company receives an order, allowing prints of single or small quantities with little to no upfront costs to the publisher

priority
a thing that is regarded as more important than another; something of the highest importance or rank

procrastination
the action of delaying or postponing something

productivity
the ability of an individual, team, or organization to work efficiently within a set timeframe in order to maximize output

prolific
producing in large quantities or with great frequency; highly productive

protagonist
the leading character in a work of fiction

public relations (PR)
the practice of deliberately managing the release and spread of information between an individual or an organization and the public in order to affect the public perception; the professional maintenance of a favorable public image; PR

purposeful marketing
a deliberate plan for moving a company from the startup phase with beginning marketing efforts to the desired phase of an established business with coordinated marketing across various channels to reach targeted audiences

Q

R

return on investment (ROI)
a performance measure used to evaluate the efficiency or profitability of an investment

return on joy (ROJ)
the measurement of happiness gained from an investment of time, money, or energy

revenue
the total amount of income generated by the sale of goods or services in relation to a company's primary operations

reverse immersion method
coined by Lydia Michaels, a multisensory technique that takes a deep-dive into research, characterization, story texture, and story setting prior to developing a plot arc, which ends in stream of consciousness writing

right brain
the right-hand side of the human brain, which is believed to be associated with creative thought and the emotions

rising action
a series of incidents in a literary plot that build toward the point of greatest interest in a dramatic structure

ROI
return on investment; a performance measure used to evaluate the efficiency or profitability of an investment

ROJ
return on joy; the measurement of happiness gained from an investment of time, money, or energy

S

S.E.O.
search engine optimization; the process of improving the quality and quantity of traffic to a website from search engines

schedule
a plan for carrying out a process or procedure at intended times

slush pile
a stack of unsolicited manuscripts that have been sent to a publishing company for consideration

small press
a publisher with annual sales below a certain level or below a certain number of titles published

structure
something arranged in a definite pattern of organization

stream-of-consciousness writing
narrative technique in fiction intended to render the flow of myriad impressions—visual, auditory, physical, associative, and subliminal—that impinge on the consciousness of an individual's thought patterns

submersion
the action or state of submerging or being submerged

supplements
something that completes or enhances something else when added to it

sustainable success
a maintainable level of ongoing favorable outcomes for the duration of an endeavor

syndrome
a group of symptoms which consistently occur together

T

tag
a label attached to someone or something for the purpose of identification

task batching
a planning process that groups similar activities together to improve focus and productivity

texture
imagery achieved through word choice, mood, and the focus of the authorial lens

theme
a central topic, subject, or message within a narrative

third person point of view
a point of view which belongs to the person/people being talked about and uses pronouns such as he, him, his, himself, she, her, hers, herself, it, its, itself, they, them, their, theirs, and themselves

time audit
an official inspection of how one passes time

time blocking
a productivity technique where a period of time is divided into smaller segments or blocks for specific tasks

time boxing
a productivity technique which allocates a fixed time period, called a timebox, within which planned activity takes place

time management
the theory that people can control time through specific activities aimed to increase effectiveness, efficiency, and productivity

traditional publishing
an agreement between an author and publisher in which the publisher offers the author a contract and, in turn, prints, publishes, and sells the author's book through booksellers and other retailers for a percentage of the royalty

U

V

vanity press
a publishing house in which authors pay to have their books published

visual learner
someone who processes information best by seeing it

visual-linguistic learner
someone who processes information best through written language, such as reading and writing tasks

voice
the rhetorical mixture of vocabulary, tone, point of view, and syntax that makes phrases, sentences, and paragraphs flow in a particular manner

W

willpower
control exerted to do something or restrain impulses

WIP
work in progress; an unfinished project that is still being added to or developed

work in progress
an unfinished project that is still being added to or developed; WIP

workaholic
a person who compulsively works hard and long hours

writer's block
the condition of being unable to think of what to write or how to proceed with writing

X

Y

Z

<u>Notable Titles by Lydia Michaels</u>

La Vie en Rose
"Heart Wrenchingly Beautiful!"

Hurt
"Hauntingly Dark! A Masterpiece!"

The Surrender Trilogy
"Drama, Betrayal, Scandal, Oh my!"

The Calamity Rayne Series
(Book #1 FREE!)
"Laugh out loud hilarious!"

Breaking Perfect
"Delicious and Dirty!"

The Jasper Falls Series
"A charming small town full of heart!"

Blind (FREE)
"Slow burn perfection!"

Protégé
"Secret Kink Society!"

Simple Man
"Unexpected Baby/Fatherhood"

The McCullough Mountain Series
(Book #1 FREE)

The Degrees of Separation Trilogy
(Book #1 FREE)

And more…

<u>NOTES</u>

NOTES

<u>NOTES</u>

NOTES

www.ingramcontent.com/pod-product-compliance
Lightning Source LLC
Chambersburg PA
CBHW080540090426
42734CB00016B/3159